Physical Medicine and Rehabilitation

STATE OF THE ART REVIEWS

Sexuality and Disability

Guest Editor:

Trilok N. Monga, MD, FRCP(C), MRCP(I)

Department of Physical Medicine and Rehabilitation
Baylor College of Medicine
  and
Physical Medicine and Rehabilitation Service
Houston Veterans Affairs Medical Center
Houston, Texas

Volume 9/Number 2   June 1995
HANLEY & BELFUS, INC.   Philadelphia

Publisher: **HANLEY & BELFUS, INC.**
210 South 13th Street
Philadelphia, PA 19107
(215) 546-7293
(215) 790-9330 (Fax)

PHYSICAL MEDICINE AND REHABILITATION: State of the Art Reviews is included in *BioSciences Information Service, Current Contents, ISI/BIOMED,* and *Cumulative Index to Nursing & Allied Health Literature.*

PHYSICAL MEDICINE AND REHABILITATION: State of the Art Reviews   ISSN 0888-7357
Volume 9, Number 2   ISBN 1-56053-184-3

PHYSICAL MEDICINE AND REHABILITATION: State of the Art Reviews is published triannually (three times per year) by Hanley & Belfus, Inc., 210 South 13th Street, Philadelphia, Pennsylvania 19107.

POSTMASTER: Send address changes to PHYSICAL MEDICINE AND REHABILITATION: State of the Art Reviews, Hanley & Belfus, Inc., 210 South 13th Street, Philadelphia, PA 19107.

The 1995 subscription price is $72.00 per year U.S., $82.00 outside U.S. (add $30.00 for air mail). Single copies $34.00 U.S., $37.00 outside U.S. (add $10.00 for single copy air mail).

Physical Medicine and Rehabilitation: State of the Art Reviews
Vol. 9, No. 2, June 1995

SEXUALITY AND DISABILITY
Trilok N. Monga, MD, FRCP(C), MRCP(I), Editor

CONTENTS

The authors introduce the volume with an overview of a wide spectrum of topics related to sexuality and the disabled: the importance of using the correct terminology, infantilization and deprivation, the role of society, personal relationships and disability, sexual abuse, politics, and others.

To understand abnormal sexual responses, clinicians must thoroughly understand the factors that promote arousal. This description of the normal sexual response cycle details the role of the central and peripheral nervous systems and the neuroanatomy and neurophysiology of erection.

This review of sexual dysfunction in men and women with spinal cord injury discusses issues such as ejaculation, semen quality, techniques to obtain erection and semen, pregnancy, labor, delivery, spasticity, and counseling for both men and women.

Stroke, the third leading cause of death in North America, leads to declines in libido, coital frequency, lubrication, and erection. Appropriate counseling can help patients cope with this multifactorial problem. However, clinicians must remember to carefully consider the attitudes of patients, many of whom were raised by parents born in the Victorian era.

Neuroendocrine dysfunction, temporolimbic epilepsy, physiatric assessment of sexuality, and clinical management are among the issues that are addressed in regard to sexual functioning in patients with traumatic brain injury. More than a dozen classes of drugs and their clinical effects are listed. The author reminds clinicians to remember the importance that patients attach to sexuality.

Most diagnoses of multiple sclerosis are made when patients are still in their reproductive years; however, the course of the disease is not affected by pregnancy. In addition to reproductive issues, the chapter covers sexual, physiologic, and psychosocial dysfunctions in patients with MS. Patient assessment is described and therapeutic interventions outlined.

Sexuality is particularly important in patients with coronary heart disease because so many of these patients return to a near normal social life. Among the many topics addressed here are anxiety, fear of pain and death, counseling, and the physiology of the sexual response.

The author focuses on issues related to sexuality in patients with arthritis, including physio-anatomic problems, psychosocial problems, and the role of the counselor in helping these patients. Sexuality in patients with scoliosis, pelvic fractures, and those who have undergone amputation also are covered.

This extensive review of sexuality in cancer patients details sexual functioning in men and, separately, in women undergoing surgery, radiotherapy, and hormonal manipulation. The author covers cancer of the prostate, colon, rectum, bladder, testicles, cervix, vulva, breast, and head and neck. Management guidelines describe the clinician's role in caring for these patients.

The authors searched the literature, surveyed leaders in the field, and collected observations from their own practice to compile this report on the relationship between chronic pain and sexuality. Factors that influence sexuality in patients with pain, the relationship between marital dysfunction and pain, and psychosexual disorders and sexual abuse are addressed.

This chapter reviews current concepts of socialization in children—from infancy through adolescence—including sexual aspects of socialization and the impact of disabilities on sexual development. Sex education for children with disabilities and sexual functioning in childhood-onset disabilities also are discussed.

The myths and benefits of sexual activity in the elderly are explored, as are topics such as the effects of societal opinion on sexuality, physiologic changes that occur with age, and the effects of chronic illness and medications on sexual function.

Once elders live in a nursing home, their sexual needs are often ignored or misinterpreted. Here, the author explores appropriate and inappropriate behavior among residents and suggests ways that staff can help to accommodate their needs. The author also broaches the issues of consent and risk of abuse, which are of particular importance in elders with cognitive or physical deficits.

Results are presented of a qualitative study of sexuality issues among women with physical disabilities. In this study, the experience of abuse emerges as an unexpectedly strong theme. Profiles of 11 women who reported abuse are described, and ways clinicians can work with such patients to prevent abuse are listed.

Aspects of reproduction, including pregnancy and delivery in women with disabilities, are addressed. Management issues of common medical problems during pregnancy and labor, such as urinary tract infection, hypotension, and autonomic hyperreflexia in spinal cord-injured women, are discussed. Other conditions, including rheumatoid arthritis, cancer, diabetes, and multiple sclerosis, are presented with regard to their effect on pregnancy and pregnancy's effect on the course of natural history of these diseases.

Various types of erectile dysfunction, including vasculogenic, neurogenic, and psychogenic, are described. Ways to evaluate impotence in physically disabled men include the monitoring of nocturnal penile tumescence, neurophysiologic testing, and examination of penile blood flow. Management approaches such as use of orthoses, vasoactive drugs, or implantation of a penile prosthesis are discussed.

Readers are updated on the psychological and psychosocial impact of disability as it pertains to sexuality and, also, on the treatment of sexual dysfunction. The chapter concludes with a summary of key elements to be included in comprehensive programs dealing with sexuality issues for the physically disabled.

CONTRIBUTORS

William P. Blocker, Jr, MD
Associate Clinical Professor, Baylor College of Medicine; Texas Methodist Hospital, Houston, Texas

Timothy B. Boone, MD, PhD
Assistant Professor of Urology, Scott Department of Urology, Baylor College of Medicine; Spinal Cord Injury Unit, Houston Veterans Affairs Medical Center, Houston, Texas

Rosie Marie Bostick, PhD
Clinical Assistant Professor, Department of Physical Medicine and Rehabilitation, Baylor College of Medicine; Houston Veterans Affairs Medical Center, Houston,Texas

David Chen, MD
Director, Spinal Cord Injury Program; Assistant Professor of Physical Medicine and Rehabilitation, Department of Physical Medicine and Rehabilitation, Northwestern University Medical School, Chicago, Illinois

Fae H. Garden, MD
Assistant Professor, Department of Physical Medicine and Rehabilitation, Baylor College of Medicine; St. Luke's Episcopal Hospital, Houston, Texas

Husam Ghusn, MD
Assistant Professor, Department of Medicine, Baylor College of Medicine; Chief, Nursing Home Care Unit, Houston Veterans Affairs Medical Center, Houston, Texas

Martin Grabois, MD
Professor and Chairman, Department of Physical Medicine and Rehabilitation, Baylor College of Medicine, Houston, Texas

Erick A. Grana, MD
Department of Physical Medicine and Rehabilitation, Baylor College of Medicine; Physical Medicine and Rehabilitation Service, Houston Veterans Affairs Medical Center, Houston, Texas

Kenneth Albert Lefebvre, PhD
Assistant Professor, Department of Physical Medicine and Rehabilitation, Northwestern University Medical School; Rehabilitation Institute of Chicago, Chicago, Illinois

Peter A.C. Lim, MD
Assistant Professor, Department of Physical Medicine and Rehabilitation, Baylor College of Medicine; Staff Physiatrist, Houston Veterans Affairs Medical Center, Houston, Texas

Manju Monga, MD
Assistant Professor, Division of Maternal Fetal Medicine, Department of Obstetrics, Gynecology and Reproductive Sciences, University of Texas Medical School at Houston, Houston, Texas

Trilok N. Monga, MD, FRCP(C), MRCP(I)
Professor, Department of Physical Medicine and Rehabilitation, Baylor College of Medicine; Chief, Physical Medicine and Rehabilitation Service, Houston Veterans Affairs Medical Center, Houston, Texas

Uma Monga, MD
Assistant Professor of Radiation Oncology, Department of Radiology, Baylor College of Medicine; Radiation Oncologist, Houston Veterans Affairs Medical Center, Houston, Texas

Maureen R. Nelson, MD
Assistant Professor of Physical Medicine and Rehabilitation and Pediatrics, Departments of Physical Medicine and Rehabilitation and Pediatrics, Baylor College of Medicine; Chief, Physical Medicine and Rehabilitation, Texas Children's Hospital, Houston, Texas

Margaret A. Nosek, PhD
Director, Center for Research on Women with Disabilities; Associate Professor, Department of Physical Medicine and Rehabilitation, Baylor College of Medicine, Houston, Texas

Henry J. Ostermann, PhD
Assistant Professor, Department of Physical Medicine and Rehabilitation, Baylor College of Medicine; Coordinator, Physical Medicine and Rehabilitation Service, Houston Veterans Affairs Medical Center, Houston, Texas

Donna M. Schramm, MD
Assistant Professor, Department of Physical Medicine and Rehabilitation, Baylor College of Medicine, Houston, Texas

Kevin G. Smith, PhD
Department of Anesthesiology, Baylor College of Medicine, Houston, Texas

Gabriel Tan, PhD
Clinical Assistant Professor, Department of Psychiatry and Behavioral Sciences, Baylor College of Medicine; Director, Pain Management and Applied Psychophysiology, Houston Veterans Affairs Medical Center, Houston, Texas

Gary M. Yarkony, MD
Vice President, Clinical Program Development, Schwab Rehabilitation Hospital; Section of Orthopaedic Surgery and Rehabilitation Medicine, University of Chicago Medical Center, Chicago, Illinois

Nathan D. Zasler, MD, FAAPM&R, FAADEP
Chief Executive Officer and Executive Medical Director, National NeuroRehabilitation Consortium, Inc.; Director, Concussion Care Center of Virginia, Richmond, Virginia

PUBLISHED ISSUES 1987–1992
(available from the publisher)

1993 ISSUES

Long-Term Consequences of Stroke
Robert W. Teasell, MD, Editor
London, Ontario, Canada

Management for Rehabilitation Medicine II
F. Patrick Maloney, MD, and Richard P. Gray, MD, Editors
Little Rock, Arkansas

Neurologic and Orthopaedic Sequelae of Traumatic Brain Injury
Lance R. Stone, DO, Editor
Downey, California

HIV-Related Disability: Assessment and Management
Michael W. O'Dell, MD, Editor
Cincinnati, Ohio

1994 ISSUES

Prosthetics
Alberto Esquenazi, MD, Editor
Philadelphia, Pennsylvania

Cancer Rehabilitation
Fae H. Garden, MD, and Martin Grabois, MD, Editors
Houston, Texas

Spasticity
Richard T. Katz, MD, Editor
St. Louis, Missouri

1995 ISSUES

Rehabilitation of Fractures
Arun J. Mehta, MB, FRCPC, Editor
Sepulveda, California

Sexuality and Disability
Trilok N. Monga, MD, Editor
Houston, Texas

The Autonomic Nervous System
Robert W. Teasell, MD, Editor
London, Ontario, Canada

Subscriptions for full year and single issues available from the publisher—
Hanley & Belfus, Inc., 210 South 13th Street, Philadelphia, PA 19107.
Telephone (215) 546-7293; (800) 962-1892. Fax (215) 790-9330.

PREFACE

This book is dedicated to one of my elderly stroke patients who was responsible for sparking my interest in sexual function and sexual concerns of people with disabilities. During my rounds one day, I was discussing with him the excellent progress he had made in his mobility and self-care activities. He listened to me carefully and at the end of my description of his progress, he had only one question to ask, and the question was put quite bluntly: "What about my sex life, doc?" That was nearly 20 years ago. I attempted to answer his question. I was vague, and the patient knew that I had little knowledge regarding sexuality problems in stroke patients. As a matter of fact, the topic of sexuality in disability was not part of the curriculum during my resident training. At that time we were only just becoming aware of the sexual problems in patients with spinal cord injury. Since then progress has been made in the study of sexual functioning in people with disability. Some progress also has been made in identifying strategies regarding management of sexuality related issues, especially in spinal cord-injured men. However, there remains a scarcity of information in regard to some fundamental questions facing people with disabilities. Many of these people wish to develop intimate relationships, have children, and be good parents. The opportunity for disabled people to have the pleasures of lasting intimate relationships, including sexual expression, pregnancy, and children continues to be limited.

Some physical medicine and rehabilitation residency training programs have now incorporated didactic lectures and workshops on sexuality in patients with spinal cord injury. However, most of the graduates in PM&R receive little education in the areas of sexuality and sexual adjustment in disabled patients, and the majority of patients with disability and their partners receive no information on this aspect of their overall functioning. As care providers, we need to look beyond the physical aspects of rehabilitation and must address quality of life issues, including sexual functioning, in disabled people.

I have attempted to include chapters on sexuality problems in most of the common diagnoses seen in the practice of rehabilitation and in primary care settings. However, our knowledge of sexual functioning in disabled people is still not only limited, but the little knowledge that is available is focused on performance issues. More research in the areas of management strategies for sexual problems, love, intimacy, and sexual expression needs to be conducted. For caregivers of physically disabled people, this book provides information on sexual activity, sexual problems, pregnancy, labor, and delivery in physically disabled persons. It also outlines some of the possible solutions to problems encountered in sexual functioning and adjustment following disability. The book is aimed at rehabilitation specialists, primary care physicians, and other professionals who provide for the needs of people with disability.

Finally, I express my heartfelt appreciation to my wife, Uma, and daughter, Manju, for their love, support, and encouragement.

Trilok N. Monga, MD
Guest Editor

TRILOK N. MONGA, MD, FRCP(C), MRCP(I)
KENNETH A. LEFEBVRE, PhD

SEXUALITY: AN OVERVIEW

From the Houston VA Medical
  Center
Houston, Texas (TNM)
  and
Rehabilitation Institute of Chicago
Chicago, Illinois (KAL)

Reprint requests to:
Trilok N. Monga, MD
Chief, Physical Medicine
  Rehabilitation Service
Houston VA Medical Center
2002 Holcombe Blvd.
Houston, TX 77030

Over the past 50 years much progress has been made in understanding the philosophy and practice of rehabilitation medicine. Traditionally, rehabilitation is defined as restoration of physical, psychological, social and vocational function in patients with physical impairment. Until recently rehabilitation has focused on physical, psychological and vocational aspects. Little emphasis has been placed on quality of life issues and sexuality in disabled persons. A patient's sexual adjustment within the functional limitations has not been studied systematically. Sexuality and the sexual needs of physically disabled persons are ignored or denied, and the disabled have been considered to be asexual by the society at large.[26,27] Furthermore, the terms *sex, sexual,* and *sexuality* are seldom defined with precision in the professional literature, and the meaning of these terms is often left to the reader's intuitive understanding.[11]

Approximately 5 million Americans (2–3% of the U.S. population) with chronic diseases and disabilities need rehabilitation services.[19] Projecting these figures globally yields an estimate of 250–300 million disabled individuals worldwide. Little information is available regarding the degree and extent of disability in disabled people. Moreover, the sexuality, sexual adjustment, and sexual practices of these people are not known. Disabled people are not only in need of rehabilitation services, but also need sexuality education that focuses on safe sex, family planning, and contraceptive options. This chapter will review some of the terminology used in the study of sexuality and discuss changing attitudes toward sexuality and sexual expression.

TERMINOLOGY

Sex, Sexual, Sexuality

Sex, sexuality, and *reproduction* are all closely interwoven into the fabric of living things. All relate to the propagation of the race and the survival of the species. Sex reflects the sum of the morphologic, physiologic, and behavioral peculiarities of living beings. It is genetically controlled and associated with sex chromosomes that typically manifest as maleness and femaleness. Thus, the term *sex* may be used to indicate chromosomal expression, to describe male and female anatomy, discuss physical or psychological attributes leading to orgasm, or merely imply penile/vaginal intercourse. Yet there can be sex without sexuality, and reproduction need not be sexual.

The current definition of sex—basically, "foreplay" followed by intercourse and ending with male orgasm in the vagina, was begun approximately 2,500 years ago to describe reproduction.[14] One of the basic problems with our definition of sex is that men have always been the "doers" and women the "done-to."[14]

Thorn-Gray and Kern[35] have described sex as a "verbal, visual, tactual and olfactory communication which expresses love and intimacy between two people."

For many people, the term *sex* evokes pleasant thoughts and sensations such as warmth, fun, lovemaking, and pleasure. On the other hand, for many people the word *disability* connotes concepts such as confinement, isolation, ugly, incapable, and painful. The emotional reaction to the concepts of sex and disability together might include such thoughts as impossibility, frustration, withdrawal, disinterest, or vulnerability.[4]

Similarly, the terms *sexual* and *sexuality* can mean different things to different people. Sexual could mean relating to, or associated with, sex as a characteristic of an organic being; having sex; participating in sex; relating to the male and female sexes or their distinctive organs or functions; or relating to the sphere of behavior associated with libidinal gratification. The term may refer to sexual drives or instincts.

Sexual behavior may be defined as an activity that may be solitary, between two persons, or in a group that induces sexual arousal. There are two major determinant of sexual behavior: the inherited sexual response patterns, a part of each individual's genetic inheritance; and the degree of restraint or other types of influence exerted on the individual by society in the expression of sexuality.

Human sexual behavior may be classified according to the number and gender of the participants. Solitary behavior involves only one individual, and sociosexual behavior involves more than one person. Sociosexual behavior may either be heterosexual or homosexual. Activities that are unusual may be labeled as deviant behavior. Sexual behavior and expression in people with disabilities is often only inadequately studied, and more work is needed in this area.

The terms *sex, sexual,* and *sexuality* may include lust, desire, and erotization.

Lust, Desire, Erotization

While discussing chronic lack of desire, Moser[29] attempted to clarify the terms *lust, desire,* and *erotization.* He described lust as a strong sexual response to an individual set of real or imagined sensory cues. He stated that lust is a basic aspect of sexual identity, set in life, unchangeable by common sex therapy techniques, and not learned in a classical sense. According to Moser, lust may also be understood as passion, and lust cues provide sexual intensity and sexual attraction between partners.

Moser[29] characterized desire as a conscious, probably hormonally mediated, perception of an interest in sex. Desire, often confused with lust, does not need to be triggered by outside stimuli. According to Kaplan,[15] feelings of sexual desire are the experiential concomitants of the physiologic activity of certain sex centers and circuits in the brain. How one develops sexual desire is an essentially unanswered question in sexology.

Erotization was seen by Moser[29] as a sexual response of variable intensity that is not as powerfully sexual as lust. It is a process by which a person learns to respond sexually to a set of cues. Erotization is amenable to change by common sex therapy techniques and has the characteristics of a learned behavior.

It is important to understand these terms for appropriate management of sex disorders. At times, what appears to be a problem with desire can actually be a problem with lust, meaning that an individual may have interest in sex but may not receive lust cues to help direct that desire.[29] The result is a person who reports no desire, but really has suppressed the desire because of the frustrations of not having found an acceptable outlet.

According to Hite,[14] the term *male sex drive* is part of the larger reproductive ideology of our society and there is no biological or physical proof of a male sex drive for intercourse. Although both males and females do have a need (sex drive) for orgasm, there is no evidence that there is anything hormonal or instinctual that drives men toward women.

Gender, Gender Identity, Gender Role

Other terms used in discussion of sex and sexuality are *gender, gender role,* and *gender identity*. Gender usually denotes male and female anatomic sex. Anatomic sex reflects the genetic and chromosomal composition of the individual. Gender identity refers to one's personally experienced sexual identity and self-awareness of being either male or female.[11] This self-awareness will then direct how or with whom one expresses this identity. The gender role reflects the behavior of the person, and this behavior indicates his/her gender identity to others.

Gender identity and gender roles develop very early in childhood. Society plays an important role in preparation and development of the gender role. The gender role may change due to impairment and disability and thus have a direct conflict with established gender identity. Partners of people with disabilities may experience the dual roles of personal care assistants and intimate partners. These challenges can create feelings of conflict for both the partner and the person with the disability and may contribute to stress in the relationship.[3]

With changing attitudes, the definitions of sexuality, gender identity, and gender roles should no longer be viewed as static, but instead should be considered as expressions of lifelong psychosocial and sexual developmental processes.[11] Furthermore, discussion of sexuality cannot be separated from the essential roles and obligations that each person has in society. Sexuality is an integral part of self-image, and self-image is an integral part of how one functions in society. The concept of sexuality should include the interpersonal aspects of one's life and the manner in which an individual discharges interpersonal responsibilities and achieves interpersonal goals.

In considering the above definitions, it becomes clear that the literature on sexuality and sexual functioning in disabled people to date has had an extremely narrow focus. Unfortunately, all too often the discussion centers on functional performance rather than the broader issues of sexuality.

SEXUALITY: HISTORICAL PERSPECTIVE

Views regarding sex and sexuality have been changing since the time of Adam and Eve. Over the centuries, attitudes toward sexuality have shifted between the extremes of sexual restraint during the Victorian era to the permissive attitude that prevailed during the 1960s. People born in the early 1900s were raised by parents who were born in the Victorian era. The attitudes, beliefs, and sexual practices of these people will be greatly different than those of children born during the sexual revolution of the 1960s and 1970s.

The emphasis in the late 1800s was on active male and passive female sexual partnership. The focus was on genital performance, female virginity, and sex role stereotyping.[11] Nudity was frowned upon, and only monogamous relationships were acceptable. The 20th century witnessed many radical changes. For example, birth control pills were introduced in the early 1960s and became widely used a decade later. By 1970, premarital sex for women was no longer as shocking as it had been only a few years earlier.[38] Also during this period, permissive media coverage was rich with sexual references for the first time.[16]

According to Francoeur,[11] sex in Western Christian thought has been viewed through the lens of a pervasive negative dualism in which one's good rational spirit/soul is opposed by one's evil, emotional, and passionate body, of which sex is a major component. Traditionally, sex has been justified by reproduction and limited to married partners. Until recently, everything associated with sex and sexual activities was viewed as some kind of "monster in the groin" that needed to be carefully restricted lest it run rampant and destroy society.[11]

Such taboos in Western culture have long impeded research concerning sexual behavior. One of the major organizations involved in the study of sex was the Institute for Sex Research at Indiana University, Bloomingdale. This research was started in 1938 by the American sexologist Alfred Charles Kinsey. Classic work by Kinsey et al.[17,18] dismantled the barrier that sex was not to be talked about or discussed in public but was only meant as a bedroom activity. He documented the variety of American sexual behavior in detailed interviews. This was probably the most comprehensive data on sexuality in its time and made the study of sex respectable in the eyes of the general public.

Kinsey used a scale from 0–6 to describe sexual behavior. At one end of the scale were people who were exclusively involved in heterosexual behavior. At the other end of the scale were people who exclusively practiced homosexual behavior. However, this work was limited to a predominantly young, middle class, healthy population. Furthermore, as helpful as the Kinsey scale was, it was still limited by the exclusion of many other potential sexual options. According to Stayton,[33] Kinsey failed to take into account autoerotic experiences and erotic experiences with nature, animals, and inanimate objects. Moreover, he failed to take into account that the entire universe may be a potential erotic "turn on."[33]

Sexual behavior data by Kinsey were complemented by Masters and Johnson's[22,23] work on human sexual response and behavioral treatments for sexual dysfunctions. Master and Johnson reported that sexual response follows a pattern of sequential stages: excitement, plateau, orgasm, and resolution.

The Hite Report[13] discusses the historical perspective of sexuality in detail.

IMPAIRMENT, DISABILITY, AND HANDICAP

The terms *impairment, disability,* and *handicap* have been used vaguely, and frequently have been incorrectly interchanged with each other. Many health care providers do not understand the meaning of these terms. The World Health Organization has attempted to define these terms as follows:

Impairment

Impairment refers to loss of function or abnormality in physiologic, psychological or anatomic structure. It implies a cellular-, organ-, or system-based diagnosis. For example, a patient with a diagnosis of diabetes mellitus has impairment of glucose metabolism, resulting from the lack of, or ineffective, insulin. This patient may need oral hypoglycemic agents, insulin, or a modified diet. Typically, he has no functional deficit and is gainfully employed. He has a positive attitude toward his health, and his family has no problems in accepting his impairment. Society may not even know that he has diabetes, an impairment.

Disability

Disability resulting from an impairment is the inability, or restriction in ability, to perform an activity within the range considered to be normal. Disability represents disturbance at the level of the individual.

To continue with the previous example, the patient may develop erectile dysfunction as a result of diabetes. This may lead to sexual disability in the sense that he cannot perform intercourse in a manner considered normal for the society in which he is living. He now has two impairments: hyperglycemia and difficulty acheiving an adequate erection. Inability to perform the sexual act becomes a disability. This disability is invisible, and the person may be able to function well within society. However, if the person develops gangrene of the foot that necessitates an amputation, the patient then has two different impairments: hyperglycemia and amputation. The resulting disability from the amputation may limit the individual's functional activities and ambulation. The person may not be able to maintain his job. If one looks beyond the boundaries of physical and vocational limitation (disability), one may find that this person has also developed *disability* in sexual functioning. This disability may include a lack of desire because of poor body image, or difficulty in performing vaginal intercourse due to problems with desired positioning.

Handicap

Handicap refers to a disadvantage that results from an impairment or disability and that limits or prevents fulfillment of a role that is considered normal for that individual. A handicap reflects the individual's interaction with and adaption to his or her environment. A broader definition of handicap includes feelings, issues, attitudes, and expectations of the society toward disabled people.

In the example above, the person's inability to maintain his job, look after his children, or maintain an active relationship with his mate could all be considered handicaps. However, it is more important to define the attitude of the spouse, family, and society toward his impairments and disability. Problems with sexual activities may be due to the fact that the spouse does not see the disabled partner as a whole person and is not willing or able to accept his limitations. However, little information is available regarding a partner's attitude toward sexuality in people with impairment and disability.

Finally, all of these issues are incorporated into the broader arena of human rights, societal values, and the entire range of problems, goals, and challenges that society assumes under the umbrella of the common good.

SEXUALITY AND DISABILITY

While it is accepted that sexuality and its prerogatives, such as childbearing and romantic relationships, are undisputed rights, it is important not to simplify or overlook the complex set of behaviors and skills that are necessary to enjoy these rights. Furthermore, as we examine sexuality in disabled people, we should not give the impression that only this societal group has problems. Problems and challenges exist at all levels of society for each individual. The ability to learn and manage what we can about our own strengths and weaknesses is multifactorial. Genetic composition, cultural background, personal and family values, and the environment in which the individual functions are all major factors.

The effects of disability will differ depending upon the age at onset of the disability. Disability starting at an early age may alter sexual orientation, sexual identity, and the biologic capacity for reproduction. Early onset of disability may interfere in spontaneous learning of sexuality and gender roles. Disabilities resulting later in life may lead to distorted body image along with sensory, cognitive, and motor deficit. These deficits will interfere in sexual expression and functioning. Gender roles may become blurred, and past patterns of sexual activity may impede the creativity needed after disability.[3]

Using the Thorn-Gray's definition[35] of sexuality as a framework, many impairments will make having a relationship difficult or impossible. For example, many stroke patients have language deficits and are unable to express, comprehend, or analyze given cues and instruction. They may have difficulty communicating their desires, feelings, and interests related to sexuality issues. Others have cognitive limitations, such as patients with traumatic brain injury (TBI). These patients may not be able to responsibly engage in sexual behavior. People with cognitive deficits, both developmental and acquired, are at higher risk for sexual exploitation and sexual abuse.[31,34]

The other component of Thorn-Gray's definition is visual expression of love and intimacy. Patients with cerebrovascular accident (CVA) and TBI may have visual deficits that could interfere in sexual expression. Although the United States has approximately 1.3 million people with impaired vision, information on sexual function in this group of patients is unavailable.

Many patients with CVA and amputation have sensory deficits. However, we do not know how these patients express love and intimacy after loss of vision or sensation of touch.

Our knowledge of sexual functioning in disabled people is not only limited, but the little knowledge available is focused on performance issues. Members of the health care community need to conduct more research in the heretofore neglected areas of love, intimacy, and sexual expression. Moreover, disabled people and those who work with them need to realistically and creatively address these limitations and broaden the definition of sexuality and sexuality-related issues.

Many impairments and disabilities interfere with social skills, body image, and self-esteem. These characteristics are considered to be central to one's ability to enjoy life and to participate in the development of relationships, intimate behavior, and preparation for pregnancy, birthing, and parenting.[7] Consequently, most people with disabilities experience difficulties in sexual expression and performance. Moreover, the spontaneity is dramatically affected and can be severely limited by the presence of a disability.[3]

SEXUAL INFANTILIZATION AND DEPRIVATION

Society generally attempts to treat people with disabilities as though sexuality and self-image do not exist. Individuals with developmental disabilities are especially likely to be treated this way. Efforts are directed at discouraging sexual expression and interest and endorsing the objective of "growing up and getting married" without ever teaching the person the skills necessary to have successful relationships. Individuals with acquired disabilities are treated without inquiry into the effects of disability on their relationships, their ability to have relationships, and their concerns about sexual function.

Moreover, it is wrong to assume that everyone has a heterosexual orientation or is comfortable with his or her orientation. A significant number of individuals have not been sexually active for some time, either by choice or because of the lack of a partner. Yet others have never had the ability to maintain a successful relationship.

Deprivation is a phenomenon that affects many people with disabilities. Areas of deprivation include lack of sex education available to people with disabilities, lack of knowledge for specific interventions, and lack of comfort in health care providers regarding dealing with issues of sexuality in these patients. The people who are deprived feel neglected by health care providers and society at large. Furthermore, insensitivity to the complications of sexual deprivation and increased sexual vulnerability results in more frequent problems and institutional denial regarding these factors.

SOCIETY, DISABILITY, AND SEXUALITY

Progress has been made in the areas of understanding the meaning, the magnitude, and management of disability. Some inroads also have been made toward prevention of primary or secondary disability. Society as a whole is more aware of the physical limitations and needs of disabled people, with the cumulative result of convincing legislators to pass the Americans with Disabilities Act (ADA) in 1990. However, many patients are frequently reluctant to seek advice. Perhaps they believe that physicians have limited knowledge of sexuality problems in disabled people. Moreover, they may feel that physicians are insensitive to specific sexuality-related issues. Many health care facilities and physician offices are not even accessible to individuals with a disability.

It is apparent that society is far behind in understanding and effectively dealing with the psychosocial impacts of disability, including sexuality. Interestingly, the ADA does not deal specifically with sexuality-related issues.

Within recent years the definition and scope of sexuality have been changing.[5,11,13,14,21] The main focus of this change has been to steer away from the traditional physical aspects of sexuality and to accept the wider, and perhaps unlimited, boundaries of sex, love, sexuality, and intimacy.

Nothing better describes this phenomenon than physician Alex Comfort's[5] comments on society's attitude toward sexuality in disabled people. He stated:

> The disabled people are people, and people are sexual. Much of our sense of person-hood comes from our ability to play a sexual role. The disabled share with the rest of us the misfortune of living in a society that has traditionally avoided and censured sex, but this hits the disabled harder than others. Moreover, virtually nobody is too disabled to derive some satisfaction and personal reinforcement from sex—with a partner if possible, alone if necessary. Human sex is widely versatile and hardly limited to the genitalia.

Similarly, Hite[13,14] states that there is no reason why physical intimacy should always consist of foreplay followed by intercourse and male orgasm. There is no reason why intercourse must always be a part of heterosexual sex. One can have sex to orgasm, or not to orgasm, genital sex, or just physical intimacy—whatever seems right to the people involved. Furthermore, if we lived in a nonpatriarchal, nonreproductively focused society, it is likely that the terms *heterosexual* and *homosexual* would become rather obscure and infrequently used.

According to Hite, sex includes intimate physical contact for pleasure; sharing pleasure with another person or one's self; learning erotic ways of touching and suggesting; and using ways of drawing another person out and aiding each other to derive pleasure. Sexuality is also simply the physical expression of feelings of love and need for another person, no matter what pattern or form the physical expression takes. Moreover, there is no standard of sexual performance against which one must measure one's own performance.

Leyson[21] has suggested use of the term *sexual celebration* instead of *sexual intercourse,* since sexual activity encompasses not only coitus in the goal-oriented model, but also a wide range of noncoital, erotic expressions, romanticism, and sensuality. The message should be that there are various ways of sexual expression and that it is acceptable to be sexual without procreation. The need to learn the skills for successful interpersonal relationships must be acknowledged as a positive goal rather than a sign of failure.

The early years of life are important in the development of interpersonal relationships and adult sexual orientation. Parents, peers, and society in general teach and condition the child about sex by indirect and often unconscious communication. In addition, some have atypical sexual experiences, such as witnessing or hearing adults engaged in sexual intercourse, or sexual contact with an older person. The effects of such experience depend upon how the child interprets these experiences and upon the reaction of adults when the experience is brought to their attention.

Many people with disabilities are raised in families that are loving, caring, supportive, and concerned, but uncomfortable or unwilling to discuss developmental or other sexuality issues.[6] These conditions provide circumstances that lead to treating the individual not only as a child but as one with no or decreased identification, interest, and potential. Sometimes there is fear that acknowledgment of sexual issues will unleash feelings, attitudes, and impulses that neither the person nor the family members can manage.

The fears directed toward disabled people reflect the fears of society in general. As we examine the problems facing the disabled, we should not treat their situation more harshly than that of their nondisabled fellow citizens. Problems with self-image, relationships and sexuality are very common. People with disabilities have an increased risk of such problems because access to educational, vocational, and cultural opportunities are restricted or absent.[32] Furthermore, role models and opportunities to express self-image or sexuality options are rare. Moreover, many people with disabilities have fixed or low incomes that may create limitations on the ability to socialize, establish relationships, and find partners.[8]

RELATIONSHIPS AND DISABILITY

There is a need to explore relationships at various levels. The relationship between the child and parent, between an adult and his or her environment, between sexual partners, and between patient and physician needs to be examined. In the context of sexuality, one usually thinks of a physical relationship among two adults rather than a social and emotional bond.

Relationships form the core of any behavior, including sexuality. In some societies or families, it is difficult to learn the skills necessary for successful relationships. The implications and consequences of such factors as single-parent households, children born out of wedlock, and other potentially stressful child-rearing approaches need to be studied so that their effects on relationship skills, sexual orientation, and sexual functioning can be known. In the absence of appropriate skills and the presence of poor or remote relationships, there is a risk of developing personality traits or behaviors that contribute to impairment and disability.

A significant number of patients with disability have dangerous or self-destructive lifestyles.[28] Many disabilities are caused by drug and alcohol use, gang violence, and domestic disputes. These problems may result from poor relationships or may lead to the breakdown of relationships and commitments. These lifestyles need to be acknowledged by health care providers so that an appropriate approach to treatment can be established. Without a good understanding of these factors, an excellent patient/physician relationship will be difficult to establish. The strengths and weaknesses of predisability relationships need to be evaluated while understanding the sexuality related issues resulting from the disability.

Many health care professionals feel uncomfortable and poorly trained in the areas of sexuality and lifestyle assessment. Staff feel that exploring and identifying destructive behaviors, habits, and sexuality problems may alienate the patient and may make it difficult to establish a good relationship with the patient and family. Furthermore, exploring this aspect of the history may be perceived as an interpersonal assault or a way of blaming the patient for his or her condition. However, it is possible to train the staff to minimize the stress of the interview. This will provide the opportunity to identify risk factors and lifestyle choices that may contribute both negatively and positively to rehabilitation outcome in general and psychosocial rehabilitation in particular.

Relationships cannot be evaluated in isolation. Many patients are seen without partners, and the information obtained may not reflect the true picture. Furthermore, the partner may take the onset of disability as an opportunity to either break the relationship or to withdraw from sexual activity in an effort to modify a relationship that was not successful or satisfying before the onset of disability.

At times, within the rehabilitation setting, we strive for the patient to achieve the premorbid level of functioning. However, this may not be right for patients who have had dysfunctional sexual or romantic relationships prior to the onset of the disability.

MULTICULTURAL SOCIETY AND HUMAN SEXUALITY

It has long been noted that culture influences sexual attitudes and behavior.[10,25] Furthermore, clinical observations show that culture has a strong impact on sexual scripts, beliefs, and behavior.[10,24] Culture may also dictate what is considered normal and dysfunctional and what sort of treatment might be acceptable. For example, some societies permit premarital coitus; others tolerate it if the individuals intend to marry. Marital coitus is usually recognized as an obligation in most societies. Extramarital coitus is generally condemned, although societies tend to be more leinient toward males than females. This double standard of behavior is also seen in premarital life.

Some believe that social class is the strongest predictor of sexual values and behavior.[9] However, others maintain that not all differences can be explained by class alone.[25] Most likely, class and ethnic origin interact in the molding of a person's sexuality and sexual expression.

Different cultures assign different meanings to sexuality, and primary sexual goals are different for cultural groups that hold the equalitarian ideology and for those that do not.[30] For example, societies with an equalitarian sexual ideology tend to emphasize that the major goals within a relationship are physical pleasure and psychological disclosure. Other components that might be considered are the interactional basis of the sexual relationship and the equality of relationships between partners.

Certain ethnic groups believe that the exchange of pleasure or communication of affection through sexual touching plays no major role in the expression of sexuality. Their major goal is heterosexual coitus in which men are permitted to engage in body-centered sexuality but sexuality for women is a powerful emotion to be feared.[30] As cited by Lavee,[20] Quijada has observed that in the cult of "virginity" women are required to be sexually pure and uncontaminated by eroticism and that sex is something to be repressed. For men, on the other hand, sexuality is a proof of manhood.

As culture influences the definition and scope of sexuality, it also formulates attitudes toward illness and dysfunction. For instance, low sexual desire and inhibited orgasm could be considered a problem in one culture but not another. In Lavee's experience, Muslim women's dysfunctions are not considered a problem unless they interfere with the man's sexual activity. For example, treatment for female orgasmic dysfunction is not sought until the women suffer from vaginismus.

When planning treatment interventions, it is very important to keep cultural differences in mind. As cited by Lavee,[20] among Asians and Chinese Americans, problem solving is supposed to occur within the family. Iranians tend to turn first to relatives, who also have a say in the diagnosis and treatment. Irish, on the other hand, tend to get help from the priest and to trust him more than the therapist. Lavee recommends that when working with clients from different cultural groups, the therapist should be aware of the possibility that he or she is not the only, or the most trusted, helper.

SEXUAL ABUSE AND THE DISABLED

People with disability may be at a greater risk than others for sexual, emotional, and financial abuse. These people find themselves in positions in which they do not feel attractive or valuable as sex partners. Furthermore, they have less opportunity to explore their sexual options and may be confused about their sexual orientation. Others may have negative feelings about their disability and feel unworthy or unacceptable as a sex partner. These feelings contribute to isolation and increased vulnerability for sexual exploitation. Rarely are such situations identified or corrected.

Staff within the health care system have both conscious and unconscious reactions to those with whom they work. Strong negative feelings of anger, frustration, and hate may develop. Similarly, positive feelings of attractiveness, nurturance, or sexual interest may arise. Health care workers and systems are often reluctant to acknowledge such feelings.[1,36]

Often, facilities are staffed by young, attractive, and healthy individuals, and patients may be attracted to the staff. Staff are routinely involved in intimate personal care and therapy activities that involve close holding and touching. Some patients will feel sexually stimulated; others may feel that staff members are making unwanted sexual advances toward them. Even in the most sensitive environment, there will still be times when such problems affect patient-staff relationships and patient care.

Professional guidelines are needed to limit or minimize patient-staff interactions that are potentially harmful or that may put the patient at risk for exploitation or abuse. Behaviors such as becoming sexually or romantically involved with patients, using recreational drugs with patients, or defining the circumstances under which social relationships can or cannot exist are appropriate issues for the health care system and professional organizations to address. People who are struggling with the redefinition of a disability are especially vulnerable and need protection from the misdirected attention or needs of caregivers.

SEXUALITY AND POLITICS

Waxman and Finger[37] comment that disabled people are denied sexual and reproductive freedom and the liberty to establish families in the form they choose. They state that "the disability rights movement has never addressed sexuality as a key political issue, though many of us find sexuality to be the area of our great oppression. We may well be more concerned with being loved and finding sexual fulfillment than getting on a bus." Waxman and Finger also cite some examples of circumstances in which a disabled person could be at a disadvantage if the government came to know that the disabled person was married.

They report that a disabled person who engaged in oral sex—even if married—would be subject to arrest in 24 states and, in some states, could be charged with a felony for having "unnatural sex." They also provide other examples where the socio-political-medical model is not tuned to the needs of the disabled in the areas of sexuality and reproduction. They conclude that (1) it is almost illegal to be severely disabled and married, (2) disabled people are denied sexual and reproductive freedom and the liberty to establish families in forms that they choose, (3) there is no other group in the United States that faces the sort of sexual and reproductive restrictions that disabled people do, and (4) disabled people are frequently prevented from marrying, bearing or rearing children, learning about sexuality, having sexual relationships, and obtaining sexual literature.

Another view point is: "A society can be measured to the extent that its members confirm one another."[2] Martin Buber's[2] guide for assessing the humaneness of a society can be used as a guiding principle in working with disabled people. However, the process of confirmation may be more complicated than it seems, because rights and opportunities usually have a cost.

Many people with a disability have basic needs that include the need to be sexual and attractive, the need to develop a positive self-image, and the desire to share affection with others in positive ways. These basic needs have implicit obligations that are sometimes overlooked. To some, the reciprocity of needs and obligations is a way of restricting or controlling behavior. To others the idea of rights and obligations being integrated is congruent with their world view. Leaders within the community of disabled people, those who work within that community, and the government need to address this balance and its implications.

Not every disabled person has the same obligations, desires, and opportunities. It may be irresponsible to encourage an individual to reproduce if the individual is unable to sustain a relationship, cannot parent, and does not have the ability to maintain a household. On the other hand, it is a violation of human rights to prohibit these activities, to limit freedom, or to deny what some consider inalienable rights. These are emotional and controversial topics.

FUTURE RESEARCH ON SEXUALITY

The body of scientific evidence that has accumulated does not address the fundamental questions facing people with disabilities who wish to form intimate friendships, have children, and be good parents. Indeed, the traditional approach to research on sexual behavior and reproduction has focused on improving the understanding of normal development and developing treatments for health problems of people without physical disabilities.[12] Authors have listed more than 70 research issues and many research directives in relation to reproductive issues for people with disabilities. These research issues include development of sexual identities and sexual relationships of people with childhood disabilities; methods of contraception available to people with physical disabilities; risks of contracting sexually transmitted diseases in patients with disabilities; and issues of fertility, marriage, pregnancy, labor, delivery, and parenting. It is important to note that one of the first initiatives of the National Center for Medical Rehabilitation Research was to set aside approximately $1 million for research on issues related to reproduction by individuals with physical disabilities.

SUMMARY

Although much progress has been made in understanding the philosophy and practice of rehabilitation medicine, little emphasis has been placed on the quality of life issues and sexuality in disabled persons. A patient's sexual function and sexual adjustment within the functional limitations has not been studied systematically. Sexual needs of physically disabled persons are often ignored. Knowledge of sexual functioning in disabled people is not only limited, but is also focused on performance issues. Members of the health care community need to do more research in the heretofore neglected areas of love, intimacy, and sexual expression in disabled persons.

REFERENCES

1. Brillhart BA, Jay H, Wyers ME: Attitudes toward people with disabilities. Rehabil Nurs 15:80–82, 1990.
2. Buber M: In Walter Kauman (trans): I and Thou. New York, Charles Scribner's Sons, 1970.
3. Cole S, Cole TM: Sexuality, disability, and reproductive issues through the lifespan: In Haseltine FP, Cole SS, Gray DB (eds): Reproductive Issues for Persons with Physical Disabilities, Baltimore, Paul H. Brooks, 1993, pp 3–21.
4. Cole TM, Cole SC: Rehabilitation of problems of sexuality in physical disability. In Kottke FJ, Lehmann JF (eds): Krusen's Handbook of Physical Medicine and Rehabilitation. 4th ed. Philadelphia, WB Saunders, 1990, pp 988.
5. Comfort A: Foreword. In Mooney TO, Cole TM, Chilgren RA (eds): Sexual Options for Paraplegics and Quadriplegics. Boston, Little, Brown & Co, 1975.
6. Cromer BA, Enrile B, Mccoy K, et al: Knowledge, attitudes and behavior related to sexuality in adolescents with chronic disability. Dev Med Child Neurol 32:602–610, 1990.
7. Deloach C, Greer BG: The third disabling myth: The sexuality of the disabled. In Deloach C, Greer BG (eds): Adjustment to Severe Physical Disability: A Metamorphosis. New York, McGraw-Hill, 1981, pp 65–99.
8. Hanks M, Poplin D: The sociology of physical disability: A review of literature and some conceptual perspectives. Deviant Behavior: An Interdisciplinary Journal 2:309–328, 1981.
9. Ficher IV, Coleman SB: Blue collar-white collar: Sexual myths and realities. In Scholevar GO (ed): The Handbook of Marriage and Marital Therapy. New York, Spectrum, 1981.

10. Francoeur RT: Human sexuality. In Sussman M, Steinmetz S (eds): Handbook of Marriage and the Family. New York, Plenum, 1987.
11. Francoeur RT: Historical and sociocultural perspectives in human sexuality. In Sexual Rehabilitation of the Spinal Cord Injured Patient. Totowa, NJ, Humana, 1991.
12. Gray DB, Schimmel AB: Future directions for research on reproductive issues for physical disabilities. In Haseltine FP, Cole SS, Gray DB (eds): Reproductive Issues for Persons with Physical Disabilities. Baltimore, Paul H. Brooks, 1993, pp 339–354.
13. Hite S: The Hite Report on Male Sexuality. New York, Alfred A. Knopf, 1981.
14. Hite S: The Hite Report. Macmillan, New York, 1976.
15. Kaplan HS: Sex, intimacy, and the aging process. J Am Acad Psychoanal 18:185–205, 1990.
16. Key WB: Subliminal Seduction. Englewood Cliffs, NJ, Prentice Hall, 1973.
17. Kinsey AC, Pomery WB, Martin CE: Sexual Behavior in the Human Male. Philadelphia, WB Saunders, 1948.
18. Kinsey AC, Pomeroy WB, Martin CE: Sexual Behavior in the Human Female. Philadelphia, WB Saunders, 1953.
19. Kottke FJ, Lehmann JF: Preface. In Kottke FJ, Lehmann JF (eds): Kruesen's Handbook of Physical Medicine and Rehabilitation. 4th ed. Philadelphia, WB Saunders, 1990, p xvii.
20. Lavee Y: Western and non western human sexuality: Implications for clinical practice. J Sex Marital Ther 17:203–213, 1991.
21. Leyson JFJ: Sociosexual and marital relationships. In Haseltine FP, Cole SS, Gray DB (eds): Reproductive Issues for Persons with Physical Disabilities. Baltimore, Paul H. Brooks, 1993.
22. Master WB, Johnson VE: Human Sexual Response. Boston, Little, Brown & Co, 1970.
23. Master WB, Johnson VE: Human Sexual Inadequacy. Boston, Little, Brown & Co, 1970.
24. McCormick NB. Sexual scripts: Social and therapeutic implications. Sex Marital Ther 2:3–27, 1987.
25. McGoldrick M: Ethnicity and family therapy: An overview. In McGoldrick M, Pearce JK, Giordano J (eds): New York, Guilford, 1982, pp 3–33.
26. Monga TN, Lawson JS, Inglis J: Sexual dysfunction in stroke patients. Arch Phys Med Rehabil 67:19–22, 1986.
27. Monga TN: Sexuality post stroke. Phys Med Rehabil State Art Rev 7:225–236, 1993.
28. Moore D, Polsgrove L: Disabilities, developmental handicaps, and substance abuse misuse: A review. Int J Addict 26:65–90, 1991.
29. Moser C: Lust, lack of desire, and paraphilias: Some thoughts and possible connections. J Sex Marital Ther 18:65–69, 1992.
30. Reiss IL: Journey into Sexuality: An Exploratory Voyage. Englewood Cliffs, NJ, Prentice-Hall, 1986.
31. Rieve JE: Sexuality and the adult with acquired physical disability. Nurs Clin North Am 24:265–276, 1989.
32. Rodgers SJ: Observation of emotional functioning in young handicapped children. Child Care Health Dev 17:303–312, 1991.
33. Stayton WR: A theory of sexual orientation: The universe as a turn on. Top Clin Nurs 1:1–7, 1980.
34. Tharinger D, Horton CB, Millea S: Sexual abuse exploitation of children and adults with mental retardation and other handicaps. Child Abuse Negl 14:301–312, 1990.
35. Thorn-Gray B, Kern L: Sexual dysfunction associated with physical disability: A treatment guide for the rehabilitation practitioner. Rehabil Lit 44:138–144, 1983.
36. Westbrook MT, Legge V, Pennay M: Attitudes toward disabilities in a multicultural society. Soc Sci Med 36:615–623, 1993.
37. Waxman BF, Finger A: The politics of sexuality, reproduction and disability. In Sexuality Update, National Task Force on Sexuality and Disability (American Congress of Rehabilitation Medicine) 4(1):1–3, 1991.
38. Wilson S, Strongi B, Robbins M, Johns T: Human Sexuality. St Paul, MN, West Publishing, 1980.

TIMOTHY B. BOONE, MD, PhD

THE PHYSIOLOGY OF SEXUAL FUNCTION IN NORMAL INDIVIDUALS

From the Scott Department
of Urology
Baylor College of Medicine
and
Spinal Cord Injury Unit
Houston VA Medical Center
Houston, Texas

Reprint requests to:
Timothy B. Boone, MD, PhD
6560 Fannin, Suite 1004
Houston, TX 77030

The arousal of libido in men and women may result from a variety of stimuli, some purely imaginary. Such neocortical influences are transmitted to the limbic system and then to the hypothalamus and spinal centers. Furthermore, normal sexual functioning depends on many factors, such as intact neural pathways, normal anatomy, normal release of neurotransmitters, and various hormones. It is imperative for the clinician to have a thorough knowledge of these factors so that a clear understanding of abnormal sexual responses can be delineated.

NORMAL SEXUAL RESPONSE CYCLE

The classic studies of Masters and Johnson divided the sexual response cycle into four phases: excitement, plateau, orgasm, and resolution.[19] These phases of the cycle vary based on the gender of the individual. The male pathway goes through excitement, plateau, orgasm, and back to baseline. The excitement phase in the male consists of vascular engorgement of the corpora cavernosa in the penis, testicular elevation, and flattening of the scrotal skin. The plateau phase includes secretions from the urethral Cowper's glands and accelerated cardiovascular responses (heart rate and blood pressure). During male orgasm, the perineal musculature contracts rhythmically, the bladder neck closes, and seminal fluid is deposited into the posterior urethra from the prostate, vas deferens, and seminal vesicles.

Women may progress from excitement to plateau with or without orgasm and remain at that state until resolution. The excitement phase in women is characterized by vaginal lubrication, clitoral enlargement, upper vaginal dilation with constriction of the lower third of the vagina, and uterine elevation. During plateau, the clitoral shaft and glans retract against the pubic symphysis, and an increase occurs in muscle tone, heart rate, respiratory rate and blood pressure. Females may experience one or multiple orgasms, with contractions of the perineal muscle, fallopian tube, and uterus.

The resolution phase in men and women slowly reverses the physiologic changes. Patients with sexual dysfunction can be classified according to specific problems during the sexual response cycle.

Central Nervous System

CORTEX AND SUBCORTICAL AREAS

Most of the understanding of the supraspinal mechanisms in sexual function and dysfunction have been derived from nonhuman primate experiments, with correlation to humans when possible. The entire cerebral hemispheric structure can be divided into four areas: idiotypic cortex, homotypical isocortex, paralimbic areas, and limbic areas.

Idiotypic Cortex. The highly specialized idiotypic cortex contains the primary sensory and motor areas. Environmental sensory input has its first relay in this zone for capturing sexual stimuli from the world.

Homotypical Isocortex. Modality-specific relays in the homotypical isocortex (association areas) transfer sensory information from the primary areas toward other parts of the cortex. Lesions in this region lead to disconnection syndromes in which cortical sensory information is not integrated with paralimbic, limbic, or associations areas, which are integral components of sexual behavior.

Paralimbic Cortex. The paralimbic cortex includes the cingulate gyrus and piriform cortex. Paralimbic structures receive cortical information from hetero-modal association areas and integrate this information with limbic inputs to emphasize the relevance of a stimulus to sexual behavior (e.g., attractiveness, libido).[20] Specific patterns of autonomic response can be associated with emotional states, and the paralimbic areas are centrally located to coordinate these responses. Electrical stimulation of the paralimbic cortex has produced erections and genital hallucinations.[16,21] Specific lesions in the piriform cortex produce hypersexuality.[20] The pathogenesis of psychosomatic disease may involve an imbalance of mental events with autonomic activity. Paralimbic areas of the brain may be a central site of psychogenic erectile dysfunction.

The Limbic System. The neural product of all of this cortical information is relayed to the limbic zone, where significant interactions with the hypothalamus occur. Limbic zone lesions cause severe alterations in sexual function. The amygdala, hippocampus, septal complex and portions of the piriform cortex make up the limbic system. The amygdala is located in the mesial temporal lobe, where it has reciprocal connections with other limbic structures and plays a central role in drive and affect. Deprivation of cortical input to the amygdala due to temporal lobe ablation in monkeys leads to loss of aggressive-aversive behavior, indiscriminate sexual activity, and oral inspection of both edible and inedible objects (Klüver-Bucy syndrome). Figure 1 shows a magnetic resonance image of a damaged temporal lobe (toxoplasmosis) in a 35-year-old patient complaining of a lack of sexual desire. This finding is consistent with Boller's impression of hyposexuality following a temporal lobe lesion.[4] The amygdala also takes part in regulation of the autonomic nervous system through the stria terminalis to the hypothalamus.

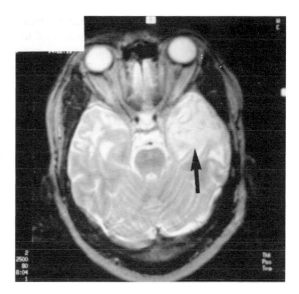

FIGURE 1. Magnetic resonance image demonstrates a temporal lobe lesion in a 35-year-old man with loss of libido.

Connections between the amygdala and the hypothalamus explain the role of the limbic system in endocrine balance and the occurrence of infertility and impotence in patients with temporolimbic epilepsy (TLE).[20] The final component of the limbic system is the hippocampus, whose primary role concerns memory and learning.

The final common pathway for the limbic system is the hypothalamus and its anterior preoptic nucleus. Lisk located this nucleus and its role in the initiation of copulation in 1967.[15] Freely moving Rhesus monkeys with lateral and dorsomedial hypothalamic electrodes were noted to have penile erections and copulatory behavior with electrical stimulation to these brain regions.[24] Stimulation of these areas also promoted ejaculation. Recent experimental work has demonstrated electrophysiologic evidence of afferent input from the dorsal penile nerve to the medial preoptic nucleus in the hypothalamus.[17] Direct projections from the hypothalamus to spinal centers for erection have been demonstrated.[11] Hypothalamic lesions placed bilaterally in humans for control of hyperkinetic movement disorders have caused erectile dysfunction and loss of libido.

FRONTAL LOBES

The frontal lobes are intimately involved with limbic and paralimbic structures. Frontal lesions may result in various behavioral abnormalities. Inferomedial frontal injury may produce disinhibition and inappropriate behaviors. On the other hand, dorsolateral frontal lesions will impair initiation of sex.[27] It should not be surprising that sexual dysfunction commonly occurs after any significant brain insult, given the propensity of frontotemporal focal cortical contusion and diffuse axonal injury.[12] Such a sexual dysfunction could also be explained in patients with cerebrovascular accident involving frontotemporal region.

CEREBRAL LATERALIZATION

Cerebral lateralization also may come into play with regard to sexual functioning. Most of the information regarding these issues comes from studies on patients with cerebrovascular accidents (see chapter 4). Some investigators believe that lesions in the right brain result in a greater degree of sexual impairment, and others hold the opposite opinion. The nondominant temporal lobe has been reported by some investigators to be the sexual activation center.[7] Furthermore, some authors have speculated that frontal involvement may be a more significant issue than laterality.

BASAL GANGLIA

The basal ganglia include the striatum and pallidum. Less is known about the basal ganglia and their role in sexual behavior than about the previously described structures. However, clinical studies have shown cognitive deficits and reduced sexual function in patients with Parkinson's disease.[4] Locomotor retardation, depression, and a neurochemical imbalance are all features of Parkinson's disease, and the precise role of each in sexual dysfunction remains to be elucidated. Basal ganglia stimulation may produce complex forms of species-specific ritualistic sexual behavior.[24]

BRAIN STEM

The brain stem conducts efferent and afferent information from the spinal cord along with the reticular activating system.[12] Brain-stem structures, like the catecholaminergically driven pontine and mesencephalic reticular activating systems, are responsible for maintaining arousal and alertness. These systems innervate limbic and frontal structures responsible for many sexually oriented behaviors along with stimulation for arousal and alertness. Activation of specific cortical and limbic structures must occur to drive libido and erectile function. Hypothalamic output traverses the brain stem in the dorsal, longitudinal fasciculus, and afferent sexual sensory input is closely associated with the spinal thalamic tract and its course through the lateral medulla and pons in route to the thalamus. Injury to brain-stem structures can result in decreased ability to prepare the patient for processing incoming information. Brain-stem damage and loss of reticular system activation can lead to lethargy, poor attention, stupor, or coma. Furthermore, damage to certain limbic and cortical structures will decrease libido and erectile potency.

In summary, supraspinal integration of neural, sensory, and hormonal pathways is complex; multiple sites in the cortex, limbic system, and brain stem are involved in normal sexual function. Knowledge of the involved supraspinal structures will help in the diagnosis and treatment of sexual dysfunction.

Peripheral Nervous System

The peripheral nervous system, including the autonomic and somatic nervous systems, comprise the remaining structures involved with sexual function. Male and female sexual organs receive sympathetic and parasympathetic innervation. The penis is innervated by three sets of nerves: pelvic (sacral parasympathetic), hypogastric-lumbar sympathetic chain (thoracolumbar sympathetic), and the pudendal (somatic) nerves (Fig. 2). Parasympathetic pathways from the sacral spinal cord (S2–S4) join sympathetic fibers from the thoracolumbar spinal cord (T10–L2) in the pelvic plexus, where postganglionic fibers form the cavernosal nerves innervating the corporal smooth muscle. The pelvic nerves also innervate the testes, prostate, seminal vesicles, and vas deferens. Preganglionic cell bodies regulating erection have been localized to the intermediolateral gray matter of the thoracolumbar spinal cord and the intermediolateral and medioventral gray

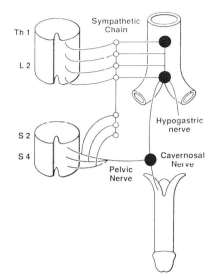

FIGURE 2. Autonomic innervation of the penis.

matter of the sacral spinal cord (Fig. 3). Branches of the pudendal nerve arising in the sacral spinal cord (S2–S4) provide sensory fibers to the penis (dorsal neve) and innervate the bulbocavernosus and ischiocavernosus muscles, which contract rhythmically during ejaculation. The pelvic floor musculature is innervated by motor fibers in the pudendal nerve arising from S2–S4.

In women, the nerve supply is a mixture of parasympathetic and sympathetic pathways. The parasympathetic nerve supply is through the pelvic nerves via the uterine and hypogastric plexus. The uterus and the ovaries receive only sympathetic innervation, and other genital structures receive mixed autonomic innervation.[12]

Neurotransmitters

Most theories regarding neurotransmitters and the physiology of sexual function are based on animal experiments and anecdotal side effects from studies of drugs in humans. Multiple neurotransmitters have been identified in corporal tissue, but the exact neurotransmitter(s) or neuromodulator(s) responsible for initiating smooth muscle relaxation and increased blood flow remain to be determined. For many years, cholinergic neurotransmission was believed to be the major effector of penile tumescence. However, atropine failed to block penile erection, as would be predicted from this cholinergic theory.[8] *Acetylcholine* released from parasympathetic pathways is not the principal or only vasodilatory transmitter triggering erection in humans. *Vasoactive intestinal polypeptide* (VIP) is also released during erection and may play a role in modulating tumescence.[19]

FIGURE 3. The location of spinal cord neurons regulating erectile function.

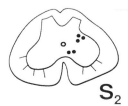

T_{12} S_2

A dose-dependent relaxation response has been demonstrated when VIP was placed on erectile tissue.[10] It is doubtful that VIP is the sole transmitter responsible for erectile function since intracorporeal injection of VIP has failed to induce erection in many men with erectile dysfunction. Penile flaccidity is maintained by the release of norepinephrine and neuropeptide Y acting via alpha-adrenergic and peptide receptors to increase anteriolar and sinusoidal smooth muscle contraction, preventing an increase in blood flow and tumescence. Therefore, *catecholamines* are not responsible for triggering erectile activity. Currently, a nonadrenergic, noncholinergic transmitter has been implicated, and recent laboratory investigations have focused on nitric oxide as the central mediator of corporal smooth muscle relaxation.[6,22] Nitric oxide released by dilator nerves and endothelium stimulates cyclic guanosine monophosphate (c-GMP) formation, and the corporal muscle relaxes. This nitric oxide–c-GMP pathway appears to be the dominant neurotransmitter system in penile erection.[13] Prostaglandins are also synthesized by corporal tissue, and prostaglandin E1 has been shown to be an effective agent for relaxation of smooth muscle in the penis. Prostaglandin E1 stimulates cyclic adenosine monophosphate formation, leading to cavernosal engorgement and tumescence.[2] Clinical studies have demonstrated its therapeutic potential.[26]

Multiple neurochemical substrates have been identified in the central nervous system, with clear linkage to sexual behavior. The ventral noradrenergic bundle in the lateral tegmentum innervates the locus ceruleus and limbic system with subsequent projection to cortical areas. Sexual arousal is facilitated by activation of this ascending noradrenergic pathway. Serotonergic pathways originate in the dorsal raphe nucleus of the brain stem and project cephalad to the forebrain while descending pathways in the spinal cord modulate reflexes involved with sexual behavior.[18,23]

The clinical availability of L-DOPA, a dopamine agonist, led to early studies with these monoamines and sexual function. Dopamine agonists improve sexual function, and antagonists suppress sexual activity.[5] Potential sites for dopaminergic mediation of sexual behavior include the nigrostriatal tract (copulation and arousal), medial preoptic area, and spinal dopamine receptors (ejaculation).[3]

Neuroendocrinology

Gonadal hormones play an important role in normal sexual maturation and sexual function. The principal male gonadal hormone is testosterone. Androgens including testosterone are secreted mainly by the cells of Leydig in the testes. Testosterone is responsible for the development of the male sexual organs, secondary sexual characteristics, and behavioral patterns. A decreased serum testosterone level may manifest as a decrease in libido and problems with erectile function. There may be loss of secondary sexual characteristics. Furthermore, neurons as well as sexual organs are targets for hormone action.

Normal sexual functioning also depends on the various hormones. The pituitary hormones involved in regulation of sexual functioning include follicle-stimulating hormone (FSH), prolactin (PRL), and luteinizing hormone (LH). These hormones regulate gonadal function; specifically, testosterone in males and estrogen in females. Testosterone secretion is regulated by the effect of LH on the cells of Leydig in the testes. FSH acts upon the seminiferous tubules, complementing the effects of LH relative to spermatozoa maturation.

In women, LH and FSH are mainly involved with the control of the menstrual cycle. Prolactin levels are suppressed in the presence of hypothalamic portal system dopamine. This hormone is increased in response to stress, in association with certain types of seizure disorders, and as a result of certain medications. Normally, an increase in PRL exerts an inhibitory effect on the hypothalamic pituitary gondal axis.[12]

Follicle-stimulating hormone and luteinizing hormones are secreted from the anterior pituitary. Cells in the arcuate nucleus of the hypothalamus secrete gonadotropin-releasing hormone (GnRH) into the portal circulation, which subsequently stimulates the release of LH and FSH. In turn, GnRH release is regulated by feedback from gonadal hormone levels, PRL, and other extrahypothalamic structures in the brain stem and limbic system.

Estrogen, progesterone, and small amounts of androgens are secreted by the ovaries. These hormones are required for normal female sexual maturation, including development of sex organs, secondary sexual characteristics, menstruation, and libido. The significant role of the hypothalamus in endocrine balance is supported by its role during sexual maturation. However, following sexual maturity, severe androgen deficiency must occur before significant changes in sexual behavior occur. Reduced libido and erectile dysfunction lag behind the loss of androgen levels.[4]

NEUROANATOMY AND NEUROPHYSIOLOGY OF ERECTION

The knowledge of neuroanatomy and physiology as it relates to sexual functioning is not well defined. As described above, multiple neural networks appear to be involved in sexual function and expression. These networks include structures in the peripheral nervous system and central nervous system. It is important to have basic knowledge of these structures so that a correct diagnosis of sexual dysfunction can be made and appropriate interventions can be instituted.

Impotence is the inability to achieve or sustain an erection of sufficient rigidity for sexual intercourse. The condition has to do with penile erection only and does not include sexual dysfunction affecting libido, ejaculation, or orgasm. A patient with normal rigidity for coitus who is unable to achieve orgasm or ejaculate is not impotent in the strictest sense of the terminology.

A common disorder affecting as many as 10 million American men, impotence is age dependent, occurring in 1.9% of 40-year-old men and 25% of 65-year-old men. The prevalence of erectile dysfunction is very high in diabetics and patients with neurological disorders. Before 1980, 90–95% of patients with erectile dysfunction were classified as having psychogenic impotence. Today, the diagnosis of psychological impotence has decreased. Diagnostic methods such as nocturnal penile tumescence monitoring, duplex penile Doppler ultrasonography, pharmacologic testing, and dynamic physiologic testing of the penile cavernous tissues during erection have provided confirmation of pathologic disorders in many patients so that the number thought to have psychogenic impotence has dropped from 90% to 25%.

Normal erectile function requires the integration of neurogenic, vascular, hormonal, and cavernosal factors. Any single factor or mixture of factors may cause erectile dysfunction, ranging from a partial decrease in rigidity to complete loss of erections. Knowledge of penile anatomy is essential to understanding the mechanisms that trigger and sustain erection. The following sections will describe the anatomy and physiology of human erectile function.

Anatomy

The penis is composed of three highly vascular cylinders at the paired corpora cavernosa and the corpus spongiosum, which surrounds the urethra and expands distally to become the glans penis (Fig. 4). The proximal corpora cavernosa rest on the ischiopubic rami and join to form the crura in the perineum, where they extend distally to the glans penis. The tunica albuginea is a thick fascial sheath surrounding each corporal body. The sponge-like interior of the corpora is made of multiple lacunar spaces lined by vascular endothelium on a lattice-like framework of smooth muscle, fibroblasts, and extracellular matrix (collagen and elastin). Tortuous helicine arteries branching from the paired cavernosal arteries provide blood flow to the erectile tissue. Subtunical veins collect venous outflow and are critical anatomic structures for the acquisition and maintenance of erection.

The pelvic plexus, which is formed by parasympathetic visceral efferent preganglionc fibers from sacral S2–S4 segments and sympathetic fibers from the thoracolumbar region, is located retroperitoneally on the lateral wall of the rectum 5–11 cm from the anal verge. Its proximity to the seminal vesicles can be used as a landmark to identify the pelvic plexus. Cavernous nerves lie adjacent to the capsular arteries and veins of the prostate gland, composing the neurovascular bundles. It is important to have a good understanding of these anatomic relationships during radical prostate and other pelvic surgery. Damage to the neurovascular bundles will cause erectile dysfunction.

In the flaccid state, active contraction of the arteriolar and sinusoidal smooth muscle shunts blood away from the sinusoids (Fig. 5). This tonically contracted state is under sympathetic modulation. Psychic stimuli or physical stimulation of the genital organs activates the autonomic nervous system to increase penile blood flow. The erect or tumescent state occurs when the main corporeal artery dilates and increases the blood flow to the sinusoidal spaces, which are enlarged by active smooth muscle relaxation. This expansion of the sinusoidal spaces leads to partial compression of the emissary veins with restricted venous outflow, thereby maintaining tumescence (*see* Fig. 5). Penile rigidity is enhanced further with contraction of the bulbocavernosus and ischiocavernosus muscles. A complex series of neurovascular events must occur to initiate a rigid erection, and this sequence requires an intact neural innervation, intact arterial supply, appropriately responsive corporal smooth muscle, and intact venous occlusive mechanism.

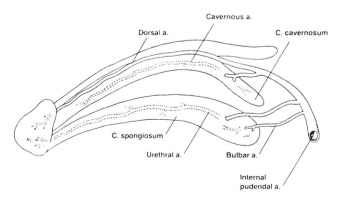

FIGURE 4.   Arterial blood supply to the penis. The cavernous arteries branch from the internal pudendal artery and run longitudinally through the corpora cavernosa. (From Orvis BR, Lue TF: New therapy of impotence. Adv Urol 1:179, 1988; with permission.)

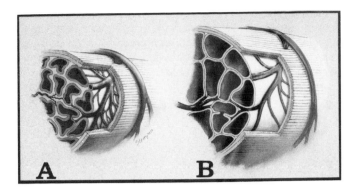

FIGURE 5.　Hemodynamics of erection. In the flaccid state, arterial blood is shunted past the sinusoids to the subtunical venous plexus *(A)*. Erection occurs with local release of nitric oxide, stimulating trabecular and arteriolar smooth muscle relaxation. Expanding blood-filled sinusoids compress the subtunical veins, preventing venous outflow to maintain the tumescent state *(B)*. (From Journal of Urology 149(5), Pt 2 of 2: 1993; P. Stempien, artist; with permission.)

Endocrine Function

Adequate androgen serum levels must be present for maintenance of sexual potency, libido, and ejaculatory function. Testosterone levels decline in men beyond the seventh decade. The decrease results from reduced testicular function and hypothalamic-pituitary dysfunction. The exact threshold at which testosterone reduction results in loss of potency is not known. Neurons and their peripheral targets are influenced by hormonal levels. Androgen-driven sexual dimorphism is important for central nervous system organization, development, and reproductive behavior. Decreased androgen levels have been shown to reduce neuron size and dendritic length in spinal cord nuclei, innervating the ejaculatory muscles.[1]

Reflex Mechanisms

Reflexogenic and psychogenic erections result from two distinct mechanisms of central nervous system regulation of penile erection. Reflexogenic penile erections occur when tactile genital stimulation is conveyed to the sacral spinal cord via the pudendal nerve. Activation of the sacral parasympathetic outflow via the pelvic nerve to the cavernosal nerve leads to relaxation of the corporal smooth muscle. These reflex erections are poorly maintained without constant tactile stimulation. Reflexogenic erections require intact S2–S4 nerve roots.

Auditory, imaginative, olfactory, or visual stimuli can induce psychogenic erections. Psychogenic erections are mediated by sympathetic or sacral autonomic outflow and require intact thoracolumbar nerve roots. Clinically, they are usually poorly sustained erections for sexual intercourse. Injury to the sacral spinal cord will abolish reflexogenic erections, but psychogenic erections may still occur through intact sympathetic innervation of the penis.

Female Sexual Function

Although the pathways for male erection have been studied in great detail, the pathways for vaginal lubrication and orgasm have been poorly described. Sensory pathways from the clitoris and vagina are present in the pudendal nerves.

Innervation of the vagina, clitoris, and fallopian tubes is provided by the pelvic hypogastric nerves. Psychogenic lubrication involves both the thoracolumbar sympathetics and sacral parasympathetics. Reflex vaginal lubrication is a function of sacral parasympathetic stimulation. Ovaries are innervated by the sympathetic nervous system. Uterine smooth muscle contraction is regulated by thoracolumbar sympathetic pathways. Activation of the somatic pudendal nerves causes contraction of the vaginal wall and pelvic floor musculature.

Women with spinal cord injuries can achieve pregnancy and deliver healthy children. Many remain amenorrheic for 6–9 months after injury, but fertility in women is not as severely affected following spinal cord injury as it is in men.[25] Spinal cord injury above T11 still allows vaginal lubrication and tumescence. Injuries between T12 and S1 are similar to complete conus medullaris lesions in men. Early sexual education is vital to reassure patients of their fertility potential and prevent unwanted pregnancies. It is important that early multidisciplinary care be given during pregnancy by the rehabilitationist, anesthesiologist, and obstetrician.

Emission and Ejaculation

Emission is a sympathetically mediated process whereby seminal and prostatic fluid is deposited into the posterior urethra from the epididymis and vas deferens. Emission is dependent on intact hypogastric sympathetic nerve function. Preganglionic neurons at T11–L2 are activated to cause smooth muscle contraction in the vas deferens and epididymis.

Ejaculation is the expulsion of fluid from the posterior urethra. Sympathetically mediated closure of the bladder neck occurs with ejaculation to prevent retrograde flow of semen into the bladder. Contractions of the bulbocavernous and ischiocavernous muscles via pudendal nerve activity compress the urethra to propel the ejaculate in an anterograde direction.

SUMMARY

Normal sexual function depends on many factors, and it is important for the clinician to thoroughly understand the neurophysiology, neuroanatomy, and neurotransmitters responsible for sexual behavior and expression. However, most of our understanding of supraspinal mechanisms and neurotransmitters as it relates to sexual function and dysfunction has been derived from nonhuman primate experiments. Further research is required in these areas to better understand human sexual behavior.

REFERENCES

1. Arnold AP, Breedlove SM: Organizational and activational effects of sex steroids on brain and behavior: A reanalysis. Horm Behav 19:469–498, 1985.
2. Bhargava G, Valcic M, Melman A: Human corpora cavernosa smooth muscle cells in culture: Influence of catecholamines and prostaglandins on cAMP formation. Int J Impot Res 2:35, 1990.
3. Bitran D, Hull EM: Pharmacological analysis of male rat sexual behavior. Neurosci Biochem Rev 11:365–389, 1988.
4. Boller F, Frank E: Sexual Dysfunction in Neurological Disorders: Diagnosis, Management, and Rehabilitation. New York, Raven Press, 1982.
5. Bowers M, VanWoert M, Davis L: Sexual behavior during L-DOPA treatment for parkinsonism. Am J Psychiatry 127:1691–1693, 1971.
6. Burnett AL, Lowenstein CJ, Bredt DS, et al: Nitric oxide: A physiologic mediator of penile erection. Science 257:401–403, 1992.

7. Cohen H, Rosen R, Golstien L: Electroencephalographic laterality changes during human sexual orgasm. Arch Sex Behav 5:189–199, 1976.
8. deGroat WC, Steers WD: Neuroanatomy and neurophysiology of penile erection. In Tanagho ET, McClure RD (eds): Contemporary Management of Impotence and Infertility. Baltimore, Williams & Wilkins, 1988, pp 3–27.
9. Gu J, Polak JM, Probert L, et al: Peptidergic innervation of the human male genital tract. J Urol 130:386–391, 1983.
10. Hedlund H, Andersson KE: Effects of some peptides on isolated human penile erectile tissue and cavernous artery. Acta Physiol Scand 124:413–419, 1985.
11. Holstege G: Some anatomical observations on the projections from the hypothalamus to brainstem and spinal cord: An HRP and autoradiographic tracing study in cat. J Comp Neurol 260:98–126, 1987.
12. Horn LJ, Zasler NS: Neuroanatomy and neurophysiology of sexual function. J Head Trauma Rehabil 5:1–13, 1990.
13. Ignarro LJ, Bush PA, Buga GM, et al: Nitric oxide and cyclic AMP formation upon electrical field stimulation cause relaxation of corpus cavernosum smooth muscle. Biochem Biophys Res Comm 170:843–850, 1980.
14. Krane RJ, Goldstein I, Saenz de Tejada I: Impotence. N Engl J Med 321:1648–1659, 1989.
15. Lisk R: Sexual behavior: Hormonal control. In Martini L, Ganong WF (eds): Neuroendocrinology. New York, Academic Press, 1967, pp 197–239.
16. MacLean P: Brain mechanisms of primal sexual functions and related behavior. In Sandler M, Gessa G (eds): Sexual Behavior: Pharmacology and Biochemistry. New York, Raven Press, 1975, pp 1–11.
17. Mallick HN, Manchanda SK, Kumar VM: Sensory modulation of the medial preoptic area neuronal activity by dorsal penile nerve stimulation in rats. J Urol 151:759–762, 1994.
18. Mas M, Zahradnik MA, Martino V, Davidson J: Stimulation of spinal serotonergic receptors facilitates seminal emission and suppression of penile erectile reflexes. Brain Res 342:128–134, 1985.
19. Masters WH, Johnson VE: Human Sexual Response. Boston, Little, Brown & Co., 1966.
20. Mesulam M: Principles of Behavioral Neurology. Philadelphia, FA Davis, 1985.
21. Penfield W, Rasmussen T: The Cerebral Cortex of Man. New York, MacMillan, 1950.
22. Rajfer J, Aronson WJ, Bush PA, et al: Nitric oxide as a mediator of relaxation of the corpus cavernosum in response to nonadrenergic, noncholinergic neurotransmission. N Engl J Med 326:90–94, 1992.
23. Rodriquez M, Castro R, Hernandez G, Mas M: Different roles of catecholamine and serotonergic neurons of the medial forebrain bundle on male rat sexual behavior. Physiol Behav 33:5 11, 1984.
24. Sachs BD, Meisel RL: The physiology of male sexual behavior. In Knobil E, Neill J (eds): The Physiology of Reproduction. New York, Raven Press, 1988, pp 1393–1482.
25. Sipski M: Spinal cord injury: What is the effect on sexual response? J Am Paraplegia Soc. J Urol 14:40–43, 1991.
26. Stackl W, Hadsun R, Marberger M: Intracavernous injection of prostaglandin E1 in impotent men. J Urol 140:66–68, 1988.
27. Walker AE: The neurological basis of sex. Neurol India 24(1):1–13, 1976.

GARY M. YARKONY, MD
DAVID CHEN, MD

SEXUALITY IN PATIENTS WITH SPINAL CORD INJURY

From the Schwab Rehabilitation
  Hospital
Section of Orthopaedic Surgery
  and Rehabilitation Medicine
University of Chicago Medical
  Center
  and
Northwestern University Medical
  School
Chicago, Illinois

Reprint requests to:
Gary M. Yarkony, MD
Schwab Rehabilitation Hospital
1401 S. California Blvd.
Chicago, IL 60608

Sexual dysfunction, fertility, and pregnancy are among the many areas addressed in a comprehensive spinal cord injury rehabilitation program. Although patients usually request information during the rehabilitation phase, this issue may arise during the acute care period.

This chapter reviews sexual dysfunction in spinal cord injured men and women and discusses management techniques.

MALE SEXUAL DYSFUNCTION

Several studies have attempted to define the importance of sexual dysfunction in spinal cord-injured (SCI) individuals in comparison to their other losses. Hanson and Franklin[76] reported that paraplegic veterans hope for legs and bowel and bladder return before hoping for sexual function and that quadriplegic veterans ranked upper extremities, bowel and bladder return, and leg return before sexual function. In a mixed rehabilitation population, Spergal et al.[144] reported that "improved sexual functioning" ranks low in importance in comparison to other outcomes. In a series of 50 veterans, Phelps et al.[122] reported that general medical condition and bowel and bladder control ranked higher as important concerns for living than sexual ability. Other sources differ: Nonmedical literature has suggested that many spinal cord injured individuals mourn the loss of sexual function more than the loss of walking.[36] Comarr[39] has stated that most patients without genital sensation sublimate their sexual gratification into that of their mates, which becomes a substitute for their own absent orgasm. These observations have not been substantiated by scientific study.

Erection and Ejaculation

Management of sexual dysfunction requires an understanding of the vascular mechanisms and neurophysiology involved in erection and ejaculation. Erections can be classified as reflexogenic and psychogenic.[171] Psychogenic stimuli can be both facilitory and inhibitory, and the degree of tactile stimulation necessary to produce a reflex erection can be diminished by psychic stimulation.

Supraspinal mechanisms[89,171] for facilitation and inhibition of erection are complex. The limbic system and hypothalamus play key roles. Lesions in the ansa reticularis may cause impotence. The visceral efferent pathways connecting the brain and spinal cord descend in the lateral columns in the area of the pyramidal tracts. The spinal centers related to erection are in the sympathetic preganglionic fibers from T11 to L2 and the parasympathetic fibers from S2 through S4.[89,171] The parasympathetic system acts synergistically with the sympathetic system to produce erections. For many years the neurotransmitter for erections had remained a mystery. It is now known that nitric oxide is involved in the nonadrenergic, noncholinergic neurotransmission. It leads to the relaxation of smooth muscle in the corpus cavernosum, resulting in penile erection.[124] The phenomenon of psychogenic erections in paraplegics with complete lower motor neuron lesions and abolished reflexogenic erections indicates that pathways for erection from the sympathetic outflow exist. Reflex erections are mediated via the sacral parasympathetics with sensory input from the pudendal nerve. Sacral parasympathetic fibers also are involved in neurologically intact individuals with psychogenic erections. T10 is the critical level for perception of gonadal pain in paraplegic men.[10] Emission is primarily under sympathetic control, followed by closure of the bladder neck and then somatic relaxation and contraction of the bulbourethral muscles for ejaculation.

Erection is a vascular phenomenon.[74,171] The penis contains vascular potential spaces between the arteries and veins, which are collapsed when the penis is flaccid.

The ability to have erections, ejaculate, and perform successful coitus after spinal cord injury has been the subject of numerous investigations and reviews.[40,70,80,152] Munro et al.[110] first reported that 74% of 84 patients were able to have erections unrelated to level of injury, 7–8% could ejaculate, and two men fathered children. Kuhn's study[90] was the only study to include observation. He noted that erections could invariably be induced if there was reflex activity before the level of the lesion and that a sharply circumscribed reflexogenic area existed that included the corona of the glans and the penile frenulum. Twenty-two of 25 patients with lesions from T2 to T12 had erections; the other three patients developed incomplete erections but reported they had full erections at other times. In a series of 200 patients, Talbot[150] reported 42.5% with reflex erections, 21% with psychic erections, and 36.5% without erections. Of those who regained sexual function, 76% did so within 6 months and almost all within a year. Erections were more common in men with injury above T11 and in incomplete lesions. Twenty-three percent (46) of the 200 patients had successful intercourse, and 10% of the whole group ejaculated. In a second study in 1955,[151] Talbot estimated a 5% rate of fertility, which is low, and noted that if erections returned, 76% began within the first 6 months and 94% in the first year of injury.

Bors and Comarr[11] reported findings of surveys in 529 patients, and Comarr[39] reported on an additional 150 patients a decade later; Comarr summarized the data from these studies in 1977[41]: They showed that 93% of reflexogenic erections occurring in upper-motor-neuron (UMN) complete lesions, 98% of reflex erections in UMN incomplete, 26% of psychogenic erections in LMN complete, and 83% of psychogenic erections in LMN incomplete. Comarr doubted their validity.[39,41] The findings were based on interviews; Comarr recorded what the injured person stated and made no attempt to verify the responses.

Zeitlin et al.[178] noted similar findings in 100 patients a year after injury. In 638 patients, Tsuji et al.[156] reported erections in 54% overall, 50% of completely injured patients, and 67% of incompletely injured patients. Other studies with similar results include those by Cibeira,[33] Joacheim and Wahle,[86] Fitzpatrick,[55] Sjogren and Egberg,[142] and Lamid.[91] The latter four studies had fewer than 60 patients, and Cibeira's had poor documentation of methodology. Lamid used nocturnal penile tumescence monitors in a small sample with various times following onset of injury, making his results difficult to interpret. Because spinal cord-injured individuals may have nocturnal erections or reflex erections that are too brief or unreliable for intercourse, the utility of these studies is limited.

The ability to ejaculate was low in all studies reviewed by Higgins.[80] For complete lesions, it was lower than 10%; for incomplete lesions, as high as 32%. Ejaculation generally is more common with lower motor neuron lesions and with more caudal lesions. Orgasms are defined poorly in the available studies.[80] Extragenital responses include headache, warm sensation, physical pleasure, and sexual excitement.[39,80,90,178]

These studies[39,80,90,178] generally relied on patient report, which is a serious methodological flaw because it limits the value of the data, but it does give a good idea of general trends. Only Kuhn's study of paraplegics included actual observation. The data also must be considered in light of the fluctuation in erectile function pointed out by several authors. Erections may not occur when desired, not be satisfactory for penetration, or not last sufficiently to satisfy the partner. It is important to note that the statistical reports do not allow for an accurate prognosis for any one patient. All spinal cord-injured patients must be evaluated individually.

Semen Quality in Spinal Cord-Injured Men

In general, ejaculates from spinal cord-injured men have decreased volume, decreased sperm counts, decreased overall and progressive sperm motility, impaired sperm membrane integrity, and poor oocyte-penetrating capabilities of the sperm.[82] In one study, only 4 of 16 (25%) patients had normal sperm penetration assays.[28] Many reasons have been postulated for the poor semen quality. Several investigators have suggested that prostatic fluid stasis and subsequent congestion affecting the testicular microenvironment may have an effect on sperm motility. Brindley[21] found a step-wise improvement in sperm motility in three men who underwent repeated electroejaculations. Roth et al.[134] found overall increasing trends in sperm concentrations, counts, and overall and progressive motilities in a series of spinal cord-injured men undergoing repeated vibratory stimulation. Urinary tract infections (UTIs) are a common complication of spinal cord injury and are believed to have an adverse effect on male fertility. Wolff et al.[173] found a significant reduction in the total sperm count, sperm velocity, and overall sperm motility of semen that high WBC counts. Unfortunately, the precise mechanism and effect of recurrent UTIs on spermatogenesis and sperm motility are not known.

Elevated scrotal temperatures are known to decrease spermatogenesis in able-bodied men. Brindley found that deep scrotal temperatures were significantly higher in men with paraplegia who were seated in wheelchairs than in noninjured controls who were seated.[19] It has been theorized that scrotal/testicular thermoregulation may be impaired after spinal cord injury.

The method of bladder management following spinal cord injury has been implicated by some researchers as a cause of poor semen quality. Ohl et al.[115] found higher sperm motility in spinal cord-injured men after sphincterotomy or in men using intermittent catheterization than in those with an indwelling catheter or who used high-pressure reflex voiding. Ohl's belief is that the higher intravesicle pressures found in reflex voiding increase the risk of prostate ejaculatory reflux with urine that may lead to reduced sperm motility and chronic inflammation.

Another reason for poor semen quality after spinal cord injury may be intrinsic damage to the testicles. Abnormal testicular histology is a common finding in spinal cord-injured men, the main finding being atrophy of the seminiferous tubules.[12] Unfortunately, no correlations have been found among testicular biopsies, level of injury, time since injury, hormonal changes, and the number of UTIs.[12,119]

Changes in the hypothalamic-pituitary-testicular axis following spinal cord injury may contribute to poor semen quality. Various researchers have reported that testosterone appears to remain normal, slightly below normal, or slightly above normal after SCI.[88,112,119] In addition, there may be subtle changes in serum follicle stimulating hormone (FSH) and luteinizing hormone (LH). If subtle changes occur in serum testosterone, FSH, and LH after spinal cord injury, this may be clinically important because all three are involved in spermatogenesis.

The presence of sperm antibodies may be a contributing factor to the difficulties of male infertility after SCI. There are two conditions that could cause the development of sperm antibodies in men with SCI. One condition is genital tract obstructions, which may occur after recurrent episodes of epididymitis.[119] Unfortunately, the reasons for the development of sperm antibodies after obstruction in men with or without SCI are not known.[81] The other condition is UTIs. Various studies have demonstrated local immune responses in able-bodied men with recurrent bacterial prostatitis.[56,140] Hirsch et al.[82] reported significant levels of antibodies in the seminal plasma of five of seven spinal cord-injured men undergoing electroejaculation.

Another potential cause of poor semen quality is the chronic use of various medications commonly required in men with SCI. Nitrofurantoin, for example, is commonly used for prophylaxis against recurrent UTIs. The administration of high doses of nitrofurantoin to rats causes temporary spermatogenic arrest. In healthy men, doses of 10 mg/kg or more produce slight to moderate spermatogenic arrest with a decrease in sperm count.[84]

Lastly, urine is known to have an adverse effect on sperm motility.[45] Urine may come in contact with sperm in spinal cord-injured men if retrograde ejaculation occurs or if there is incontinence of urine during intercourse. Retrograde ejaculation has been reported to occur in 37–100% of spinal cord-injured men undergoing electroejaculation.[119,136]

Techniques to Restore Erections

INTRACAVERNOUS INJECTIONS OF VASOACTIVE SUBSTANCES

Virag[161,162] first reported the use of intracavernous injections of papaverine to restore erections, stating that its use was discovered accidentally during a surgical

TABLE 1.   Techniques to Restore Erections in Spinal Cord-Injured Men

Intracavernous injections of vasoactive substances
  Papaverine
  Papaverine plus phentolamine
  Prostaglandins

Vacuum tumescence constriction therapy

Penile prostheses
  Semirigid
    Hinged
    Malleable
    Articulating
  Inflatable
    Multicomponent
    Self-contained

procedure[105] (Table 1). Further studies of its therapeutic effects led to the conclusion that penile prosthesis and revascularization procedures could be avoided if a proper nonsurgical therapy was available. This technique bypasses psychological, neurologic, and hormonal influence by acting locally on the penile vasculature.[96] Brindley[20,23] described the use of intracavernous injection of phenoxybenzamine; however, this drug is not available in an injectable form in the United States. Further studies by Brindley[24] showed that drugs that relax smooth muscle can cause an erection to some degree and that papaverine and phenoxybenzamine are currently being used therapeutically. He suggested that short-acting substances such as thymoxamine, phentolamine, and verapamil, which cause brief erection, can be used for teaching purposes or for brief assessment of the erectile function.

The majority of studies on this technique have used combinations of papaverine and phentolamine in various concentrations.[64,114,141,174,179] Zorgniotti and Lefleur[179] described injection at the posterolateral aspect of the base of the penis with a 28.5-gauge needle without aspiration. Sidi et al.[141] studied 100 men, and all of the 17 men with spinal cord injuries responded. The dose ranged from 0.1–1.0 mL of a combination containing 25 mg/mL papaverine and 0.83 mg/mL phentolamine. Two spinal cord-injured patients had sustained erections requiring treatment. Sidi recommends papaverine injections alone in neurogenic patients. Nellans et al.[114] studied 69 spinal cord-injured patients of mixed etiology and noted side effects in 14.5% and a good response in 14 of 15 with neurologic impotence. Some patients noted decreased effectiveness of the medication with time. Lue and Tanagho[96] recommend injection with a 25-gauge needle with a rubber band at the base, followed by pressure for 2 minutes. Although doses as high as 120 mg of papaverine have been used, they recommend starting with 3 mg (0.1 mL) in neurogenic impotence and progressing at 3- mg increments. Satisfactory responses at low dosages such as this have been consistent with the clinical experience at our hospital, particularly in patients with partial or inconsistent reflex erections that were not sufficient nor reliable for intercourse. The majority of successful injections require fewer than 12 mg.[175]

Minor side effects include transient pain and paresthesias, ecchymosis, and fibrotic changes at the site of injection. Infection, although not reported to be a risk in the general population,[2] has been reported in two spinal cord-injured individuals.[96] The most serious complication is priapism. There is a higher risk of priapism with the combination of papaverine and phentolamine in neurologic patients.[92] However, Stief and Watterauer[147] recommend the combination, because papaverine alone has caused fibrosis of intracavernous tissue after repeated dosages in monkeys. There are numerous treatment options to manage priapism.[22,95,96] The treatment depends on the duration. Aspiration both removes the drug and decreases intracavernous pressure; it is considered by many to be the first-line treatment. Adrenergic agents may be added, but their judicious use is recommended due to hypertensive episodes and the danger of cardiac ischemia. Surgical shunting procedures may be necessary in severe cases.

Prostaglandins currently are being studied as an alternative to these medications. Prostaglandins may be injected alone or in combination with papaverine.[62] Prostaglandin use in combination with calcitonin gene-related peptide[49] and papaverine and phentolamine and prostaglandin combinations[5,163] also have been studied. These combinations will probably rarely be used in spinal cord injury due to the response of papaverine alone.

Neither drug is FDA-approved for these purposes.[2] A signed informed consent should be obtained before their use. Unreliable patients may perform multiple injections, resulting in priapism.[168] Topical minoxidil, a direct relaxant of arterial smooth muscle, has a high level of activity in neurogenic impotence. Further studies are needed to determine the clinical utility of minoxidil.[29]

MECHANISM OF ACTION

Papaverine,[87,169] a non-specific smooth muscle relaxant, acts by decreasing resistance to arterial inflow and increasing resistance to venous outflow. The filling of sinusoids passively obstructs venous outflow. Phentolamine,[87,169] an alpha adrenergic blocker, acts by decreasing resistance to arterial inflow. Its effectiveness is less than that of papaverine, and it does not increase resistance to venous outflow. The combination of the two drugs is stable in solution for 40 days.[8]

VACUUM TECHNIQUES

Vacuum tumescence constriction therapy (VTCT)[172] describes the use of external devices that create a vacuum and cause an erection-like state that is maintained by a constricting band. The penis is placed in a rigid tube, a pump creates the needed vacuum and fills the corpora with blood, and a constricting band at the base of the penis maintains the erection for up to 30 minutes. These devices generally are effective but result in decreased blood flow while the rubber band is in place.[111] During erections the penile temperature falls, and there is congestion of extracorporal penile tissue. The penis may pivot since it is only rigid distal to the constrictive band. The ejaculation may be trapped proximal to the band. Many similar devices are available, some with mechanisms to limit the degree of vacuum created. The side effects of these devices include bruising of the penis, penile petechiaes, pain, and pain with orgasm.[44]

Intracavernous injections of papaverine and phentolamine and VTCT have been combined to augment partial erections.[100] The time to produce an erection was diminished and blood flow increased during the constriction interval. However, there were no SCI patients in this study.

PENILE PROSTHESES

Many types of penile prostheses are available. The two basic designs are semirigid and inflatable. Semirigid prostheses can be hinged, malleable, or articulating. Inflatable penile prostheses can be multicomponent or self-contained.

These devices may be used in spinal cord-injured individuals for both impotence[65,68,85,94,133] and maintenance of external catheters.[77,133,143,158] Melman and Hammond[102] first reported use of the Small-Carrion prosthesis primarily for maintaining a condom catheter. Drawbacks of these devices include a high erosion rate as well as risk of infection and mechanical problems.[37,65,76,77,133] Perkash et al.[120] recommends a semirigid hinged prosthesis. Although not always successful, it may enhance self-esteem by decreasing the fear of condom loss. The ability to use it for sexual intercourse is another benefit.

Green and Sloan[68] stressed the importance of combining psychosexual counseling with surgical treatment. Green recommends implantation of prostheses when there is a stable bladder program, a recent urologic x-ray examination, sterile urine, and no decubiti. Results were reported in 40 patients; six patients had inflatable prostheses and 34 had semirigid rods. Of 35 patients available for follow-up, 31 reported satisfactory intercourse, and four stated that their semirigid prostheses were not rigid enough for intercourse.

Penile prostheses should be used judiciously in spinal cord-injured patients. The rate of infection in the general population is 2%, but it is 7% in the spinal cord-injured population. The erosion rate in the general population is 1% but 11% in the spinal cord-injured population.[37] Clearly defined criteria must be developed for their usage.

OTHER METHODS

Sacral anterior root stimulators[26,27] were developed as a way to obtain urinary continence, but they also may produce erection, which can last the duration of the electrical stimulation. It is doubtful that this device will be implanted solely for erectile dysfunction.

Yohimbine,[108,128] an alpha$_2$-adrenergic blocker given orally, has been studied for the treatment of impotence. In a placebo-controlled double-blind partial cross-over study, Reid et al.[128] showed yohimbine to be as effective as sex and marital therapy in psychogenic impotence. This beneficial effect was proposed to be due to its enhancement of sympathetic outflow. Morales et al.[108] studied yohimbine in patients with organic impotence. There was no statistically significant difference between yohimbine and placebo. Despite this, the authors feel that due to its safety and ease of administration, it may be used in patients who reject more invasive methods. There is no documentation of its benefits in spinal cord-injured patients. Further study of this agent is needed.

Methods to Obtain Semen

Guttman and Walsh[73] described the use of intrathecal neostigmine methyl sulfate (Prostigmin) to obtain semen for sperm analysis, to check the motility, concentration, and cytology of sperm following hormone treatment, or for artificial insemination. Neostigmine is a reversible acetylcholine esterase inhibitor. The drug was given via lumbar puncture, and positive results were obtained in 58.2% of patients. The majority of negative results occur with lesions between T10 and L4. Side effects included headache, sweating, vomiting, and one death, which occurred at a previously tolerated dosage. Pregnancies using this technique have been reported by Spira in 1956,[146] Chapelle et al. in 1976,[31] and Otani et al. in 1985.[118] Chapelle believes that segments of T11, T12 and L1 must be intact for this technique to be successful. This technique largely has been abandoned.[58]

Chapelle et al.[30] have reported on the use of subcutaneous physostigmine, which differs from neostigmine in that it can cross the blood-brain barrier and can be given by subcutaneous injection. Peripherally acting parasympathetic blockers are used to inhibit the peripheral effects such as nausea and vomiting. Chapelle feels that this technique is as effective as intrathecal neostigmine but with fewer side effects. Francois and Maury[58] reported that Chapelle documented 27 pregnancies from 80 paraplegics using this technique. A dose of 2 mg of physostigmine sulfate is injected subcutaneously and followed by masturbation 15 minutes later. This may be followed by an additional 1 mg of physostigmine after 30 minutes if there is no response. For side effects, metoclopramide was used, if necessary, with atropine. For the procedure to be successful, T11, T12 and L1 must be intact. The most common side effects are orthostatic hypotension, tachycardia, nausea, and vomiting. Autonomic dysreflexia was not observed.

Vibratory stimulation of the penis may induce reflex ejaculation, and pregnancies have been reported from this technique. Comarr[39] described a patient using a "Swedish massager" to obtain sperm and inseminate his wife with the condom-collected ejaculation. Tarabulcy[152] reported that Whelan had used a vibrator to obtain semen from spinal cord-injured men, but no details of the technique were reported. Brindley[16,18] studied this technique further and reported success in 12 of 21 men using the Ling 201 vibrator, which originally was designed for industrial use, or the Pifco vibrator for home use. He refined this technqiue further and in 1984 reported positive results in 48 of 81 men, mostly with complete lesions using the Ling vibrator at 80 Hz and 2.5 mm.[22] This technique was rarely successful in the first 6 months following onset of injury and failed in all patients without reflex hip flexion after stroking the bottom of the foot. He reported 11 pregnancies in eight couples. Vibratory ejaculation was felt to produce better sperm quality than electroejaculation. Sarkarati et al.[136] used the Ling vibrator and was successful in eight of 33 patients, one within the first 6 months after injury. Vibratory ejaculation was accompanied by rhythmic reflex contraction of anal and genital muscles and abdominal contractions. In a study in which a vibrator was used at 60–80 Hz, Szasz[149] reported success in 14 of 17 men with lesions above T12/L1 and failure in five men with lesions below this level. The major side effect of this technique is autonomic dysreflexia, which may prevent successful completion of the clinical trial. A recent review indicates that up to 60% of spinal cord-injured men may respond to this technique.[4] It is our experience that higher complete levels of injury are most responsive.

Electroejaculation, obtaining semen by electrical stimulation electrodes in the rectum, may be successful where vibratory stimulation fails or autonomic dysreflexia prohibits its usefulness[22] (Table 2). Brindley[17] described the goal of electroejaculation to be stimulation of the proper nerve fibers and as few as possible of the wrong ones, with the least possible risk of thermal and electrolytic damage to the rectal mucosa. The technique stimulates myelinated sympathetic efferent fibers of the hypogastric plexus.[24] Electroejaculation may be successful within the first 6 months following injury. Numerous techniques have been described, and there is some debate in the literature as to the electrical safety of various methods used.

The first report in spinal cord-injured men, by Horne et al.,[83] obtained sperm by electroejaculation in 13 of 18 patients, 10 by electrical stimulation and three by masturbation. The five failures with both techniques were in men with lesions below T11. A urethral sound was used and placed in the region of the seminal

TABLE 2.   Comparison of Electroejaculation and Vibratory Ejaculation

Electroejaculation	Vibratory Ejaculation
Greater success than vibration	Less retrograde emission
Used with intact T10-L2 spinal cord	Better quality semen
Decreased risk of dysreflexia	L-S reflexes must be intact
Generally succeeds in conus, caudal lesions	Fails in first 6 months
	Fails in complete conus, caudal lesions

vesicles or prostate. Current was sinusoidal or faradic, 45 or 60 mA and 90 V. Stimulation was followed by massage of the seminal vesicles and prostate. Massage without electrical stimulation was unsuccessful in all but one case. Potts[123] and Ravan et al.[125] reported unsuccessful attempts at electroejaculation. Bensman and Kottke[7] reported successful electroejaculation using a rectal diathermy probe in three patients, two with cervical lesions and one with a flaccid T12 lesion. All sperm was obtained from the urine and was nonmotile. Frankel et al.[60] reported the hemodynamic effects of rectal electroejaculation and noted hypertensive headache and a rise in plasma noradrenaline and prostaglandin E.

David et al.[46] used a Grass stimulator and a custom-designed rectal probe and obtained specimens in four of six patients with upper-motor neuron lesions, of which three were incomplete. Sperm motility was poor, with a high percentage of abnormal cells. The first reported pregnancy using semen obtained by electroejaculation from a T12 paraplegic of 3 years' duration was reported by Thomas et al.[154] in 1975. The baby died within 24 hours of birth. Francois et al.[59] reported the next live birth in 1977 after electroejaculation and successful electroejaculation in 13 of 31 patients; the baby lived. Brindley summarized his results in 154 men in 1984.[23] Sixty-nine patients had external success (spermatozoa at the meatus, not necessarily motile), and 28 had retrograde success with sperm in the next urine. Semen was obtained by electroejaculation in 21 of the 34 men for whom the vibrator failed. He reported 11 pregnancies in eight couples, three by electroejaculation, seven by vibration, and one by masturbation.

Martin et al.[101] and Warner et al.[166] refer to their technique of electroejaculation as *rectal probe electrostimulation* (RPE). These authors feel that the technique is safer than Brindley's because the intensity of current is lower and the sinusoidal wave form is safer than the rectangular wave form. They described a modified Foley catheter with a port in the prostatic urethra to prevent retrograde ejaculation. Success was reported in 20 patients. Retrograde ejaculation occurred in six patients, antegrade in four, both in 10, and none in two. Nine patients below L2 could not tolerate the stimulation.

Using RPE in 12 men, Halstead et al.[75] reported antegrade ejaculation in nine and retrograde ejaculation in one. Sperm suitable for insemination was obtained from four of the men. Repeated attempts yielded an improvement in sperm quality. Sarkarati et al.[136] used the equipment developed by Brindley and had success in eight of 22 men with lesions from C6 to T12; however, no improvement occurred with repeated attempts and the samples had low quality. Bennett et al.[6] reported positive results in seven of 13 men with cervical lesions, 14 of 21 thoracic, one in three lumbar, or 13 of 20 complete and eight of 17 incomplete. They reported pregnancies in four of 10 patients and felt that the best results were obtained in thoracic levels. Recurrent urinary tract infections or epididymitis appeared to negatively affect the ability to ejaculate.

These studies are difficult to compare due to the various methods used, although the many reported pregnancies make this procedure promising. Electroejaculation appears to succeed on a large proportion of men because it requires survival of the T10–L2 segments. Reflex function in the lumbar cord is not necessary. Pregnancies that are confirmed by paternity testing are a concern in evaluating techniques reported to enhance fertility. Further study is needed to compare the various devices available for safety and efficacy.

Counseling Male Spinal Cord-Injured Patients

Thorough physical evaluation is an important adjunct to a counseling program.[42,43] The patient and staff dealing with the patient should be aware of the physiological changes that occur and likely functional outcomes. Awareness on the part of the patient should greatly enhance reintegration into the community. It is unclear at what time following injury a counseling program is most effective. The rehabilitation phase has been reported to be the time at which patients are most likely to desire information regarding sexual functioning.[106] A sexual counseling program is a mandatory part of any rehabilitation program and can be accomplished through both individual and group therapy.[36,51,103]

Management of sexual dysfunction is an integral part of rehabilitation of spinal cord-injured individuals. The first step is counseling the patient and his partner. Spinal cord-injured individuals should be provided with both general information in regard to sexual functioning after spinal cord injury as well as more specific guidelines based on the physical examination and experience with other individuals with injuries at that level. Written or audiovisual materials may assist in this process. It is important to note that erectile functioning may not return for 6–12 months, and aggressive intervention should be limited initially. Spinal cord-injured individuals should be aware prior to discharge of the possibilities to restore both erectile functioning and fertility. Services in our center generally are initiated 6 months after injury. This allows for natural recovery and avoids the disappointment of vibratory ejaculation failing during the initial trial. Patients are shown videos of the techniques to restore erection and are allowed to decide which technique they prefer unless specific medical conditions prevent its use. A medical work-up is required of patients who do not have spinal cord injury as an obvious cause of sexual dysfunction. They must be aware of the risks of each technique, particularly of scarring and priapism from intracavernous injections and the decreased blood flow from constrictive rings around the penis with vacuum tumescence constriction therapy. Informed consent is obtained prior to penile injections. Patients generally choose the technique they consider the most natural or safest.

From semen collection, we begin with the Ling vibrator 6 months after injury and then try commercially available vibrators. The Ling is used initially because of the good response reported in the literature allowing for the best initial results. Patients may be given vibrators for home use, although the autonomic dysreflexia is a limiting factor. Electroejaculation with the equipment developed by Seager and Halstead is then used if there is no response or the patient develops autonomic dysreflexia. This may become the first choice if home units become available. Evaluation for sexually transmitted disease is required when fertilization is requested. Consultation with a gynecologist may be needed for insemination, especially when a low sperm count is involved.

Recent advances have improved the possibilities for sexual rehabilitation after spinal cord injury. Further study is needed to determine the long-term risks and benefits of these techniques and to provide adaptive devices that spinal cord-injured patients can manage independently.

FEMALE SEXUAL FUNCTIONING

Sexual adjustment after a spinal cord injury is an important part of the person's psychological and social rehabilitation.[9,15] This adjustment may take several years after injury. Women have been reported to have less impairment in sexual function and identification after disability than men.[170] Disability may lead to post-injury divorce, further complicating adjustment.

Counseling

The woman's self-concept and degree of perceived independence following injury may affect a woman's participation as a sexual partner.[54] Counseling[35,71,131,155] may play an important part in the adaptation process. A woman must acknowledge that sexuality is an integral part of her being and be encouraged to experiment with her sexual expression. Counseling may be needed on a short- or long-term basis. Issues in counseling may be related to problems such as positioning, contractures, management of menstrual periods, or dealing with bladder and bowel incontinence. Other areas that may require long-term counseling include presentation and perception of self and social skills, communication and cuing during sexual activity, and the impact of the injury on the marriage and family.[131] Counseling may be helpful prior to conception to help the spinal cord-injured woman prepare for the difficulties she may encounter in caring for a child.

In spite of the absence of genital sensation, other erogenous areas such as the breasts, shoulders, neck, or mouth may enhance the sexual experience.[155] Women report orgasm in spite of reports that it is not possible with complete lesions of the spinothalamic tracts.[116] Phantom orgasms have been reported in the dreams of paraplegics.[107] Orgasms[61] may be described as similar to that of able-bodied women or as a wide variety of psychological experiences such as pleasant, relaxful, and glowing feelings.[15] Vaginal lubrication may occur reflexly with lesions at T9, not at all with lesions between T10 and T12, and psychogenic lubrication may occur in lesions below T12.[9]

Although amenorrhea may occur following a spinal cord injury, its occurrence is not uniform, and menstruation generally returns in 1 year.[35] Reports of secondary amenorrhea after a spinal cord injury range from 50–60%.[3,38] Axel[3] reported a return of menses in a mean of 5 months. Comarr reported that the majority will have return of menses within 6 months, but one woman's delay was 30 months. Women at or near the climacteric may become menopausal. Charlifue et al.[32] reported amenorrhea in 60% of 218 women. The median time for normal menses to return was 5 months, with 89% by 12 months.

Pregnancy, Labor, and Delivery

There are numerous reports of pregnancy in spinal cord-injured women. These reports date back to 1906 and note painless labor and cesarean section without anesthesia.[165] Unfortunately, the reports generally are in the form of case studies[1,14,47,53,63,66,72,78,93,98,99,109,113,117,131,137,145,148,160,165,167] and reviews.[9,34,157,159] Currently there are no controlled studies resulting in guidelines for optimal management.

Women may sustain a spinal cord injury during pregnancy. They may not be aware that they are pregnant or are unable to inform the staff of this due to associated brain injury. Pregnancy during the acute phase may limit radiologic evaluation and surgical treatment of the injured spine, necessitating conservative spine management.

Goller and Paeslack[66] have reported two cases in which the fetus may have sustained cranial injuries at the time of the accident in which the mother was rendered paraplegic. This may have been due to direct trauma, the mother's anorexia, or hypoxemia. In a second series[67] based on a questionnaire of 45 pregnancies at the time of injury, there were 31 healthy babies. Five children were born with malformations or disability. There were five miscarriages, two abortions, one death due to lung immaturity, and one stillbirth due to placenta previa. Insufficient data exists to analyze the abnormalities in these births, which are most likely multifactorial. They also reported that 147 normal children were born to 130 spinal-cord injured women whose pregnancies began after injury. There were also 10 miscarriages, three abortions, and five stillbirths. The authors noted an increase in premature and small-for-date children in this group but no problems with malformations.

Robertson and Guttman[129,130] have reported their experience in 25 spinal cord-injured women giving birth to 33 children. Several of their observations generally are well accepted. It is well known that the uterus can contract with the nerve supply severed. Because labor will be painless with lesions above T10, examination may be necessary to determine the onset of labor. Premature labor is more common, and premature delivery may occur in unfavorable surroundings without competent medical care. The authors recommended that the examination begin at the 28th week, with hospital admission if the cervix is effaced, and routine admission by the 35th week. Home tokadynamometry and patient instruction in uterine palpation also may be helpful.[69]

Greenspoon and Paul[69] recommend a team approach in dealing with these pregnancies. A team including the primary care physician, neurologist, rehabilitation personnel, obstetrician, anesthesiologist, and urologist is recommended. The delivery facility should be able to perform invasive hemodynamic monitoring and the neonatal unit care for a premature infant. The management of the patient includes (1) recognition and treatment of autonomic dysreflexia, (2) the ability to support respiration in cervical lesions, (3) prevention of unsupervised delivery, (4) surveillance for urinary tract infections, (5) treatment of anemia, (6) skin care to prevent pressure ulcers, (7) maintenance of normal bowel function, (8) counseling, and (9) contraception and sterilization.

Autonomic dysreflexia during labor has generated numerous reports and much controversy. Obviously the first step is awareness of this condition by the labor and delivery team. Autonomic dysreflexia must be differentiated from preeclampsia (Table 3). There are recent reports of intraventricular hemorrhage with resultant neurologic deficits[99,160] and death,[1,160] indicating that unrecognized autonomic dysreflexia still results in morbidity and mortality.

Although autonomic dysreflexia generally occurs in lesions of T6 and above, one case associated with labor was reported at T10.[63] Monitoring the situation may require an intraarterial catheter, cardiac monitoring, the ability to administer antihypertensive medication, fetal monitoring because maternal hypotension may cause fetal hypoperfusion, and appropriate anesthesia. Cardiac arrhythmias may occur in the mother due to the dysreflexia, although they are not considered a general manifestation of the dysreflexia and not solely due to the pregnancy.[72]

Reserpine 2 weeks prior to the expected date of delivery has been suggested as a means to prevent the occurrence of autonomic dysreflexia.[137] Based on a cystometrogram in the same patient, Saunders and Yeo[137] suggested that

TABLE 3. Differentiating Autonomic Dysreflexia and Toxemia

Autonomic Dysreflexia	Toxemia of Pregnancy
Blood pressure rises with contractions	Hypertension, proteinuria, edema
Blood pressure falls between contractions	Blood pressure increase not episodic
Headache, piloerection	Blood increase not associated with uterine
Bradycardia	contractions, bowel or bladder
No response to magnesium sulfate	

cystometrograms can predict dysreflexia during delivery, but guidelines were lacking. Nitroglycerine has been given intravenously during cesarean section in hypertensive women, but it has not been studied in spinal cord injury. Nitroprusside has been used, but epidural anesthesia was required, and concerns exist about the metabolic effects of cyanide that has been detected in fetal blood after maternal exposure to nitroprusside.[121,126] Young[176] reported the use of diazepam, diphenhydramine, and promethazine, none of which is used commonly to treat dysreflexia. This resulted in numerous letters suggesting that continuous epidural anesthesia or spinal anesthesia would have been more appropriate.[98,145] These letters were based on reports by Stirt et al.,[148] Ciliberti et al.,[34] and Abouleish[1] of success with epidural anesthesia. Many believe epidural anesthesia to be the method of choice because it blocks the reflex arc. It is easy to perform and control and beneficial in that it prevents the syndrome. Epidural anesthesia has been reported to improve patient comfort[167] and to be preferable to spinal anesthesia because of difficulties in controlling the level of block and the increased risk of hypotension.[148] There are reports of epidural anesthesia failing with spinal anesthesia succeeding, probably due to difficulties with placement of the epidural catheter. Nath et al.[113] suggested that if autonomic dysreflexia cannot be controlled, prompt delivery by cesarean section may be the most expedient method of management.

Other suggestions to prevent autonomic dysreflexia include avoidance of external restraints, an indwelling catheter to prevent bladder distension particularly during the later stages of pregnancy, and use of anesthetic ointments during examination and manipulation of the catheter.

Early mobilization after delivery is encouraged to prevent deep venous thrombosis. Physical therapy to assist lower extremity functions should be available.

Urologic complications have been noted as a result of pregnancy. Although ileal conduits are used less frequently, obstruction may occur.[47] Urinary infection may lead to pyelonephritis or septicemia.[14] It should not be assumed that normal patterns of voiding will resume after delivery. Increased residual urines have resulted, and the loss of reflex bladder function has occurred with the need for indwelling catheters.[164] An indwelling catheter may facilitate bladder management as pregnancy progresses.

Management of anemia with oral iron may exacerbate constipation and require modification of the bowel program.[135] Folate deficiencies may be present in women being treated for seizure disorders.

The rehabilitation team may be helpful to the obstetrician. Consultation may be obtained in regard to positioning for comfort and treatment of pressure ulcers. The rehabilitation facility may be an appropriate site to manage the patient during pregnancy.[93] After delivery, our center has admitted the mother and child to the same room. This facilitates bonding and allows the mother to learn to care for the infant as part of her rehabilitation.

Spasticity

Spasticity may be both beneficial and problematic to men and women with spinal cord injuries. Beneficial effects include maintenance of muscle bulk, decreased lower extremity edema, and enhanced pulmonary functioning. Spasticity may interfere with functional skills, result in falls during ambulation or transfers, and be uncomfortable.

The foundation of management is sound basic medical care.[104] Because spasticity may be exacerbated by urinary tract infections, bladder stones, ingrown toenails, bowel impactions, or pressure ulcers, proper prevention and care of these conditions is essential. An adequate range of motion program is an essential ingredient in the treatment of spasticity.

Four medications are generally used, either alone or in combination for treatment of spasticity.[50,177] Baclofen (Lioresal, Geigy Pharmaceuticals, Summit, NJ), a γ-aminobuteric acid derivative acting directly on the spinal cord, is generally the first-line drug. There are no studies of its usage in pregnant women, and the manufacturer advises that its usage in pregnancy should be considered only if the benefit clearly justifies the potential risk to the fetus. Adverse effects have been seen in animal studies.[84] A single case report demonstrates that baclofen is excreted in breast milk at one thousandth of the ingested dose and should not reach toxic levels in the newborn.[52] Baclofen should be tapered when discontinuing its use to avoid hallucinations, anxiety, and tachycardia that may occur with sudden cessation.

Diazepam (Valium, Roche Products, Manati, Puerto Rico) is another centrally acting drug indicated for spasticity. Diazepam and its metabolites cross the placenta and accumulate in the fetal circulation.[121] Although the association between diazepam and oral clefts has been questioned,[132] other malformations demonstrated include inguinal hernia, cardiac defects, pyloric stenosis, and hemangiomas.[121] The floppy infant syndrome also occurs.[138] Diazepam is excreted in breast milk and may reach high levels in breast-fed infants.

Clonidine (various manufacturers), a centrally acting α-adrenergic agonist used to treat hypertension, has been shown to be beneficial in the treatment of spasticity.[50] Clonidine crosses the placenta extensively and is generally considered free of teratogenic risk. It is not known to be deleterious for fetal growth, mortality, and morbidity. There may be a long-term behavioral teratogenicity manifesting as hyperactivity and sleep disturbances. No data exist on fetal hemodynamics.[13] Clonidine is excreted in breast milk. In a small series there were no adverse effects on newborns.[79]

Dantrolene (Dantrium, Norwich Eaton Pharmaceuticals, Norwich, NY) acts directly on muscle to decrease release of calcium from the sarcoplasmic reticulum. A major drawback of its usage is hepatotoxicity. Its safety in pregnancy has not been established, and it should not be used by nursing mothers.[84] Dantrolene has been studied in pregnant women as a prophylactic agent to prevent malignant hyperthermia. When given 5 days before and 3 days after delivery, it was not felt to be deleterious to the fetus and newborn. There was no long-term follow-up on the newborn.[139]

SUMMARY

Management of sexual functioning after spinal cord injury should be considered a routine part of the rehabilitation process. Because both the physical and psychological impact of the spinal cord injury can affect sexual functioning, it is essential that all team members be aware of the changes that result and the management techniques that are available.

REFERENCES

1. Abouleish E: Hypertension in a paraplegic parturient. Anesthesiology 53:348–349, 1980.
2. Abramowicz M (ed): Intracavernous injections for impotence. Med Lett Drugs Ther 29:751:95–96, 1987.
3. Axel SJ: Spinal cord injured women's concerns: Menstruation and pregnancy. Rehabil Nurs 7:10–15, 1982.
4. Beckerman H, Becher J, Lankhorst GJ: The effectiveness of vibratory stimulation in anejaculatory men with spinal cord injury. Paraplegia 31:689–699, 1993.
5. Bennett AH, Carpenter AJ, Barada JH: An improved vasoactive drug combination for a pharmacological erection program. J Urol 146:1564–1565, 1991.
6. Bennett CJ, Seager SW, Vasher EA, McGuire EJ: Sexual dysfunction and electroejaculation in men with spinal cord injury: Review. J Urol 139:453–457, 1988.
7. Bensman A, Kottke FJ: Induced emission of sperm utilizing stimulation of the seminal vesicles and vas deferens. Arch Phys Med Rehabil 47:436–443, 1966.
8. Benson GS, Seifert WE: Is phentolamine stable in solution with papaverine? J Urol 140:970–971, 1988.
9. Berard EJT: The sexuality of spinal cord injured women: Physiology and pathophysiology, a review. Paraplegia 22:99–112, 1989.
10. Bors E: Perception of gonadal pain in paraplegic patients. Arch Neurol Psychol 63:713–718, 1950.
11. Bors E, Comarr AE: Neurological disturbances of sexual function with special reference to 529 patients with spinal cord injury. Urol Surv 10:191–222, 1960.
12. Bors E, Engle ET, Rosenquist RC, Hollinger VH: Fertility in paraplegic males: A preliminary report of endocrine studies. J Clin Endocrinol 10:381–398, 1950.
13. Boutroy MJ: Fetal effects of maternally administered clonidine and angiotensin-converting enzyme inhibitors. Dev Pharmacol Ther 13:199–204, 1989.
14. Bradley WS, Walker WW, Searight MW: Pregnancy in paraplegia: A case report with urologic complication. Obstet Gynecol 10:573–575, 1957.
15. Bregman S, Hadley RG: Sexual adjustment and feminine attractiveness among spinal cord injured women. Arch Phys Med Rehabil 57:448–450, 1976.
16. Brindley GS: Electroejaculation and the fertility of paraplegic men. Sex Disabil 3:223–229, 1980.
17. Brindley GS: Electroejaculation: Its technique, neurological implications and uses. J Neurol Neurosurg Psychiatry 44:9–18, 1981.
18. Brindley GS: Reflex ejaculation under vibratory stimulation in paraplegic men. Paraplegia 19:299–302, 1981.
19. Brindley GS: Deep scrotal temperature and the effect on it of clothing, air temperature activity, posture and paraplegia. Br J Urol 54:49–55, 1982.
20. Brindley GS: Cavernosual alpha-blockage: A new technique for investigating and treating erectile impotence. Br J Psychiatry 143:332–337, 1983.
21. Brindley GS: Physiology of erection and management of paraplegic infertility. In Haregrave TB (ed): Male Infertility. Berlin, Springer Verlag, 1983, pp 261–279.
22. Brindley GS: New treatment for priapism. Lancet 2:220–221, 1984.
23. Brindley GS: The fertility of men with spinal cord injuries. Paraplegia 22:337–348, 1984.
24. Brindley GS: Pilot experiments on the action of drugs injected into the human corpus cavernosum penis. Br J Pharmacol 87:495–500, 1986.
25. Brindley GS: Sexual and reproductive problems of paraplegic men. In Clarke JR (ed): Oxford Reviews of Reproductive Biology. Oxford, England, Clarendon Press, 1986.
26. Brindley GS, Polkey CE, Rushton DN: Sacral anterior root stimulators for bladder control in paraplegia. Paraplegia 20:365–381, 1982.
27. Brindley GS, Polkey CE, Rushton DN, Caudozo L: Sacral anterior root stimulators for bladder control in paraplegia: The first 50 cases. J Neurol Neurosurg Psychiatry 49:1104–1114, 1986.
28. Buch JP, Zorn BH: Evaluation and treatment of infertility in spinal cord injured men through rectal probe electroejaculation. J Urol 149:1350–1354, 1993.
29. Cavallini G: Minoxidil versus nitroglycerin: A prospective double-blind controlled trial in transcutaneous erection facilitation for organic impotence. J Urol 146:50–53, 1991.
30. Chapelle PA, Blanquart F, Peuch AJ, Held JP: Treatment of anejaculation in the total paraplegic by subcutaneous injection of physostigmine. Paraplegia 21:30–36, 1983.
31. Chapelle PA, Jondet M, Durand J, Grossiord A: Pregnancy of the wife of a complete paraplegic by homologous insemination after an intrathecal injection of neostigmine. Paraplegia 14:173–177, 1976.
32. Charlifue SW, Gerhart KA, Menter RR, et al: Sexual issues of women with spinal cord injuries. Paraplegia 30:192–199, 1992.

33. Cibeira JB: Some conclusions on a study of 365 patients with spinal cord lesions. Paraplegia 7:249–254, 1970.
34. Ciliberti BJ, Goldfein J, Rovenstine EA: Hypertension during anesthesia in patients with spinal cord injuries. Anesthesiology 15:273–279, 1954.
35. Cole TM: Sexuality and physical disabilities. Arch Sex Behav 4:389–403, 1975.
36. Cole TM, Chilgrem R, Rosenberg P: A new programme of sex education and counseling for spinal cord injured adults and health care professionals. Paraplegia 11:111–124, 1973.
37. Collins KP, Hackler RH: Complications of penile prosthesis in the spinal cord injury population. J Urol 140:984–985, 1988.
38. Comarr AE: Observations on menstruation and pregnancy among female spinal cord injury patients. Paraplegia 3:263–272, 1966.
39. Comarr AE: Sexual function among patients with spinal cord injury. Urol Int 25:134–168, 1970.
40. Comarr AE: Sexual concepts in traumatic cord and cauda equina lesions. J Urol 106:375–378, 1971.
41. Comarr AE: Sexual function in patients with spinal cord injury. In Pierce PS, Nickel VH (eds): The Total Care of Spinal Cord Injury. Boston, Little, Brown, & Co, 1977, pp 171–180.
42. Comarr AE, Vique M: Sexual counseling among male and female patients with spinal cord and/or cauda equina injury, Part 1. Am J Phys Med 57:107–122, 1978.
43. Comarr AE, Vique M: Sexual counseling among male and female patients with spinal cord and/or cauda equina injury, Part 2. Am J Phys Med 57:215–227, 1978.
44. Cookson MS, Nadig PW: Long-term results with vacuum constriction device. J Urol 149:290–294, 1993.
45. Crich JP, Jequier AM: Infertility in men with retrograde ejaculation: The action of urine on sperm motility and a simple method for achieving antegrade ejaculation. Fertil Steril 30:572–576, 1978.
46. David A, Ohry A, Rozin R: Spinal cord injuries: Male infertility aspects. Paraplegia 15:11–14, 1977–78.
47. Daw E: Pregnancy problems in a paraplegic patient with an ileal conduit bladder. Practitioner 211:781–784, 1973.
48. Devenport JK, Swenson JR: An unusual cause of autonomic dysreflexia [abstract]. Arch Phys Med Rehabil 64:485, 1983.
49. Djamilian M, Stief CG, Kuczyk M, Jonas U: Follow-up results of a combination of calcitonin gene-related peptide and prostaglandin E1 in the treatment of erectile dysfunction. J Urol 149:1296–1298, 1993.
50. Donovan WH, Carter RE, Rossi D, et al: Clonidine effect on spasticity: A clinical trial. Arch Phys Med Rehabil 69:193–194, 1988.
51. Eisenberg MG, Rustad LC: Sex education and counseling program on a spinal cord injury service. Arch Phys Med Rehabil 57:135–140, 1976.
52. Erikkson G, Swahn CG: Concentrations of baclofen in serum and breast milk from a lactating woman. Scand J Clin Lab Invest 91:185–187, 1981.
53. Ferguson JE, Catanzorite VA: Clinical management of spinal cord injury. Obstet Gynecol 64:588–589, 1984.
54. Fitting MD, Salisbury S, Davies NH, Mayclin DK: Self-concept and sexuality of spinal cord injured women. Arch Sex Behav 7:143–156, 1978.
55. Fitzpatrick WF: Sexual function in the paraplegic patient. Arch Phys Med Rehabil 55:221–227, 1974.
56. Fjallbrant B, Nilsson S: Decrease of sperm antibody titer in males and conception after treatment of chronic prostatitis. Int J Fertil 22:255–256, 1977.
57. Floth A, Schramek P: Intracavernous injection of prostaglandin E1 in combination with papaverine: Enhanced effectiveness in comparison with papaverine plus phentolamine and prostaglandin E1 alone. J Urol 145:56–59, 1991.
58. Francois N, Maury M: Sexual aspects in paraplegic patients. Paraplegia 25:289–292, 1987.
59. Francois N, Maury M, Jouannet D, et al: Electroejaculation of a complete paraplegic followed by pregnancy. Paraplegia 16:248–251, 1978–79.
60. Frankel HL, Mathias CT, Walsh JT: Blood pressure, plasma cathecholamines, and prostaglandins during artificial erection in a male tetraplegic. Paraplegia 12:205–211, 1974.
61. Geiger RL: Neurophysiology of sexual response in spinal cord injury. Sex Disabil 2:257–266, 1979.
62. Gerber GS, Levine LA: Pharmacological erection program using prostaglandin E1. J Urol 146:786–789, 1991.
63. Gimovsky ML, Ojeda A, Ozaki R, Zerne S: Management of autonomic hyperreflexia associated with a low thoracic spinal cord lesion. Obstet Gynecol 153:223–224, 1985.

64. Girdley FM, Bruskewitz RC, Feyzi J, et al: Intracavernous self-injection for impotence: A long-term therapeutic option? Experience in 78 patients. J Urol 140:972–974, 1988.
65. Golgi H: Experience wiht penile prostheses in spinal cord injury patients. J Urol 121:288–289, 1979.
66. Goller H, Paeslack V: Our experience about pregnancy and delivery of the paraplegic women. Paraplegia 8:161–166, 1970.
67. Goller H, Paeslack V: Pregnancy, damage and birth complications in the children of paraplegic women. Paraplegia 10:213–217, 1972.
68. Green BG, Sloan SL: Penile prostheses in spinal cord injured patients: Combined psychosexual counseling and surgical regimen. Paraplegia 24:167–172, 1986.
69. Greenspoon JS, Paul RH: Paraplegia and quadriplegia: Special considerations during pregnancy and labor and delivery. Am J Obstet Gynecol 155:738–741, 1986.
70. Griffith ER, Tomko MA, Timms RJ: Sexual function in spinal cord injured patients: A review. Arch Phys Med Rehabil 54:539–543, 1973.
71. Griffith ER, Trieschmann RB: Sexual functioning in women with spinal cord injury. Arch Phys Med Rehabil 56:18–21, 1975.
72. Guttmann L, Frankel HL, Paeslack V: Cardiac irregularities during labour in paraplegic women. Paraplegia 3:144–151, 1965.
73. Guttmann L, Walsh JT: Prostigmin assessment test of fertility in spinal man. Paraplegia 9:39–50, 1971.
74. Guyton AC: Textbook of Medical Physiology. 7th ed. Philadelphia, WB Saunders, 1986.
75. Halstead LS, VerVoort S, Seager SWJ: Rectal probe electrostimulation in the treatment of anejaculatory spinal cord injured men. Paraplegia 25:120–129, 1987.
76. Hanson RW, Franklin MR: Sexual loss in relation to other functional losses for spinal cord injured males. Arch Phys Med Rehabil 57:291–293, 1976.
77. Hanson TJ, Merritt JL: Penile prostheses in spinal cord injured patients. In International Medical Society of Paraplegia, Annual Scientific Meetings Proceedings. Edinburgh, September 3–5, 1985.
78. Hardy AG, Worrell DW: Pregnancy and labour in complete tetraplegia. Paraplegia 3:182–186, 1965.
79. Hartikainen-Sorri AL, Heikkinen JE, Koivisto M: Pharmokinetics of clonidine during pregnancy and nursing. Obstet Gynecol 69:598–600, 1987.
80. Higgins GE: Sexual response in spinal cord injured adults: A review of the literature. Arch Sex Behav 8:173–196, 1979.
81. Hirsch I, Lipshultz LI: Medical treatment of male infertility. Urol Clin North Am 14:307–322, 1987.
82. Hirsch IH, Sedor J, Callahan HJ, Staas WE: Antisperm antibodies in seminal plasma of spinal cord-injured men. Urology 39:243–247, 1992.
83. Horne HW, Paull DP, Munro D: Fertility studies in the human male with traumatic injuries of the spinal cord and cauda equina. N Engl J Med 239:959–961, 1948.
84. Huff BB (ed): Physicians' Desk Reference. 43rd ed. Oradell, NJ, Medical Economics, 1989.
85. Iwatsubo E, Tanaka M, Takahashi K, Akatsu T: Non-inflatable penile prosthesis for the management of urinary incontinence and sexual disability of patients with spinal cord injury. Paraplegia 24:307–310, 1986.
86. Joacheim KA, Wahle H: A study on sexual function in 56 male patients with complete irreversible lesions of the spinal cord and cauda equina. Paraplegia 8:166–172, 1970.
87. Jeunemann KP, Lue TF, Fournier GR Jr, Tanagho EA: Hemodynamics of papaverine- and phentolamine-induced penile erection. J Urol 136:158–161, 1986.
88. Kikuchi TA, Skowsky WR, El Toraei I, Swerdloff R: The pituitary gonadal axis in spinal cord injury. Fertil Steril 27:1142–1145, 1976.
89. Krane RJ, Siroky MB: Neurophysiology of erection. Urol Clin North Am 8:91–102, 1981.
90. Kuhn RA: Functional capacity of the isolated human spinal cord. Brain 73:1–51, 1950.
91. Lamid S: Nocturnal penile tumescence studies in spinal cord injured males. Paraplegia 23:26–31, 1985.
92. Lee M, Sharifi M: Information and treatment with intracavernous injections of papaverine and phentolamine [letter]. J Urol 137:1008–1110, 1987.
93. Letcher JC, Goldfine LJ: Management of a pregnant paraplegic patient in a rehabilitation center. Arch Phys Med Rehabil 67:477–488, 1986.
94. Light JK, Scott FB: Management of neurogenic impotence with inflatable penile prosthesis. Urology 17:341–343, 1981.
95. Lue TF, Hellstrom WJG, McAninich TW, Tanagho EA: Priapism: A refined approach to diagnosis and treatment. J Urol 136:104–108, 1986.

96. Lue TF, Tanagho EA: Physiology of erection and pharmacological management of impotence. J Urol 137:829–835, 1987.
97. Macrodantin capsules. In Physicians' Desk Reference. 47th ed. Montvale, NJ, Medical Economics, 1993, pp 1877–1878.
98. McCunniff DE, Dewon D: Pregnancy after spinal cord injury. Obstet Gynecol 63:757, 1984.
99. McGregor JA, Meeuwsen J: Autonomic hyperreflexia: A mortal danger for spinal cord damaged women in labor. Am J Obstet Gynecol 151:330–333, 1985.
100. Marmar JL, DeBenedictis TJ, Praiss DE: The use of a vacuum constrictor device to augment a partial erection following an intracavernous injection. J Urol 140:975–979, 1988.
101. Martin DE, Warner H, Crenshaw TL, et al: Initiation of erection and semen release by rectal probe electrostimulation. J Urol 129:637–642, 1983.
102. Melman A, Hammond G: Placement of the Small-Carrion penile prosthesis to enable maintenance of an indwelling condom catheter. Sex Disabil 1:292–298, 1978.
103. Melnyk R, Montgomery R, Ouer R: Attitude changes following a sexual counseling program for spinal cord injured persons. Arch Phys Med Rehabil 60:601–605, 1979.
104. Merritt JL: Management of spasticity in spinal cord injury. Mayo Clin Proc 56:614–622, 1981.
105. Michal V, Kramar R, Pospichal J, Hejhal L: Arterial epigastricocavernous anastomosis for the treatment of sexual impotence. World J Surg 1:515–520, 1977.
106. Miller SB: Spinal cord injury: Self-perceived sexual information and counseling needs during the acute, rehabilitation and post-rehabilitation phases. Rehabil Psychol 33:221–226, 1988.
107. Money J: Phantom orgasm in the dreams of paraplegic men and women. Arch Gen Psychiatry 3:373–382, 1960.
108. Morales A, Condra M, Owen JA, et al: Is yohimbine effective in the treatment of organic impotence? Results of a controlled trial J Urol 137:1168–1172, 1987.
109. Mulla N: Vaginal delivery in a paraplegic patient. Am J Obstet Gynecol 73:1346–1348, 1957.
110. Munro D, Horne HW Jr, Paull DP: The effect of injury to the spinal cord and cauda equina on the sexual potency of men. N Engl J Med 239:904–911, 1948.
111. Nadig PW, Ware JC, Blumoff R: Non-invasive device to produce and maintain an erection-like state. Urology 27:126–131, 1986.
112. Naftchi NE, Viau AT, Sell GH, Lowman EW: Pituitary-testicular axis dysfunction in spinal cord injury. Arch Phys Med Rehabil 61:402–405, 1980.
113. Nath M, Vivian JM, Cherny WB: Autonomic hyperreflexia in pregnancy and labor: A case report. Am J Obstet Gynecol 134:390–391, 1979.
114. Nellans RE, Ellis LR, Kramer-Levien D: Pharmacological erection: Diagnosis and treatment applications in 69 patients. J Urol 138:52–54, 1987.
115. Ohl DA, Bennett CJ, McCabe M, et al: Predictors of success in electroejaculation of spinal cord injured men. J Urol 142:1483–1486, 1989.
116. Ohry A, Deleg D, Goldman J, et al: Sexual function, pregnancy and delivery in spinal cord injured women. Gynecol Obstet Invest 9:281–291, 1978.
117. Oppenheimer WM: Pregnancy in paraplegic women: Two case reports. Am J Obstet Gynecol 110:784–786, 1971.
118. Otani T, Kondo A, Takita T: A paraplegic fathering a child after an intrathecal injection of neostigmine: Case report. Paraplegia 23:32–37, 1985.
119. Perkash I, Martin DE, Warner H, et al: Reproductive biology of paraplegics: Results of semen collection, testicular biopsy and serum hormone evaluation. J Urol 134:284–288, 1985.
120. Perkash I, Kabalin JN, Lennon S, Wolfe V: Use of penile prostheses to maintain external condom catheter drainage in paraplegic spinal cord injury patients. Paraplegia 30:327–332, 1992.
121. Petrie RH (ed): Perinatal Pharmacology. Oradell, NJ, Medical Economics, 1989.
122. Phelps G, Brown M, Chen J, et al: Sexual experience and plasma testosterone levels in male veterans after spinal cord injury. Arch Phys Med Rehabil 64:47–52, 1987.
123. Potts IF: The mechanism of ejaculation. Med J Australia 1:495–497, 1957.
124. Rajfer J, Aronson WJ, Bush PA, et al: Nitric oxide as a mediator of relaxation of the corpus cavernosum in response to nonadrenergic, noncholinergic neurotransmission. N Engl J Med 326:90–94, 1992.
125. Ravan RL, Howley TF, Nova HR: Electroejaculation. J Urol 87:726–729, 1962.
126. Ravindran RS, Cummins DF, Smith IE: Experience with the use of nitroprusside and subsequent epidural analgesia in a pregnant quadriplegic patient. Anesth Analg 60:61–63, 1981.
127. Reame NE: A prospective study of the menstrual cycle and spinal cord injury. Am J Phys Med Rehabil 71:15–21, 1992.
128. Reid K, Surridge DHC, Morales A, et al: Double-blind trial of yohimbine in treatment of psychogenic impotence. Lancet 2:421–423, 1987.

129. Robertson DNS: Pregnancy and labour in the paraplegic. Paraplegia 10:209–212, 1972.
130. Robertson DNS, Guttmann L: The paraplegic patient in pregnancy and labor. Proc R Soc Med 56:381–387, 1963.
131. Romano MD: Counseling the spinal cord injured female. In Sha'ked A (ed): Human Sexuality and Rehabilitation. Baltimore, Williams & Wilkins, 1981, pp 157–166.
132. Rosenberg L, Mitchell AA, Parsells JL, et al: Lack of relation of oral clefts to diazepam use during pregnancy. N Engl J Med 309:1282–1285, 1983.
133. Rossier AB, Fam BA: Indication and results of semi-rigid penile prosthesis in spinal cord injury patients: Long-term followup. J Urol 131:59–62, 1984.
134. Rossier AB, Ruffieux M, Ziegler WH: Pregnancy and labor in high traumatic spinal cord lesions. Paraplegia 7:210–216, 1971.
135. Roth E, Chen D, Ling E, et al: Analysis of semen collected using vibratory stimulation in spinal cord injured males. J Am Paraplegia Soc 53:528–536, 1992.
136. Sarkarati M, Rossier AB, Fam BA: Experience in vibratory and electroejaculation techniques in spinal cord injury patients: A preliminary report. J Urol 138:59–62, 1987.
137. Saunders D, Yeo J: Pregnancy and quadriplegia—the problem of autonomic dysreflexia. Aust N Z J Obstet Gynaecol 8:152–154, 1968.
138. Schlumpf M, Ramseier H, Abriel H, et al: Diazepam effects on the fetus. Neurotoxicology 10:501–516, 1989.
139. Shime J, Gare D, Andrews T, et al: Dantrolene in pregnancy: Lack of adverse effects on the fetus and newborn infant. Am J Obstet Gynecol 159:831–834, 1988.
140. Shortliffe LM, Wehner N, Stamey TA: The detection of a local prostatic immunological response to bacterial prostatitis. J Urol 125:509–515, 1981.
141. Sidi AA, Cameron JS, Duffy LM, Lange PH: Intracavernous drug-induced erections in the management of male erectile dysfunction: Experience with 100 patients. J Urol 135:704–706, 1986.
142. Sjogren K, Egberg K: The sexual experience in younger males with complete spinal cord injury. Scand J Rehabil Med Suppl 9:189–194, 1983.
143. Smith AD, Sazama R, Lange PH: Penile prosthesis: Adjunct to treatment in patients with neurogenic bladder. J Urol 124:363–364, 1980.
144. Spergel P, Rosenthal D, Albert BW: Sex-rehabilitation issue: What priority and when? [abstract]. Arch Phys Med Rehabil 57:562, 1976.
145. Spielman FJ: Portorient with spinal cord transection: Complications of autonomic hyperreflexia. Obstet Gynecol 64:147, 1984.
146. Spira R: Artificial insemination after intrathecal injection of neostigmine in a paraplegic. Lancet 1:670–671, 1956.
147. Stief CG, Watterauer V: Erectile responses to intracavernous papaverine and phentolamine: Comparison of single and combined delivery. J Urol 140:1415–1416, 1988.
148. Stirt JA, Marco A, Conklin KA: Obstetric anesthesia for a quadriplegic patient with autonomic hyperreflexia. Anesthesiology 51:560–562, 1979.
149. Szasz G: Vibratory stimulation of the penis in men with spinal cord injury. Presented at the 12th annual scientific meeting of the American Spinal Injury Association, San Francisco, March 13–15, 1986.
150. Talbot HS: A report on sexual function in paraplegics. J Urol 61:265–270, 1949.
151. Talbot HS: The sexual function in paraplegia. J Urol 73:91–100, 1955.
152. Tarabulcy E: Sexual function in the normal and in paraplegia. Paraplegia 10:201–208, 1972.
153. Tawil EA, Gregory JG: Failure of the Jones prosthesis. J Urol 135:702–703, 1986.
154. Thomas RJS, McLeigh G, McDonald IA: Electroejaculation of the paraplegic male followed by pregnancy. Med J Aust 2:798–799, 1975.
155. Thorton CE: Sexual counseling of women with spinal cord injuries. Sex Disabil 2:267–277, 1979.
156. Tsuji I, Nakajima F, Morimoto J, Nounaka Y: The sexual function in patients with spinal cord injury. Urol Int 12:270–280, 1961.
157. Turk R, Turk M, Assejeu V: The female paraplegic and mother-child relations. Paraplegia 21:186–191, 1983.
158. Van Arsdalen KN, Klein FA, Hackler RH, Brady SM: Penile implants in spinal cord injury patients for maintaining external appliances. J Urol 126:331–332, 1981.
159. Verduyn WH: Spinal cord injured women, pregnancy and delivery. Paraplegia 24:231–240, 1986.
160. Verduyn WH: A deadly combination: Induction of labor with oxytocin/pitocin in spinal cord injured women, T6 and above. Proceedings of the 15th annual meeting of the American Spinal Injury Association, April 3–5, 1989.
161. Virag R: Intracavernous injection of papaverine for erectile failure. Lancet 2:938, 1982.

162. Virag R, Frydman D, Legman M, Virag H: Intracavernous injection of papaverine as a diagnostic and therapeutic method in erectile failure. Angiology 35:79–87, 1984.
163. Von Heyden B, Donatucci CF, Kaula N, Lue TF: Intracavernous pharmacotherapy for impotence: Selection of appropriate agent and dose. J Urol 1149:1288–1290, 1993.
164. Wanner MB, Rageth CJ, Zach GA: Pregnancy and autonomic hyperreflexia in patients with spinal cord lesions. Paraplegia 25:482–490, 1987.
165. Ware HH: Pregnancy after paralysis—report of three cases. JAMA 102:1833–1834, 1934.
166. Warner H, Martin DE, Perkash J, et al: Electrostimulation of erection and ejaculation and collection of semen in spinal cord injured humans. J Rehabil Res Develop 23:21–31, 1986.
167. Watson DW, Downey GO: Epidural anesthesia for labor and delivery of twins of a paraplegic mother. Anesthesiology 52:259–261, 1980.
168. Watters GR, Keogh EJ, Earle CM, et al: Experience in the management of erectile dysfunction using the intracavernosal self-injection of vasoactive drugs. J Urol 140:1417–1419, 1988.
169. Weiner N: Drugs that inhibit adrenergic nerves and block adrenergic receptors. In Gilman AG, Goodman LS, Rall TW, Murad F (eds): The Pharmacological Basis of Therapeutics. 7th ed. New York, Goodman & Gilman, 1985, pp 181–214.
170. Weiss AJ, Diamond MD: Sexual adjustment, identification and attitudes of patients with myelopathy. Arch Phys Med Rehabil 47:245–250, 1966.
171. Weiss HD: The physiology of human penile erection. Ann Intern Med 76:793–799, 1972.
172. Witherington R: External aids for treatment of impotence. J Urol Nurs 6:1–7, 1987.
173. Wolff H, Politch JA, Martinez A, et al: Leukocytospermia associated with poor semen quality. Fertil Steril 53:528–536, 1990.
174. Wyndaele JJ, DeMeyer JM, DeSy WA, Claessens H: Intracavernous injection of vasoactive drugs, an alternative for treating impotence in spinal cord injury patients. Paraplegia 24:271–275, 1986.
175. Yarkony GM, Chen D, Palmer T, Roth ET: Management of impotence due to spinal cord injury with low-dose papaverine [abstract]. J Am Paraplegia Soc 16:145, 1992.
176. Young BK, Katz M, Klein SA: Pregnancy after spinal cord injury: Altered maternal and fetal response to labor. Obstet Gynecol 62:59–63, 1983.
177. Young RR, Delwaide PJ: Drug therapy: Spasticity. N Engl J Med 304:28–33, 96–99, 1981.
178. Zeitlin AB, Cottrell TL, Lloyd FA: Sexology of the paraplegic male. Fertil Steril 8:337–344, 1957.
179. Zorgniotti A, Lefleur R: Auto-injection of the corpus cavernosum with a vasoactive drug combination for vasculogenic impotence. J Urol 133:39–41, 1985.

TRILOK N. MONGA, MD, FRCP(C), MRCP(I)
HENRY J. OSTERMANN, PhD

SEXUALITY AND SEXUAL ADJUSTMENT IN STROKE PATIENTS

From the Department of Physical
  Medicine and Rehabilitation
Baylor College of Medicine
  and
Physical Medicine and
  Rehabilitation Service
Veterans Affairs Medical Center
Houston, Texas

Reprint requests to:
Trilok N. Monga, MD, FRCP(C)
Chief, Physical Medicine and
  Rehabilitation Service
Houston VA Medical Center
2002 Holcombe Blvd.
Houston, TX 77030

Cerebrovascular accident (CVA) is the third leading cause of death in North America. CVA leaves many of its survivors with long-term physical and psychological disabilities. The incidence of stroke declined during 1945–1980.[20,21,37] However, a recent rise in the hospitalization rate for stroke has been reported.[8,39,47] Since 1970, mortality due to stroke has been declining, but the prevalence of stroke is increasing, and there has been no decline in morbidity. Despite its increasing prevalence, few studies have comprehensively examined the long-term effects on physical functioning, quality of life, and sexuality issues following stroke.

During the acute stages of stroke, the patient and the family are concerned with survival. Once past the acute stage, the first question usually relates to when or if the patient will walk again. Most patients will be able to walk with a cane or a brace, and 50–75% of the patients will become independent in basic activities of daily living. However, the remaining 25–50% of the patients will need moderate to total assistance. An even more disturbing finding is that the overall quality of life after stroke is poor, even in young people who would be expected to have better recovery than older patients.[6] In a study on quality of life 4 years after stroke, Neimi et al. found that, despite recovery good enough for discharge from the hospital, resumption of activities of daily living, and return to work, the quality of life of 83% of patients had not been restored to the prestroke level.[59] Deterioration for older patients was significantly more than for younger patients. Similar results have been reported by other investigators. Astrom et al. found a marked reduction in patients' overall satisfaction with quality of life 1 year after stroke.[2] Soderback and colleagues concluded that the consequences of stroke for function and personal activities were considerable even after 3 years.[70]

Until recently, little information has been available on sexual functioning and sexual adjustment in stroke patients. Most of the studies on sexuality in stroke patients have involved either a small sample size or included subjects younger than 60.[7,22,33,63] In other studies, the only specific sexual behavior assessed was frequency of coitus, with very little reference to attitudes or psychological functioning.[33,63]

An 85-year-old patient who has suffered a stroke today was born in the early 1900s to parents who were born in the Victorian era. When addressing sexuality issues in these patients, one should consider the prevailing attitudes toward sexual expression during this earlier era.[51] Also, the changes in sexual behavior in aging patients should be considered since stroke is common in this age group. Age, however, is only one of the many factors contributing to the decline of sexual functioning. Understanding the physiologic changes of aging and sexuality in the elderly is a prerequisite to any discussion regarding sexuality in stroke patients. Since the classic work by Kinsey et al.,[21,22] various investigators have studied sexual functioning in the elderly.[4,9,10,14,38,39,47,48] It can be concluded that sex continues to play an important role in the lives of many elderly people. Sexuality in aging has recently been reviewed by Kleitch and O'Donnell,[34] and is also presented in chapter 12 of this issue.

MAGNITUDE OF THE PROBLEM

Various authors have reported a marked decline in many aspects of sexuality.[6,7,41,50,54,59,66,67] Muckleroy, however, has stated that although stroke patients commonly experience change in sexual activity, change is not necessarily a problem.[57] According to Muckleroy, it is rare for either partner to view this decline as a significant one. Stroke may affect both physical and psychosocial aspects of sexuality. For example, many patients with cerebrovascular accidents have erectile dysfunction, while others have fear of rejection from the partner to the extent that they withdraw from all kinds of sexual encounters (Table 1).

Libido

The profound effect of stroke on patients' libido has been well documented.[50] The earliest study, by Kalliomaki et al., described sexual behavior in stroke patients younger than 60.[33] According to these authors, CVA tends to diminish libido as well as frequency of coitus. In their study, the decline was more common in patients with right-sided paralysis than in those with left-sided weakness. The study was based on personal interviews with patients, and it appears that spouses were not involved in the study.

TABLE 1.   Sexuality in Stroke Patients

Decline in libido	Orgasmic difficulties
Decline or cessation of coital activity	Poor satisfaction with sexual activity
Lack of or poor erection	Lack of enjoyment with sexual activity
Absence of ejaculation	Hypersexuality
Poor vaginal lubrication	

In a study of 25 stroke patients, Goddess, Wagner, and Silverman also found that decline in libido was more prevalent in patients with dominant hemispheric lesions.[22]

In a study of elderly stroke patients (mean age at onset, 68 years), 75% of the men and 60% of the women reported normal libido prior to stroke, but only 21% of men and 12% of the women had normal libido after stroke.[54]

However, Bray et al. did not observe a decline in libido.[7] Ford and Orfirer reported that 60% of their patients did not experience loss of libido after CVA.[17]

Coital Frequency

Various studies have reported a decline in the frequency of intercourse for stroke patients. Many stroke patients stop having intercourse completely. Sadoughi et al. studied sexual adjustment in 55 chronically ill and physically disabled patients, 12 of whom had a history of stroke.[63] Although the authors did not report the sexual problems in the various subgroups separately, 78% of the patients experienced a decline of sexual activity after the onset of their disability.

In another study, nine men (11%) and ten women (29%) reported no coital activity before their CVA while 50 men (64%) and 19 women (54%) ceased all coital activity after stroke.[54] Sjogren, Damber, and Liliequist noted that the decrease in intercourse appeared to be more common in men than in women.[67] In their study, 72% of the men and 59% of the women reported a cease or decrease in frequency of intercourse (Among the men, 41% ceased coital activity and 31% had a decrease in frequency; the numbers were 17% and 42%, respectively, for women.) The authors also noted marked changes in foreplay, with 31% of the men and 27% of women ceasing activity that is commonly termed *foreplay*. In another study by Sjogren,[68] the changes in frequency of intercourse were related to the degree of cutaneous sensibility impairment and levels of dependence in activities of daily living, but not with degree of motor impairment. On the other hand, the degree of motor impairment was a main factor causing sexual dysfunction in a study by Fugl-Meyer.[19]

Arousal

Problems with erection in men and vaginal lubrication in women have been reported in patients with CVA. In a study by Sjogren and Fugl-Meyer, 64% of the men had difficulty achieving erections after stroke, compared with 21% reporting such problems before stroke.[69] Monga et al. reported that 73 men (94%) had normal erection before stroke versus only 30 men (38%) after CVA.[54] In the same study, 63% of the women had normal vaginal lubrication before stroke, and only 29% reported normal lubrication after stroke.

Ejaculation and Orgasm

Problems with ejaculation and orgasm are also common in stroke patients. Bray et al. reported that only one of 11 women experienced orgasm after stroke, versus five women who regularly had orgasms before the stroke.[7] In the study by Monga et al., most women became anorgasmic after stroke, and premature ejaculation was prevalent in men following stroke.[54] Fifteen women (43%) and four women (11%) had normal orgasm before and after stroke, respectively. Similarly, 17 (22%) and 57 (35%) men reported premature ejaculation before and after stroke, respectively. Other studies[65,67] have reported similar problems to a greater or lesser extent.

Enjoyment and Satisfaction with Sexual Activity

Other findings regarding sexuality after stroke include declined leisure activities,[42,68,73] enjoyment with sexual activity, and satisfaction with the level of sexual activity.[54] Sjogren et al. found a decline in mutual verbal and nonverbal responsiveness, a decrease in frequency of caressing and touching with the intention of having sex, and a decrease in intimate caressing or foreplay following stroke.[65] They noted that 31% of men and 27% of the women had ceased foreplay altogether. "Spectatoring" occurs when these patients remove themselves from an active sexual role and are instead preoccupied by attempts to observe and evaluate their own and their partners' performance. Decline in foreplay activity also was reported by Boldrini.[6]

Sexuality in Aphasic Patients

Information regarding sexual problems in aphasic patients is limited. Some studies have reported that impairment of language skills plays a role in sexual changes of patients affected with CVA.[32,43,76] Kinsella and Duffy[32] stressed that a sudden loss of ability to communicate effectively influenced several aspects of life, including the marital relationship. Wiig focused on the sexual readjustment in 100 persons with aphasia.[76] It was reported that physically intact aphasic patients with relatively good auditory comprehension and nonverbal communication ability exhibited the least problems with sexual adjustment, irrespective of expressive language ability. Wiig's findings implied that sexual readjustment was easier for aphasic patients if they could interpret other people correctly. Her results indicated that men, especially right hemiplegics, questioned their adequacies and capabilities, whereas female aphasics were primarily concerned about their attractiveness.

Long-term Effects of CVA on Sexuality

Few studies have been published on the long-term effects of CVA on sexuality.[27,54,59,68,75] In their study on adjustment to life after stroke, Sjogren et al. reported that while changes in coital frequency were temporally independent, changes in leisure activities were less pronounced for people who were examined later than 12 months after stroke.[68] They commented that patients with previously known arterial hypertension, myocardial infarction, or diabetes mellitus had changed relatively little in their sexual function and lifestyle compared to those without these ailments. This probably represents a prestroke decline in sexual functioning.

In a prospective long-term study of life after stroke conducted in Sweden, Viitanen et al. reported that 61% of 62 stroke patients with a follow-up of 4–6 years experienced a decreased general and/or domain-specific satisfaction with life.[75] Twelve patients (19%) had decreased in four or more aspects, while 14 (23%) had decreased in only one aspect. Except for contact with friends, where 85% were as satisfied before as after the stroke, changes in all of the items of domain-specific life satisfaction were significantly associated with changes in global life satisfaction. Reduced satisfaction with sex life was noted in 42 of 62 married patients. Whether these results can be generalized to all patient populations is difficult to state.

In another study on sexual adjustment of men who have had strokes, Hawton reported that interest in sex returned for the majority of 35 patients.[27] The patients had been living with a partner and had been sexually active before the stroke. The interval between the onset of stroke and the interviews averaged 6.2 months (SD = 5.4). The shortest interval was 3 months and, with the exception of three patients, the interviews took place within 1 year of the stroke. This kind of experience has not been reported by other investigators.[54] Hawton comments that the men

TABLE 2.   Factors Influencing Sexuality in Stroke Patients

Fear of having another stroke	Severity of disability
Fear of rejection by the partner	Contractures and spasticity
Fear of poor performance	Cognitive deficits
Concomitant medical conditions	Poor coping skills
Side effects of medications	

who reported full return of their previous interest in sex tended to be younger than those whose interest in sex did not return or had returned partially. In this study, only two patients were older than 70.[27]

Nature of the Problem

Sexual dysfunction in stroke patients is complex and multifactorial (Table 2). There are two parameters of impairment in stroke patients: dysfunction and disfigurement. Both may vary from minor to major in terms of severity of physical loss and problems with body image and self-esteem. The sexual problems in these patients are never a consequence of stroke alone; rather, they may be due to a variety of associated medical conditions, such as diabetes, hypertension, and coronary artery disease. A multitude of psychosocial factors are also involved, including role changes, loss of self-esteem, and fear of rejection by the spouse. Other factors that may influence sexual functioning are incontinence, poor coping skills, and cognitive, sensory, and motor deficits.

None of the above factors have been systematically investigated, and subjective loss of potency in men has not been objectively verified by penile plethysmography. In one study, cessation of sexual intercourse was most common among patients who did not regain independence after their strokes.[68]

Sidedness of Lesion

Kalliomaki et al. reported that impairment of sexual interest was more common with dominant hemispheric lesions than with nondominant hemispheric involvement;[33] however, Sjogren et al. reported no significant correlation between side of lesion and in any of the sexual parameters they investigated.[67] Similarly, Boldrini concluded that the side of hemispheric lesion did not play a crucial role in determining changes in sexual life after stroke.[6] Monga et al. reported a lesser decline in sexuality, as measured on an index of sexual function, among women with right-sided lesions.[54] In this study, the sexual function of four groups (left and right hemispheric lesions in men and women) was compared. A single index of sexual function before and after was established: the sexual function data thus produced had a minimum value of eight points and a maximum value of 30 points. Twenty-six diabetic patients were excluded from the analysis. Sexual function of the four groups was comparable before CVA. Although there was a decline in sexual function for all groups after CVA, the sexual function of the four groups after CVA was not comparable. The women with right-sided lesions had a less marked decline in index of sexual function than any of the other three groups. No significant difference between men with right and left lesions in the degree of sexual function was noted. However, there was a marked difference between women having left and right lesions in the severity of decline of sexual function, with the latter showing a much smaller decline. The authors concluded that the severity of cognitive deficits may contribute to this sexual decline.[54] Their conclusion was based upon a finding, previously reported by Inglis et al.,[29] that right-sided lesions in women did not reveal cognitive deficits as severe as the left-sided lesions in women or both right- and left-sided lesions in men. In summary, there is no general agreement about the incidence of sexual disturbance as a function of the side of lesion. Patients who had a higher frequency of sexual activity before stroke were more likely to resume sexual intercourse after their stroke.[27]

Alcohol

Alcohol can contribute to the decline in sexual performance, particularly in men. As a central nervous system depressant, alcohol can cause erectile problems. Hawton reported that up to 80% of chronic alcoholics experienced a decreased sex drive and ejaculation dysfunction.[27]

Medications

Antihypertensives, antidepressants, and hypnotics can contribute to erectile difficulties and ejaculatory dysfunction. Sexual dysfunction, particularly impotence, has been reported with the use of all antihypertensive agents. However, many patients with hypertension already have pelvic vasculature insufficiency related to atherosclerotic changes[38] and may have had preexisting vascular impotence.

Thiazide diuretics are commonly prescribed in the treatment of hypertension and heart failure. In a randomized placebo-controlled trial of the effect of thiazide diuretics on quality of life, Chang reported that patients taking diuretics experienced greater sexual dysfunction than controls.[10] The sexual problems encountered were decreased libido, difficulty gaining and maintaining an erection, and difficulty with ejaculation.

Hagan, Wallin, and Baer[26] reported a positive correlation between antihypertensives and erectile dysfunction; however, there was no such association in Sjogren's study.[67] Other medications that may influence sexual performance include anxiolytics, antihistamines, muscle relaxants, and cimetidine.

In a study by Boldrini, patients who had aphasia, severe debilitating illnesses, urologic disorders, and patients receiving any medication that could have caused sexual dysfunctioning were excluded from the evaluation.[6] Yet, most of the patients of both genders reported a decline in sexual activity. The authors did not report whether patients with diabetes mellitus were excluded. However, these findings suggest that most of the changes in sexual functioning after stroke are a direct result of stroke rather than other underlying medical conditions or medications.

In the above study, both partners were interviewed separately. In 24 cases (27%), there was disagreement on answers about the frequency of intercourse. Sixteen patients reported a higher frequency of intercourse than their spouse, and eight patients reported a lower frequency than their spouse. Overall, it appears that men exaggerated the performance. This points to the subjective nature of the available data on sexual functioning in stroke patients. Furthermore, most of the information regarding prestroke sexual activity may have been subject to the vagaries of memory.

Fear of Another Stroke

One of the main factors identified in the decline of sexual function was the fear that sexual intercourse might precipitate another stroke.[54] Other investigators have also found that fear is one of the factors responsible for the decline of sexual functioning.[6,32,67]

The reasons for this fear appear to be similar to those reported in patients with myocardial infarction. Block, Macden, and Hinsley[5] studied patients with acute myocardial infarction and reported that the average frequency of sexual intercourse declined from the preinfarction rate. The decline did not correlate with measures of patients' health or activity levels or the results of exercise tests. The authors found the main reason for reduction in sexual activity to be psychosocial, the principal factors being depression, fear of relapse, or fear of sudden death. Although sudden death does occur during intercourse in patients with myocardial infarction, it is very rare. Ueno[74] reported that the occurrence of death during intercourse or shortly thereafter was 0.6% of all deaths. Sudden death during or after intercourse has not been reported in stroke patients.

Fear of Rejection or Failure

Besides the fear of having another stroke or myocardial infarction, these patients also fear rejection by their spouse and fear performance failure.[34] Masters and Johnson,[45,46] Rykken,[62] and Starr[71] suggested that a major cause of sexual dysfunction in aging men is the fear of failure and that its accompanying anxiety becomes a self-fulfilling prophecy. In time, men often will withdraw from sexual activity with their spouse altogether.

Autonomic Dysfunction

Autonomic nervous system dysfunction as a factor leading to sexual decline in stroke patients was suggested by Monga et al. in their study of cardiovascular effects of exercise in stroke patients.[52] They reported a significantly smaller increase in both systolic and diastolic blood pressure with upper limb exercises compared to age- and sex-matched controls. No such difference was noted with lower limb exercises. They concluded that a lack of normal response may suggest an underlying autonomic dysfunction.

In another study involving stroke patients, autonomic nervous system functioning was examined and compared with an age-matched control group of normal elderly people.[53] Abnormalities of skin temperature on the hemiparetic side versus the normal side were noted; no such findings were present in the controls. Similarly, abnormalities in Valsalva maneuver and heart rate variation with change of posture were detected in some stroke patients. The abnormalities were more marked in patients who had symptoms of autonomic nervous system dysfunction. It was concluded that these findings suggest autonomic system dysfunction in stroke patients.

Altered Self-image

Stroke often leads to a loss of status and a diminished self-image. Men often experience a decline in their authority in the family, which negatively influences their relationship with their spouses.[6] Reduced self-esteem resulting from inability to perform intercourse according to expectations has been reported.[7,68] Not surprisingly, the incidence of depression is high, occurring in 20–60% of these patients. Decrease in the frequency and firmness of erections may be a clinical manifestation of depression, with resultant decline in sex drive and desire. Beaumont reported that depressed men suffer erectile dysfunction and that some depressed women report difficulty reaching an orgasm.[3]

Coping Skills and Role Changes

Coping with the stress of stroke and its outcome is becoming increasingly recognized in relation to quality of life and sexual functioning. Stress is viewed as a dynamic unfolding process rather than a static unitary event. It leads to a disturbed person-environment relationship that exceeds one's current personal resources.[40] Similarly, coping is a dynamic process designed to manage a situation through regulation of distressing emotions and taking action to change the situation.

Sjogren et al. contend that sexual dysfunctions in hemiplegics may be explained in terms of poor coping skills rather than by endocrine deficits.[67] According to these authors, there was no organic background for common sexual dysfunction; therefore, they concluded that the dysfunction was a result of a change in sex role, the custodial attitude of the partner, and dependency in self-care. According to Sjogren, a stroke patient may become distressed and less willing to initiate a sexual encounter while his spouse has to assist him with toiletting and other self-care activities. Other investigators also have identified the role change and role conflict as contributing factors that influence sexual function in stroke patients.[13,19,23] The patient's spouse may abruptly become the wage earner, family decision maker, and household manager, in addition to having the responsibility to providing care. Social isolation, such as reduced contact with friends, fewer social interactions, and lack of time for leisure activities may add to further frustrations and influence sexual relationships with the partner. Marron[44] cautioned that rejection of the stroke patient by the partner may reflect previous marital discord within the couple.

Hypersexuality

Although hyposexuality is common in stroke patients, some patients may present with hypersexuality. Monga et al. have described hypersexuality and deviant sexual behavior as a complication following stroke.[55] Symptoms in these patients were similar to the findings described in the Kluver-Bucy syndrome.[36] Kluver and Bucy described behavior changes as a result of bilateral temporal lobectomies in rhesus monkeys. These changes included increased sexual activity, marked changes in dietary habits, and antisocial behavior. Hypersexuality has been described in both animals and humans with temporal lobe lesions and seizures.[4,16,64] Andy demonstrated that temporal lobe or limbic system seizures may induce hypersexuality in early stages of seizure development.[1] Patients described by Monga et al. had involvement of temporal lobe lesions. However, in two cases the lesion was extending into the frontal lobe, and these patients also had a history of seizure activity.[55] Management of these patients is more difficult and rehabilitation outcome tends to be poor due to the difficulty of partners accepting and coping with such a problem.

ASSESSMENT

The degree of functional alteration and change in physical appearance are important to assess because they may predict the severity of impact on emotional response and sexuality (Table 3). It is recommended that assessment should include an in-depth interview of both partners to determine sexual history and sexual behavior and functioning before the onset of stroke. Because vascular disease is one of the major causes of impotence in patients older than 40, a prestroke history of erectile difficulties will be important in an overall assessment of the patient. Furthermore, low penile brachial pressure has been reported in patients who have erectile problems and as an indicator of a major future vascular event.[56]

Any psychosocial disorders, such as depression and anxiety, and other factors that may interfere with sexual functioning should be noted. Patients and

TABLE 3. Assessment of Sexuality in Stroke Patients

Thorough history and physical examination	History of alcohol consumption
Pre- and poststroke sexuality	Interview with both partners
Cognitive and functional status	Need for current medications
Prestroke marital problems	Side effects of current medications
Past and present psychosocial functioning	Personal preferences of sexual expression
Coping skills	

spouses should be interviewed together and separately so the clinician can determine how the couple has been coping with stresses resulting from stroke, with special reference to the sexuality-related concerns. Interviewing separately also provides insight into the partners' preferences about methods of sexual expressions. This also may help to unmask some of the concerns about perceived extramarital relationships on the part of the healthy partner. Sometimes it is possible that both partners do not desire sexual activity as part of the relationship.

The medical history should include details of past and present medical diagnoses, history of any surgical procedures, drug usage, endocrine function, and other neurologic deficits or diseases. Special note should be made of diseases that may influence sexuality (e.g., diabetes mellitus, renal failure, chronic obstructive pulmonary disease). History of excessive alcohol consumption and use of antidepressants, tranquilizers, sedatives, and hypotensives should be explored.

There is a relatively high incidence of depression in these patients. Significant decrease in the frequency and firmness of nighttime erections occurs in depressed elderly men. Thus, it is important that past or present history of depression should be considered in the assessment of sexuality in stroke patients. It is also important to examine penile sensitivity in elderly people because it may be a factor in their sexual behavior.[15]

In men who have problems achieving satisfactory erections and who have a strong desire to remain sexually active, further investigations should be considered, including urodynamics, penile biothesiometry, dorsal nerve somatosensory evoked potentials (SSEP), and nocturnal penile tumescence (NPT) (Table 4). However, the absence of NPT should not lead to the conclusion that the dysfunction is wholly or even partially organic in nature, since it could be due to an underlying depression. There is no information available regarding the use of NPT in the evaluation of sexuality in male stroke patients. Measurement of serum testosterone levels may not be of much help either in diagnosis or management of the patient, because the relationship between testosterone levels and sexuality in older men has been found to be only modest.[9] When Sjogren et al. measured serum testosterone levels in stroke patients, they found the values within the predicted range.[67] Responses to HCG-stimulation also were adequate.

The traditional organic versus psychogenic approach to sexual dysfunction in stroke patients is a gross oversimplification. Most sexual problems encountered by stroke patients result from a complex interaction of psychological and physical factors, including the side effects of medication.

TABLE 4. Sexuality Assessment in Selected Patients

Urology consultation
Penile biothesiometry
Dorsal nerve somatosensory evoked potentials
Nocturnal penile tumescence

TABLE 5.   Management Approaches to Sexuality in Stroke Patients

Remove communication barriers	Retrain cognitive and perceptual deficits
Reassure patients regarding the following:	Adjust medications
Acceptance	Manage depression
Performance	Improve coping skills
Safety	Suggest alternative positions
Improve functional status	

Management

Because sexual problems in stroke patients are multifactorial, the management of these patients requires a multifaceted approach (Table 5). The first and most important task for those who are caring for these patients is to be aware of sexual dysfunctioning in stroke patients. Sexual counseling and discussion should not be left to the orderlies and in the hands of staff members who feel uncomfortable in discussing sexual issues with the disabled. Conine and Evans[11] remind us that stroke patients will discuss sexual concerns with people with whom they feel comfortable.

Before sexual counseling can begin, assessment of the cause or causes of sexual dysfunction should be carried out. An erection occurring during the morning or sleep may indicate that impotence is not organic.

In preparing for the discussion of sexuality with elderly patients, counselors must carefully consider their own feelings and attitudes toward sexuality so that the information and counseling provided is free from judgment and bias. Mims and Swenson[49] have developed a sexual model "to provide a frame-work for self assessment, for client assessment, and for intervention." According to these authors, the development of behaviors regarding sexuality is based on personal experience and societal influence. They explained that the "life experience level" involves the development of personal destructive and intuitively helpful behaviors that may result in conflicting messages regarding sexuality. The authors believe that attaining the "basic level" awareness is necessary to assist other individuals with sexual concerns. This awareness is created by the interaction of perceptions, attitudes, and cognition and that awareness is fluid and constantly changing due to the changes in sexual norms.[49]

It is this author's opinion that the topic of sexuality should be discussed early during the recovery from stroke and that it should not be delayed. The most appropriate time might be when the patient is going home for a weekend pass, or it may be sooner if the patient mentions concerns regarding sexual function. Most patients welcome an open and honest discussion of this topic and welcome any suggestions that one may be able to provide.

Several concerns need to be addressed, including problems with self-image, self-esteem, communication barriers within the partners, problems related to sensory/perceptual deficits, weakness, contractures, and bowel and bladder incontinence. The fear of having another stroke or a heart attack, fear of rejection, and fear of performance also need to be discussed.

Permission-giving is a fundamental intervention,[28] and reassurance should be provided that concerns and questions following stroke are normal. Furthermore, patients should be reassured regarding the safety of exercises and intercourse. There is no available data to indicate that sexual intercourse will or may precipitate another stroke; moreover, exercises within limits of fatigue have been found to be safe.[52] The patient should be asked to notify the physician of any shortness of breath, chest pain, or dizziness experienced during exercise, and the clinician needs to be cautioned in prescribing unsupervised exercises with the upper limbs.

Medications may need to be adjusted or changed to drugs with fewer side effects on sexual function. Empirical use of antidepressants and tranquilizers should be discouraged. If spasticity is considered to be interfering in sexual performance, dantrolene sodium could be tried to relieve some of the increased tone.

In young stroke patients, counseling needs to include questions regarding contraceptive options, pregnancy, labor, delivery, and parenting. There is no information available regarding the last three areas of concern. Oral contraceptives are contraindicated due to the increased risk of thrombophlebitis. A diaphragm may be difficult to insert because of poor coordination and balance. Use of condoms may be the most practical means of contraception; however, this may require the partner's cooperation.

This author had to deal with one patient in whom the question of child custody was raised. The patient was a young woman with a history of left-sided cerebral hemorrhage leading to right-sided hemiparesis and expressive aphasia. The patient was admitted to the rehabilitation unit for assessment and intensive training in child care. The patient was found to be independent in activities of daily living, ambulation, and household chores. She was also able to demonstrate the ability to care for the child. However, custody of the child was denied. The decision was based upon the fact that the patient would not be able to seek help in case of an emergency due to her aphasia.

Attempts should be made to improve the functional status of patients and make them as independent as possible. Female patients with history of vaginal dryness and dyspareunia may be relieved of symptoms with a local estrogen preparation.

Patients with chronic obstructive pulmonary disease (COPD) may fear becoming dyspnic during sexual activity. Attempts should be made to minimize performance anxiety. The partner can be taught to be sensitive to changes in breathing and to learn the COPD partner's limits by close observation.[25] Furthermore, the couple may find coughing during intercourse a source of frustration and may need encouragement to share their feelings of guilt and resentment with each other. Placing a box of tissues nearby for fits of coughing should become part of preparation for sexual activity.[75] Patients with COPD could be instructed in controlled breathing. There are basically two methods: pursed-lip breathing and diaphragmatic breathing. Pursed-lip breathing is carried out by inhaling through the nose and exhaling through pursed lips; exhalation should be twice as long as inhalation. Diaphragmatic breathing involves conscious use of the diaphragm. In these patients, sexual activity must be planned and paced to take advantage of times the patient has maximum energy.[14] However, this may take away the pleasure of having spontaneous sexual encounters.

If depression has been diagnosed, it should be treated by medication or, if required, by psychotherapy. Partners of stroke patients with sensory deficits should be encouraged to explore erogenous zones in which sensation remains intact. Various means of sexual expression, such as hugs, kisses, caresses, and verbal affection need to be explained to the couple.

The need for marital counseling should be assessed and provided. Sjogren has emphasized the importance of role changes and increased dependency in self-care as major factors contributing to the decline in frequency of intercourse and interference with positive attitudes toward sexuality.[65] Once the problem of custodial care has been identified, it is possible to find alternative ways of providing care to maintain the previous relationship and sex roles.

Unlike in spinal cord-injured patients, the role and need for penile implantation has not been examined in stroke patients and, similarly, no reports of papaverine injections in stroke patients have been identified. However, a urology consultation is in order if there is any question of a prostatic problem or if patients are keen to explore the possibility of having any of these procedures.

Information regarding alternate sexual positions for couples in which one partner has residual physical impairments should be provided. Conine and Evans[11] and Fugl-Meyer[19] offer suggestions on methods for enhancing sexual performance in male hemiplegics. Both suggest that the patient should lie on the affected side so that the unaffected arm is free to caress the partner. In this position, with a pillow wedged behind the male's back, a rear entry is easiest. The female partner may need encouragement to increase her active participation. If this position is not possible, the man can remain supine during intercourse and the woman can adopt a top superior position. The authors have provided more details as how to manage with the problem of incomplete erection and perform hand stimulation.[11] Costello Smith[12] also recommends that stroke patients assume a mutual side-lying or supine position, with their partners, to facilitate intercourse. Patients with shoulder pain should avoid the side-lying position in favor of a supine position. McCormick, Riffer, and Thompson[48] have schematically outlined several alternate positions for these patients. The partner may need to be reminded that the patient may neglect stimuli from the affected side because of perceptual and sensory deficits.

Many options, suggestions, and recommendations have been put forward concerning the treatment and management of sexual problems in stroke patients; however, no information is available to confirm that the above approaches are effective in the management of sexual dysfunction. There is a need for further research regarding the outcome of various treatment approaches, including sexual counseling.

SUMMARY

A marked decline in many aspects of sexuality has been reported in stroke patients. The common problems that have been identified include a decline in libido and coital frequency, a decline in vaginal lubrication and orgasm in women, and poor or lack of erection and ejaculation in men. Patients experience lack of enjoyment and poor satisfaction with sexual activity following stroke. The decline appears to be multifactorial. The major factors influencing sexuality include poor coping skills, psychosocial adjustment to the impairment and disability resulting from stroke, fear of having another stroke, and, to a certain extent, the severity of sensory, perceptual, and cognitive deficits. The first step in management is a complete assessment of the medical, functional, and psychosocial status of the patient. To determine sexual history and behavior before and after stroke, an in-depth interview with both partners should be carried out and followed by appropriate interventions. Interventions should focus on reassurance, adjustment of medications, counseling regarding coping skills, and alternate positioning and means of sexual expressions and satisfaction.

No information is available regarding the value of urodynamics, penile biothesiometry, dorsal nerve SSEP, and nocturnal penile tumescence in the diagnosis of impotence in stroke patients.

REFERENCES

1. Andy OJ, Velamati S: Temporal lobe seizures and hypersexuality. Appl Neurophysiol 41:13–28, 1978.
2. Astrom M, Asplund K, Astrom T: Psychosocial function and life satisfaction after stroke. Stroke 23:527–531, 1992.
3. Beaumont G: Sexual side of cloipramine (Anafranil). J Int Med Res 5(suppl 1):37–44, 1977.
4. Blumer D, Walker AE: Sexual behavior in temporal lobe epilepsy. Arch Neurol 16:37–43, 1967.
5. Block A, Maeder J, Haissly J: Sexual problems after myocardial infarction. Am Heart J 90:536–537, 1975.
6. Boldrini P, Basaglia N, Calanca MC: Sexual changes in hemiparetic patients. Arch Phys Med Rehabil 72:202–207, 1991.
7. Bray GP, De Frank RS, Wolfe TL: Sexual functioning in stroke patients. Arch Phys Med Rehabil 62:286–288, 1981.
8. Brederick JP, Phillips SJ, Whisnant JP, et al: Incidence rate of stroke in the eighties: The end of the decline in stroke? Stroke 20:577–582, 1989.
9. Brown WA, Monti PM, Corriveau DP: Serum testosterone and sexual activity and interest in men. Arch Sex Behav 7:97–103, 1978.
10. Chang SW, Fine R, Siegel D, et al: The impact of diuretic therapy on reported sexual function. Arch Intern Med 151:2402–2408, 1991.
11. Conine TA, Evans JH: Sexual reactivation of chronically ill and disabled adults. J Allied Health 11:261–270, 1982.
12. Costello Smith P: The sexual recovery of stroke patients. Sexual Med Today 5:6–11, 1981.
13. Crossman L, London C, Barry C: Older women caring for disabled spouses: A model for supportive services. The Gerontologist 21:464–470, 1981.
14. Curgian LM, Gronkiewicz CA: Enhancing sexual performance in COPD. Nurse Pract 13:34–38, 1988.
15. Edwards AE, Husted JR: Penile sensitivity, age and sexual behavior. J Clin Psychol 32:697–700, 1976.
16. Falconer MA, Hill D, Meyer A, et al: Treatment of temporal lobe epilepsy by temporal lobectomy: Survey of findings and results. Lancet 1:827–835, 1955.
17. Ford AB, Orfirer AP: Sexual behavior and chronically ill patient. Med Aspects Human Sex 1:51–61, 1967.
18. Freeman JT: Sexual capacities in aging male. Geriatrics 16:37–43, 1961.
19. Fugl-Meyer AR, Jaasko L: Post-stroke hemiplegia and sexual intercourse. Scand J Rehabil Med 7:158–166, 1980.
20. Garraway WM, Whisnant JP, Drury I: The continuing decline in the incidence of stroke. Mayo Clin Proc 58:520–523, 1983.
21. Glllum RF, Gomez-Martin O, Kottke TE, et al: Acute stroke in a metropolitan area, 1970 and 1980: The Minnesota Heart Survey. J Chronic Disabil 38:891–898, 1985.
22. Goddess ED, Wagner NN, Silverman DR: Post-stroke sexual activity of CVA patients. Med Aspects Hum Sex 13(3):16–29, 1979.
23. Goldstein V, Regnery G, Wellin E: Caretaker role fatigue. Nursing Outlook 29(1):24–30, 1981.
24. Griggs W: Sex and the elderly. Am J Nurs 78.1352–1354, 1978.
25. Hahn K: Sexuality and COPD. Rehabil Nurs 14:191–195, 1989.
26. Hagan MJ, Wallin JD, Baer RM: Anti-hypertension therapy and male sexual dysfunction. Psychosomatics 21:234–237, 1980.
27. Hawton K: Sexual adjustment of men who had strokes. J Psychosom Res 28.243–249, 1984.
28. Herring BE: Sexual changes in patients and partners following stroke. Rehabil Nurs Mar–Apr:28–30, 1985.
29. Inglis J, Ruckman M, Lawson JS, et al: Sex differences in cognitive effects of unilateral brain damage. Cortex 18:257–275, 1982.
30. Kinsey AL, Gebhard PH: Sexual Behavior in the Human Female. Philadelphia, WB Saunders, 1953.
31. Kinsey AC, Pomeroy WB, Martin CE, Gebhard PH: Sexual Behavior in the Human Male. Philadelphia, WB Saunders, 1948.
32. Kinsella GH, Duffy FD: Psychosocial readjustment in the spouses of aphasic patients: A comparative survey of 79 subjects. Scand J Rehabil Med 11:129–132, 1979.
33. Kalliomaki JL, Markkanen TK, Mustonen VA: Sexual behavior after cerebral vascular accident: Study on patients below age 60 years. Fertil Steril 12:156–158, 1961.
34. Kleitsch EC, O'Donnell PD: Sex and aging. Phys Med Rehabil State Art Rev 4:121–134, 1990.

35. Kling A, Hutt PJ: Effect of hypothalamic lesions on amygdala syndrome in cats. Arch Neurol Psychiatry 79:511–517, 1958.
36. Kluver H, Bucy PC: Preliminary analysis of functions of temporal lobes in monkeys. Arch Neurol Psychiatry 42:979–1000, 1939.
37. Kotila M: Declining incidence and mortality of stroke? Stroke 15:255–259, 1984.
38. Krane R: Sexual function and dysfunction. In Walsh P, Gittes RF, Perlmutter AD, Stamey TA (eds): Campbell's Urology. 5th ed. Philadelphia, WB Saunders, 1986, pp 700–735.
39. Kuller LH: Incidence rates of stroke in eighties: The end of decline in stroke? Stroke 200:841–843, 1989.
40. Lazarus RS: Stress, Appraisal and Coping. New York, Springer, 1984.
41. Leshner M, Fine HL, Goldman A: Sexual activity in older stroke patients. Arch Phys Med Rehabil 55:578–579, 1974.
42. Lobi MLC, Phillips TF, Cresham GE: Psychosocial disability in physically restored long term stroke survivors. Arch Phys Med Rehabil 61:56–71, 1980.
43. Malone PE: A preliminary investigation of changes in sexual relations following strokes. In Brookshire R (ed): Clinical Aphasiology: Proceedings of a Conference. Minneapolis, BBK Publishers, 1975.
44. Marron KR: Sexuality with aging. Geriatrics 37:135–138, 1982.
45. Masters WH, Johnson VE: Human Sexual Response. Boston, Little Brown & Company, 1966.
46. Masters WH, Johnson VE: Human Sexual Inadequacy. Boston, Little Brown & Company, 1970.
47. Mayo NE, Goldberg MS, Levy AR, et al: Changing rates of stroke in the province of Quebec, Canada: 1981–1988. Stroke 22:590–595, 1991.
48. McCormick GP, Riffer DJ, Thompson MM: Coital positioning for stroke afflicted couples. Rehabil Nurs 11:17–19, 1986.
49. Mims FH, Swenson M: Sexuality: A Nursing Perspective. New York, McGraw-Hill, 1980.
50. Monga TN: Sexuality post stroke. Phys Med Rehabil State Art Rev 7:225–236, 1993.
51. Monga TN: Sexuality Update. National Task Force on Sexuality and Disability, American Congress of Rehabilitation 3(1), 1990.
52. Monga TN, DeForge DA, Williams J, Wolfe LA: Cardiovascular responses to acute exercise in patients with cerebrovascular accident. Arch Phys Med Rehabil 69:937–940, 1988.
53. Monga TN, Miller T, Biederman HJ: Autonomic nervous system dysfunction in stroke patients [abstract]. Arch Phys Med Rehabil 68:630, 1987.
54. Monga TN, Lawson JS, Inglis J: Sexual dysfunction in stroke patients. Arch Phys Med Rehabil 67:19–22, 1986.
55. Monga TN, Monga M, Raina MS, Hardjasudarma M: Hypersexuality in stroke. Arch Phys Med Rehabil 67:415–417, 1986.
56. Morley JE, Korenman SG, Kaser FE, et al: Relationship of penile brachial pressure index to myocardial infarction and cerebrovascular accidents in older men. Am J Med 84:445–448, 1988.
57. Muckleroy RN: Sex counseling after stroke. Med Aspects Hum Sex 11:115–116, 1977.
58. Newman G, Nichols CR: Sexual activities and attitudes in older persons. JAMA 173:33–35, 1960.
59. Niemi ML, Laakasonen R, Kotila M, Waltimo O: Quality of life 4 years after stroke. Stroke 19:1101–1107, 1988.
60. Pfeiffer E, Verwoerdt A, Wang HS: Sexual behavior in aged men and women: 1 observation on 254 community volunteers. Arch Gen Psychiatry 19:753–758, 1968.
61. Renshaw DC: Geriatric sex problems. J Geriatr Psychiatry 17:123–148, 1984.
62. Rykken DE: Sex in the later years. In Silverman P (ed): The Elderly as Modern Pioneers. Bloomington, IN, Indiana University Press, 1988, pp 158–182.
63. Sadoughi W, Leshner M, Fine HL: Sexual adjustment in chronically ill and physically disabled population: Pilot study. Arch Phys Med Rehabil 52:311–317, 1971.
64. Savard R, Walker E: Changes in social functioning after surgical treatment for temporal lobe epilepsy. Soc Work 10:87–95, 1965.
65. Sjogren K: Sexuality after stroke with hemiplegia. II. With special regard to partnership adjustment and to fulfillment. Scand J Rehabil Med 15:63–69, 1983.
66. Sjogren K: Leisure after stroke. Int Rehabil Med Suppl 7:140, 1980.
67. Sjogren K, Damber JE, Liliequist B: Sexuality after stroke with hemiplegia. I. Aspects of sexual function. Scand J Rehabil Med 15:55–61, 1983.
68. Sjogren K, Fugl-Meyer AR: Sexual problems in hemiplegia. Int Rehabil Med 3(11):28–31, 1981.
69. Sjogren K, Fugl-Meyer AR: Adjustment to life after stroke with special reference to sexual intercourse and leisure. J Psychosom Res 26:409–417, 1982.

70. Soderback I, Ekholm J, Caneman G: Impairment/function and disability/activity 3 years after cerebrovascular incident or brain trauma: A rehabilitation and occupational therapy view. Int Disabil Stud 13:67–73, 1991.
71. Starr BD, Weiner MB: The Starr-Weiner Report on Sex and Sexuality in the Mature Years. New York, McGraw-Hill, 1981.
72. Thienhaus OJ: Practical overview of sexual function and advancing age. Geriatrics 43(8):63–67, 1988.
73. Trudel L, Fabia J, Bouchard JP: Quality of life of 50 carotid endarterectomy survivors: A long term follow-up study. Arch Phys Med Rehabil 65:310–312, 1984.
74. Ueno M: The so-called coital death. Jpn J Legal Med 17:535, 1963.
75. Viitanen M, Fugl-Meyer KS, Bernspan B, Fugl-Meyer AR: Life satisfaction in long term survivors after stroke. Scand J Rehabil Med 20:17–24, 1988.
76. Wiig EH: Counseling the adult aphasic for sexual readjustment. Rehabil Counsel Bull 17(2):110–119, 1973.

NATHAN D. ZASLER, MD, FAAPM&R, FAADEP

TRAUMATIC BRAIN INJURY AND SEXUALITY

From National NeuroRehabilitation
  Consortium, Inc.
  and
Concussion Care Center
  of Virginia
Richmond, VA

Reprint requests to:
Nathan D. Zasler, MD
Executive Medical Director
National NeuroRehabilitation
  Consortium, Inc.
11653 Rutgers Drive, Suite 100
Richmond, VA 23233

Among civilians in the United States, accidental death is the fourth most frequent cause of death, exceeded only by coronary artery disease, cancer, and cerebral vascular disease. The primary cause of death to both males and females age 15–24 is accidental injury.[9] Civilian statistics on traumatic brain injury suggest that, at least conservatively, 2 million individuals per year incur TBI, and approximately a quarter of these require hospitalization[1] Most deaths associated with traumatic brain injury occur at the time of injury or within the first several hours thereafter. Among individuals who survive more severe neural insults to the brain, about 50,000–70,000 will be left with permanent neurologic impairments that significantly impede their ability to return to their earlier way of life. Epidemiologic analysis is complicated by the lack of consistency regarding how brain injury is defined, differences in screening methodologies for TBI, and differences in populations studied—facts that must be taken into consideration when reviewing the literature on this topic. In civilians, motor vehicle accidents account for about half of all TBI; falls are the second most common mechanism of injury, with an incidence of about 20%. Violence, including gunshot wounds and assaults, accounts for 12%; and recreational injuries, 10%.[12] Males typically are injured two to three times more frequently than females. Males age 15–24 have the highest rate of injury. The frequency distribution of TBI relative to age is trimodal, with young adults having the highest frequency. The other two peaks occur in infants and in the elderly.

Traumatic brain injury may adversely affect the expression of sexuality due to a variety of factors. Physical, cognitive-behavioral, and linguistic-pragmatic sequelae can have an adverse impact on the expression of sexuality. Brain injury may produce sexual dysfunction at the genital level and nongenital level.[45] Ultimately, the mediating factors in these functional alterations include disruption of neuroanatomic pathways and/or aberrations in neurophysiologic function as a result of the TBI. One must understand the basic neuroanatomic pathways and neurophysiologic mechanisms involved in the mediation of sexual function to better comprehend the effect of brain injury on sexuality. The knowledge base relative to sexual neuroanatomy is still far from an exacting science, even for normal sexual function. Multiple neural networks seem to be involved in sexual expression and function. These networks are felt to include structures in both the autonomic and somaticperipheral nervous system, the brain stem, subcortex, and cortex[19,40] (see chapter 2).

Appropriate neuromedical and rehabilitative intervention should be available to these patients to allow for maximal reintegration into preinjury sexual lifestyles at the personal, family, and community level. To provide a comprehensive approach to the problem and to minimize any resultant functional impairment, professionals must address the area of sexuality as they do other functional areas of human "performance," including mobility, activities of daily living, and bowel/bladder function.[43]

Professionals must be willing to discuss sexuality concerns rather than "sweep sexuality under the carpet." As rehabilitationists, we must address this issue to be truly holistic in our approach to patient-centered care. Experience has shown that appropriate early, yet graduated, intervention allows for a smoother transition and adjustment to potential postinjury sexuality issues.

SEXUAL FUNCTIONING IN TBI: A REVIEW OF THE LITERATURE

There is a dearth of clinical studies examining specific issues related to sexual dysfunction following traumatic brain injury. Some of the more methodologically sound studies examining sexuality issues from a holistic perspective have been performed in the last 5 years (Table 1).

Bond was one of the first researchers to examine issues of psychosocial changes arising from severe brain injury via interview assessments.[7] He found that no relationship exists between posttraumatic amnesia, level of physical disability, or the level of cognitive impairment and level of sexual activity. Specific sexual function patterns were not examined in this study.

Rosenbaum and Najenson interviewed wives of wartime neurotrauma patients with brain and spinal cord injuries.[38] The authors used a four-part questionnaire to explore areas of family life, interpersonal behavior, marital roles, and disturbance of mood. Thirty wives enrolled in the study, of whom 10 were married to men with TBI and six to men with paraplegia. The remaining 14 women were married to men who fought in the war but did not sustain any injuries. All groups studied were at least 1 year postinjury and/or postwar involvement. Reduced sexual function and emotional distress were present more often in the wives of men with brain injury relative to the wives of uninjured men. The greatest level of mood disturbance also occurred in wives of men with brain injury. No relationship was found between the site of injury and the reported sexual dysfunction. Among the wives of persons with TBI, being a "sexual partner to husband" was ranked as

TABLE 1.   Research on Sexual Function Following Traumatic Brain Injury

Authors and Year Published	Conclusions
Bond, 1976	No association between level of impairment and level of sexual activity
Rosenbaum and Najenson, 1976	TBI > SCI relative to reduction in sexual function and emotional distress in relatives
Oddy, Humphrey, and Uttley, 1978	50% decrease/50% increase in sexual intercourse
Oddy and Humphrey, 1980	Approximately 50% of spouses less affectionate toward injured partner
Lezak, 1978	High frequency of altered libido
Weddell, Oddy, and Jenkins, 1980	Behavioral changes were common, affecting expression of affection
Kosteljanetz, Jensen, and Norgard, 1981	53% reduced libido; 42% erectile dysfunction
Mauss-Clum and Ryan, 1981	47% altered libido; 42% of wives with no sexual outlet
Miller, Cummings, McIntyre, et al., 1986	Correlation between sexual behavior and neuropathology
Kreutzer and Zasler, 1989	Majority reported negative changes in sexual behavior
Garden, Bontke, Hoffman, 1990	Majority reported decline in frequency of intercourse
O'Carroll, Woodrow, and Maroun, 1991	Approximately 50% of male patients were dysfunctional
Sandel, Derogatis, Williams, 1993	Decreased orgasm and libido, frontal and right hemisphere lesions; reported better sex

significantly less important in actual life than in ideal or normal marital life. The role of "handling family matters outside the home" had, conversely, increased significantly in importance in their actual lives as compared to their perception of their normal role. Wives of survivors of TBI also noted tense relationships with their husband's parents; this was mainly due to overprotective tendencies on the part of the in-laws, which was theorized to be due to "slipping back to the old parent-child relationship."

In a secondary analysis by the same authors, a 22-item mood inventory was used to assess the relationship between mood disturbance and sexual functioning. Data analysis revealed that greater levels of mood disturbance were associated with decreased levels of sexual activity. Additionally, negative attitudes toward perceived sexual changes were associated with a lower mood level.

Oddy, Humphrey, and Uttley studied 50 adults with TBI who were at least 6 months postinjury and had a minimum of 24 hours of posttraumatic amnesia.[36] Half of the 12 married patients reported an increase in coital frequency, and half reported a decrease. None of the spouses reported any sexual problems persisting into the fifth and sixth months. Despite the fact that many patients had personality changes, there was no evidence that at this stage in the recovery process the patient's family or marital relationships were prone to increased friction.

In a subsequent study, Oddy and Humphrey investigated alterations in sexual behavior 1 year postinjury.[35] No significant change was found in sexual behavior. Only one patient noted any problems. Just under 50% of spouses reported that they were significantly less affectionate toward their injured spouses. At 2 years of follow-up, only one spouse and two patients reported their marital relationships to be less satisfactory than prior to the accident. Oddy et al. followed-up their original group of patients to 7 years postinjury; however, data regarding sexual activity were not included.[34]

Lezak reported that many patients with TB suffered from completely absent libido and some from increased sexual drive.[27] Alterations in sexual interest and other behavioral problems reportedly contributed to family and marital difficulties. Lezak theorized that spouses were sexually frustrated because many patients with brain injury no longer had full capacity for empathy and interpersonal sensitivity and thus could rarely satisfy their mate's needs for sexual pleasure or affection. Typical emotional changes in family members of patients characterologically altered by TBI, including but not limited to depression, anxiety, and obsessive ruminations, have an impact on marital and familial relations. Lezak also noted that many patients made incessant sexual demands regardless of whether they could be satisfied. The sexual performance of individuals with TBI was often a one-sided act carried out without regard for the partner. She also acknowledged several common family problems, including spousal feelings of entrapment and isolation, concerns of abandonment by the extended family on the part of the immediate family, relatives being critical of the immediate caretaker, and the potential for familial abuse, including the spouse and dependent children, by the patient.

Social adjustment 2 years after severe TBI was assessed by Weddell et al.,[41] who interviewed relatives of a group of patients having completed a rehabilitation program. Although no direct inquiries were made regarding sexuality issues, personality changes were examined. Irritability was listed as the most frequent behavioral alteration, followed by alterations in expression of affection. Other common behavioral sequelae included childishness, disinhibition, and increased talkativeness.

One of the best early studies on alterations in sexual function following brain injury was conducted by Kosteljanetz et al.[20] on a group of 19 postconcussional patients. A majority of patients (58%) reported posttraumatic sexual dysfunction; 53% reported reduced libido; and 42%, a lesser but still significant percentage, experienced erectile dysfunction. Eleven percent reported problems sexually in areas unrelated to their history of TBI. A positive correlation was noted between reports of sexual dysfunction and intellectual impairment. Increased plasma concentrations of follicle stimulating hormone (FSH) were observed in 37% of the patients, suggesting a reduced spermatogenesis. No major evidence could be obtained by laboratory testing or radiologic evaluation of major hypothalamic-pituitary dysfunction.[20]

A survey of wives and mothers of men with brain injury, not necessarily posttraumatic, by Mauss-Clum and Ryan found that a large proportion of the survivors were either disinterested in sex or preoccupied with it. A total of 42% of the wives reported that they had no sexual outlet.[32]

Kreutzer and Zasler administered the Psychosexual Assessment Questionnaire (PAQ) to 21 men who were sexually active following TBI.[23] The majority reported negative changes in sexual behavior, including decreased libido, erectile dysfunction, and decreased frequency of intercourse. Common personality changes included depression and reduced self-esteem and sex-appeal. There did not seem to be any relationship between the level of change in affect and alterations, negative or positive, in sexual behavior. Interestingly, despite these negative changes, there was evidence that the quality of the marital relationship was preserved.

Garden, Bontke, and Hoffman studied 11 men and four women at least 2 months following TBI. Both the spouses and the patients completed a sexual history and function questionnaire. Although a variety of factors were assessed, including libido; frequency of intercourse; time spent in foreplay; sexual attractiveness; erectile, ejaculatory, and orgasmic capabilities; and marital adjustment; only a few significant correlations were found. Frequency of intercourse decreased for 75% of the women and 55% of the men. Interestingly, although male genital sexual dysfunction was rarely reported, female spouses reported a significant decline in their ability to achieve orgasm after their partner was injured.[14]

O'Carroll, Woodrow, and Maroun examined the psychosexual and psychosocial sequelae of the TBI in a series of 36 patients followed for up to four years after injury.[33] Using several previously validated scales, including the Golombok Rust Inventory of Sexual Satisfaction (GRISS), General Health Questionnaire (GHQ), and Hospital Anxiety and Depression Scale (HAD), they assessed both patients and partners. Approximately half of the men scored within the dysfunctional range on the psychosexual profiles. The major psychosexual complaint was decreased frequency of sexual intimacy. A large percentage of patients demonstrated significant emotional distress, anxiety and/or depression (61%, 25%, and 22%, respectively). Of the partners evaluated, the percentages were 41%, 18%, and 6%, respectively. Findings did not seem to correlate with severity of neurologic insult; however, age and time following injury were related to degree of psychosexual dysfunction. The authors recommended focusing further research efforts on the efficacy of early counseling, education, behavioral sex therapy, and environmental manipulation in patients with TBI.

Hypersexuality (which may follow surgical intervention or be related to anticonvulsant medication) and homosexual behavior also have been reported following brain injury. Kluver-Bucy syndrome associated with anterior bitemporal injury and/or limbic system involvement has been reported as a posttraumatic sequela. The neurobehavioral correlates of KBS typically include hypersexuality, placidity, visual agnosia, hyperorality, and hypermetamorphosis, bulimia, and severe memory disturbance.[15] A small study by Miller et al. examined the incidence of hypersexuality and altered sexual preference following brain injury.[30] They found that in eight selected patients, four had hypersexuality and four had altered sexual preference following various brain insults. The investigators further speculated that medial basal-frontal or diencephalic injury was associated with hypersexual behavior and that limbic system injury was associated with altered sexual preference.

Neuroendocrine Dysfunction and Sexuality

Neuroendocrine dysfunction following TBI has received some attention in the scientific literature. Anterior hypopituitarism is not a common clinical entity in survivors of TBI; however, it can be seen on occasion, and clinicians should be familiar with its clinical correlates.[22] Hypothalamic injury more commonly induces clinical hypopituitarism than direct pituitary damage.[21] The exact effects of clinical and subclinical hypopituitarism on sexual function following TBI are yet to be clarified.

A study reported by Clark et al. in 1988 suggests that hypogonadotrophic hypogonadism may occur more frequently than previously suspected following brain injury. The vast majority of men in the study (88%) demonstrated acute hypotestosteronemia within 7–10 days following injury. More strikingly, 24% still had low testosterone levels and associated complaints of erectile dysfunction and hyposexuality 3–6 months postinjury.[10]

Lee and Zasler conducted a prospective study to evaluate pituitary-gonadal function and associated parameters in 21 men with severe TBI during acute inpatient rehabilitation.[24] Serum concentrations of testosterone, follicle-stimulating hormone (FSH), and luteinizing hormone (LH) were measured within 1 week after the patient was transferred to the rehabilitation unit. A total of 14 of 21 patients (67%) had abnormally low testosterone levels. One patient had a subnormal FSH level, and one had a supranormal level. Three patients had subnormal LH levels, and two had supranormal levels. There was no correlation between the severity of brain injury and the levels of testosterone, FSH or LH. Neither were there statistically significant correlations with an array of clinical parameters and neuroendocrine abnormalities that were examined. The investigators concluded that the high incidence of hypotestosteronemia in survivors of severe TBI was seemingly more related to accompanying physiologic stressors rather than structural or neurochemical disruption of the hypothalamic-pituitary-gonadal axis.

Even after relatively less severe neural insults, case reports occasionally document rare sequelae, such as acquired growth hormone deficiency due to pituitary damage, which may affect overall development, including sexual growth and secondary sexual characteristics.[42] Clinical conditions such as precocious puberty following TBI also have been reported.[29]

Temporolimbic Epilepsy and Psychosexual Behavior

Given the incidence of temporolimbic epilepsy (TLE) following TBI, it is important for clinicians to be familiar with this clinical entity and its potential neurobehavioral manifestations, including but not limited to issues of sexual dysfunction. There is general agreement that estrogens lower seizure threshold, a particularly relevant fact in dealing with women with posttraumatic TLE during menses and/or pregnancy. TLE is theorized to have its effects on the hypothalamic-pituitary-gonadal axis through alterations in central dopamine levels. The alterations (decrease) in central dopamine levels—being prolactin-inhibiting—associated with TLE may produce a secondary hyperprolactinemia.[17]

Although much has been written about TLE, the groups of patients that formed the bases of these studies were typically quite heterogeneous. Herzog found that 40–58% of men with TLE were impotent or hyposexual and that up to 40% of women had menstrual irregularities.[17] Another study by Herzog found that 28 of 50 women (56%) with TLE had menstrual problems. Polycystic ovarian syndrome was associated with predominantly left-sided lateralization of interictal epileptic discharges, and hypogonadism was more commonly found with right-sided discharges. Hyposexuality occurred more often in women with predominantly right-sided interictal discharges and was associated with low serum LH levels.[18]

Blumer reported that 70% of patients with TLE reported sexual problems.[2] The most chronic alteration in sexual behavior was hyposexuality (58%). In particular, the inability to experience orgasm was noted by respondents; 20 patients reported sexual responses less than once per year. The hyposexuality noted in Blumer's study was theorized to be clearly associated with the onset and course of the TLE. Anecdotal observations suggest that mesial temporal involvement may be correlated with libidnal alterations in TLE; however, no well-controlled studies have confirmed this finding.[3,5]

Summary of the Literature

It becomes readily apparent to even the novice clinician that the literature in the area of TBI and sexuality/sexual function is significantly sparse. Few studies focus specifically on sexual behavior and, in the few that do, the results have been somewhat disparate. At best, many of the commonly quoted studies are anecdotal reports that do not provide information to relate to patients and families or any empirical evidence on which to guide clinical decision making. Given the cornucopia of sequelae of TBI, including physical, emotional, cognitive, and behavioral changes, it is not surprising that alterations occur in sexuality as well as sexual function. As of now, we only have a general sense of the magnitude of this area of functional deficit, which is unfortunate given the importance of sexuality to most people.

PHYSIATRIC ASSESSMENT OF SEXUALITY ISSUES

Traumatic brain injury can result in sexual problems due to a number of factors, including nongenital and genital dysfunction. Genital dysfunction may result in erectile dysfunction, ejaculatory problems, orgasmic dysfunction, problems with vaginal lubrication, and vaginismus. Nongenital problems that may adversely affect sexual intimacy include sensorimotor deficits, linguistic-pragmatic deficits, perceptual deficits, limited joint range of motion, neurogenic bowel/bladder dysfunction, dysphagia with or without problems controlling secretions, motor dyspraxias, posttraumatic behavioral deficits, and alterations in self-image and self-esteem.[43]

Not much literature is available that might help neurorehabilitationists gain an appreciation for the clinical assessment of sexual function in an individual following a traumatic brain injury. Professionals working with this unique group of patients must have an appreciation for the appropriate neuromedical assessment and management of these functional deficits. One protocol that has been proposed is the GRASP (General Rehabilitation Assessment Sexuality Profile), which divides assessment into the sexual history, sexual physical examination, and clinical diagnostic testing[43] (Table 2).

TABLE 2. General Rehabilitation Assessment Sexuality Profile (GRASP) for Clinical Evaluation of Neurogenic Sexual Dysfunction

Sexual history	Interview patient and partner, if possible
	Assess preinjury medical status
	Assess preinjury sexual status
	Assess preinjury sexual status and performance
	Delineate sexuality concerns
	Provide privacy
	Take time in the interview
	Use appropriate vocabulary
	Clarify sexual preference
Sexual physical exam	Assess general mobility
	Assess ADLs
	Evaluate general hygiene
	Examine genitalia
	Perform neurologic assessment: rectal exam, sensory testing, lumbosacral reflex arc testing
Clinical sexual diagnostic testing	Urodynamics
	Male: penile biothesiometry, dorsal nerve SSEP, NPT, and ICP
	Female: photoplethysmography, thermal clearance, and heat electrode
	Neuroendocrine evaluation: FSH, LH, PRL with testosterone (male) and estradiol and dehydroepiandrosterone (female)

Sexual History

A good sexual history defines needs, expectations, and behavior. It also identifies problems, misconceptions, and areas for education, counseling, and reassurance in relation to sexuality issues. When applicable and possible, interviews should be conducted with both the patient and the partner. The assessment should include demographic and personal information. A past medical history is essential to clarify any and all medical disorders that could potentially affect sexual function. Premorbid sexual functioning, practices, and relationships should be explored. Partners of both sexes should be questioned about their specific genital function. Patients and couples should be questioned regarding their specific concerns in areas such as birth control, fertility, genital dysfunction, and alterations in libido. Sexuality issues may not be important for all patients, and this fact must be recognized by clinicians. Key points regarding interviewing include providing a private atmosphere, not rushing the interview, being frank yet empathetic, using nondirective techniques, and using vocabulary appropriate to the patient's educational and cultural background. One should avoid putting the patient in conflict with moral or ethical beliefs. Lastly, the status of an individual's sexual preference should never be assumed and should always be discussed. Ultimately, the interview can serve as a foundation for demonstrating to patients that they have a right to be a sexual being just like anyone else and that sexual expression resulting in intimacy, not necessarily vaginal intercourse, is the goal of the process.[45]

The Sexual Physical Examination

The sexual physical exam really begins when the clinician first sees the patient. Mobility deficits may give clues as to physical limitations that may adversely affect sexuality and sexual function. The flexibility of the hips and degree of adductor spasticity are of particular importance. During the examination, the clinician should note the patient's general hygiene status and use of adaptive equipment. The genitals should be examined from both a neurologic and nonneurologic standpoint. In women, the genitalia should be inspected first, followed by a bimanual examination. If the primary physician does not feel comfortable performing a bimanual exam, a referral should be made to a qualified physician. The vaginal walls should be evaluated for tone and mucosal alterations. In men, the penis should be palpated for the presence of plaques as found in Peyronie's disease. Testicular presence in the scrotal sacs should be assessed, as should size and consistency. In both men and women, the clinician should check distribution of hair in the genital region and in locations of secondary sexual hair growth to rule out possible primary or secondary endocrinopathies. The neurologic assessment of the genitalia should include a rectal exam, sensory testing, and assessment of lumbosacral reflex integrity. The skilled clinician can use the information from bedside testing to guide recommendations and to prognosticate genital sexual function relative to the neurologic insult in question.[43]

Clinical Sexual Diagnostic Testing

Urodynamics may be of value in obtaining a better understanding of the integrity of the innervation of genital sexual organs. Afferent neurologic assessment can be accomplished with penile biothesiometry and/or dorsal nerve somatosensory evoked potentials (DNSSEP). Penile biothesiometry, which measures the vibration perception threshold of the skin of the penis, is performed with a portable hand-held electromagnetic vibration device that has a fixed frequency and variable amplitude. DNSSEP provides an objective physiologic assessment of the entire pudendal nerve afferent pathway. Efferent neurological assessment, whether motor or autonomic, can be accomplished in a gross manner via nocturnal penile tumescence (NPT) and/or response to intracavernosal pharmacotherapy (ICP).[37]

The clinical sexual assessment in women is less sophisticated. Evaluation has been conducted with a variety of techniques, including but not limited to photoplethysmography, thermal clearance, and heat electrode techniques, which have been used to assess vaginal hemodynamics via indirect evaluation of blood flow parameters in the vaginal wall.[26] The above techniques can be used to treat orgasmic and arousal deficits via biofeedback training.[26,43]

The initial laboratory evaluation should include assessment of FSH, LH, prolactin, and free testosterone in males. Given the pulsatile cycle of the release of these hormones, it has been suggested that three samples be obtained approximately 20 minutes apart and then be combined for a single measurement. In women, the same hormones and estradiol and dehydroepiandrosterone should be assessed. Due to normal menstrual variations, the best time for testing is the early follicular phase. An awareness of appropriate neuroendocrine tests relative to specific clinical presentations is paramount for any practitioner working with these patients. Clinicians should keep in mind that other factors may contribute to neuroendocrine abnormalities, the most common in patients with TBI being medications and, in the acute setting, physiologic stress factors.[19,43]

CLINICAL MANAGEMENT

Clinicians managing sexual dysfunction must consider the many issues that may directly or indirectly contribute to alterations in sexual function following TBI, including neuroendocrine and nongenital and genital dysfunction. Clinicians should be aware of how subjective complaints may provide clues to guiding treatment. Additionally, adequate knowledge regarding the potential benefits and side effects of pharmacologic agents in TBI patients is critical in optimizing outcome. There are also multiple issues related to sexuality following TBI that require management through counseling, including matters of birth control, sex education, competency to engage in sexual activity, sexual abuse, and sexual "release."

Genital Dysfunction

Genital sexual dysfunction after TBI may take a number of potential forms. Men may have erectile, ejaculatory, and/or orgasmic dysfunction. The present state of the art in neurologic management of erectile dysfunction focuses on one of three main treatment categories: penile prostheses, intracavernosal pharmacotherapy, and external management. Enteral agents have been used, including noradrenergic agonists such as yohimbine (5.4–6.0 mg PO, TID),[31] as have drug classes such as dopamine agonists. Work is ongoing relative to the efficacy of enteral agents in patients with TBI. Problems with premature ejaculation should be addressed behaviorally first to assess how much of the problem is functionally based. Methods such as the "squeeze" technique, which involves application of pressure to the penile shaft just proximal to the glans penis when the man feels that he is about to ejaculate, can be taught to prolong the plateau phase of the sexual cycle. On occasion, medication might be considered for men experiencing premature ejaculation; this might include topical anesthetics to the penile shaft (5–10% lidocaine) or anticholinergic (imipramine 100–200 mg/day) and sympatholytic medication (phenoxybenzamine 10 mg BID–TID) administered orally. Orgasmic dysfunction is generally approached from a behavioral standpoint in both men and women.

Women may complain of alterations in vaginal lubrication and/or orgasmic dysfunction. Inadequate vaginal lubrication can generally be addressed with artificial lubrication with water-soluble products. Behavioral therapy including imagery and body exploration/sensitization training may benefit some women who have arousal or orgasmic dysfunction.

Neuroendocrine dysfunction may occur following TBI; however, the general clinical experience has been that this phenomena is relatively rare in TBI patients. In postpubertal girls, cyclic administration of oral estrogen-progesterone preparations will restore the menstrual cycle, maintain secondary sexual characteristics, and reduce the risk for osteoporosis. In postpubertal boys, hypogonadism may be treated with intramusuclar testosterone (200–400 mg) replacement typically given every 2–4 weeks. In cases of delayed puberty, treatment should begin during adolescence. Boys are typically treated with human chorionic gonadotropin (HCG) (500–1,000 USP units 3×/week for the first 3 weeks, followed by 500 USP units 2× week for 1–2 years); this is followed by maintenance therapy with testosterone.[8] In girls, cyclic estrogen and progesterone therapy is instituted to establish menses and secondary sexual characteristics.[43] Relevant neuroendocrine issues are summarized in Table 3.

Physicians should know how certain medications may produce iatrogenic sexual dysfunction. Antipsychotic medications, antihypertensives, and anticholinergic medications are some of the more common "culprits." Other drugs, including H2-blockers, may produce adverse effects through their antiandrogenic

TABLE 3. Posttraumatic Neuroendocrine Dysfunction: Clinical Presentation and Laboratory Evaluation

Clinical Syndrome	Clinical Presentation (Possible Symptoms)	Neuroendocrine Evaluation
Male postpubertal sexual dysfunction	Decreased libido Impotence Ejaculatory dysfunction Infertility	FSH, LH, PRL, free testosterone R/O associated medical conditions
Female postpubertal sexual dysfunction	Oligomenorrhea Amenorrhea Virilization Galactorrhea Decreased libido Recurrent spontaneous abortions	FSH, LH, PRL, estradiol, and DHEA R/O associated medical conditions
Male prepubertal sexual dysfunction	Delay in secondary sexual characteristics Precocious puberty	FSH, LH, PRL, free testosterone
Female prepubertal sexual dysfunction	Delay in secondary sexual characteristics Precocious puberty	FSH, LH, PRL, estradiol, and DHEA
Sexual dysfunction associated with TLE	Male: impotence, decreased libido, and endocrine disturbances Female: menstrual irregularities, endocrine disturbances, and polycystic ovarian syndrome	Same as above Same as above R/O drug side effect

TABLE 4.   Sexual Pharmacology: Drug Class and Clinical Effect

Drug Class	Clinical Effect
Anorexiants Amphetamines	(–) decreased libido, impotence, ejaculatory dysfunction, anorgasmia
Anticholinergics Oxybutynin Scopolamine	(–) inhibited erection and ejaculation, decreased libido
Anticonvulsants Carbamazepine and phenytoin	(–) impotence and decreased libido
Antidepressants Nortriptyline Doxepin	(–) decreased libido, delayed orgasm in women, ejaculatory and erectile dysfunction
Antihypertensives Beta-blockers, methyldopa, and clonidine	(–) impotence, decreased libido, and ejaculatory dysfunction
Antiparkinsonian Levodopa, bromocriptine and amantadine	(+) generally increase libido, may also improve erectile function
Antipsychotics Haloperidol, droperidol, thioridazine, thiothexene	(–) impotence, decreased libido, ejaculatory dysfunction, priapism
Antispasticity Baclofen, Valium	(–) impotence, ejaculatory dysfunction, and menstrual irregularities
Diuretics Thiazides	(–) decreased libido and impotence
Estrogens	(–) decreased libido
H₂-antihistamines Ranitidine	( ) decreased libido, erectile dysfunction
Nonsteroidal antiinflammatory Naproxen	(–) erectile problems and anejaculation
Noradrenergic agonists Yohimbine, activating TCSs	(+) increased libido in both sexes
Phenoxybenzamine	(–) ejaculatory dysfunction
Progestins Medroxyprogesterone/ cyproterone	(–) decreased libido, impotence
Serotonergic agonists Trazodone, sertraline, paroxetine	(–)/(+) in general, decreased libido; however, reports of increased libido in females has occurred

effect and increased central prolactin. Anticonvulsant medication such as phenytoin may decrease circulating levels of sex hormone via induction of hepatic enzyme systems, resulting in a relative secondary hypogonadism. Assessment of medications and appropriate substitutions to optimize sexual functioning is a critical part of the physician's role in the management of sexuality issues in patients with TBI (Table 4).

Nongenital Dysfunction

Other areas of nongenital neurologic impairment must be assessed relative to treatment options, whether pharmacologic, surgical, or compensatory. Sensorimotor deficits, cognitive-behavioral deficits, language-based alterations, changes in libido, and neurogenic bowel and bladder dysfunction can be addressed by the clinician as they impact upon the ability for sexual expression.[43] Libidinal changes can be managed behaviorally and pharmacologically. Hormonal treatment and/or serotonergic agents can be used for hypersexuality.[16,28]

Medroxyprogesterone acetate has been used in varying doses to suppress both aggressive behavior and sexual arousal: 100–200 mg/week, typically preceded by a loading dose of 400 mg/week over the first 2–3 weeks.[4,25] Clinically, serotonergic agents such as trazodone hydrochloride have shown some benefit for suppression of libido in doses typically ranging 3.0–5.0 mg/kg of body weight. Other newer agents, including selective serotonergic reuptake inhibitors (SSRIs) such as paroxetine and sertraline, may also work in this application. Noradrenergic agonists and/or hormonal supplementation have been used for hyposexuality, particularly in males.[43]

Clinicians should be aware that patients with temporolimbic epilepsy may present with alterations in neuroendocrine status and sexual function. The presence of characteristic "temporal lobe personality" traits such as circumstantiality, viscosity, and obsessionalism in combination with altered sexuality, even in the absence of "clinical" seizures and/or electrographic seizures, suggests consideration for treatment with a psychoactive anticonvulsant such as carbamazepine or valproate.[16] Patients with Kluver-Bucy syndrome have also shown hypersexual behaviors as part of this symptom complex that respond favorably to psychotropic anticonvulsants such as carbamazepine.[39]

Counseling Issues

There are numerous controversial issues pertaining to sexuality in TBI patients that have an impact on medical, ethical and legal fronts. Among these issues are matters pertaining to sex education, including birth control, sexually transmitted disease, sexual abuse, and methods for obtaining sexual gratification (sexual release) including but not limited to masturbation. Other questions that may arise include decisions regarding sterilization and more germane and socially "acceptable" issues such as dating, marriage, sexual preference, child-rearing, and psychosocial behavior.

Quite frequently, patients assume that they will be unable to find a compatible sexual companion because they have had a brain injury. Various recommendations can be provided to maximize community reintegration, including attending church/synagogue functions, meetings of head injury survivors, local organization social gatherings; or participating in dating services for persons with disabilities such as Handicapped Introductions and DateAble.[13] Prior to attempting mroe aggressive community reentry efforts, professionals can assist clients by teaching or "reteaching" the psychosocial graces that may many times be adversely affected by significant TBI. Responsible decisions regarding sexual relations are critical for both single and married patients with brain injury, and ongoing follow-up is essential to ensure compliance with the recommendations and satisfaction with sex life.

Generally, patients who are competent and have the capacity to understand and remember the ramifications of their actions are probably capable of being sexually active in a responsible fashion. Given the ever-present fear of AIDS, sexually active men and women should be instructed in the appropriate use of condoms. Ethical issues arise when dealing with patients demonstrating poor "sexual judgment" or uncontrollable sexual behaviors, including indiscriminant masturbation or hypersexuality. The professional may need to consider the need for and advise chemical or surgical sterilization. Given the variability in state laws regarding competency/capacity issues and decisions regarding sterilization, the professional consult legal counsel regarding each case.

Families and patients should be counseled regarding alternatives for sexual release, particularly in patients without active sexual partners. Masturbation should be discussed as a potential option so long as it is done in an appropriate social context. For clients requiring external stimulation to aid in successful masturbation, sexual stimuli can be provided with erotic reading materials, pictures, videotapes, and telephone sex services. Even though many of these suggestions may not be acceptable to some patients due to their moral and/or religious beliefs, they should be discussed with all patients and families, as appropriate.

Some health care professionals and family members have advocated, as well as condoned, the use of sexual surrogates and prostitutes to address the sexual frustrations of patients with TBI who might otherwise never find sexual partners.[44] Although there are differences between surrogates and prostitutes, many state laws do not make a legal distinction. In an era of high awareness regarding sexually transmitted diseases and legal liability, most professionals seem to be more conservative in using these approaches.

It is not uncommon for patients who were heterosexual prior to injury to turn to or at least experiment with homosexual lifestyles after injury because it may become the only way to demonstrate their sexual feelings and "vent" sexual needs. Professionals should counsel patients and family members regarding dealing with alterations in sexual preference. These changes in preference are more commonly a result of lack of heterosexual partners (for heterosexual patients) than a result of organically based alterations in sexual preference due to the TBI itself. Appropriate counseling for heterosexuals and homosexuals should be available. Clinician-counselors should always ask about the patient's sexual preference. All patients, regardless of sexual preference, should be counseled on high-risk sexual practices.

Sexual abuse is an issue that occurs on occasion in patients with TBI. Although abuse is poorly documented due to a general trend toward not studying things that make us feel uncomfortable, clinicians must recognize abuse when they see it. Health care professionals are legally and morally obligated to ensure that the proper authorities are notified if a person with TBI, a family member, an attendant, or an acquaintance is engaged in sexual misconduct and/or abuse. If sexual abuse is suspected, proper measures should be taken to remove the patient from the environment in question or remove the suspected perpetrator from the patient's immediate milieu.[44]

SUMMARY

Professionals are just beginning to explore and understand the neurologic and functional ramifications of traumatic brain injury on sexual function. Presently, there is a relative dearth of information on how to base decisions regarding prognostication, assessment, or treatment; however, the knowledge base is expanding slowly. Better acknowledgment of the importance of sexuality and sexual function to quality of life may stimulate researchers and clinicians to allocate more resources to investigate many of the unresolved issues. In the interim, clinicians and researchers should remain cognizant of the importance of sexual expression relative to other areas of human function following TBI.

REFERENCES

1. Annegers JF, Grabow MD, Kurland LT, Laws ER: The incidence, causes, and secular trends of head trauma in Olmsted county, Minnesota: 1935–1974. Neurology 30:912–919, 1980.
2. Blumer D: Changes of sexual behavior related to temporal lobe disorders in man. J Sex Res 6:173–180, 1970.
3. Blumer D: Hypersexual episodes in temporal lobe epilepsy. Am J Psychiatry 126:1099–1106, 1970.
4. Blumer D, Migeon C: Hormone and hormonal agents in the treatment of aggression. J Nerv Ment Dis 160:127–137, 1975.
5. Blumer D, Walker AE: Sexual behavior in temporal lobe epilepsy. Arch Neurol 16:31–43, 1967.
6. Boller F, Frank E: Sexual dysfunction in neurological disorders: Diagnosis, Management and Rehabilitation. New York, Raven, 1982, pp 9–23.
7. Bond MR: Assessment of psychosocial outcome of severe head injury. Acta Neurochir 34:57–70, 1976.
8. Buvat J, Lemaire A, Buvat-Herbaut M: Human chorionic gonadotropin treatment of non-organic erectile failure and lack of sexual desire: A double-blind study. Urology 6:216–219, 1987.
9. Chicago National Safety Council Statistics Department: Accident Facts. Chicago, Chicago National Safety Council, 1989.
10. Clark J, Raggatt P, Edwards O: Hypothalamic hypogonadism following major head injury. Clin Endocrinol 29:153–165, 1988.
11. Cohen H, Rosen R, Goldstein L: Electroencephalographic laterality changes during human sexual orgasm. Arch Sex Behav 5:189–199, 1976.
12. Frankowski RF, Annegers JF, Whitman S. The descriptive epidemiology of head injury in the United States. In Becker DP, Povlishock JT (eds): Central Nervous System Status Report. Bethesda, MD, National Institute of Neurological and Communicative Disorders and Stroke, 1985, pp 33–44.
13. Garden FH: Dating services for the disabled. Sexuality Update Newsletter (American Congress of Rehabilitation Medicine) 1(1):4, 1988.
14. Garden FH, Bontke CF, Hoffman M: Sexual functioning and marital adjustment after traumatic brain injury. J Head Trauma Rehabil 5(2):52–59, 1990.
15. Gerstenbrand F, Poewe W, Aichner F, Saltuari L: Kluver-Bucy syndrome in man: Experiences with posttraumatic cases. Neurosci Behav Rev 7:413–417, 1983.
16. Gualtieri CT: Neuropsychiatry and Behavioral Pharmacology. New York, Springer-Verlag, 1991.
17. Herzog A: Endocrinological aspects of epilepsy. In Neurology and Neurosurgery Update Series. Princeton, NJ, Continuing Professional Education Center. 5(11), 1984.
18. Herzog AG, Seibel MM, Schomer DL, et al: Reproductive endocrine disorders in women with partial seizures of temporal lobe origin. Arch Neurol 43:341–346, 1986.
19. Horn LJ, Zasler ND: Neuroanatomy and neurophysiology of sexual function. J Head Trauma Rehabil 5(2):1–13, 1990.
20. Kosteljanetz M, Jensen TS, Norgard B, et al: Sexual and hypothalamic dysfunction in post-concussional syndrome. Acta Neurol Scand 63:169–180, 1981.
21. King LR, Knowles HC, McLaurin RL, et al: Pituitary hormone response to head injury. Neurosurgery 9:229–235, 1981.
22. Klingbeil GEG, Kleine P: Anterior hypopituitarism: A consequence of head injury. Arch Phys Med Rehabil 66:44–46, 1985.
23. Kreutzer JS, Zasler ND: Psychosexual consequences of traumatic brain injury: Methodology and preliminary findings. Brain Injury 3:177–186, 1989.
24. Lee SC, Zasler ND, Kreutzer JS: Male pituitary dysfunction following severe traumatic brain injury. Brain Injury 8:571–577, 1994.
25. Lehne GK: Brain damage and paraphilia: Treatment with medroxyprogesterone acetate. Sex Disabil 7:145–157, 1986.
26. Levin RJ: The physiology of sexual function in women. Clin Obstet Gynecol 7:213–252, 1980.
27. Lezak ML: Living with the characterologically altered brain injured patient. J Clin Psychiatry 39:592–598, 1978.
28. McConaghy N, Balszczynski A, Kidson W: Treatment of sex offenders with imaginal desensitization and/or medroxyprogesterone. Acta Psychiatr Scand 77:199–206, 1988.
29. Maxwell M, Costas DK, Ellenbogen RG, et al: Precocious puberty following head injury. Case report. J Neurosurg 73:123–129, 1990.
30. Miller BL, Cummings JL, McIntyre H, et al: Hypersexuality or altered sexual preference following brain injury. J Neurol Neurosurg Psychiatry 9:867–873, 1986.
31. Morales A, Surridge DHC, Marshall PG, Fenemore J: Non-hormonal pharmacological treatment of organic impotence. J Urol 128:45, 1982.

32. Mauss-Clum N, Ryan M: Brain injury and the family. J Neurosurg Nurs 13:165–169, 1981.
33. O'Carroll RE, Woodrow J, Maroun F: Psychosexual and psychosocial sequelae of closed head injury. Brain Injury 5:303 313, 1991.
34. Oddy M, Coughlan T, Tyerman A, Jenkins D: Social adjustment after closed head injury: A further follow-up seven years later. J Neurol Neurosurg Psychiatry 48:564–568, 1985.
35. Oddy M, Humphrey M: Social recovery during the first year following severe head injury. J Neurol Neurosurg Psychiatry 43:798–802, 1980.
36. Oddy M, Humphrey M, Uttley D: Subjective impairment and social recovery after closed head injury. J Neurol Neurosurg Psychiatry 41:611–616, 1978.
37. Padma-Nathan H: Neurologic evaluation of erectile dysfunction. Urol Clin N Am 15:77–80, 1988.
38. Rosenbaum M, Najenson T: Changes in life patterns and symptoms of low mood as reported by wives of severely brain-injured soldiers. J Consult Clin Psychol 44:881–888, 1976.
39. Stewart JT: Carbamazepine treatment of a patient with Kluver-Bucy Syndrome. J Clin Psychiatry 46:496–497, 1985.
40. Walker AE: The neurological basis of sex. Neurol India 24:1–13, 1976.
41. Weddell R, Oddy M, Jenkins D: Social adjustment after rehabilitation: A two year follow-up of patients with severe head injury. Psycholog Med 10:257–263, 1980.
42. Yamanaka C, Momoi T, Fufisawa I, et al: Acquired growth hormone deficiency due to pituitary stalk transection after head trauma in childhood. Eur J Pediatr 152:99–101, 1993.
43. Zasler ND, Horn LJ: Rehabilitative management of sexual dysfunction. J Head Trauma Rehabil 5:14–24, 1990.
44. Zasler ND, Kreutzer JS: Family and sexuality after traumatic brain injury. In Williams J, Kay T (eds): Impact of Head Injury on the Family System: An Overview for Professionals. Baltimore, Paul Brookes, 1990, pp 253–370.
45. Zasler ND: Sexuality in neurologic disability: An overview. Sex Disabil 9:11–27, 1991.

ERICK A. GRANA, MD

SEXUALITY ISSUES IN MULTIPLE SCLEROSIS

From the Physical Medicine and
  Rehabilitation Service
Houston VA Medical Center
  and
Department of Physical Medicine
  and Rehabilitation
Baylor College of Medicine
Houston, Texas

Reprint requests to:
Erick A. Grana, MD
Physical Medicine and
  Rehabilitation Service (117)
Houston VA Medical Center
2002 I lolcombe Blvd.
Houston, TX 77030

Multiple sclerosis (MS) is a progressive disease whose prevalence varies widely throughout the world. All of the areas with the highest incidence are located in the higher latitudes in both the northern and southern hemispheres, although studies in the southern hemisphere are scarce. There are an estimated 250,000–350,000 cases of physician-diagnosed MS in the United States.[1] The disease is marked by loss of myelin and plaque formation in the white matter of the central nervous system (CNS). The clinical presentation is dependent on the location and extent of this demyelination. Because demyelinating plaques may develop anywhere within the CNS, the resultant disabilities may be diffuse and intermittent until permanent nerve damage has occurred. As any chronic illness, MS can have a tremendous impact on sexuality. Affected patients have several characteristics that make them especially prone to developing sexual dysfunction. Most diagnoses are made in patients aged 20–40,[7] when most patients are still in their reproductive years. Since MS is a disease with multiple clinical presentations and an unpredictable course, it may affect the sexual life of a patient in several different ways. The pathologic lesion may disrupt the transmission of neural impulses from the CNS to the genitalia. Decreased sensibility or paresthesia may interfere with the perception of pleasurable sensations and also diminish the capacity to achieve a sexual response through direct stimulation. Lesions in the brain may affect the mechanisms regulating libido. Sexual functioning also may be affected indirectly by the presence of symptoms such as weakness, fatigue, spasticity, incoordination, bowel and bladder incontinence, and decreased vision. Sex life may also be influenced by psychological changes such as anxiety, depression, changes in body image, and self-respect. In addition, the partner of an individual coping with a chronic disease such as MS also can experience changes in sexual ability and interest.

SCOPE AND NATURE OF THE PROBLEM

The few studies that have been carried out regarding this subject have all reported a high incidence of sexual dysfunction in both sexes and at all stages of MS[11,16-20,29,32,33] (Table 1). In a survey of 249 MS patients, Lilius et al.[16] found that sex life in general had changed for 91% of the men and 72% of the women. More than half (52%) of all the patients reported that their sex life was either unsatisfactory or had ceased entirely. Valleroy and Kraft[32] reported sexual dysfunction in 56% of their female patients and 75% of their male patients. Interestingly, only 4% of the 217 patients studied reported sexual dysfunction as their major disability. No correlation has been found between the incidence of sexual dysfunction and duration or severity of disease, suggesting that plaque location and/or psychological changes are the main factor determining whether sexual dysfunction occurs in a given individual. Even among early and mild cases of MS, rather pronounced sexual problems are fairly common.[18,33]

The clinical course of multiple sclerosis can vary tremendously. This variability in presentation makes prediction of sexual status very difficult. Sexual functioning in patients with MS can be affected by many factors. Demyelinating plaques can directly alter the normal physiology of the sexual response. Other generalized symptoms such as weakness, fatigue, spasticity, or loss of sensation can also influence sexual functioning. Bowel and bladder incontinence can become a major barrier. Cognitive and psychological problems also may have significant deleterious effects upon sexual activity. The reported prevalences for different sexual problems in MS patients are listed in Table 2. Decreased ability to maintain an erection is by far the most common problem in men. Fatigue, loss of sensation, and decreased orgasm seem to be the most common problems in women.

Genital Dysfunction

Sexual problems associated with MS may be due to upper motor neuron lesions in the brain stem or above the lumbar region of the spinal cord (blocking psychogenic erection) or to lower motor neuron lesions interfering with reflex erection in men. Lilius et al.[16] found that the frequency of sexual disturbances in

TABLE 1.   Studies of Sexual Dysfunction in Patients with Multiple Sclerosis

Authors	Year	Patients
Ivers and Goldstein[15]	1963	91 women, 53 men
Miller et al.[25]	1965	91 men
Vas[43]	1969	37 men
Lilius et al.[21]	1976	134 women, 115 men
Smith[37]	1976	?
Lundberg[23]	1981	25 women
Minderhoud et al.[26]	1984	39 women, 35 men
Szasz et al.[39]	1984	47 women, 26 men
Valleroy and Kraft[42]	1984	149 women, 68 men
Kirkeby et al.[18]	1988	29 men

TABLE 2.   Prevalence of Sexual Problems in Patients with Multiple Sclerosis

Problem	Incidence	References
Difficulty with erection	26–80%	15, 18, 21, 23, 25, 26, 37, 39, 42, 43
Difficulty with ejaculation	37–77%	18, 21, 26, 42
Fatigue	51–68%	42
Decreased sensation	48–55%	42
Decreased orgasm	33–48%	21, 23, 26, 42
Decreased libido	27–48%	21, 23, 42
Decreased vaginal lubrication	5–21%	21, 26
Dyspareunia	8–12%	23, 26

their study corresponded to the occurrence of pyramidal tract symptoms and bladder disturbances. They concluded that the occurrence of sexual disturbances depends on the location of plaques in the central nervous system.

MALE SEXUAL DYSFUNCTION

The most common sexual problem in men with MS is erectile dysfunction. Estimates of the incidence of erectile dysfunction in these patients range from 26% to 80%.[11,16,19,20,28,32,33] Erectile dysfunction in MS may be caused by lesions involving the thoracic spine and autonomic fibers or by psychogenic factors. In most of the studies, the erectile problems were identified by means of questionnaires, thus making it difficult to differentiate between neurogenic and psychogenic causes. There is, however, some evidence that sexual dysfunction is caused by neurogenic lesions. Vas[33] found evidence of autonomic disturbances in the form of abnormal patterns of sweating in impotent MS patients. He suggested that impotence was caused by lesions of the thoracic or lumbar segments of the spinal cord. Kirkeby et al.[14] performed electrophysiologic tests of nerve function measuring pudendal evoked potentials and bulbocavernous reflexes in 29 MS patients with complaints of erectile dysfunction. They found that subjective erectile problems were accompanied by abnormal nerve function in 90% of the patients. They also found a poor correlation between disability scores (a measure of disease severity) and reduced sexual function. Goldstein et al.[9] also found abnormal sacral evoked potentials among patients with sexual disturbances and functional disturbances of the bladder, indicating the presence of damage in the lumbosacral area of the spinal cord.

Other sexual problems reported by male MS patients include problems with ejaculation, decreased sensation, and decreased libido.[16,20,32] In general, decreases in other sexual activities such as masturbation and nocturnal erections paralleled the decreases in frequency of, and satisfaction derived from, intercourse.[20]

FEMALE SEXUAL DYSFUNCTION

One of the most common sexual complaints of female MS patients is a reduction in the ability to obtain orgasm. Lilius et al.[16] reported that 33% of their patients had this problem, while Minderhoud et al.[20] found an incidence of 48%. Other sexual difficulties experienced by female MS patients include decreased sensation, decreased libido, and difficulties with vaginal lubrication.[16,18,20,32] Sensory abnormalities in the genital region may produce anesthesia, dysesthesia (sometimes painful), and paresthesias. Inadequate vaginal lubrication also may result in painful intercourse. A decrease in libido may be associated with the genital sensory dysfunction, but in some cases it develops at different times.

Lunberg[18] noted correlation between sexual dysfunction and genital sensory symptoms as well as loss of sacral cord reflexes. He concluded that sexual disturbances in female patients with MS were related to anatomic lesions of the central nervous system.

Other Physiologic Dysfunctions

Motor Deficits. Weakness, fatigue, ataxia, and spasticity are common complaints of MS patients that can preclude "normal" sexual function. Decreased mobility by itself has not been found to correlate with sexual dysfunction.[16,32] Fatigue and motor weakness do not appear significantly more often among individuals with perceived sexual dysfunction. Spasticity, on the other hand, is strongly associated with sexual dysfunction.[16,32] Adductor spasticity is a fairly common problem with significant sexual functional implications, interfering with positioning.

Sensory Deficits. Normal sexual function requires intact sensation in the genital region. Decreased sensibility may interfere with the perception of pleasurable sensations, and it would be expected to result in a loss of libido and interest in sexual activity. Decreased sensation was reported to be one of the most common sexual problems in the survey done by Valleroy and Kraft.[32] In this study, the incidence of libido correlated with decreased sensibility. External dysesthesia might make direct genital contact unbearable. But, fortunately, this symptom, when reported, seemed to be transitory. Vaginal dyspareunia also has been reported in these patients.[17]

Bowel and Bladder Incontinence. Bowel and bladder disturbances may be problematic. The inconvenience of dealing with an indwelling catheter or the possibility of embarrassment due to incontinence may preclude sexual activity. Several authors have found a significant correlation between bladder symptoms and sexual dysfunction.[9,16,19,20,32] This is not surprising considering that the lateral columns of the spinal cord, a frequent site of involvement in MS, carry the neurologic pathways of both of these functions. Still, the chance of sexual dysfunction among patients without bladder symptoms is nearly 50%.[12]

Cognitive Deficits. Lesions in the brain may interfere with the mechanisms regulating sexual libido. Deficits of higher level neuropsychological function will also produce significant obstacles in normal social interactions. This may have a significant impact in sexual functioning, particularly when stable relationships have not been previously established.

Effect of Drugs. Many pharmacologic agents are associated with alteration of sexual function. Chronic alcohol abuse, beta blockers, diuretics, antidepressants, vasodilators, hypnotics, antihistamines, and tranquilizers are all associated with impotence.[5] Tranquilizing drugs may have a depressant effect on the sympathetic nervous system, resulting in problems with ejaculation. Phenoxybenzamine, sometimes used in the management of bladder dysfunction, may produce retrograde ejaculation. Some antispasmodic medications may cause a reduction in sex drive.

Psychosocial Dysfunctions

For patients with MS, there may be marked changes in feelings about the body and the self due to changes in physical appearance, abilities, and social interactions. In a recent study, about half of the MS patients showed dissatisfaction with their body image or with self-image.[26] That dissatisfaction correlated with their degree of disability and duration of disease. Disruptions in body image, with low self-esteem, may compound any neurophysiologic changes. It seems that physically disabled patients who are engaged in activities that increase their self-esteem, such as sex, have fewer medical complaints and feel less need for medical or social support.[2] MS patients may also show marked depression and anger. They may be hesitant or unwilling to undertake sexual activity, experiencing anxiety about ability to perform and fear of failure.

The relationship between the patient and the partner greatly affects sexual health. A decrease in sexual performance can become an early symptom of stress within the relationship.[13] Kalb et al.[12] decribed three aspects of the relationship that may be disrupted:

1. Level of Intimacy. The couple who was previously close is now unable to share the disease and thus experience feelings of alienation and abandonment that may intrude on sexual intimacy.
2. Gender Roles. With role changes (e.g., breadwinner or homemaker), the partner may view the patient as less masculine or feminine and, therefore, less attractive.
3. Caretaking Activities. The partner and caretaker may harbor feelings of anger or guilt that can interfere with sexual activity. On the other hand, the patient may be anxious or angry about becoming increasingly dependent.

The couple should be reassured of the normality of these feelings and assisted with coming to terms with the changes imposed on their relationship. The need for more intensive therapy must be identified so that adequate referrals can be made in a timely manner.

PATIENT ASSESSMENT

Physicians working with MS patients should expect sexual dysfunction in a sizable proportion of these patients, even if they have mild symptoms. Since patients might want to discuss their sexual concerns but expect the health care provider to initiate the discussion, it is important to overcome whatever reticence or uneasiness one may have in discussing sexually related subjects. Patients should be asked specific questions relating to sexual dysfunction. Components of a sexual history should include the nature of the problem, concerns about the marriage or interpersonal relationship, and previous ways of sexual expression. A history and physical examination are essential in ruling out any concurrent entity that may be exacerbating the sexual dysfunction. Diabetes mellitus, in particular, must be ruled out. Specific note of all medications taken by the patient should be made since the number of drugs that may affect sexual activity is large. Laboratory studies that are of help in evaluating patients with sexual dysfunction include measurements of follicle-stimulating hormone (FSH) and luteinizing hormone (LH) as screening tests for evidence of adequate gonadal function and, also, prolactin levels to identify early pituitary tumors. Male MS patients with impotence will benefit from referral to a urologist to distinguish organic from psychogenic components. Psychologic evaluation must be conducted by a psychiatrist with experience treating sexual dysfunction, and it should include the patient's partner.

A five-point sexual functioning scale for MS patients was developed by Szasz et al.[29] (Table 3). This scale has the advantage that it can be used to grade patients in the process of routine collection of data for the Minimal Record of Disability in MS.[27] However, the scale does not indicate the nature of the sexual problems, and control data for this scale is needed.

TABLE 3.   Sexual Function Scale in Multiple Sclerosis

0	As sexually active as before and/or not experiencing sexual problems
1	Sexually less active than before and/or experiencing some sexual problems but not concerned (does not consider this an issue)
2	Sexually less active than before and/or experiencing some sexual problems and concerned (would like to regain former pattern of sexual activity)
3	Sexually inactive and concerned (still wishes to regain previous sexual pattern)
4	Sexually inactive and not concerned (given up).

Adapted from Szasz G, Paty D, Lawton-Speer S, Eisen K: A sexual functioning scale in multiple sclerosis. Acta Neurol Scand 70:37–43, 1984.

THERAPEUTIC INTERVENTIONS

Suggested interventions for some of the most common physical problems affecting sexual function in MS are presented in Table 4, which is adapted from Dewis and Thornton.[4]

Bladder problems may be treated by using adequate hygiene in order to avoid bladder infections. Emptying the bladder before intercourse removes the fear of loss of bladder control. It is also useful to decrease fluid intake for 2–3 hours prior to sexual activity. Repositioning of the catheter by taping it out of the way on the leg may be helpful. It may be necessary to clamp and disconnect the catheter prior to sexual intercourse. Pharmacologic agents that reduce bladder motility also may be of value.

Fatigue can be reduced by using techniques of energy conservation and by resting frequently during the day. By recognizing that fatigue can be a major obstacle, couples can often overcome this problem by experimenting with different

TABLE 4.   Therapeutic Interventions

Problem	Suggested Intervention
Bladder	Using adequate hygiene to avoid infections
	Preparing for sexual activity by emptying bladder
	Decreasing fluid intake for 2–3 hours prior to sexual activity
	Repositioning catheter by taping out of the way or clamp and disconnect prior to sexual intercourse
	Using pharmacologic agents to reduce bladder motility
Fatigue	Using energy conservation techniques
	Resting frequently during the day
	Experimenting with different positions and different times of day
	Dopamine agonists such as amantadine
Impotence	Pharmacotherapy
	Vacuum suction devices
	Intracavernosal injections of papaverine
	Penile implants
Sensation	Decreased sensation can be treated with a vibrator to increase genital stimulation
	Hypersensitivity to touch can be treated with a topical anesthetic
Vaginal lubrication	Using sterile, water-soluble lubricants
Weakness or spasticity	Experimenting with different positions
	Taking a warm bath prior to sexual activity to reduce spasticity
	Using pharmacotherapy for spasticity
	Using an obturator block when hip adductor spasticity interferes with sexual activity

positions and different times of the day to increase strength. Treatment with dopamine agonists such as amantadine may be helpful.

Several therapeutic interventions for the treatment of impotence, such as pharmacotherapy, penile implants, vacuum suction devices, and intracavernosal injections of papaverine, are available. The evaluation and treatment of impotence is reviewed in detail elsewhere in this issue.

The presence of weakness or spasticity may require experimentation with a variety of positions. Women with weak pelvic muscles should use coital positions that minimize the need for thrusting the pelvis. Reduction of spasticity by either medications or physical modalities could be helpful. An obturator block may be necessary in cases with severe hip adductor spasticity interfering with sexual activity.

Women who experience decreased vaginal lubrication should use a sterile, water-soluble lubricant jelly. Nonwater-soluble lubricants should never be used, because they may cause urinary tract infection. Decreased sensation can be treated with the use of a vibrator to increase the amount of genital stimulation.[30] A topical anesthetic may be helpful in patients with hypersensitivity to touch.

COUNSELING REGARDING REPRODUCTION

Young women in the reproductive age group are at highest risk for the development of MS. They are often faced with difficult decisions regarding childbearing and ask their physicians a number of questions regarding the advisability of pregnancy. Counseling of these women involves considering a number of issues such as risks of recurrence, fertility, possible effects of pregnancy on the disease, ability to deal with the stress of raising a family, and ability to care for children.

Although the complicated interactions between genetics and environment are not totally understood, it appears that there is an increased risk of contracting MS among first-degree relatives of patients. About 10–15% of patients with the disease will have an affected family member.[10] The risk of a patient's child having MS may be as high as 3%.[24,25] Although this risk is low, it is still significantly increased over the risk for the general population, which is estimated to be 0.1%.

Fertility does not appear to be affected by MS;[32] nor does the ultimate course of the disease appear to be affected by pregnancies.[8,15,22,31] No association has been found between disability and timing of pregnancy relative to onset of MS.[34] For a more comprehensive review of these issues, see chapter 15.

Very little is known about parenting by individuals with physical handicaps and its impact on children. The consensus of opinion has been that physical disability in a parent has deleterious effects on the development of children.[3,10,23] Aspects of child development that have been cited to be at risk include personality adjustments, sex role identification, body image, interpersonal relationships, and parent-child relations. Olgas, however, found no significant relationship in general between multiple sclerosis in parents and body image in children.[21]

SUMMARY

Although a limited number of studies focus on sexual dysfunction of MS patients, the available literature suggests that sexual problems are common in both sexes and that they may occur at any stage of the disease. Reasons for altered sexual responses in MS patients are multiple and complex. Many organic and psychosocial factors are involved. Since sexual problems are common in these patients, a sexual history must be included as part of the medical evaluation. If sexual dysfunction is present, a discussion of viable therapeutic options should be encouraged. Help and support in many areas of the sexual relationship might assist MS patients in coping with their disabilities.

The ultimate course of the disease is not affected by pregnancy. The decision to start a family should therefore be based on the disability level at the time, ability to care for children in later years, and the ability to deal with the stress of raising a family.

REFERENCES

1. Anderson DW, Ellenberg JW, Leventhal CM, et al: Revised estimate of the prevalence of multiple sclerosis in the United States. Ann Neurol 31:333–336, 1992.
2. Anderson TP, Cole T: Sexual counseling of the physically disabled. Postgrad Med 58:117–123, 1975.
3. Buck FM, Hohmann GW: Child adjustment as related to severity of paternal disability. Arch Phys Med Rehabil 63:249–253, 1982.
4. Dewis ME, Thornton NG: Sexual dysfunction in multiple sclerosis. J Neurosci Nurs 21:175–179, 1989.
5. Drug Facts and Comparisons. Facts and Comparisons, St. Louis, 1993.
6. Ebers GC: Genetic factors in multiple sclerosis. Neurol Clin 1:645–654, 1983.
7. Ellison GW, Vissher BR, Graves MC, Fahey JL: Multiple sclerosis. Ann Intern Med 101:514–526, 1984.
8. Ghezzi A, Caputo D: Pregnancy: A factor influencing the course of multiple sclerosis? Eur Neurol 20:115–117, 1981.
9. Goldstein I, Siroki MB, Sax DS, Krane RJ: Neurourologic abnormalities in multiple sclerosis. J Urol 128:541–545, 1982.
10. Hilbourne J: On disabling the normal: Implications of physical disability for other people. Br J Soc Work 3:497–504, 1973.
11. Ivers RR, Goldstein NP: Multiple sclerosis: A current appraisal of symptoms and signs. Proc Mayo Clin 38:457–463, 1963.
12. Kalb RC, La Rocca NG, Kaplan SR: Sexuality. In Scheinberg LC, Holland NJ (eds): Multiple Sclerosis: A Guide for Parents and Their Families. New York, Raven, 1987, pp 177–195.
13. Keller S, Buchanan DC: Sexuality and disability: An overview. Rehabil Dig 15:3–7, 1984.
14. Kirkeby HJ, Poulsen EU, Petersen T, Dorup J: Erectile dysfunction in multiple sclerosis. Neurology 38:1366–1371, 1988.
15. Leibowitz U, Antonovsky A, Kats R, Alter M: Does pregnancy increase the risk of multiple sclerosis? J Neurol Neurosurg Psychiatry 30:354–357, 1967.
16. Lilius HG, Valtonen E, Wikstrom J: Sexual problems in patients suffering from multiple sclerosis. Scand J Soc Med 4:41–44, 1976.
17. Lundberg PO: Sexual dysfunction in patients with multiple sclerosis. Sex Disabil 1:218–222, 1978.
18. Lundberg PO: Sexual dysfunction in female patients with multiple sclerosis. Int Rehabil Med 3:32–34, 1981.
19. Miller H, Simpson CA, Yeates WK: Bladder dysfunction in multiple sclerosis. BMJ 1:1265–1269, 1965.
20. Minderhoud JM, Leemkius JG, Kremer J, et al: Sexual disturbances arising from multiple sclerosis. Acta Neurol Scand 70:299–306, 1984.
21. Olgas M: Relationship between parents' health status and body image of their children. Nurs Res 23:319–324, 1974.
22. Poser S, Poser W: Multiple sclerosis and gestation. Neurology 33:1422–1427, 1983.
23. Romano MD: Preparing children for parental disability. Soc Work Health Care 1:309–315, 1976.
24. Sadovnick AD, MacLeod PMJ: The familial nature of multiple sclerosis: Empiric recurrence risks for first, second, and third degree relatives of patients. Neurology 31:1039–1041, 1981.
25. Sadovnick AD, Baird PA: Reproductive counseling for multiple sclerosis patients. Am J Med Genet 20:349–354, 1985.
26. Samonds RJ, Cammermeyer M: Perceptions of body image in subjects with multiple sclerosis: A pilot study. J Neurosci Nurs 21:190–194, 1989.
27. Slater RJ, Raun NE (eds): Symposium on a Minimal Record of Disability for Multiple Sclerosis. Acta Neurol Scand Suppl 101:1–217, 1984.
28. Smith BH: Multiple sclerosis and sexual dysfunction. Med Aspects Hum Sex 10:103–104, 1976.

29. Szasz G, Paty D, Lawton-Speer S, Eisen K: A sexual functioning scale in multiple sclerosis. Acta Neurol Scand 70:37–43, 1984.
30. Stone B, Melman A: Management of sexual and bladder dysfunction in multiple sclerosis. J Neurol Rehabil 3:167–175, 1989.
31. Thompson DS, Nelson LM, Burns A, et al: The effects of pregnancy in multiple sclerosis: A retrospective study. Neurology 36:1097–1099, 1986.
32. Valleroy ML, Kraft GH: Sexual dysfunction in multiple sclerosis. Arch Phys Med Rehabil 65:125–128, 1984.
33. Vas CJ: Sexual impotence and some autonomic disturbances in men with multiple sclerosis. Acta Neurol Scand 45:166 182, 1969.
34. Weinshenker BG, Hader W, Carriere W, et al: The influence of pregnancy and disability from multiple sclerosis: A population-based study in Middlesex County, Ontario. Neurology 39:1438–1440, 1989.

WILLIAM P. BLOCKER, Jr, MD

CORONARY HEART DISEASE AND SEXUALITY

From the Department of Physical
Medicine and Rehabilitation
Baylor College of Medicine
and
Texas Methodist Hospital
Houston, Texas

Reprint requests to:
William P. Blocker, Jr., MD
Texas Methodist Hospital
Smith Tower, Suite 1421
6560 Fannin Street
Houston, TX 77030

Cardiovascular disease remains the primary cause of death in the United States. Approximately 69 million of the more than 250 million individuals (28%) in the U.S. have cardiovascular diseases. Of these, 170,000 are expected to lose their lives each year.[16]

Coronary heart disease is a problem not only in this country, but worldwide. In worldwide, randomly selected postmortem studies of individuals dying from accidental causes, McGill[30] and Tageda[39] found that approximately an eighth of the world's population already had coronary artery disease. Assuming that the world's population was approximately 5 billion in 1994, we can then project that approximately 600 million of the world's population currently have arterial sclerotic changes in the coronary vessels.[3]

Life expectancy following a myocardial infarction has improved during the past decade due to multiple factors, including (1) improved medications for medical management (thrombolytic agents, new drugs for the management of cardiogenic shock, and cardiac dysarrthymias), (2) the use of pericutaneous transluminal coronary angioplasties (more than 200,000 per year), and (3) more frequent use of coronary bypass surgeries (more than 350,000 per year). In the patients with end-stage cardiac disease, cardiac transplants can often extend life expectancy by several years. As a consequence of the increased number of patients surviving, 75–85% of the postmyocardial infarction patients will be able to return to their former jobs (with some restriction of their physical activities)[45] and a near normal social life.

SEXUAL ACTIVITIES IN CORONARY PATIENTS

The literature on the sexual activities of patients experiencing a myocardial infarction and undergoing surgical treatment with pericutaneous transluminal angioplasty, coronary bypass, or cardiac transplant shows that, due to a number of factors, the results remain variable. Among the factors resulting in sexual dysfunction common to all of these individuals are (1) limitation of cardiac function, (2) angina pectoris, (3) surgical incisional pain, (4) side effects of medication, (5) psychological problems, (6) inappropriate attitudes, and (7) aging.[27]

As a result of cardiac disease and other associated problems, sexual dysfunction is a common problem in these patients. In several studies of large groups of patients who have experienced a myocardial infarction, it was found that 10–15% of men have experienced impotence and 40–70% experienced diminished frequency and quality of their sexual activities.[40] In women, the information regarding sexual functioning is somewhat sparse; however, 65–75% will have some degree of diminished sexual performance[34] (Fig. 1).

In patients who have had pericutaneous transluminal angioplasty, the primary problem is angina. The angina is often relieved, allowing patients to resume a normal sexual life.

The prevalence of sexual problems after coronary bypass surgery ranges from 30–57%.[13,19,44] Some investigators have reported improved sexual functioning after the surgery.[12] Cain et al.[7] report that although 63% of patients had problems with sexual activity prior to surgery, only 18% had any form of sexual dysfunction at the end of a 3-month period post surgery. Similar improvement was noted in home relationships, social life, and recreational activities.

Thurer[41] studied the long-term sexual response to coronary bypass surgery and reported that up to 4 years after surgery, 70% of his patients experienced worsening of sexual function.

In a study of physical, psychological, social, and economic outcomes among patients with coronary artery bypass surgery, Jenkins et al.[18] reported that half of the patients did not experience any change in level of satisfaction with sexual functioning after the surgery compared with 1 year before surgery. The remainder were about equally divided between those reporting better or worse levels of satisfaction.[18]

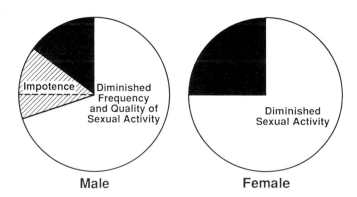

FIGURE 1.   Sexual activity following myocardial infarction. (Adapted from Whitehouse FA: Cardiovascular disability. In Garret JF, Levine E (eds): Psychology Practice and Physical Disability. New York, Columbia University Press, 1962.)

In a sample of 17 women undergoing surgery, Althof[2] concluded that female sexual response differs from what is known about male adaptation to coronary artery bypass surgery. Women in this study did not demonstrate a significant decline in frequency of intercourse 1 year after surgery. The most common problem was decline in desire. These patients also did not harbor the sexual fears commonly seen in men, such as sudden death during intercourse or performance anxiety.[2]

The data available on sexual dysfunction in pre- and postcardiac transplant patients are sparse. Personal communications with the Baylor College of Medicine/ The Methodist Hospital Transplant Center suggest that no man and few women were sexually active prior to cardiac transplant. The transplant patients were sexually dysfunctional because of chest pain and breathlessness, which precluded any physical stress. A small percentage of postcardiac transplant patients are capable of being sexually active; some have been able to indulge in competitive sports.

FACTORS INVOLVED IN CHANGES IN SEXUALITY IN POSTCORONARY PATIENTS

A number of factors may be involved with changes in sexuality in coronary patients,[27] including (1) psychological changes, (2) vasculogenic erectile dysfunctions, (3) a fear of developing cardiac symptoms associated with the sexual act, (4) fear of a so-called "coital death" during sex, (5) limited cardiac function, (6) angina pectoris, (7) surgical incisional pain, (8) side effects of medication, and (9) inappropriate attitudes.

Psychological Problems

The psychological impact of a cardiac event may at least temporarily alter the patient's sense of body image, undermine their self-esteem, and cast doubt on their attractiveness or ability to be a bread winner contributing to their family's welfare and economic support.[7] Studies[4] have shown that following a myocardial infarction, patients experience three primary psychological disorders: anxiety, denial, and depression. During the first 5 days following a myocardial infarction, approximately half of the individuals will experience both anxiety and denial. About 20% will develop a chronic anxiety, and 10% will develop a chronic depression that will influence their sexual activity (Fig. 2). Both anxiety and depression will affect the sexual life of the patient's mate. The psychological impact after a myocardial infarction usually is self-limited and may be treated by proper counseling. However, the anxiety associated with sex and the fear of coital death remains a severe problem in some patients.

Anxiety

Any patient experiencing a myocardial infarction will experience severe anxiety that will be proportional to the magnitude of the symptoms (pain, shortness of breath, nausea) and the psychological make-up of the particular patient. In 10% of patients, this anxiety will become chronic and persist for months or years.

Anxiety varies with the sex of the patient and the nature of his or her care. In a man, anxiety may be related to his ability to continue working and supporting his family. He will wonder what the future will be like, if he will have a second heart attack, or if he will be able to remain sexually active. In a woman, her concerns may be similar, and she also might be concerned with her body image as a woman. She might wonder if she will be regarded as less desirable. In both sexes, there is fear of chest pain, a second coronary, or death during intercourse.

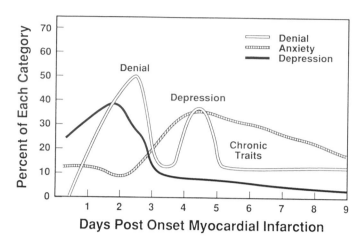

FIGURE 2.   Psychological stages in postmyocardial infarction experiences in nine patients.

If a patient has had cardiac surgery, he or she might fear incisional pain or dehiscence of the chest wound. Women often feel that the chest scar is disfiguring.

Denial
In about 30–50% of patients, after the immediate crisis is over, there will be some denial that they really experienced a life-threatening myocardial infarction. In fewer than 5% of patients, however, this denial will persist for at least 13–14 days.[29]

Depression
The most chronic and clearly established cause of sexual dysfunction is depression.[9] As noted in Figure 2, depression becomes apparent at a later date following the patient's myocardial infarction but can persist for many months, thus suppressing normal sexual arousal.

Reactive depression may often be severe in postmyocardial infarction patients. In the postcoronary bypass patients, depression appears to subside quickly; however, in cardiac transplant patients, depression remains persistent in a high percentage throughout their lives.

Fear of Death
Fear of "coital death" is common among patients who have had a myocardial infarction. The number of patients who have experienced "coital death," according to DeSilva and Lowe[11] and Ueno,[42] is relatively small (less than 1%). Coital death happens most often in an intoxicated patient committing adultery with a younger sexual partner in unfamiliar surroundings.[23] It is for this reason that death occurring during sexual intercourse in cardiac patients has been termed "motel cardiac death."[36]

Most deaths in cardiac patients who died during sexual activity have been attributed to a cerebral hemorrhage and far fewer to cardiac dysarrythmias. Blocker[4] and Kopel[25] found that about 30% of sexual partners or spouses of postcoronary patients were fearful of causing the death of their partner during sexual activities.

Fear of Pain

Patients often fear two types of possible pain during intercourse: angina pectoris and incisional pain.[6]

Anginal pain in postmyocardial patients prior to a coronary bypass was present in 30% of patients during sexual activities. Following coronary bypass in the same patients, anginal pain was present in only 5% or less.

A second fear of pain is sternal incisional pain. Pain in the sternal incisional area, although bothersome and sometimes a serious problem, usually subsides 6–8 weeks after surgery in patients who are sexually active. Fear of wound dehiscence is unwarranted because the sternum is surgically wired for stabilization at the time of surgery.

THE PHYSIOLOGY OF SEXUAL RESPONSE AND PHYSICAL WORK CAPACITY

The physiologic responses of humans during sexual activities are similar, but individual variations in the magnitude and the duration occur. These variations are the result of age, associated medical problems, disabilities, sexual attractions, and the feeling of comfortable intimacy with their sex partners.

Masters and Johnson[29] identified four phases of the sexual cycle: the excitement phase, plateau phase, orgasmic phase, and desolution. The excitement phase begins when the sexual partners are physically or psychologically stimulated and is accompanied by the individual developing a tachycardia, a tachypnea, and some increase in blood pressure. At the same time, there is increased muscle tension, which persists throughout the sexual act. During this stage, there is penile erection and vaginal lubrication. The plateau phase is an advanced stage of the excitement phase. During this phase, there is vasocongestion of the body, including the primary sexual organs, continued tachycardia and tachypnea, and muscle tension. In the orgasmic stage, men ejaculate and women experience rhythmic contractions of the vagina and perineal muscles. There are significant physiologic response variations between studies[5,31] during sexual activity. In older, healthy adults, the maximum heart rate tends to vary between 114–166 beats per minute and systolic blood pressure rises up to 168 or more.[26] However, these changes in heart rate and blood pressure are of short duration and tend to occur immediately preceding an orgasm. It is during this period that patients develop ectopic heart beats and ST changes, particularly in postcoronary patients. During the fourth phase, resolution, the body returns to its relaxed state. The heart rate decreases, the heart muscles become more relaxed, the blood pressure drops, and, if the patient had ST changes, they normalize. If the patient is prone to have ectopic heart beats, however, they may persist (Figs. 3 and 4).

Metabolic output in healthy young men during intercourse in the missionary position varies from 3.3–5.5 mets for at least a few seconds during orgasm.[19] Skinner found that among middle-aged, married men, the peak cost of sexual activity does not exceed 4 mets.[37] Bohlen et al.[5] measured oxygen uptake, pulse, and blood pressure during various sexual activities, such as masturbation, foreplay, intercourse with the man on top, and intercourse with the woman on top, and found that intercourse in a familiar position had lower metabolic cost than intercourse in an unfamiliar position.[5] The mean maximal heart rate and systolic blood pressures do not differ in cardiac patients and normal subjects. However, dysarrhythmias such as premature ventricular heart beats, premature atrial heart beats, and supraventricular tachycardias can be provoked by sexual activities. In

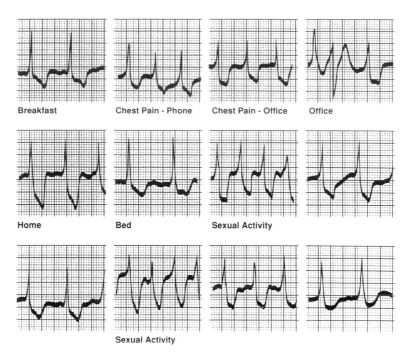

Breakfast   **Chest Pain - Phone**   **Chest Pain - Office**   **Office**

Home   **Bed**   **Sexual Activity**

Sexual Activity

FIGURE 3. Electrocardiogram of postmyocardial 52-year-old man. Marked displacement of ST segment and an occasional premature contraction occurring at office and during sexual activity. Adapted from Blocker WP, Cardus D (eds): Rehabilitation in Ischemic Heart Disease. New York, S. P. Medical & Scientific Books, 1983.

a study of 24 postcoronary patients, four of the patients developed significant arrhythmias, including ventricular bigemenies, supraventricular tachycardias with couplets, and frequent premature ventricular contractions. One patient had Wolf Parkinson syndrome, 7% had premature atrial contractions, and 28% developed ST depressions.[37]

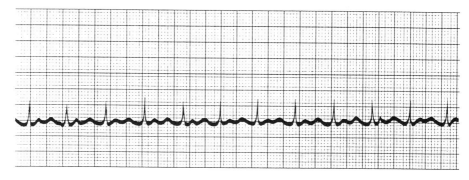

FIGURE 4. Electrocardiogram taken during sexual activity in a normal woman, probably at peak of orgasm. Cardiac rate 200 heart beats per minute (Del Mar Avionics, Irvine, California). Adapted from Blocker WP, Cardus D (eds): Rehabilitation in Ischemic Heart Disease. New York, S. P. Medical & Scientific Books, 1983.

During sexual intercourse, an adult requires approximately 4–5 mets of energy, and walking on a treadmill at 3 miles per hour at a 5% grade will simulate the physical activity of sexual intercourse. Therefore, a treadmill test may be used to determine if the patient will develop angina, which would preclude safe sexual activity.[27]

Studies by Hellerstein and Friedman[17] and Kopel[25] that evaluated the cardiac status of patients using the Holter monitor during sexual activity have shown that ischemic ST changes and serious dysarthemias occur in some but not in most patients. The mean maximum heart rate in their patients was 117 beats/minute (range 90–140). The rate in the time surrounding the maximum heart rate (2 minutes before and 2 minutes after orgasm) averaged 92 beats/minute. Kavanagh and Shephard have reported similar peak pulse rates of middle-aged men during normal sexual relations with a familiar partner.[21] The use of Holter monitors during sexual activity will be of value to reassure both the patient and the physician that sexual activity in postcoronary patients is safe.

Types of Sexual Dysfunction

Sexual dysfunction in healthy or coronary patients are to some extent similar and may be divided based on the gender of the patient.

Female sexual dysfunctions include the following:[32]

Preorgasemia.   Women who have never experienced an orgasm.

Secondary Nonorgasemia.   Women who experience orgasm by masturbation but not by intercourse.

Dyspareunia.   Women who experience disabling pain during intercourse.

Sexual Aversion.   Women who are repulsed or terrified by the sexual act.

Vaginismus.   Spasm of the muscles surrounding the vagina during attempted penile penetration.

Male sexual dysfunctions include:[43]

Primary Impotence.   An inability to have ever maintained a penile erection for sexual intercourse.

Secondary Impotence.   Ability to secure an erection on some occasions. Secondary impotence is often caused by the use of alcohol or drugs, the result of anxiety, or fear of having a heart attack during intercourse.

Premature Ejaculation.   In some men, ejaculating before they may wish becomes a major problem. Premature ejaculations are often a behavioral disorder, which can be treated.

A number of drugs may induce sexual dysfunction, and many of these drugs are used by patients who have experienced a myocardial infarction. Drugs specifically known to decrease libido, produce impotence, or interfere with ejaculation include tranquilizers, antihypertensives, beta blockers, antidepressants, thiazide diuretics, phenothiazines, monoamine oxidase inhibitors, and ganglion blocking agents.[10,35]

Among the drugs most commonly used in postcoronary men that can produce erectile failure are digitoxin and estradiol. In both men and women, the sexual drive may be diminished through antidepressant and antihypertensive drugs. Approximately 25% of all heart transplant patients experience a secondary erectile dysfunction but have continued sexual desire. In posttransplant patients, the most probable cause of dysfunction is immunorepressive treatment programs (Table 1).

TABLE 1.   Commonly Prescribed Medications Compromising Sexual Function

Medication	Effects
Antianginals	
Propranolol	Decreased libido, impotence
Antihypertensives	
Clonidine, guanabenz, guanadrel, labetalol, lisinopril, mecamylamine, methyldopa, metyrosine, penbutolol, phenoxybenzamine hydrochloride, prazosin, ramipril, rauwolfia, rescinnamine, reserpine terazosin	Impotence, sexual dysfunction, ejaculatory dysfunction
Antilipemics	
Clofibrate	Impotence, decreased libido
Anticonvulsants	
Carbamzepine, ethosuximide, paramethadione, primidone, trimethadione	Impotence, vaginal bleeding
Antidepressants	
Bupropian hydrochloride	Impotence
Clomipramine dehydrochloride	Ejaculation failure, impotence
Fluxetine hydrochloride	Sexual dysfunction
Trancypromine sulfate	Impotence
Diuretics	
Chlorothiazide	Failure of erection, poor erection
Hydrochlorothiazide	Decreased libido, impotence
Spironolactone	Impotence, decreased libido
Antipsychotics	
Acetophenazine maleate, chlorpromazine hydrochloride, chlorprothixene, clozapine, fluphenazine, mesoridazine, molindone, perphenazine, pimozide, promazine, thioridazine, thiothixene, trifluoperazine	Inhibited or abnormal ejaculation, impotence
Cerebral stimulants	
Amphetamine sulfate, benzphetamine, dextrophtamine, diethylpropion, fenfluramine mazindol, methamphetamine, phenmetrazine, phentermine	Impotence, altered libido
Antiparkinsonian agents	
Carbidopa-levodopa	Excessive and inappropriate sexual behavior
Selegiline hydrochloride	Sexual dysfunction
Anticholinergics	
Clidinium bromide, dicyclomine hydrochloride, glycopyrrolate, nexocyclium, hyoscyamine, isopropamide iodide, mepenzolate, methantheline bromide, methscopalamine bromide, oxyphencyclimine, oxyphenonium bromide, propantheline bromide	Impotence

From Data from Nursing '92 Drug Handbook. Springhouse, PA, Springhouse, 1991.

PROGRAMS FOR IMPROVING SEXUAL FUNCTION

A change in normal sexual needs and function occurs in postcoronary patients. These changes may result from one or many different causes, some psychological and some physical. Because the causes of these sexual dysfunctions are different, the approaches must be varied according to need. If the sexual dysfunction persists for more than 6–7 months, further investigations need to be considered.[24]

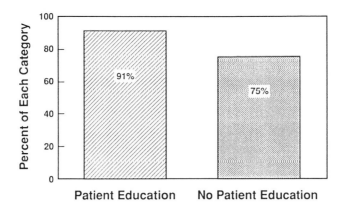

FIGURE 5. Benefits of psychological counseling in normalizing sexual activities in postmyocardial patients. Adapted from Kopel KF: Sexual activities in the coronary patient. In Blocker WP, Cardus D (eds): Rehabilitation in Ischemic Heart Disease. New York, S. P. Medical & Scientific Books, 1983.

Counseling

Psychological counseling soon after myocardial infarction may facilitate the patient's ability to attain a more near normal sexual lifestyle, provided that no organic cause is present[24] (Fig. 5). Psychological counseling following a myocardial infarction should begin early in the patient's illness. In most cases following a myocardial infarction, patients experience a short period of denial that they have had a heart attack, followed by a longer period of anxiety and depression.[6] The period of denial is usually self-limited; however, the problems of anxiety and depression may become chronic if not properly treated.

Anxiety not only manifests itself during the myocardial infarction, but in some cases may last many months, particularly with reference to individuals engaging in sexual intercourse. The anxiety may manifest itself in many ways, including an inability to perform the sexual act. Patients fear that they may have a second heart attack or may die during sexual intercourse, and male patients have anxiety concerning whether they will be able to obtain or sustain an erection. The patient's inability to obtain an erection may be psychological or physiologic.[43]

It is important to assure patients that they will be able to resume a normal sexual life after a short period following their myocardial infarction. This period is variable but normally lasts approximately 2 months. Hugging, cuddling, or noncoital foreplay activities are relaxing, pleasurable, of low metabolic cost, and without danger to patients. Patients should be encouraged to participate in these activities. Patients should also be assured that it is improbable that they will die during intercourse with their usual mate and in friendly surroundings.

There is no increase in mortality associated with a gradual but full return to premorbid levels of activity, including sexual activity.[13,17] A study by Uno[42] in Japan found that death during intercourse occurred in only 0.6% of the 559 post-coronary patients studied. An American study by Silber and Katz[36] on coital death, which they referred to as "motel cardiac deaths," occurred in only 0.5% of the postcoronary patients they studied. Of the patients who died during sexual intercourse, death was usually a result of ventricular fibrillation, asystole, or a rupture of the ventricle.

TABLE 2.   Patient Guidelines for Sexual Activity after a Heart Attack

In terms of energy expended conjugal intercourse is comparable to climbing one or two flights of stairs or taking a brisk walk. It is usually safe to resume sexual intercourse 6–12 weeks after having a heart attack. However, your physician should be your guide since each person's recovery phase is different.

To minimize the expenditure of energy while the heart is healing, the following guidelines might be helpful:

1. Avoid intercourse after a heavy meal, when intoxicated, or when fatigued.

2. Avoid intercourse when it is uncomfortably hot or cold or in unfamiliar surroundings.

3. You may find during recovery that alternate positions require less exertion since any position requiring prolonged use of the arms and legs for body support involves muscular activity, which may be too tiring. Such positions include partners lying side by side or the person who has had the heart attack lying on the back. These not only require less exertion but also may provide a more enjoyable experience for both partners.

4. Notify your physician if rapid breathing or a rapid heart rate persists longer than 15 minutes after intercourse.

5. If you experience chest pain during intercourse, take nitroglycerin, when prescribed, before you again engage in intercourse. If chest pain persists, notify your physician.

6. Men may experience a temporary absence of spontaneous erections following a myocardial infarction that is most likely due to the physical strain and emotional exhaustion that accompany a heart attack. Generally, this problem resolves quickly as your overall level of activity increases.

7. Openly discuss with your physician any questions you may have concerning sexual activity.

To lessen patients' anxiety with reference to the sexual act, they should be given specific guidelines (Table 2), which should include the following:

1. Postcoronary patients should have intercourse preferably with a familiar lover or spouse. Extramarital sex, according to Cantwell,[8] increases the chances of experiencing a serious cardiac disorder during sexual intercourse.

2. Sexual intercourse should not follow excessive eating or drinking of alcoholic beverages.

3. The sex act should not follow a very hot or cold bath.

4. The couple should have sex in a cool environment (72–78° F).

5. The woman astride the male is the least physically taxing position for both partners.

6. Should patients experience shortness of breath or chest pain, sex should be immediately discontinued and patients should take a niitroglycerin tablet. Some patients prefer to take a nitroglycerin tablet before sex.

The most chronic psychological problem following a myocardial infarction is depression. Kavan and Elsassar[20] found that 45% of postmyocardial infarction patients develop a depressive disorder during the first 8–10 days following their heart attack. Those who became depressed early in their disease often tended to continue to have this problem for 3 or more months.

One of the problems in depressed patients is a diminished interest in all pleasures, including sex. Counseling should include reassurance of their denial that they have had a myocardial infarction. Denial usually responds to assurance and fortunately is usually self-limited.

The medical treatment of anxiety and depression may require some forms of drug therapy. Anxiety usually responds well to alprazolam (Xanax) in daily dosages of 1.54–4.0 mg per day or lorezepam (Ativan), 0.5–1.0 mg three times per day. Management of depression may entail psychological intervention as well as drug therapy and antidepressants. Fluxetone hydrochloride (Prozac) in daily dosages of

25–80 mg per day or paroxetine (Paxil), 20–50 mg per day, have been found to have the least undesirable side effects. Should these drugs not be effective, one of the stronger tertiary amines with their orthostatic and anticholernagic and arrhythmic side effects may be used.

Treatment of Organic Causes of Impotence

Boone[6] stated, "Sexual health cannot be separated from total health." Yater[46] has shown that a number of systemic diseases can coexist in patients who have had a myocardial infarction or a coronary bypass. The systemic diseases that play a part in male impotence include (1) diabetes mellitus, (2) multiple sclerosis, (3) amyotrophic lateral sclerosis, (4) tabes dorsalis, (5) hypopituitarism, (6) lead poisoning, (7) pituitary tumors, (8) pernicious anemia, (9) occlusion of aortic bifarcation, and (10) hypogonadism. Only a limited number of these systemic diseases can be treated with a return of normal sexual potency. However, most male impotence can be treated with the use of penile devices.

Impotence Due to Endocrine Failure

Endocrine therapy has been extensively used by Margoles et al.[28] Margoles and his group gave Afrodex, a combination of 5 mg of nux vomica extract, 5 mg of methyl testosterone, and 5 mg of yohibine hydrochloride, to 4,000 impotent men 41–60 years old. Fair to excellent results were obtained in 80%. However, this was not a well-designed double-blind study. A later double-blind study[12] found that Afrodex was three times more effective than a placebo. Some patients are reluctant to use this preparation because of the potential for methyl testosterone toxicity. Other drugs have been used in hypogonadal men with endocrine failure, with poor to fair results as described by Margoles.[28]

Penile Dysfunction, Surgical Treatment, and Penile Devices

Penile dysfunction is often due to local problems,[27] including priapism, corpus cavernosum leakage, and Peyronie's disease. These disorders often respond well to surgery.

Surgical treatment of erectile failure has been described by Gorm and Green[12] and is also reviewed in chapter 16 of this issue. The treatment of erectile failure often responds to devices such as penile implants, of which there are four in common usage: (1) Scott's inflatable prosthesis, (2) Subrini's prosthesis (silastic penile implant), (3) Small-Carrion prosthesis, and (4) the Jones prosthesis. Other more technically difficult surgeries include arterial surgeries to improve erection. Many of these surgical approaches to help individuals obtain a normal erection are new, and only time will show whether they are of great value.

Penile devices exist that produce and/or maintain an erection. They are known as vacuum erection devices and can produce an erection that lasts approximately 30 minutes.

CONCLUSION

Sexual activity following a coronary heart attack is not a high-risk activity and is not only normal but desirable for a healthy lifestyle. Sexual counseling must involve both the patient and his or her sexual partner.

In the beginning of the sexual act, most patients will become oversensitive to their heart actions. They may be expected to experience an occasional missed heart beat and tire more easily than before the heart attack. Patients should be assured that there is no alarm unless they experience angina or shortness of breath.[15]

The question that may patients ask is when can they resume sexual activity safely. According to Hackett and Cassem,[15] the best time is when patients can exert themselves sufficiently to increase their heart rate to 120 beats per minute in the absence of beta blocker therapy and not experience angina pectoris.

If one is to believe the number of books on the healing power of sex, perhaps the human organism will function better with positive emotions such as fun, excitement, exercise, and sex. Be that as it may, postmyocardial infarction patients may have a better quality of life if they include love, intimacy, and sex.

REFERENCES

1. Abranov LA: Sexual life and sexual frigidity among women developing myocardial infarctions. Psychosom Med 38:418–425, 1976.
2. Althof SE, Coffman CB, Levine SB: The effects of coronary bypass surgery on female sexual, psychological, and vocational adaptation. J Sex Marital Ther 10:176–184, 1984.
3. Blocker WP: Stastitical studies. In Blocker WP, Cardus D (eds): Rahabilitation in Ischemic Heart Disease. New York, S. P. Medical and Scientific Books, 1983, pp 7–29.
4. Blocker WP: Cardiac rehabilitation. In Halstead L, Grabois M (eds): Medical Rehabilitation. New York, Raven Press, 1985, pp 181–192.
5. Bohlen JG, Held JP, Sanderson MO, Patterson RP: Heart rate, rate pressure product and oxygen uptake during four sexual activities. Arch Intern Med 144:1745–1748, 1984.
6. Boone T, Kelley R: Sexual issues and research in counseling the myocardial infarction patient. Cardiovasc Nurs 4(4):65–75, 1990.
7. Cain N, Harrison SCW, Sharples LD, Wallwork J: Prospective study of the quality of life before and after coronary artery bypass grafting. BMJ 302:511–516, 1991.
8. Cantwell JD: Sex and the Heart. Med Aspects Hum Sex 15:18–23, 1981.
9. Cassem NH, Hackett TP: Physiological rehabilitation of myocardial infarction patients in the acute phase. Heart Lung 2:382–388, 1973.
10. [Reference deleted.]
11. DeSilva RA, Lown B: Ventricular premature beats, stress, and sudden deaths. Psychosomatics 1913:140–153, 1978.
12. Gorm W, Green R: Penile Dysfunction Due to Local Causes in Impotence. New York, Plenum Press, 1981, pp 149–166.
13. Green AW: Sexual activity and the postmyocardial infarction patient. Am Heart J 89:246–252, 1975.
14. Gundle GJ, Bozman BR, Tate S, et al: Psychosocial outcome after coronary artery surgery. Am J Psychiatry 137:1591–1594, 1980.
15. Hackett TP, Cassem NH: Psychological aspects of rehabilitation after myocardial infarction. In Wenger, Hellerstein H (eds): Rehabilitation of the Coronary Patient. New York, John Wiley & Sons, 1984, pp 437–451.
16. Heart Stroke Facts 1992. Dallas, American Heart Association, 1992.
17. Hellerstein H, Friedman E: Sexual activity and the post coronary patient. Arch Intern Med 125:981–999, 1970.
18. Jenkins CD, Stanton BA, Savageau JA, et al: Coronary artery bypass surgery: Physical, psychological, social, and economic outcomes six months later. JAMA 250:782–788, 1983.
19. Johnson BL, Fletcher BF: Dynamic electrocardiographic recording during sexual activity in recent post myocardial infarction and revascularized patients. Am Heart J 98:736–741, 1979.
20. Kavan MG, Elsasser GN: Depression after acute myocardial infarction. Postgrad Med 89:83–89, 1991.
21. Kavanagh T, Shephard RJ: Sexual activity after myocardial infarction. Can Med Assoc J 116:1250–1253, 1977.
22. Kornfeld DS, Heller SS, Frank KA, et al: Psychological and behavioral responses after coronary artery bypass surgery. Circulation 66:24–28, 1982.
23. Klein SW: Sex and the coronary patient. Practical Cardiol 4:140–143, 1978.
24. Koller R, Kennedy J, Butler J: Counseling the coronary patient on sexual activity. Postgrad Med 51:133–136, 1972.
25. Kopel KF: Sexual activities in the coronary patient. In Blocker WP, Cardus D (eds): Rehabilitation in Ischemic Heart Disease. New York, S. P. Medical and Scientific Books, 1983, pp 293–296.

26. Larson JL, McNaughton, et al: Heart rate and blood pressure responses to sexual activity and stair climbing test. Heart Lung 9:1025–1030, 1980.
27. Mackey FG: Sexuality in coronary artery disease. Postgrad Med 80:58–72, 1986.
28. Margoles R, Sangree H, et al: Clinical studies on the use of Afrodex in the treatment of impotence. Curr Therapeut Res 9:213–219, 1967.
29. Masters WJ, Johnson VE: Human Sexual Response. Boston, Little, Brown & Co., 1966.
30. McGill HS, Strong JP: The geographic pathology of arteriosclerosis. Ann N Y Acad Sci 2(part 2):149–158, 1968.
31. Nemec ED, Mansfield L, Kenedy JW: Heart rate and blood pressure responses during sexual activity in normal males. Am Heart J 92:274–277, 1976.
32. Novak E, Novak ER: Problems of sex life. In Gynecology. Baltimore, Williams & Wilkins, 1962, pp 571–577.
33. Nursing '92 Drug Handbook. Springhouse, PA, Springhouse, 1991.
34. Papadopoulos C: Sexual concerns and needs of post coronary patients' wives. Arch Intern Med 140:38–41, 1980.
35. Pollock ML, Schmidt DH: Heart Disease and Rehabilitation. 2nd ed. New York, John Wiley & Sons, 1986.
36. Silber EN, Katz LV: Cardiac Activity and Sexual Response. New York, MacMillan Press, 1980, pp 1252–1274.
37. Skinner JB: Sexual relations and cardiac patient. In Pollock ML, Schmidt DH (eds): Heart Disease and Rehabilitation. 2nd ed. New York, John Wiley & Sons, 1986, pp 583–589.
38. Stern MJ: Sexual activity after myocardial infarction. Hum Sex 119, August 1978.
39. Tageda C, Strong JP: Distribution of coronary and arteriosclerosis, race and sex. Int Acad Pathol 18(5): 1968.
40. Tardif GS: Sexual activity after a myocardial infarction. Arch Phys Med Rehabil 70:763–766, 1989.
41. Thurer S: The long term sexual response to coronary bypass surgery: Some preliminary findings. Sex Disabil 5:208–212, 1982.
42. Ueno M: The so-called "coital deaths." Jpn J Legal Med 17:333–340, 1963.
43. Wagner G, Green R: General Medical Disorders and Erectile Failures Impotence. New York, Plenum Press, 1981, pp 37–50.
44. Westaby S, Sapsford RN, Bentall HH: Return to work and quality of life after surgery for coronary artery disease. BMJ 27:1028 1031, 1979.
45. Whitehouse FA: Cardiovascular disability. In Garret JF, Levine E (eds): Psychology Practice and Physical Disability. New York, Columbia University Press, 1962, pp 85–124.
46. Yater WM: Symptoms Diagnosis. 5th ed. New York, Appleton Century, 1942.

PETER A.C. LIM, MD

SEXUALITY IN PATIENTS WITH MUSCULOSKELETAL DISEASES

From the Department of Physical
  Medicine and Rehabilitation
Baylor College of Medicine
  and
Physical Medicine and
  Rehabilitation Service
Veterans Affairs Medical Center
Houston, Texas

Reprint requests to:
Peter A.C. Lim, MD
Staff Physiatrist
Physical Medicine and
  Rehabilitation Service (117)
Veterans Affairs Medical Center
2002 Holcombe Blvd.
Houston, TX 77030

In the United States, musculoskeletal conditions make up the largest single category of diseases that result in impairment of self-care, ambulation, or ability to carry on the usual activities of daily living (Fig. 1).[40]

Arthritis is the leading musculoskeletal condition, with a prevalence of 30.8 million cases (1990) in noninstitutionalized civilians. There is a significant correlation with age and sex. The rate of arthritis in men 65–75 years old is 373.3 per 1,000 persons; in comparison, the rate is 25.8 in men younger than 45. The incidence is even higher in women: 472.2 in women 65–75 and 35.8 in women younger than 45. Joint replacements, often performed in situations of endstage degenerative or inflammatory arthritis, are also becoming common. Patients in this category represent a group with unique needs in the practice of physical medicine and rehabilitation. The U.S. National Center for Health Statistics records 816,000 artificial hip joint and 521,000 knee joint replacements in its survey of procedures performed in 1988.[53]

Peripheral vascular disease affecting the lower limb, particularly in diabetic patients, accounts for a large number of amputations each year. The 1990 figures by the U.S. National Center for Health Statistics show that 183,792 noninstitutionalized civilians were using an artificial leg or foot. Upper limb amputations may be related to congenital birth deficiencies or from causes such as trauma and tumors. A total of 39,384 persons were reported to be using an artifical arm or hand in 1990.[53]

The literature on sexuality in connection with musculoskeletal condtions such as the above

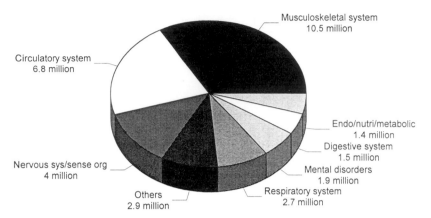

FIGURE 1.   Major disease categories limiting activity (number affected each year in the United States). (Adapted from Kottke FJ, Lehmann JF, Stillwell GK: Preface. In Kottke FJ, Lehmann JF, Stillwell GK (eds): Krusen's Handbook of Physical Medicine and Rehabilitation. 4th ed. Philadelphia, WB Saunders, 1990, p xxix.)

is, in general, limited, with an exception perhaps for arthritis. A few references are available concerning spinal scoliosis, fractures of the pelvis, and postsurgical resections of the pelvis as a result of tumors. Sexuality is an area of great significance when considering quality of life and activities of daily living, and it is a worthwhile field for further research.

SEXUALITY AND ARTHRITIS

Blake et al.[6] compared people with osteoarthritis, rheumatoid arthritis, and ankylosing spondylitis with arthritis-free matched controls. Both groups showed very similar rates of satisfaction and dissatisfaction with the quality of their current sexual adjustment. The two groups had similar concerns, behavior, and receptivity to sexual rehabilitation. However, 58% of the arthritis patients reported decrease in sexual satisfaction (over the time from onset of illness to present) versus 42% in the control group. Also, 38% of the patients versus 21% of the controls reported loss of sexual pleasure.

Yoshino and Uchida's study[58] on married women with rheumatoid arthritis indicated that more than half had experienced a decrease in sexual desire since onset of their illness. More than 60% stated that both they and their spouses were unsatisfied with their sexual relationship. In Currey's patients with osteoarthrosis of the hip,[19] 81% of women and 46% of men reported sexual difficulties due to arthritis.

Studying men and women with ankylosing spondylitis and rheumatoid arthritis, Elst et al.[26] demonstrated that both sexes tend to score similarly to healthy controls on a sexual motivation scale that includes enjoyment potential, orgasmic intensity, preferred frequency of intercourse, and length of foreplay. Men and women with rheumatoid arthritis, however, tended to show more aversion to sexual interaction than healthy controls, suggesting that they had more sexual concerns. The results also suggested that the more disabled patients (who had a greater number of joints involved) had less sexual motivation than the other patients.

Cohen[16] commented that ". . . sexual satisfaction is the result of the interplay of significant social, cultural, religious, emotional, relationship, reproductive, and

TABLE 1. Arthritis and Sexuality

Problems	Management
Medical issues	
Pain	Counseling
Physical limitations	Medications and timing
Fatigue	Physiotherapeutic modalities
Medications	Exercise
Genital lesions	Positions and techniques
	Surgery
Psychosocial issues	Social/administrative policy
Depression/anxiety	
Loss of self-esteem	
Inability to perform role	
Restricted opportunity	
Physical separation	

biological factors." Hence it is not surprising that arthritis-free controls also had concerns over sexual performance, loss of satisfaction, and receptivity to sexual rehabilitation.

These studies indicate that the presence of arthritis significantly affects sexual desire and satisfaction. However, one should keep in mind that sexuality is indeed a complex issue, either with or without an associated musculoskeletal disease.

Specific problems in arthritis affecting sexuality are outlined in Table 1 and are addressed below.

Medical Problems

Pain

Although relatively less intense than in many acute conditions, pain in patients with chronic arthritis does result in a greater impact and suffering due to its continuous and unrelenting nature.[24] The pain of arthritis has been described in varied terms, such as "a continual companion with no consideration of personal or social engagements,"[45] "a toothache that never goes away,"[52] "exhausting,"[21] "depressing,"[22] "an antiaphrodisiac,"[24] "inhibiting sexual activity,"[60] and, in general, as adversely affecting sexual function and satisfaction.[11,12,16,26,28,58,60]

Blake et al.[6] reported joint pain as contributing to loss of sexual satisfaction in 66% of men and 39% of women, while Currey[19] listed pain as the cause of sexual difficulties in 49% of his respondents. Pain may affect the joints involved in sexual activity, such as the hips, sacroiliac, and knee joints. Pain may also be generalized.[22] It interferes with genital intercourse when the hips and pelvic joints are affected or with kissing and caressing when the temporomandibular or hand and arm joints are painful.[18,30] Sjogren's syndrome is a relatively common association with inflammatory arthritis; it may result in a dry atrophic vaginitis, causing dyspareunia, and xerostomia, inhibiting oral-genital activity.[23] The anger, hostility, and denial mechanisms used by patients for managing their pain can create difficulties with family and professional relationships.[9]

Conversely, sexual activity can have an analgesic effect.[21] After sexual intercourse, there can be relief of pain, discomfort, and depression for up to 6–8 hours.[23] This may be due to endorphins or to the psychological benefits of caring and being cared for.[17]

PHYSICAL LIMITATIONS

Stiffness of the joints has been reported as contributing to loss of sexual satisfaction in as many as 66% of men and 28% of women with arthritis.[6] Stiffness has also been implicated as the cause for sexual difficulties in 74% of patients with osteoarthritis of the hip.[19] Arthritic hip involvement can limit abduction and external rotation,[17,60] with severe pain when such motions are attempted.[22,60] This limitation is particularly significant when flexion contractures in adduction have occurred or when there is fusion of the hip by disease or surgery.[22,23] It can produce a major mechanical impediment[22,23,45,60] to women during genital intercourse, particularly with the customary frontal missionary position with the woman on her back.[17,23,28] Total bilateral hip immobility may preclude entry entirely.[22] Perineal hygiene can be seriously restricted by the inability to obtain good access to the area.[23]

Limitations of spinal and knee movements can pose problems with positioning during intercourse.[17,45,58] Deforming hand arthritis is not only aesthetically unpleasing but affects dexterity for stroking, caressing, and manipulating genitalia.[17] Although stiffness of the joints occurs frequently in both rheumatoid arthritis and osetoarthritis, it is especially prevalent in ankylosing spondylitis, reported by 82% of a group of these patients.[9] Patients can have great difficulty in achieving tolerable positions, approximation of genitals to their partner's, and in making thrusting movements during sexual intercourse. Wheelchairs and orthotic devices such as braces also can physically interfere with approximation of bodies during sexual activity.[30]

FATIGUE

Fatigue is a common problem in patients with arthritis. It decreases desire and capability for sexual functioning in both men and women and contributes to loss of sexual satisfaction.[6,21,24] Fatigue was reported by 39% of women and 57% of men in a group of arthritic patients (significantly more than in arthritis-free controls) and can be used as an indirect measure of disease activity.[6] Fatigue is often intermittent and sometimes results in a misunderstanding as the partner observes the patient to be active during the day, yet complaining of fatigue and, hence, not desiring to participate in sex a little later.[8]

MEDICATIONS

The side effects of drugs used to treat arthritis, including corticosteroids, have been implicated for causing fatigue and decreasing libido.[3,23] Loss of libido or sexual desire has been reported to occur in 22–50% of arthritic patients.[6,19,58]

The number of drugs taken by patients with arthritis is sometimes remarkable, with potential toxicities and a high incidence of noncompliance, especially in patients with rheumatoid arthritis.[24] Besides the expense and difficulty of taking many doses, the side effects of corticosteroids in particular are a problem; they can cause alterations in physical appearance such as moon face, truncal obesity with buffalo hump and thin extremities, ecchymoses, acne, hirsutism, cataracts, occasional peripheral gangrene, and osteoporosis predisposing to pathologic fractures.[23]

These physical changes compound the issue of loss of physical attractiveness due to deforming arthritis and lead to further withdrawal from attempts at interpersonal interactions and sexual expression.[45] Many men on prolonged therapy with corticosteroids are unable to achieve an erection, but in most cases this recovers with withdrawal of the drug.[22] On the other hand, sexual activity has been reported to be therapeutic, increasing natural cortisone by stimulation of adrenal cortex.[18] The associated physical activity is definitely beneficial.[18]

Immunosuppressives may result in undesirable alteration of physical appearance such as hair loss. Other toxic effects of these drugs include mouth and genital ulcers. Cyclophosphamide may cause cystitis. Gold compounds can also produce mouth and genital ulcers.[23] To avoid effects on the fetus, men taking methotrexate may need to be advised to stop the drug 3 months before attempting conception.[2] Drugs such as methyldopa, used in the treatment of hypertension, can cause impotence or problems with ejaculation. Narcotics such as codeine may decrease libido and sexual responsiveness. The nonsteroidal antiinflammatory drugs are not known to cause sexual problems, and antianxiety drugs such as diazepoxide may actually help the patient.[8]

GENITAL LESIONS

Some arthritides are associated with involvement of the genitals, such as Reiter's syndrome with urethral discharge, cervicitis, and balanitis; Behçet's syndrome with ulcerative lesions of the external genitalia and recurrent balanitis; and Sjogren's syndrome with keratoconjunctivitis sicca, xerostomia, and atrophic vaginitis.[17,22] Decreased vaginal secretion can cause dyspareunia, and genital ulcers can be painful with sexual intercourse, but the aesthetic effects of these lesions are also a considerable psychological barrier. Avoidance of sexual contact, or use of a condom, may at times need to be advised with active infections.[8] As with other conditions, limited manual dexterity and movement of the hands as a result of arthritis can lead to inadequate toileting and less than pleasing personal hygiene.[17,45]

Psychosocial Problems

DEPRESSION AND ANXIETY

Rheumatoid arthritis sufferers may present with personality traits common to other patients with chronic painful, disabling diseases such as chronic low back pain and multiple sclerosis.[24] They have higher scores in the triad of hypochondriasis, depression, and hysteria on the Minnesota Multiphasic Personality Inventory and Tennessee Self-Concept Scales.[47] Depression is a frequently occurring issue that has been suggested as an important predictor of sexual functioning[42]; it can result in loss of sexual interest and desire.[4,17,22]

Depression may arise from the persistent pain,[9,22,23] immobility, altered sex roles, frustration from the inability to perform simple tasks, or employment difficulties and subsequent financial issues.[9] Anxiety is an associated finding, especially in patients with established rheumatoid arthritis.[4] It may include an uncertainty of the future as well as being directly related to sexuality in terms of patients' ability to satisfy themselves and their partner.[6] The partner may have fears that the arthritis is transmissible or may be anxious that he or she might be causing the spouse pain during sexual activity.[8]

LOSS OF SELF-ESTEEM

The importance of self-esteem, self-image, or self-worth cannot be overemphasized, because it affects us all, in all of our dealings with others. A low self-esteem can lead to withdrawal from relationships for fear of being rejected or, conversely, to a promiscuity to prove one's desirability.[24] Severe arthritis can cause a low self-esteem by virtue of its deforming nature on the body, as can the physical side effects of drug treatments.[23] The assaults of the advertising world as to the desirability of an unrealistically perfect body cause great doubts to patients' self-image.[22]

Losses in independence, in personal expectations of productivity and employment, in relationships with family, friends, and lovers, the stresses of coping with chronic pain, disability, and extended periods of hospitalization are other psychologic pressures on patients.[45,48,54,57] Ehrlich wrote that "enactment of sexual roles can be affected by alterations in perception of self, perception of self by others, and patient's idea of what this perception of self by others may be." It is therefore not surprising in the situation of a vulnerable self-esteem that the patient may be less then confident in sexual overtures or that a potential partner's responses are misunderstood.[22]

INABILITY TO PERFORM AN EXPECTED ROLE

Although roles have become somewhat blurred in today's society, it is generally expected that the man is physically strong and plays the role of breadwinner. The woman is expected to either contribute to the family income or be a full-time homemaker and mother.[22,28,30] Severe arthritis may not allow the performance of these roles, or patients might be placed on a disability income[24] by an employer who would rather not go through the efforts of job modification or substitution. The loss of expected roles or diminished income and, in a way, the diminishing of one's identity, can transfer to sexual performance and functioning.[23,28] It also can cause increased general stress on the patient, family,[9] and, in particular, the spouse.[30]

RESTRICTED OPPORTUNITIES

Lost or decreased mobility as a result of disease and illness can cause social isolation and loss of independence.[3,9,30] This limits the opportunities for meeting potential sexual partners and, subsequently, the chance for sexual activity.[4] The physical inability to participate in activities such as sports, dancing, and other courting rituals often leads to withdrawal and a preference for a solitary lifestyle.[45] Architectural and design barriers still exist and many social settings remain inaccessible to wheelchairs. This necessitates a greater effort and motivation to go somewhere new or even to leave home at all.

Unmarried people who are dependent on parents or nurses for transportation and daily care, or who are living at home, may find further constraints to their freedom of activities and privacy. In regard to opportunities for sexual encounters, they are totally dependent on the attitudes toward sexuality and the goodwill of their caretakers.[28,30]

PHYSICAL SEPARATION

Physical separation from their sexual partner is a reality that happens with long periods of hospitalizations for rehabilitation or multiple surgery. Third party payors or insurance plans usually do not allow overnight leave from the hospital. Hospitals themselves do not cater for privacy and are barriers to intimacy.[22,23] Older patients living in institutions such as nursing homes may not be allowed to share a bed or room with their sexual partner, and privacy is often limited.[5] Families and society itself may have reservations about any sexual activity, even masturbation.[34,35]

Juvenile Rheumatoid Arthritis

Children with arthritis of juvenile onset deserve special attention because they may not have yet learned the interpersonal skills, protocols, and requirements of healthy adult sexuality before the start of their disease.[17] These patients may have to do their learning with the added disadvantages of the stigmata of the disease, including micrognathia, short neck, severe leg length discrepancies, hand and foot deformities, waddling gait, and visual difficulties.[23]

Despite the handicaps, these children as adults reflected sexual behavior comparable to their healthy peers in one study.[32] They even had a higher income than the local average in one report, with a majority in professional, skilled, or semiskilled employment.[33] Although chronic or serious disease in adolescents can disrupt healthy psychological development, a study comparing adolescents with either oncologic, cardiac, rheumatic, diabetic disease, or cystic fibrosis with healthy adolescents revealed marked similarities on measurements of self-esteem and trait anxiety. Apparently, chronically ill children learn to live with their disability and develop effective coping mechanisms, which may include a healthy form of denial. During periods of illness, however, there can be high levels of situational anxiety and, particularly in rheumatic patients, more disruption of body image than healthy or other ill adolescents with less visible evidence of disease.[38,59]

There may be implications to sexuality related to the overwhelmed parents of a disabled child. They may not give as much physical contact in the form of stroking or fondling the child, who thus may not learn to enjoy these pleasurable sensations that later become a part of sexual expression. These children also may not receive appropriate information regarding developmental changes occurring during adolescence, such as menstruation or masturbation.[41]

Management of Sexual Problems in Arthritis

Table 1 outlines strategies for the management of sexual problems related to arthritis.

INFORMATION AND COUNSELING

Many patients with arthritis, even the elderly, are open to discussing sexual functions related to their illness. Unfortunately, sexuality is seldom addressed by their health care providers.[7,23,60] A survey[6] on arthritis patients showed that 39% were interested and willing to learn different ways of sexual expression. For health care providers who would be counselors it was recommended that actual practice in interviewing patients is an important component of becoming effective at discussing treatment options for sexual adjustment.[7]

The Counselor's Attitudes and Views. Many health care professionals are reluctant to deal with their patient's sexuality issues because of personal discomfort and insufficient expertise.[16] However, attitude matters because it may either encourage adjustment and growth, or it may inhibit sexual expression.[56] The counselor needs to be aware and comfortable with his or her own sexuality, accept a wide range of sexual behaviors as normal, and believe that it is possible to respect and deal with different moral, religious, and aesthetic values without compromising one's own. The counselor should be nonjudgmental, quietly encouraging, sensitive, and realistic yet tactful. A good knowledge of the sexual responses, the effects of disability, disease, drugs, aging, and society on sexuality is essential.[16,29,43,56]

Who Should Be the Counselor. The counselor of choice by patients is usually the physician,[19,49,58,60] preferably one of like-sex, but may be a nurse,[45] social worker, or a therapist[56] working with the patient. In occasional recalcitrant situations, such as when behavior modification therapy is required, referral to a marriage counselor or psychiatrist may be appropriate.[22]

What Should Be Asked. The counseling session may begin with a systematic review of the history and physical examination. Questions related to sexuality should be introduced at an appropriate juncture.[23,28,31] Information should be obtained about sexual adjustment prior to onset of symptoms, during exacerbation, and present adjustment.[31] The best guide to sexual adjustment is an analysis of the sexual relationship prior to illness, which, if important and satisfying previously, will continue to be an important and realistic goal.[60]

Areas to explore include frequency of intercourse, satisfaction, positional variations, willingness to experiment, and ability to discuss sexual problems with the partner. The type of contraception used is important because pregnancy is still an issue with younger arthritis patients. Other questions to ask include family roles, desire for children, body image and feelings of sexual attractiveness, cultural differences, and fears of both the patient and spouse.[45] It cannot be recommended enough that the partner be included in the counseling.[31]

Occasionally, it is necessary to discern the presence of psychogenic illness and secondary gain. Pain and the disease itself allow an excuse for avoiding unwanted sexual activity.[22] At times, the information from the spouse might reveal that more of the problem is with the partner than the patient.[8]

What to Tell the Patient. A stepwise approach that has been suggested is to follow the PLISSIT model, which can be useful for defining levels of intervention.[16] The P is for Permission, LI is for Limited Information, SS is for Specific Strategies, and IT is for Intensive Therapy. Further information can be obtained from the referred text.[1]

Counseling should take into account the religious, cultural, social, and disease-related history of the individual patient. Information provided to the patient on the type of arthritis, course, prognosis, and effects on daily activities including sexuality is usually appreciated and helpful.

Contraception options and advice should be provided, taking into account the patient's ability to manipulate or tolerate the chosen method as well as the partner's willingness and ability to assist.[28] Condoms and diaphragms may be difficult to place. Oral contraceptives predispose to thrombosis, especially in some patients in whom it is already a potential complication of their disease or treatment.[23] Intrauterine devices may cause heavier menstrual periods that are a problem for someone who is wheelchair-dependent.[28]

Most women develop remissions of arthritis during pregnancy, but the extra weightbearing, hormonal, gait, and postural changes may actually worsen established deformities. Respiration may be compromised by the growing uterus if the costovertebral joints are involved, as in ankylosing spondylitis. Drug treatment or chemotherapy may be harmful to the fetus. A cesarean section delivery should always be anticipated as a possibility, especially when there is already hip involvement.[22] Concerns about the effects of the disease and medications on childbearing and nursing should be addressed in conjunction with the obstetrician and pediatrician.[54] A patient taking corticosteroids may need a higher dose because of the maximal stresses of delivery. In the postpartum period, there can be flare-ups of rheumatoid arthritis or systemic lupus erythematosus.[8]

The would-be parent should be informed that there is little evidence that rheumatoid arthritis and other connective tissue disorders are genetically transmitted, although the relatively less serious generalized arthritis and gout may have a genetic component.[22] The few studies available have not proven the belief that disability in a parent influences a child's psychological adjustment. In one study that compared the adjustment of children reared by fathers with either severe (quadriplegia) or less severe (paraplegia) physical disability, it was found that both groups developed into well-adjusted, adequately functioning adults as measured by the Minnesota Multiphasic Personality Inventory and the Sixteen Personality Factor Questionnaire. Neither body image nor sex role development was affected by the severity of the father's disability.[10]

Patients and spouses should be counseled on different aspects of sexual expression. Although genital intercourse is possible in the majority, foreplay, body contact, and stimulation of the secondary erogenous zones can be very enjoyable and even bring on a noncoital orgasm.[29,43] Stimulation of the breasts is particularly pleasurable with women.[43] Prosthetic devices and vibrators can be useful aids. Oral-genital sexual activity is possible for many and may be mutually acceptable. Sexual gratification includes enjoying the stimulating of the partner and experiencing feelings of adequacy and the satisfaction of being able to give pleasure to another person.[29] Activities such as holding, touching, kissing, and just being close are all emotionally gratifying.[34]

Older women also need to know that it is normal to continue to have sexual feelings and needs; they often have an increased need for closeness and touching.[5] Many marriages are based on mutual affection, love, and self-esteem,[29] and simple expressions of these by themselves may be adequately satisfying to both parties. Tenderness and companionship in the relationship should be stressed.[23]

The physician should be sensitive to and help preserve the patient's sexual identity. Aids such as splints are often rejected as markers of disability, and the doctor may need to give permission for such devices not to be worn every night or on every social occasion.[13]

MEDICATIONS AND TIMING

Sexual activities can be planned around times when the pain is minimal, when feeling least fatigued, and around periods of maximum effectiveness of pain medication.[18,21,23,36,45] Analgesic or antiinflammatory medications can be taken 30–60 minutes before sexual activity. The patient and partner should both be involved in the planning of the sexual encounter to improve compliance.[24] They need to understand that sexual activities need not be spontaneous to be enjoyable and that the time for preparations and anticipation can even ultimately heighten pleasure.[22,23,36]

Adequate medication should be used to control other associated problems of arthritis, such as inflammation and ulceration of the oral and genital tracts.[30] Intraarticular corticosteroid injections into the joints that are usually used in sexual activity has been recommended.[8]

PHYSIOTHERAPEUTIC MODALITIES

Moist heat from warm baths, showers, or compresses 10–15 minutes before sexual activity[42] is effective for relieving pain and muscle spasms, easing stiffness, improving joint motion, and promoting relaxation.[18,23,36,60] In addition, warm baths and showers can aid with personal hygiene and comfort prior to sex or can be part of the foreplay when performed along with the partner. Heat lamps can be used, and cold application may be helpful in others. Massage, vibration, and self-hypnosis can reduce pain and allow relaxation.[21,30]

Pillows and cushions can be placed under painful joints or limbs[28,36] but need to be removed after sex to avoid contractures.[8,45] Sterile water-soluble lubricants are useful in the dry vaginitis of Sjogren's syndrome[23] or can be used simply to improve lubrication. Orthotic splints can be used to stabilize, support, or protect unstable or painful joints.[30]

EXERCISE

Simple range of motion exercises to limber or warm up can follow application of moist heat.[23,36,60] Exercises should be nonweightbearing, and the patient should not exercise to the point of fatigue or pain.[22,45] Abduction exercises of the hips and flexion at the knees are recommended for the woman, and back and arm exercises for the man.[8]

POSITIONS AND TECHNIQUES

Most arthritis patients can find a comfortable position for intercourse through good communication and some experimentation. An excellent guide to position options is available from the Arthritis Foundation.[2] The customary frontal position requires hip mobility, but other positions are possible and may even be preferable.[60] Rear approaches are possible when abduction of the hip is precluded but flexion is possible.[22] Different positions of intercourse can relieve the woman from being underneath or the man from having to bear weight on painful arms or legs.[28]

Kegel exercises for developing pelvic musculature to increase vaginal grip on the penis can help women who want genital intercourse but for whom pelvic thrusting is painful or restricted. Water beds can also help with repetitive thrusting movements.[18] Pillows and cushions to support painful limbs should be kept handy.[28,36] Manual and oral methods of stimulation and gratification may be mutually enjoyable,[6,18,22,28] although a patient survey on alternative sexual techniques[6] ranked experimentation with positions of intercourse as the most acceptable and oral-genital sex as the least acceptable option.

Muscle relaxation techniques and mental imagery can be helpful for promoting comfort,[45] and sufficient rest and avoiding a heavy work schedule[8] prior to the "date" can conserve energy for the sexual activity. Makeup for women, use of toiletries, a stylish haircut, and dressing in attractive colors with a good cut and design helps an arthritic patient maintain a positive self-image of his or her personal appearance.[2,4,5]

SURGERY

Synovectomy still has a role in selected areas, such as the wrist, to relieve intractable pain.[60] Sexual problems related to hip disease, however, may be of primary importance to a younger patient, even more so than walking itself. Sexual difficulty may itself be a legitimate indication for surgery, especially joint replacement.[3,23,28,58]

In one study, 57% of patients claimed some relief of sexual difficulty after surgical treatment that included arthroplasty, osteotomy, excision, or arthrodesis of the hip.[19] Another study of sexually active patients reported that of those who expressed severe sexual difficulty related to hip disease, 43% of the women and 48% of the men had either complete or considerable relief of their sexual problem, with 95% and 91% respectively having relief of pain after total hip replacement.[55]

Following hip replacement, exaggerated abduction and external rotation and especially flexion, adduction, and internal rotation can dislodge the femoral head prosthesis from the acetabular cup. The patient needs counseling on these restrictions, and variable periods of abstinence from sexual intercourse ranging from 6–12 weeks are usually advocated.[8,21–23] The optimal position subsequently is supine, with side-lying and posterior entry being contraindicated due to adduction and flexion, respectively, at the hips.[8]

The surgical release of contracted adductor tendons to allow for intercourse and perineal hygiene may be a consideration in nonambulatory patients.[8] Rarely, a long abstinence from sexual activities is necessary when the patient has severe osteoporosis related to prolonged corticosteroid therapy.[8,21]

Social and Administrative Policy

Comprehensive management of severe disabling arthritis often requires long hospital stays and separation of the patient from the spouse.[22] Some hospitalization plans already allow for overnight passes, and a few hospitals, especially in the rehabilitation setting, have private or family rooms. Use of these privileges should be encouraged by the physician when appropriate.

SEXUALITY AND AMPUTATION

Problems with Sexuality in Amputees

Sexuality in amputees is a neglected subject. This is possibly due to the older age of the majority of amputees and the reluctance of health professionals to bring up what is often felt to be an embarassing subject. It is assumed, on the other hand, that younger patients do not have sexual problems.[29]

The available literature deals mainly with sexuality in surgical (dysvascular and, less frequently, because of tumor) and traumatic amputees, with a serious lack of information on congenital limb deficiencies. There appear to be several recurring problems that influence sexual activity. These include positioning and balancing, phantom sensation, phantom pain, depression, and other emotional issues. Distortion of body image and medical problems related to the original disease process are the other common issues.[18,29,50]

During sex play and intercourse, positioning might present a challenge due to poor balance, for instance, in an older man with an above-knee amputation. There can also be decreased mobility after the loss of a limb. Others are unable to assume their usual coital position due to inability to bear weight on a painful upper or lower limb stump. Loss of a dominant upper limb decreases ease of sexual foreplay, including caressing and manual stimulation.[18,29]

Phantom sensation, which is experienced by 35% of all amputees,[18] can be most perturbing when one forgets and leans on a limb that is no longer there. Phantom pain, on the other hand, is a serious problem that occurs more commonly than often realized by health care professionals. It occurred in one survey in more than 90% of veterans who were amputees.[51] It is most often seen in surgical amputees, especially when there was limb pain preoperatively. It can be severe, increasing with time in 5–10% of patients. In some cases, healthy areas of the body can act as trigger zones for the phantom or stump pain.[18]

The psychological and emotional effects of an amputation are considerable, with many patients equating the loss of a limb to loss of manhood or femininity. There is distortion of body image and the feeling of no longer being whole. The mourning period for the lost body part sometimes can be pathologically prolonged. Depression and anxiety are often present; feelings of dependency and frustrations over lack of mobility and subsequent enforced isolation are not uncommon.[21]

Amputees who have diabetes or who have undergone bilateral lumbar sympathectomy have a higher incidence of neurogenic impotence. Retrograde ejaculation or inability to ejaculate is often present. Blood flow also may be an issue, with microvascular disease in diabetes interfering with normal engorgement of the penile cavernous sinuses.[25]

Management

Changes in position for intercourse may sometimes be all that is needed—for example, from the man above to the woman above or switching sides to lie on. This frees up use of the normal arm and avoids weightbearing on the amputated stump.[18,29] Phantom limb is a common phenomenon, and providing information regarding this before the operation to the patient is helpful.

Phantom pain can be a more difficult problem; the host of recommended treatment approaches[18,50] is indicative of its sometimes intractable nature. With referred pain, such as may occur from impacted or loaded bowels or impinged nerves, the management begins with treatment of these problems. Local measures include intermittent pressure on the stump, massage, moist or dry heat, and ultrasound to the stump. Transcutaneous electrical nerve stimulation (TENS) with one electrode on the stump and the other near the sensory nerve root of the painful dermatome can be used before and during sex.[18] Low-dose tricyclic antidepressants, especially amitriptyline, may be very useful by helping with both sleep and pain.

EMG muscle tension feedback helps in relieving stump spasms. Sympathetic blocks or acupuncture[46] provides help in some patients. Behavioral and relaxation techniques such as biofeedback, guided fantasy, and hypnosis have been attempted. Medications including beta blockers and benzodiazepines may help to control pain. With the last drug category, caution must be exercised due to the potential for addiction. Diazepam itself can also produce diminished libido. When there is triggering of pain from healthy areas, good communication between the patient and partner will help avoid this problem.[18] A poor prosthetic fit may cause nociceptor sensitization; prosthetic refitting and gait correction may provide the solution.[50]

Psychotherapy for depression and anxiety is helpful although, in most cases, the passing of time improves matters. A period of mourning for the lost limb is natural, but after the prosthesis is fitted, its use mastered, and independence regained, mood, self-esteem, and interest in sex usually improve. Encouragement and reassurance by the partner, family, and physician on personal attractiveness and independence will be supportive. Counseling on changes to be expected with amputation and options for positioning should be recommended for all patients. In more difficult cases where adjustment is not proceeding well, intensive psychotherapy and medications for depression or premorbid issues may be necessary.[18,21,50]

When an organic cause for impotence is present, counseling may be required for extragenital means of sexual expression. For patients with erectile problems, penile shells, penile implants of various designs, and vacuum pump systems (such as the ErecAid) to produce an erection can allow for genital intercourse. The technique of "stuffing" the penis into the vagina, the process of which may or may not produce a reasonable erection, can still be satisfying for some patients.[18]

SEXUALITY AND SCOLIOSIS

One study[15] was available on sexuality in women with mostly class III scoliosis 4 or more years after treatment. Half of the patients were treated conservatively by bracing and the other half by posterior fusion surgically. There was no significant difference in psychological adjustment, except higher Global Sexual Satisfaction Inventory (GSSI) scores, a scale that reflects the individual's subjective judgment concerning quality of sexual activity in those with scoliosis compared to controls without scoliosis. This means that individuals with scoliosis claimed greater overall sexual satisfaction. This finding was thought to possibly be reflective of denial in the face of subconscious feelings of impairment and related sexual conflicts, or it may have been due to the higher motivation for intimacy (a stronger pull for closeness with others) in subjects with scoliosis. The controls had greater subconscious self-esteem and freedom from body image disturbance.[15]

Women treated by spinal fusion claimed better sexual adjustment and had higher GSSI scores than the braced group; they also had less subconscious impairment of self-esteem and body image. The findings were not related to the severity of the scoliotic curves.[15]

SEXUALITY AND PELVIC FRACTURES

With the frequency of road traffic accidents and high speeds of motorized vehicles, fractures of the pelvis are becoming more common and severe.[39] Significant pain can arise from the sacroiliac joint or from a fixation across the pubic symphysis and interfere with sexual function in men.[44] Although lateral compression injuries rarely produce any problems, when there is tilting of the pubic rami towards the perineum, dyspareunia can result. With open pelvic fractures in women, a pelvic examination is mandatory, because there can be vaginal injury along with involvement of the rectum, bowel, and urinary bladder.[37]

Impotency is another major problem in pelvic fractures. The articles reviewed[14,27,39] quoted incidences ranging from 2.6% to 80% from various other sources. Within the authors' own patients, there appeared to be a higher incidence of persistent impotence associated with urethral injury, with rates of 26–43%.[14,27,39] However, the study producing the highest number, 43%[39] had a broader definition of impotence that included failure to achieve orgasm, retrograde ejaculation, or failure to ejaculate. Impotency is more common particularly after complete rupture of the membranous urethra.[14,27] The possible causes of impotence in these patients include interruption of the blood supply, neurogenic injury especially to the nervi erigentes, or psychological concerns.[14,39]

SUMMARY

Concern with sexuality is not merely an issue with the disabled. A great number of nondisabled people struggle with problems and worries of the same nature.[6] Sexuality in musculoskeletal conditions is an important issue, however, in part because of the large numbers of people it does or will affect.

REFERENCES

1. Annon JS: The Behavioral Treatment of Sexual Problems. Vol. 1. New York, Harper & Row, 1976, pp 48–119.
2. Arthritis Foundation: Living and loving: Information about sexuality and intimacy [pamphlet]. Atlanta, Arthritis Foundation, 1993.
3. Baldursson H, Brattstrom H: Sexual difficulties and total hip replacement in rheumatoid arthritis. Scand J Rheumatol 8:214–216, 1979.
4. Baum J: A review of the psychological aspects of rheumatic diseases. Semin Arthritis Rheum 11:352–361, 1982.
5. Bernhard LA, Dan AJ: Redefining sexuality from women's own experiences. Nurs Clin North Am 21:125–136, 1986.
6. Blake DJ, Maisiak R, Alarcon GS, et al: Sexual quality-of-life of patients with arthritis compared to arthritis-free controls. J Rheumatol 14:570–576, 1987.
7. Blake DJ, Weaver W, Maisiak R, et al: A curriculum in clinical sexuality for arthritis health care professionals. Psychosomatics 31:189–191, 1990.
8. Brassell MP, Katz WA: Sexuality and arthritis. In Katz WA (ed): Diagnosis and management of rheumatic diseases. 2nd ed. Philadelphia, JB Lippincott, 1988, pp 71–976.
9. Brown GMM, Dare CM, Smith PR, Meyers OL: Important problems identified by patients with chronic arthritis. S Afr Med J 72:126–128, 1987.
10. Buck FM, Hohmann GW: Child adjustment as related to severity of parental disability. Arch Phys Med Rehabil 63:249–253, 1982.
11. Chamberlain MA: Socioeconomic effects of ankylosing spondylitis. Int Rehabil Med 3:94–99, 1981.
12. Chamberlain MA: Socioeconomic effects of ankylosing spondylitis in females: A comparison of 25 female with 25 male subjects. Int Rehabil Med 5:149–153, 1983.
13. Chamberlain MA, Ellis M, Hughes D: Joint protection. Clin Rheum Dis 10:727–742, 1984.
14. Chambers HL, Balfour J: The incidence of impotence following pelvic fracture with associated urinary tract injury. J Urol 89:702–703, 1963.
15. Clayson D, Luz-Alterman S, Cataletto MM, Levine DB: Long-term psychological sequelae of surgically versus nonsurgically treated scoliosis. Spine 12:983–986, 1987.
16. Cohen M: Sexuality and the arthritic patient—how well are we doing? [editorial].J Rheumatol 14:403–405, 1987.
17. Cole TM, Cole SS: Rehabilitation of problems of sexuality in physical disability. In Kottke FJ, Lehmann JF, Stillwell GK (eds): Krusen's Handbook of Physical Medicine and Rehabilitation. 4th ed. Philadelphia, WB Saunders, 1990, pp 988–1008.
18. Conine TA, Evans JH: Sexual reactivation of chronically ill and disabled adults. J Allied Health 11:261–270, 1982.
19. Currey HLF: Osteoarthrosis of the hip joint and sexual activity. Ann Rheum Dis 29:488–493, 1970.
20. Derogatis LR: Psychological assessment of psychosexual functioning. Psychiatr Clin North Am 3:113–131, 1980.
21. Ducharme S, Gill K, Biener-Bergman S, Fertitta L: Sexual functioning: Medical and psychological aspects. In DeLisa JA (ed): Rehabilitation Medicine: Principles and Practice. 2nd ed. Philadelphia, JB Lippincott, 1993, pp 763–782.
22. Ehrlich GE: Sexual problems of the arthritic patient. In Ehrlich GE (ed): Total Management of the Arthritic Patient. Philadelphia, JB Lippincott, 1973, pp 193–208.
23. Ehrlich GE: Sexual problems of the arthritic. In Comfort A (ed): Sexual Consequences of Disability. Philadelphia, George F Stickley Co, 1978, pp 61–83.
24. Ehrlich GE: Social, economic, psychologic, and sexual outcomes in rheumatoid arthritis. Am J Med 75(6A):27–34, 1983.
25. Ellenberg N: Impotence in diabetes: The neurogenic factor. Ann Intern Med 75:213–219, 1971.
26. Elst P, Sybesma T, van der Stadt RJ, et al: Sexual problems in rheumatoid arthritis and ankylosing spondylitis. Arthritis Rheum 27:217–220, 1984.
27. Gibson GR: Impotence following fractured pelvis and ruptured urethra. Br J Urol 42:86–88, 1970.
28. Greengross W: Sex and arthritis. Rheumatol Rehabil (suppl):68–70, 1979.
29. Griffith ER, Trieschmann RB, Hohmann GW, et al: Sexual dysfunctions associated with physical disabilities. Arch Phys Med Rehabil 56:8–13, 1975.
30. Hamilton A: Sexual problems of the disabled. In Nichols PJR (ed): Rehabilitation Medicine: The Management of Physical Disabilities. 2nd ed. London, Butterworths and Co, 1980, pp 286–302.
31. Halstead LS: Aiding arthritic patients to adjust sexually. Med Aspects Hum Sex 85–86, April 1977.

32. Herstein A, Hill RH, Walters K: Adult sexuality and juvenile rheumatoid arthritis. J Rheumatol 4:35–39, 1977.
33. Hill RH, Herstein A, Walters K: Juvenile rheumatoid arthritis: Follow-up into adulthood—Medical, sexual and social status. Can Med Assoc J 114:790–796, 1976.
34. Hobson KG: The effects of aging on sexuality. Health Soc Work 9:25–35, 1984.
35. Kain CD, Reilly N, Schultz ED: The older adult. A comparative assessment. Nurs Clin North Am 25:833–848, 1990.
36. Katzin L: Chronic illness and sexuality. Am J Nurs 90:54–59, 1990.
37. Kellam JF, McMurtry RY, Paley D, Tile M: The unstable pelvic fracture. Operative treatment. Orthop Clin North Am 18:25–41, 1987.
38. Kellerman J, Zeltzer L, Ellenberg L, et al: Psychological effects of illness in adolescence. I. Anxiety, self-esteem, and perception of control. J Pediatr 97:126–131, 1980.
39. King J: Impotence after fractures of the pelvis. J Bone Joint Surg 57A:1107–1109, 1975.
40. Kottke FJ, Lehmann JF, Stillwell GK: Preface. In Kottke FJ, Lehmann JF, Stillwell GK (eds): Krusen's Handbook of Physical Medicine and Rehabilitation. 4th ed. Philadelphia, WB Saunders, 1990, p xxix.
41. Krajicek MJ: Developmental disability and human sexuality. Nurs Clin North Am 17:377–386, 1982.
42. Lipe H, Longstreth WT, Bird TD, Linde M: Sexual function in married men with Parkinson's disease compared to married men with arthritis. Neurology 40:1347–1349, 1990.
43. MacRae I, Henderson G: Sexuality and irreversible health limitations. Nurs Clin North Am 10:587–597, 1975.
44. Majeed SA: Grading the outcome of pelvic fractures. J Bone Joint Surg 71B:304–306, 1989.
45. Malek CJ, Brower SA: Rheumatoid arthritis: How does it influence sexuality. Rehabil Nurs 9:26–28, 1984.
46. Monga TN, Jaksic T: Acupuncture in phantom limb pain. Arch Phys Med Rehabil 62:229–231, 1981.
47. Polley HF, Swenson WN, Steinhilber R: Personality characteristics of patients with rheumatoid arthritis. Psychosomatics 11:45–49, 1970.
48. Rogers MP, Liang MH, Partridge AJ: Psychological care of adults with rheumatoid arthritis. Ann Intern Med 96:344–348, 1982.
49. Sadoughi W, Leshner M, Fine HL: Sexual adjustment in a chronically ill and physically disabled population: A pilot study. Arch Phys Med Rehabil 52:311–317, 1971.
50. Sherman RA, Tippens JK: Suggested guidelines for treatment of phantom limb pain. Orthopedics 5:1595–1600, 1982.
51. Sherman RA, Sherman CJ: Prevalence and characteristics of chronic phantom limb pain among American veterans: Results of a trial survey. Am J Phys Med 62:227–238, 1983.
52. Smith LL: Helping to manage the emotional effects of arthritis. Health Soc Work 4:134–150, 1979.
53. Statistical Abstract of the United States 1993. 113th ed. The Reference Press, 1993.
54. Swezey RL, Weiner SR: Rehabilitation medicine and arthritis. In McCarty DJ (ed): Arthritis and Allied Conditions. 10th ed. Philadelphia, Lea & Febiger, 1985, pp 692–721.
55. Todd RC, Lightowler CDR, Harris J: Low friction arthroplasty of the hip joint and sexual activity. Acta Orthop Scand 44:690, 1973.
56. Vemireddi NK: Sexual counseling for chronically disabled patients. Geriatrics 33:65–69, 1978.
57. Vershys HP: Physical rehabilitation and family dynamics. Rehabil Lit 41:58–65, 1980.
58. Yoshino S, Uchida S: Sexual problems of women with rheumatoid arthritis. Arch Phys Med Rehabil 62:122–123, 1981.
59. Zeltzer L, Kellerman J, Ellenberg L, Dash J, Rigler D: Psychologic effects of illness in adolescence. II. Impact of illness in adolescents—Crucial issues and coping styles. J Pediatr 97:132–138, 1980.
60. Zurier RB: Rheumatoid disease; an overview. Conn Med 39:348–353, 1975.

UMA MONGA, MD

SEXUALITY IN CANCER PATIENTS

From the Radiation Therapy
    Service
Veterans Administration Medical
    Center
Houston, Texas

Reprint request to:
Uma Monga, MD
Radiation Therapy Service
Houston VA Medical Center
2002 Holcombe Blvd.
Houston, TX 77030

The outcome of cancer treatment with surgery, radiotherapy, and chemotherapy has traditionally been assessed on the basis of disease-free survival. However, neoplastic disease and its treatment can interfere with many of the cellular, anatomic, physiologic, behavioral, and social processes that contribute to normal sexual and reproductive function. Thus, it is important that those treating cancer patients today should look beyond survival and address quality of life issues including sexual function.

Although controversy exists regarding the extent and nature of sexual problems in cancer patients, most reports confirm that cancer and its treatment have deleterious effects on sexual function. The incidence of sexual dysfunction following various cancer treatments ranges from 40–100%.[48]

Efforts are being made to refine surgical techniques and modify chemotherapy and radiotherapy regimens to reduce sexual morbidity and improve quality of life while retaining the primary objective of cure. This chapter reviews the impact of cancer and its treatment on sexuality in patients with a diagnosis of cancer.

Sexuality is a complex process. Sexual function may be disrupted by many physiological and psychological factors (Table 1). While age at the time of diagnosis, other medical conditions, and their management, affect sexual function, diagnosis of cancer and its management has a profound impact. Anxiety, depression, and emotional state all affect sexual function. Pain medication may also influence the sexual response. Cancer treatment may damage the central or peripheral nervous system and affect the endocrine system, thus altering the sexual response.

TABLE 1.   Factors Influencing Sexual Function

Physiologic	Cancer	Psychological
Aging	Cancer-related	Self-esteem
Medical conditions	Effects on gonads in Hodgkins disease	Coping skills
Diabetes mellitus	Cancer treatment-related	Depression
Hypertension	Surgery	Anxiety
Cerebrovascular accident	Body image	Body image
Arthritis	Neurovascular bundle damage	Relationships
Atherosclerotic heart disease	Radiotherapy	Role responsibility
Medical treatment	Vascular compromise	
Antidepressants	Effects on gonads	
Antihypertensives	Chemotherapy	
	Effects on gonads	

SURGERY AND SEXUAL FUNCTIONING

Many cancer patients report sexual problems following surgery. These may result from damage to the autonomic nervous system, vascular compromise of the genitals, or endocrine effects. Postoperative disfigurement and a change in body image also may influence sexual functioning.

Pelvic Surgery in Men

Various pelvic and retroperitoneal operative procedures may impair erection and ejaculation. The physiology of penile erection and ejaculation has been outlined in chapter 2. Briefly, the pelvic plexus is formed by parasympathetic visceral efferent preganglionic fibers that arise from the sacral center (S2–S4) and sympathetic fibers from the thoracolumbar region via the hypogastric nerve. The pelvic plexus is located retroperitoneally on the lateral wall of the rectum 5–11 cm from the anal verge. Branches of the pelvic plexus provide innervation to the rectum, bladder, prostate, seminal vesicles, urethra, and corpora cavernosa. Intraoperatively, the seminal vesicles can be used to identify the pelvic plexus. The cavernous nerves travel from the pelvic plexus toward the posterolateral base of the prostate gland. They lie in close association with the capsular arteries and veins of the prostate in the lateral pelvic fascia outside the prostate capsule and outside Denonvilliers' fascia. The cavernous nerves and the capsular vessels of the prostate gland form the neurovascular bundle. The cavernous nerves can be identified intraoperatively as they travel posterolateral to the prostate on the anterolateral surface of the rectum.

Radical pelvic surgery may be necessary in patients with prostate, bladder, or rectal cancer. Interruption of parasympathetic innervation during radical pelvic procedures, such as total prostatectomy and cystectomy, have been reported to cause erectile dysfunction.[44,146,204,208] Sympathectomy during retroperitoneal operations may lead to an inability to ejaculate. This is the principal morbidity following retroperitoneal lymphadenectomy for testicular tumors.[45,104,179]

PROSTATE CANCER

Prostate cancer is the most commonly diagnosed cancer in elderly men. Approximately 80% of cases occur in men older than 65.

Treatment for early stage prostate cancer is either surgery or radiotherapy. Erectile dysfunction has been frequently reported following radical proctectomy; 80–95% of patients were reportedly unable to achieve adequate erection for vaginal penetration.[42,57,90,129,195,197] In 1982, Walsh and Donker[195] demonstrated that impotence often followed radical prostatectomy due to injury to the branches of the pelvic plexus that innervate the corpora cavernosa. They proposed modifications in surgical technique to avoid this complication. In their study with nerve sparing prostatic surgery, 259 of the 320 patients with prostate cancer were potent preoperatively and 192 (74% of the 259) remained potent postoperatively. Return of potency was gradual, taking up to a year or more for many men. Potency was correlated with the age of the patient and the stage of the disease. Potency returned in 93% of patients with stage A1 disease versus 56% of patients with stage B2 disease.[200]

In another study, Walsh et al.[196] assessed the quality of erections in patients with preservation of one neurovascular bundle. Although 69% of the patients met the usual criteria of potency, only 32% reported normal rigidity. The authors concluded that potency can be maintained following radical prostatectomy in 69% of patients even when it is necessary to widely excise one neurovascular bundle.

Others have reported similar results with nerve sparing procedures for sexual preservation.[100,131] Quinlan reported that age, clinical and pathologic stage of the tumor, and extent of nerve preservation correlated with potency after surgery. Patients older than 70 had only a 22% chance of postoperative potency even after sparing of bilateral neurovascular bundles. Extension of cancer through the prostatic capsule and seminal vesical invasion (stage C) had a significant impact on postoperative potency in that it required more extensive surgery.[131]

Various studies have shown that nerve sparing modifications do not compromise the adequacy of tumor removal.[195,200] Bigg[21] questioned the efficacy of nerve sparing prostatectomy in preserving erectile ability and achieving good surgical margins in patients with bulky, clinical stage B2 cases. Only 20% of men with stage B2 disease achieved the dual goals of clear margins and preservation of erectile function.

Colorectal Cancer

Cancer of the colon and rectum is the second most common cancer in North America. Surgery remains the mainstay of treatment and includes resection of the tumor and pelvic lymphadenectomy. Operative procedures such as abdominoperineal resection and retroperitoneal lymphadenectomy may damage the autonomic nervous system, causing erectile dysfunction and problems with ejaculation.

The prevalence of erectile difficulties following standard abdominoperineal resection has been reported to be 15–100%.[13,70,96,149,204] Patients undergoing low anterior resection had a lower incidence (20–30%) of erectile problems than those who had abdominoperineal resection (45–55%).[74,92,96,149] The critical site of parasympathetic damage is at the level of the prostatic plexus.

Hojo[78] reported the effect of wide iliopelvic lymphadenectomy on survival, micturition, and sexual function in patients with carcinoma of the rectum. He concluded that wide iliopelvic lymphadenectomy was successful in decreasing the incidence of local recurrence and in prolonging survival. However, there was an increased incidence of bladder dysfunction and sexual impotency. In another study, Hojo et al.[79] examined 134 patients with rectal cancer who underwent pelvic lymphadenectomy with selective preservation of the pelvic autonomic nerves; 31% of the patients recovered erectile function, and only 19% recovered normal ejaculatory function in the first postoperative year. The authors concluded that preservation of male sexual function is difficult, requires a high degree of nerve preservation, and should be restricted to patients with Dukes' A and B carcinomas.

Impaired emission is also common after abdominoperineal resection because of dissection in the presacral area and area between the seminal vesicles and rectum.[149,182,209] The incidence of impaired emission increases with the extent of the dissection.[182]

CARCINOMA OF THE BLADDER

Erectile dysfunction has been documented in patients undergoing radical cystectomy.[11,157,191] The prevalence of erectile problems is 70–100%. Dry orgasm is always experienced after radical cystectomy. Sexual desire is usually not altered by these surgical procedures.[80]

Schover[157] assessed 73 men preoperatively and 6 months following radical cystectomy with ileal conduit diversion and found that while 20% of the patients were sexually inactive before the surgery, 50% were inactive postoperatively. Similarly, 35% and 91% had some erectile dysfunction preoperatively and postoperatively, respectively.

With nerve sparing radical cystectomy, 83% of men had recovery of erections; however, the recovery was not good in patients who subsequently required complete urethrectomy.[201]

TESTICULAR TUMORS

Testicular tumors typically affect young men. Treatment usually includes unilateral orchidectomy and sometimes retroperitoneal lymphadenectomy, followed by radiotherapy for seminomatous tumors and chemotherapy for nonseminomatous tumors.

Bilateral retroperitoneal lymph node dissection (RLND) usually damages the sympathetic ganglion. Sympathetic input is responsible for contraction of the prostate and seminal vesicles during emission, as well as for closure of the bladder neck at emission. Dry orgasms following RLND may be due to retrograde ejaculation or lack of smooth muscle contraction. Bracken[24] described patients with retrograde ejaculation secondary to surgical damage of the paraaortic sympathetic nervous system. Attempts have been made to preserve fertility and prevent dry orgasm by modifying RLND and sparing the crucial sympathetic ganglion.[51,85,163] Schover[163] reported a 38% prevalence of dry orgasm (either retrograde ejaculation or a failure of ejaculation) in their patients who underwent RLND. Donohue[51] reported no dry orgasm in 75 patients who underwent nerve-sparing RLND. This procedure does not cause erectile dysfunction. Takasaki et al.[178] concluded that unilateral retroperitoneal lymph node dissection without injury to the superior hypogastric plexus preserved ejaculatory function.

The effect of unilateral orchidectomy on mean sperm density and fertility is not clear because many patients have low counts before any treatment.

Pelvic Surgery in Women

Since most studies of sexuality following pelvic surgery have been carried out in women who have had several types of treatment, it is difficult to assess the specific effects of surgery on sexual function in women. Furthermore, the literature reveals that most studies used frequency of intercourse as the only indicator of the quality of sexual function. The prevalence of sexuality problems in women after treatment for gynecologic cancer varies from 0% to nearly 100%.[1] So far, research indicates that sexuality undergoes the greatest disruption after gynecological cancer.[2,3]

Schover et al.[159] found that cancer treatment was frequently followed by disturbances of libido and orgasmic function. Postmenopausal women were more likely to have decreased desire and arousal or to have dyspareunia.

CANCER OF THE CERVIX

Treatment approaches for invasive cervical cancer include radical hysterectomy or radiation therapy. Radical hysterectomy for invasive early-stage cancer of the cervix includes removal of uterus, cervix, and upper third to half of the vagina-surrounding ligaments and pelvic lymph-node dissection. Impaired sexual function occurs in 6–42% of patients undergoing radical hysterectomy.[159]

In a prospective study of women who had cervical conization, no impairment of sexual desire, frequency of coital activity, or ability to achieve a satisfactory orgasm was found.[89] In a case-control study of sexual function in women 6 months after radical surgery for cervical cancer, the patients had a significantly less positive view of themselves as sexual partners than did the control group.[183]

Attempts have been made to compare the relative incidence of sexual problems in patients with cervical cancer after surgery or radiotherapy.[159,187] No significant difference in sexual function between surgery and radiation therapy could be found 6 months after treatment. However, at 1 year of follow-up, both groups reported decreased sexual interest and postcoital bleeding. Patients treated with radiation therapy reported more problems with arousal (29% versus 6%) and dyspareunia (22% versus 0%) than patients treated with surgery.

In Schover's study,[159] 26 women were interviewed and completed questionnaires before radical hysterectomy and 6 months and 1 year postoperatively. These patients did not report any significant change in their ability to reach orgasm from masturbation, noncoital stimulation, or intercourse. Sexual desire, arousal, and satisfaction with sexual activity were maintained at pre-illness levels. However, at 1 year of follow-up, 10% of the women reported dyspareunia.

CARCINOMA OF THE VULVA

Simple vulvectomy is removal of the labia majora and minora; radical vulvectomy includes removal of the vulva, clitoris, and femoral and inguinal lymph nodes. During radical vulvectomy, parts of the urethra, vagina, and anus are sometimes removed. Marked dyspareunia due to scarring and narrowing of the vagina is common in these patients. These procedures may result in loss of erogenous tissue, leading to loss of desire, difficulty in reaching orgasm, and lack of pleasurable genital sensations.[6]

Stellman[174] reported that patients with simple vulvectomy were no more sexually functional or satisfied with their sexual function than were those with radical vulvectomy. However, others report that better preservation of sexual function was achieved with wide local excision than with radical vulvectomy in patients with "in situ disease."[4,50]

In a prospective study of 10 women undergoing radical vulvar surgery, Weijmar[203] reported that half of the patients regained the ability to achieve orgasm. However, they experienced increased unpleasant sensations during intercourse. Despite these problems, sexual satisfaction and level of sexual activity recovered to pretreatment levels in these five patients.

In a study of the effects of vulvectomy on 15 women with an age range of 50–70, Andersen and Hacker[4] found a marked postoperative reduction in sexual activity. Many women had persistent numbness, to the point that some were unable to recognize penile penetration. Many of the patients felt that the information provided to them regarding sexuality was either absent or falsely reassuring.

Stellman et al.[174] compared patients who had vulvectomy for early-stage carcinoma of the vulva to patients in whom the hysterectomy was performed for stage II endometrial carcinoma. This allowed them to compare groups with the diagnosis of cancer, a similar 5-year survival rate, and removal of a genital organ. Postvulvectomy patients were more likely to be depressed, anxious, and not sexually active; they also had serious problems with their body image.

Moth et al.[123] also found a marked reduction in coital frequency in patients following vulvectomy. Most patients stopped coital activity because of dyspareunia. Other symptoms included hyperesthesia, irritation, and pruritus, all of which became worse during intercourse. Many of the partners reported negative feelings about their physical disfigurement.

The clitoris may need to be sacrificed in cases of vulvar cancer, and this may cause problems in arousal and achievement of orgasm. However, in one report the loss of the clitoris was not associated with inability to achieve orgasm following various surgical procedures for vulvar cancer.[4]

Carcinoma of the Rectum

In women, abdominoperineal resection for rectal cancer sometimes includes hysterectomy and excision of the posterior vaginal wall. Pelvic lymphadenectomy may damage the autonomic nervous system. However, very little information is available regarding sexual function in women undergoing pelvic lymphadenectomy.

In a study of 18 women who were sexually active before the diagnosis of rectal carcinoma, 78% reported loss of sexual desire, 44% noted decreased overall satisfaction with sexual functioning, and 34% experienced dyspareunia.[39] Dyspareunia is most likely due to pelvic adhesions after surgery.

Disfigurement and Sexual Decline

Surgical intervention in patients with breast cancer, gynecologic cancer, and cancer of head and neck area may result in body disfigurement. Some of these changes are visible, such as loss of the nose or jaw, and some are not visible.

Disfigurement from any cause produces psychosocial problems, altered body image, anxiety, and depression. Premorbid psychological status, stability of the relationship, and coping skills will influence postoperative psychological function. Psychosocial dysfunction is one of the major factors influencing sexual problems in cancer patients. Low sexual desire is more common in patients who are depressed and coping poorly with their cancer.[158]

Breast Cancer

Breast cancer in the most common malignancy in women. It is now widely accepted that comparable survival rates can be obtained in early-stage disease following either modified radical mastectomy or breast-conserving surgery and radiation. A number of investigators have compared psychological and sexual function outcomes following these two approaches.[26,37,153,155] Some believe that sexual morbidity in breast cancer patients and their partners is more widespread, complex, more disruptive, and less willfully identified than had previously been speculated.[152] Others hold the viewpoint that a woman's overall psychological health, satisfaction with spousal relationship, and premorbid sexual life are far stronger predictors of postcancer sexual satisfaction than the extent of damage to her breast.[155]

Unfortunately, the available data on sexuality after breast cancer treatment are nonspecific. Most of the studies simply ask about overall satisfaction with sex or coital frequency. Patients have not been assessed on a longitudinal basis to better understand the natural history of these problems.

Renneker[137] and Bard[15] were the first to describe the profound psychological distress associated with disfigurement following the standard Halsted radical mastectomy. Other studies have confirmed that a significant number of women undergoing radical mastectomy experience psychosocial and sexual problems.[22,43,83,99,111,122,128,173,206] The reported prevalence of sexual problems, including decreased coital frequency and anorgasmia following mastectomy, ranges from 21–30%.[17,60] Marital problems are significantly more frequent in patients who had mastectomy for breast cancer than those with benign breast disease.[122]

Miller[115] concluded that almost 25% of mastectomy patients routinely experience disruptive mood and psychosocial dysfunction for up to 1 year after the initial surgery. Many women and their partners suffer from depression, anxiety, suicidal thoughts, sexual problems, lower self-esteem, and family maladjustment.

Various authors have confirmed the presence of a postmastectomy depression complex.[43,55,102,111,122] However, some studies have shown that women with early-stage breast cancer do not show any significant difference in psychiatric disorders, sexual problems, or marital happiness than other women with similar demographics.[188,205]

The negative impact can be intensified by distress caused by a fear of rejection by the partner, fear of performance failure, and fear of pain and discomfort during sexual activities. All these areas of concern will compromise sexual excitement, arousal, and orgasm.

A positive body image and self-esteem are critical for optimal psychological and sexual functioning.[87] Breast conservation may positively influence body image and self-esteem. Some recent studies[16,88,110,189] found less psychosocial morbidity with breast preservation surgery than with radical procedures. Breast conservation[99,173] and reconstruction[47] have been shown to preserve body image and maintain a perception of sexual attractiveness. They also contributed positively to the perception that the sexual partner's reactions were unchanged.

In a review of 12 studies on the effectiveness of breast conservation and reconstruction in preventing or ameliorating sexual problems in cancer patients, Schover[155] concluded that the impact of these modifications is subtle and may relate to the woman's perception of being less desirable rather than how often she has intercourse. She states that women whose breasts are conserved have more positive feelings about their bodies.

Although breast reconstruction procedures may restore a woman to a near normal appearance, these procedures are not without limitations. Each procedure has operative risks and potential for infection. The incision site may be quite painful, and some scarring is inevitable. Although reconstructive procedures are available, only a small number of patients choose to have the surgery.[154] In a study by Gerard,[62] sexual arousal and responsiveness was quicker in patients who had reconstructive surgery than in those who did not. Patients who have undergone reconstructive surgery reported improved body image.

A detailed assessment of the effect of breast reconstruction on a woman's sexual desire, feeling of sexual attractiveness, comfort with nudity in sexual situations, and range of sexual practices needs to be carried out.[155]

Lymphedema, one of the complications of radical mastectomy and radiation, causes disfigurement, pain, and disability. Psychosocial problems in patients with lymphedema are yet to be studied.

The reactions after breast surgery are clearly not the exclusive responsibility of either the patient or her partner but are rather an intricate interweaving of their personalities, habits, attitudes, and defenses, as well as a reflection of the quality of the relationship as a whole.[40] There is a paucity of information regarding the partner's reaction to breast cancer. Some partners may withdraw from making sexual requests for fear of physically hurting their spouses. Other partners appear to be disturbed by the physical appearance after surgery.[69] Body image distractions can also block arousal and excitement in men.[152] A man may withdraw affection and sexual energy as a form of self-protection. The frequency of intercourse and degree of satisfaction may only be a part of the more "malignant" process of withdrawal.

Wellisch et al.[206] reported the response to a self-report questionnaire administered to 31 men. Men who were involved in the decision process for treatment were more satisfied with their sex life. The better the men felt about the relationship, the less disrupted was the sexual interaction. These findings dictate the need for involving partners in decision making and early rehabilitation efforts. Stillerman[175] reported similar findings. In their study, reactions of the partner were more dependent on the patient's depression, anxiety, and body image.

Wabrek and Wabrek[193] identified some practical aspects of the physical environment that might inhibit resumption of sexual activity, such as particular positions in bed that could make sexual relations less comfortable.

The relationship between age and positive feelings about one's breasts is not clear. However, one's self-image and view of sexuality is critical for sexual arousal and responsiveness. In general, a young woman's psychological and sexual adaptation is more negatively affected by breast cancer surgery than an older woman's.[17] However, the older woman may feel equal distress but may be too self-conscious to express it.[67]

RECTAL CARCINOMA

Patients with colostomies or ileostomies may have emotional problems that impair sexual enjoyment. These patients face issues of changed body image and problems related to the colostomy itself. Many patients have difficulty adjusting to the odor, dealing with cleanliness, and may fear stool leakage.[125] Sutherland[177] concluded that the sexual impact of ostomy far exceeds the extent of physical handicap. Depression and anger are common emotional reactions and may contribute to a pattern of sexual avoidance.

In a study by Gloeckner,[65] 24 of 40 patients with ostomy reported feeling less attractive during the first year after surgery; 68% of the 24 patients reported improvement at follow-up (mean, 4.6 years).

It has been noted that men seek help for ostomy care from their wives. This new role of care provider may strain the intimate sexual relationship. On the other hand, women prefer to rely on nurses for advice and care. They tend to hide their ostomy by keeping their clothes on during intercourse or preferring the rear approach. Nilsson,[124] in his study on sexual adjustment in ileostomy patients before and after conversion to continent ileostomy, found that patients had better sexual adjustment after conversion.

Head and Neck Cancer

Although head and neck cancers are not common (they account for approximately 5% of all malignant tumors), they are often described as one of the most emotionally traumatic types of cancers.[27,53,91] Head and neck cancers usually require surgery and/or radiotherapy. Patients may develop swallowing or speech problems in addition to facial disfigurement.

Most studies report reduced self-esteem, social isolation, and fear of rejection.[23,49,56,61,75,97,121,130] However, very little information is available regarding the impact of disfigurement on sexual function, body image, and sexual relationships.

Dhillon[49] reported that 43% of the patients who had hemimandibulectomy for head and neck cancer became "social recluses." This was significantly greater than 11% of patients who had laryngectomy.

Monga et al.[119] examined sexuality and sexual adjustment in 20 patients with head and neck cancer. Derogatis Inventory of Sexual Functioning was used to assess sexual arousal, behavior, drive, fantasy, and orgasm. Severity of disfigurement was assessed as described by List.[106] Although only six patients were considered to have extensive disfigurement, the majority of patients were experiencing sexual problems. A total of 33% reported having no sex drive; 40% had ceased having intercourse; 60% were experiencing erectile problems, and 50% reported to have no orgasm. However, the majority performed masturbation. Although 50% were satisfied with their current sexual partner, only 20% were satisfied with their current sexual functioning.

The severity of disfigurement may have a negative influence on sexual function. MacGregor[109] stated that "looking at one another is our basic form of conversation" and that a person can be rejected or accepted on the basis of facial appearance alone. The relationship between severity of disfigurement and sexuality has been provided by Gamba.[61] Worsening of sexual function was more common in patients with extensive disfigurement than those who were considered to have mild disfigurement (74% vs 39%). A total of 45% of the patients reported problems with self-image. Again, this was more common in patients with extensive disfigurement (57% vs. 25%).

Excessive alcohol consumption is common in head and neck cancer patients. Alcohol produces both long- and short-term effects on sexuality. In general, with small amounts of alcohol, there is a release of inhibition that leads to a false perception of enhanced sexuality. Large amounts of alcohol produce erectile difficulties. Impotence results from chronic intake of alcohol. It is possible that some of the erectile problems reported in these patients are due to excessive drinking and predate the diagnosis of cancer.

Patients often have problems with swallowing and may need nasogastric or gastric tube feeding. Problems with breathing are also very common, requiring temporary or permanent tracheostomy. Some patients lose their voice and have problems with speech, necessitating electronic devices and other help for communication. Patients may prefer to eat alone in order to avoid embarrassment due to altered eating habits. Similarly, patients with tracheostomy may be embarrassed by the accompanying hissing sound, and some patients fear suffocation during sexual intercourse. This can lead to isolation and psychosocial problems. None of these factors have been examined in relation to sexuality in head and neck patients.

RADIOTHERAPY AND SEXUAL FUNCTIONING

Radiotherapy is one of the major modalities for treating cancer. It is often the primary modality given before or after surgery. Although radiotherapy cures cancer, it is not free from side effects. Some of the significant side effects are related to sexuality and reproduction. Improved techniques and a better knowledge of side effects have resulted in a decreased incidence of side effects.

Radiotherapy in Men

PROSTATE CANCER

Erectile impotence has been reported following pelvic irradiation for prostate cancer. The reported prevalence has varied from 10–84% in patients undergoing radiation therapy.[12,14,68,133,138] Although the cause of erectile dysfunction due to radiation therapy is not clear, dysfunction is believed to be caused by constriction of vessels following radiation. Men with prostate cancer are elderly and often have complex medical problems such as diabetes mellitus and peripheral vascular disease, leading to preexisting erectile problems unrelated to cancer.[184] Decline in libido and sexual performance also has been documented.[14]

In a retrospective study, Goldstein[68] reported that radiation therapy leads to fibrosis and stenosis of the pelvic arteries and may accelerate existing arteriosclerosis. Mittal,[118] in a small prospective case series, did not confirm these findings.

Men with excellent health and sexual function prior to treatment had a lower incidence of erectile problems following radiotherapy than men with less adequate sexual function and risk factors for cardiovascular disease.[12,14,184] In a prospective study by Banker,[14] only 27% of patients with normal pretreatment sexual function developed erectile problems, versus 54% in patients who had "borderline" erectile rigidity and coital frequency before treatment.

Prognosis for sexual preservation is better in younger than elderly patients. Men younger than 60 are often sexually active and, with early-stage disease, have a better chance of maintaining sexual potency.[14,210] Potency was preserved after definitive external beam irradiation in 50–60% of patients with adenocarcinoma of the prostate versus 85–93% of patients following radioactive implantation of the prostate.[77,95]

TESTICULAR TUMORS

Information on the effects of radiation on the human testis is limited because the testis is rarely directly irradiated in the clinical setting. However, the testis may receive a significant amount of scatter radiation during pelvic irradiation, and this can lead to infertility and impotence[82] (Table 2).

TABLE 2.   Effects of Testicular Failure

Hormonal	Physical	Sexual
↓ Testosterone	Testicular atrophy	Loss of libido
↑ Leutinizing hormone	Oligospermia	Erectile difficulties
↑ Leutinizing hormone-releasing	Azoospermia	Slow response
hormone	Sterility	Poor response
↑ Follicle-stimulating hormone	Sperm abnormalities	Impotency
		Ejaculatory problems
		Painful
		Dry
		Scanty

Effects on the germ cells are dose-dependent and are related to the stage of maturation at the time of irradiation.[143,211] Type B spermatogonia are the most radiosensitive; type A spermatogonia are more resistant because of their long cell cycle time.

Rowley ct al.[143] irradiated normal human testicles with a single dose of 8–60 cGy and found that morphologic and quantitative changes were seen following single doses as low as 10 cGy. Spermatocytes showed morphologic signs of injury with single doses of 4–6 cGy. Single doses in the range of 8–25 cGy produced moderate oligospermia, and azoospermia was noted with doses of 78–600 cGy. Azoospermia was temporary; recovery was eventually complete in all cases.[143] The single dose required for permanent sterilization is probably in the range of 6–9.5 Gy.[66,108]

Slanina et al.[170] reported long-term side effects of radiation in patients with Hodgkin's disease. The authors concluded that patients undergoing mantle or inverted Y radiation received between 5–15 rad of scatter radiation to the testis per treatment, with a total dose of 100–300 rad. This resulted in aspermia as early as 2 months postradiation. Some of the patients remained azoospermic for a long period.

According to Shamberger,[165] gonadal function was retained in 50% of patients if irradiation was remote from the gonads. In comparison, if the irradiation field included the thighs and abdomen, all of the patients became azoospermic. Testicular shielding can reduce radiation doses to the testicles, but small doses due to internal body scatter can still reach the testicles. Following a total midpelvic dose of 36.5 Gy, the total testicular dose was 1.2–1.6 Gy as compared to a dose of 2.8–3.3 Gy outside the testicular shield.[117]

A dose of 75–600 cGy may damage the Sertoli and Leydig cells, with a resultant increase in levels of follicle stimulating hormone (FSH) and luteinizing hormone-releasing hormone (LHRH). The level of serum testosterone decreases a few weeks after radiation and returns to normal in 6–12 months.[181] Patients with reduced serum testosterone may experience loss of sexual desire or difficulty achieving erection. Urethral irradiation may cause painful ejaculation.[160]

The sperm cells of the testis are more sensitive to fractionated irradiation than they are to single doses.[143] This is thought to be mainly due to the long cell cycle time of the primitive stem cells.

The effect of conventionally fractionated irradiation on testicular function in men with Hodgkin's disease was studied by Shapiro.[166] Gonadal function was compromised at doses as low as 50 cGy. At a cumulative dose of 200 cGy, testicular dysfunction persisted for 3 years.[166]

According to Thachil et al.,[180] giving 2,500 rad to the periaortic area in 20 fractions over 4 weeks resulted in 13% of the total dose being given to the upper scrotum. In a retrospective analysis of 22 patients treated with irradiation for stage I seminoma, seven patients were aspermic and 11 were severely oligospermic. Ejaculation was preserved in these patients.

In a review of the literature on the effects of fractionated pelvic irradiation on fertility, Ash[9] found that 15–30 cGy produced transient azoospermia. Azoospermia may be permanent after a total fractionated dose of 140–300 cGy.[72,143] Furthermore, ionizing radiation produces genetic mutations, which are cumulative to a high degree.[82]

In normal men, sperm count recovery requires 9–18 months after a dose of 8–100 cGy, 30 months after 200–300 cGy, and 5 years or more after 400–600 cGy.[143] The individual may remain infertile because the recovered sperm may be of low quality or contain genetic abnormalities.

Recovery of germ cells is also dose-dependent and occurs as long as 30 months after completion of treatment.[28,37] Hahn et al.[72] reported that recovery occurred 21–41 weeks after doses of 60–140 cGy.

Although sexual problems are common in cancer patients, it is not clear if declines in sexual function are the result of treatment or if they existed prior to intervention. Most studies on sexual function have been based on retrospective evaluations using simple questionnaires.

In a prospective study, Zinreich et al.[210] used the Derogatis Inventory for Sexual Functioning to demonstrate that 27 of 43 patients (63%) were impotent prior to radiotherapy. In another study by the same authors, the Derogatis questionnaire was given to 27 patients with adenocarcinoma of the prostate prior to and 1 year following radiation therapy. Seventeen of the 27 patients were considered to be impotent prior to treatment. Only three of the 10 patients who were potent prior to treatment maintained their potency after radiotherapy. Interestingly, four patients who were impotent prior to therapy became potent after completion of radiation therapy.

Several studies have reported a low pretreatment semen count.[25,33,135,147,170] Infertility after therapy should not be simply attributed to treatment itself, since it may be related to preexisting deficient spermatogenesis or sperm transport.[180]

Thachil[180] studied pretreatment sperm counts in patients with testicular tumors and compared the results with normal, healthy age-matched patients who were hospitalized for minor operations. The mean sperm density was 24.7 in 42 semen samples provided by the patients, and it was 73.8 in semen provided by 43 controls. The mean density was not significantly different between patients with seminomas versus nonseminomas. There was more suppression in patients with stage II and III than in those with stage I disease. These results indicate that 52% of patients with germinal testicular tumors had subfertile sperm density before any treatment.

Pelvic Irradiation in Women

Pelvic irradiation in women may cause ovarian failure (Table 3). Cessation of ovarian function is dose- and age-dependent. The oocytes in the primitive follicle are more sensitive to radiation damage than oocytes in mature follicles. There is depletion of oocytes and cessation of ovulation. There is lack of estradiol and progesterone from granulosa and theca cells, respectively, because they are dependent on oocyte proliferation. This results in premature menopausal symptoms, including loss of libido, dyspareunia, and postcoital bleeding.

Irradiation permanently damages the basal cell layer of the vaginal epithelium, the endothelium of small vessels in the genital area, and the fibroblasts of the connective tissues in the subepithelium. Dryness and thinning of the vaginal walls are due to the effects of estrogen deprivation. Due to gradual fibrosis, most women experience some narrowing of the upper vagina, which leads to dyspareunia. Intercourse may cause small vaginal ulceration and postcoital bleeding and irritation.

TABLE 3.   Effects of Ovarian Failure

Hormonal	Physical	Sexual
↓ Estrogen	Amenorrhea	Loss of femininity
↓ Progesterone	Sterility	Loss of libido
↑ Follicle-stimulating hormone	Vaginal dryness	Loss of orgasm
↑ Leutinizing hormone	Vaginal fibrosis	Lack of pleasure
↑ Leutinizing hormone-releasing	Vaginal stenosis	Dyspareunia
hormone	Vaginal ulceration	Postcoital bleeding

Permanent cessation of menses occurs in more than 95% of women younger than 40 who receive a dose in the range of 500–1,000 cGy; however, only 375 cGy will cause amenorrhea in almost all women older than 40.[126]

Cole[41] reported results of ovarian ablation in patients with breast cancer. A single dose of 450 cGy produced permanent amenorrhea in 67% of women younger than 40 and in all women older than 49.

Cust et al.[46] reported on the consequences of total body irradiation on sexual function. In their study, 33 of 36 women who responded to a questionnaire experienced vaginal dryness that profoundly affected sexual function. Eighteen women experienced difficulty with intercourse, and 16 reported decline in sexual desire. Anxiety regarding sterility, femininity, and appearance was common. Although hormone replacement abolished the symptoms in 24 women, vaginal dryness continued to be a problem in three.

Vose[192] studied the long-term sequelae of total body irradiation in 50 patients who had undergone bone marrow transplant for lymphoid malignancy; 37% reported a subjective diminution in sexual desire and sexual function. However, the effects of chemotherapy and radiation therapy could not be separated.

Attempts have been made to compare sexual function in patients treated with pelvic radiotherapy with function in patients treated with hysterectomy. Most studies have reported a higher prevalence of sexual dysfunction in patients treated with radiotherapy versus hysterectomy.[159,164] However, Vincent[187] did not find significant difference in sexual function in such patients.

Controversy exists regarding whether estrogen replacement in postmenopausal patients is safe. However, there is evidence that when estrogens are replaced in postmenopausal women, they live longer,[54] have fewer cardiovascular problems, have decreased osteoporosis, and have improvement of the climacteric symptoms. Estrogen replacement will decrease thinning and dryness of vaginal walls, and it also may increase vaginal blood supply. A recent review suggests that conjugated estrogens in a daily dose of 0.625 mg do not increase the relative risk of breast cancer.[54] Moreover, women who used estrogen therapy had less mortality from breast cancer than women who had no hormonal therapy.[76]

CHEMOTHERAPY AND SEXUALITY

Most of the chemotherapeutic agents have side effects against reproductive tissues. These effects can be classified as immediate, early, or late. It is estimated that approximately 52,000 patients will be treated for cancer during their reproductive years or prior to puberty. Since many of these patients survive, the effects of chemotherapy on gonadal function are of great significance.

Chemotherapy in Men

Testicular function is susceptible to injury by many chemotherapeutic agents, mainly alkylating agents. There is progressive depletion of the germinal epithelium lining of seminiferous tubule.[132] Although morphologic structure of Sertoli and Leydig cells is maintained, the cells are functionally impaired.[37,116,132,139] Serum testosterone is decreased, and LHRH, LH, and FSH are increased. Testicular atrophy occurs, with oligospermia or azoospermia.

The effects of nitrogen mustard on testes were first reported by Spitz in 1948.[172] Since then, other chemotherapeutic agents, such as chlorambucil, cyclophosphamide, and procarbazine, have been shown to be toxic to testes.[101,114,139] Azoospermia and severe oligospermia are usually seen after intensive chemotherapy.[58,139]

Alkylating agents are most often implicated. A cumulative dose of 18 g of cyclophosphamide has been reported to consistently produce azoospermia. Testicular biopsies after treatment have shown a loss of germinal epithelium;[37,167] the effects appear to be dose-dependent.

Combination chemotherapeutic agents also have a profound impact on spermatogenesis.[34,35,94,190] Up to 80% of men receiving nitrogen mustard, vincristine, procarbazine, and prednisone (MOPP) develop testicular atrophy.[35,167] Cyclophosphamide, vincristine, procarbazine, and prednisone (COPP) cause irreversible germinal aplasia. In one study, azoospermia was noted in all patients during treatment with nitrogen mustard, vinblastine, procarbazine, and prednisone (MVPP), and only 6% of the patients recovered active spermatogenesis.[34]

In 10 leukemic patients, Kreuser et al.[94] noted that a polychemotherapy regimen produced azoospermia and elevated FSH in all patients during treatment. All of these patients recovered during the second year with normal sperm density and FSH levels.

During treatment of soft tissue sarcoma, cyclophosphamide and doxorubicin produce irreversible testicular damage in men older than 40 or in men receiving concomitant irradiation proximal to the gonads.[113]

Testicular function after chemotherapy for testicular cancer with vinblastine, bleomycin and cisplatin may be reversible within 2–3 years.[52,94,94a] However, these patients may have low serum testosterone due to a congenital abnormality in the remaining testicle.

The effects of chemotherapy on prepubertal and pubertal testes include irreversible azoospermia,[30,207] germinal aplasia, elevated serum gonadotropin, decreased testosterone, and gynecomastia.[168] However, in two autopsy studies no histological abnormalities were noted in the testes of these patients.[8,112]

Rustin et al.[144] reported that the initial size of the testicular tumor and duration of chemotherapy are related to the recovery of spermatogenesis. They studied 59 men whose germ cell tumors were treated with POMB/ACE (cisplatin, vincristine, methotrexate, bleomycin, actinomycin D, cyclophosphamide, and etoposide). About 80% of patients with small tumors and fewer then six months of treatment recovered spermatogenesis, and 12 pregnancies subsequently occurred. Of patients with larger tumors or treatment lasting longer than six months, only 32% recovered spermatogenesis.

Endocrine dysfunction secondary to chemotherapy can result in a decrease in sexual desire and erectile dysfunction.[52] Infertility usually occurs immediately after treatment.

Some chemotherapeutic drugs cause autonomic neuropathy, which may explain some of the sexual problems in these patients. No information is available on the association of autonomic neuropathy with erectile dysfunction after chemotherapy.

Chemotherapy in Women

Ovarian failure resulting from chemotherapy has been reported.[7,19,32,63,93,140,202,207] Examination of the ovaries in these patients frequently reveals arrest of follicular maturation or frank destruction of ova and follicles.[116,171] Amenorrhea and menopausal symptoms are common due to lack of estrogen with resultant vaginal dryness and loss of elasticity. Patients experience dyspareunia due to vaginal dryness and vaginal irritation during chemotherapy. Ovarian androgens promote sexual desire in women; however, the effects of chemotherapy on androgen production are not clearly understood. Loss of sexual desire is quite common during chemotherapy treatment and afterward. The underlying factors for this decline in sexual desire are not known.

Breast cancer patients who receive adjuvant chemotherapy may have amenorrhea. Ovarian dysfunction appears to be age- and dose-dependent. Stillman[176] concluded that chemotherapy in girls up to 17 years of age was not a major cause of ovarian dysfunction. Patients older than 35–40 at the time of treatment are much more likely to develop permanent amenorrhea after moderate doses of chemotherapy.[202] In younger patients, alkylating agents may accelerate the onset of menopause.[71] Overall, at least half of the women treated with a single alkylating agent develop permanent ovarian failure and amenorrhea.[19,116]

In a group of 84 women and 62 men treated with chemotherapy for various childhood cancers, Li et al.[105] studied 286 pregnancies. There was no increase in congenital malformations. Other investigators have also found no increase in congenital malformations in women previously treated for trophoblastic neoplasms.[142,185]

HORMONAL MANIPULATION AND SEXUALITY

Hormonal Therapy in Men

Hormonal therapy with estrogens and LHRH antagonists may be prescribed for patients with metastatic prostate cancer to reduce the circulating serum testosterone. There is no evidence that one drug is superior to another for preservation of sexual function. The effects are similar to those produced by surgical orchiectomy. Therapy with estrogen compounds results in a decline in libido, poor arousal, and difficulty in achieving erection or orgasm. Reduced semen volume has also been reported.[156]

There appears to be no significant relationship between the level of testosterone and the severity of sexual problems. For example, Peeling[127] reported that 15–20% of men could function normally after hormonal treatment despite reduced serum testosterone levels to near zero. The use of estrogenic compounds has declined. Luteinizing hormone-releasing hormone agonists, such as busereline, provide an alternate to estrogen compounds. These drugs do not have estrogenic side effects, such as gynecomastia and cardiovascular toxicity.[127]

Hormonal Therapy in Women

Hormones are prescribed to patients with breast cancer and, sometimes, those with endometrial cancer. Menopause, whether natural or related to treatment, may cause hot flushes, dryness and thinning of vagina, and decreased sexual activities.

Breast cancer patients with positive estrogen receptors may be given tamoxifen, a drug with both antiestrogenic and estrogenic effects. Tamoxifen inhibits the growth of estrogen-positive receptor breast cancer cells and may produce estrogenic changes in the vaginal mucosa of postmenopausal women.[86,107]

MANAGEMENT GUIDELINES

A diagnosis of cancer is a very emotional event, and many questions are likely to arise. Attempts should be made to anticipate and prevent psychosocial and sexual problems. A complete pretreatment assessment and appropriate counseling may help to prevent these problems.

TABLE 4.   Assessment

Past Medical History	Psychosocial Behavior	Sexual Behavior	Adjustment to the Diagnosis of Cancer
Diabetes mellitus	Alcohol abuse	Perception of own sexuality	By the patient, spouse, and family
Hypertension	Drug abuse	Satisfaction with relationship	
Atherosclerotic heart disease	Smoking	Marital satisfaction	To household activities, work, finances
	Communication skills	Sexual function	
Cerebrovascular accident	Coping skills	Satisfaction with sexual function	To treatment and its side effects
Surgery	Depression	Sex drive	To the prognosis
Medications	Anxiety	Practices of sexual expression	

According to Schover,[158] 73% of the patients referred for sexual consultation were seen only once or twice. It is estimated that about 10–20% of cancer patients have severe sexual problems that require the skills of a trained sex therapist and that only a few patients will require medical consultation by a urologist or gynecologist.

Assessment

During the initial history and physical, the patient should be assessed for the extent of the disease and the psychosocial environment (Table 4). Inquiry should be made regarding the sexual functioning, relationships with sexual partner(s), and any history of marital or psychological problems prior to the diagnosis of cancer. If the patient has a committed relationship, it is helpful to include both partners in the session. Some of the sensitive aspects of sexuality, such as masturbation and extramarital relationships, also need to be discussed, while respecting the patient's privacy.

At follow-up, it is important to establish which phase of the sexual response cycle (desire, excitement, and orgasm) has been most severely affected. The investigation and management of impotency are described in chapter 16.

Schain[152] reported that women who are young or have a history of psychiatric morbidity or sexual and substance abuse are at higher risk for postoperative sexual problems. She reports that it is important to determine preoperatively if there is any compromise of three critical factors: psychological, physiologic, or rational.

Prevention

Timely discussion of psychosocial and sexual issues related to cancer and its treatment may prevent sexual problems (Table 5). Opinion differs regarding the

TABLE 5.   Prevention

Provide information and education	Provide reconstructive surgery and devices
Provide counseling and rehabilitation	Breast reconstruction
	Vulvar reconstruction
Preserve sexual physiology	Vaginal reconstruction
Sympathetic and parasympathetic nerves	Facial prosthetic devices
Vascular supply	Preserve body image and function
Preserve gonadal function	Breast conservation
Oral contraceptives	Limb sparing surgery
Oophoropexy	Correct hormonal and other deficiencies
Shielding	Estrogen replacement
Preserve reproductive capacity	Testosterone replacement
Sperm banking	Provide support for stress and emotional needs

best time at which this aspect of care should be discussed. Some believe that discussion should take place early during the course of management, because this may reduce the patient's anxiety. Others feel that at the time of diagnosis, the patient and family are more concerned with survival, pain, and suffering than sexual function and that sexuality related questions should be addressed at the time of follow-up. This author believes that each case should be handled individually. The patient and family need to know that the oncologist and other team members are available to answer any questions or concerns, including sexual issues. This relationship must be developed early in the course of the first interview.

Irrespective of timing, every effort should be made to provide accurate information regarding prognosis, survival, and side effects of proposed treatment.

To minimize the emotional and psychological impact of treatment, the couple should be provided with information regarding potential effects of the treatment. The patient and partner should understand that narcotics, antiemetics, and general fatigue may influence the sexual response cycle. Options for rehabilitation should be discussed at the time that treatment decisions are made.

When surgery is indicated, attempts should be made to perform nerve-sparing procedures whenever feasible. It is also important to minimize disfigurement when possible. The possibility of nerve generation, partial excision of the neurovascular bundle, or cavernous grafts needs to be explored in high-risk patients in whom surgical procedures are likely to damage the autonomic nervous system or neurovascular bundle.

Radiation therapy should be immaculately planned and should be accompanied by shielding of the testicles. Oophoropexy should be considered in young women.[103,134] The effects of the loss of hormone production due to ovarian failure or natural menopause can be minimized by estrogen therapy. Oral contraceptives have been used to prevent ovarian failure. In a study by Chapman and Sutcliffe,[36] five of six women who had discontinued oral contraceptives resumed normal menstrual cycles. However, similar experience has not been reported by Whitehead et al.[207] The ability of oral contraceptives to prevent ovarian failure awaits further documentation.[10]

In men, testosterone can be replaced and will help patients with loss of libido and erectile problems. Sometimes hormones cannot be given because of the site and type of cancer.

Counseling

It is important for patients to differentiate between sexuality and physical sexual performance. Sexual function may be altered; however, sexuality is a physiologic and psychological component of the person based on genes, hormones, and life experiences. Sexuality may be influenced, but cannot be destroyed, by illness and environmental factors. Patients need to understand that, while physical intimacy is desirable, there are other means of sexual expression that will provide satisfaction and pleasure.

Sex is often viewed as an activity restricted to the young, healthy, and attractive. Patients should recognize that beauty is not only one's physical appearance but is also a combination of individual talents, behavior, maturity, kindness, and sense of humor. Even if body image changes, other factors are important in psychosocial functioning.

Patients should be encouraged to focus on their positive features. Various counseling models have been reported.[29,161,162] Schover suggests that patients

TABLE 6.   Patient and Family Education

Regarding particular cancer and its prognosis
Regarding cancer treatment and its side effects
Regarding the impact of side effects on sexuality
Regarding solutions to the side effects on sexuality
Regarding sexual rehabilitation

For both sexes	*For women*	*For men*
Sexual counseling	Estrogen replacement	Testosterone replacement
Sex therapy	Water-base vaginal lubrication	Vacuum constrictive devices
	Vaginal dilators	Corpus cavernosa injection
	Vaginal reconstruction	Penile prosthesis

should create a "healthy illusion" by disguising the changes cancer has made and drawing attention to their best points. It is important for patients to overcome depression, anxiety, negative thoughts, and try to rebuild self-esteem and overcome communication barriers. Therapeutic interventions should include restructuring old attitudes about sexuality and learning pleasuring activities through techniques of sensate focus and behavioral prescription. For cancer patients, Schover has outlined some keys for staying sexually healthy.[161,162] Components of counseling are listed in Table 6.

Pretreatment Semen Cryopreservation

Patients undergoing chemotherapy should have counseling regarding pretreatment semen analysis, cryopreservation, and the possibility of in vitro fertilization.[64,151] Because cancer itself may have an adverse effect on fertility before treatment, sperm banking may be a poor guarantee of future reproductive capacity. Furthermore, in one report,[136] only 23% of 62 patients had post-thaw semen analyses favorable for fertility. The major abnormalities were decreased post-thaw motility and decreased sperm density.[135,136] Prognosis is better with a sperm density of greater than $20 \times 10^6/mL$ and post-thaw motilities greater than 30%.

Patients should be reassured that pregnancies conceived after cytotoxic chemotherapy have about the same chance for successful outcome as do normal pregnancies and that there is no increase in the risk of congenital malformations.

Reconstruction

In patients undergoing mastectomy, options for breast reconstruction should be discussed. Similarly, a prosthesis should be offered to patients with head and neck disfigurement resulting from cancer or surgery. Procedures for vaginal reconstruction using split-thickness skin grafts, myocutaneous grafts, and transpositional skin flaps have been described.[73] However, many women do not resume sexual activity after pelvic exenteration even if vaginal reconstruction has been performed.[120,186] After radical vulvectomy, some women benefit with split-thickness flap grafts to repair vaginal stenosis. Various techniques have been reported for vulvar reconstruction in patients with radical vulvectomy.[20,81,145]

Dyspareunia

Dyspareunia has been reported in women following removal of rectum and bladder.[80] Dyspareunia may result from decrease in vaginal size and reduced lubrication. Nonestrogen topical lubricants, suppositories, and vaginal moisturizers may be used in the management of patients with painful coitus. According to Fordney,[59] women with a history of dyspareunia can benefit from exercises that relax the muscles that surround the vaginal entrance. A series of graduated-size vaginal dilators have been used to give these patients a sense that it is possible to relax vaginal musculature and facilitate intercourse.

General Techniques

Patients and their partners can be taught a variety of relaxation techniques that can help minimize disruptive thoughts before or during sexual activities.

Men who undergo RLND and have impaired emission can be treated by sympathomimetic agents to induce ejaculation.[85] Patients with ostomy can be provided with some specific suggestions so that they can better prepare for sexual encounters. Examples of suggestions include (1) ascertaining that the pouch is securely attached, (2) wearing an attractive pouch, and (3) emptying the pouch prior to sexual activity.

CONCLUSION

Cellular, anatomic, physiologic, and psychosocial changes in cancer patients can influence their sexual functioning. Although controversy exists regarding the magnitude and nature of sexual problems in cancer patients, most reports confirm that cancer and its treatment have deleterious effects on sexual function. It is important to provide sexual rehabilitation so that this important aspect of quality of life can be restored.

REFERENCES

1. Andersen BL: Sexual functioning morbidity among cancer survivors. Cancer 55:1835–1842, 1985.
2. Andersen BL, Andersen B, deProsse C: Controlled prospective longitudinal study of women with cancer: I. Sexual functioning outcomes. J Consult Clin Psychol 57:683–691, 1989.
3. Andersen BL, Andersen B, deProsse C: Controlled prospective longitudinal study of women with cancer: II. Psychological outcomes. J Consult Clin Psychol 57:692–697, 1989.
4. Andersen BL, Hacker NF: Psychosexual adjustment after vulvar surgery. Obstet Gynecol 62:457–462, 1983.
5. Andersen BL, Jochimsen PR: Sexual functioning among breast cancer, gynecologic cancer, and healthy women. J Consult Clin Psychol 53:25–32, 1985.
6. Andreasson B, Moth J, Jensen SB, Bock JE: Sexual function and somatopsychic reactions in vulvectomy-operated women and their partners. Acta Obstet Gynecol Scand 65:7–10, 1986.
7. Andrieu JM, Ochoa-Molina MR: Menstrual cycle, pregnancies and offspring before and after MOPP therapy for Hodgkin's disease. Cancer 52:435–438, 1983.
8. Arneil GC: Cyclophosphamide and the prepubertal testis. Lancet 2:1259–1260, 1980.
9. Ash P: The influence of radiation on fertility in man. Br J Radiol 53:271–278, 1980.
10. Averette HE, Boike GM, Jarrell MA: Effects of cancer chemotherapy on gonadal function and reproductive capacity. CA 40:199–209, 1990.
11. Bachers ES: Sexual dysfunction after treatment for genitourinary cancers. Semin Oncol Nurs 1:18–24, 1985.
12. Bagshaw MA, Cox RS, Ray GR: Status of radiation treatment of prostate cancer at Stanford University. NCI Mongr 7:47–60, 1988.
13. Balslev I, Harling H: Sexual dysfunction following operation of carcinoma of the rectum. Dis Colon Rectum 26:785–788, 1983.
14. Banker FL: The preservation of potency after external beam radiation for prostate cancer. Int J Radiat Oncol Biol Phys 15:219–220, 1988.
15. Bard M, Sutherland AM: Psychological impact of cancer and its treatment: IV. Adaptation to radical mastectomy. Cancer 8:656–672, 1955.
16. Bartelink H, van Dam F, van Dongen J: Psychological effects of breast conserving therapy in comparison with radical mastectomy. Int J Radiat Oncol Biol Phys 11:381–385, 1985.

17. Becker H: Psychodynamic aspects of breast cancer: Differences in younger and older patients. Psychother Psychosom 32:287–296, 1979.
18. Beiler DD, Wright DJ, Reddy GN: Radical external radiotherapy for prostatic carcinoma. Int J Radiat Oncol Biol Phys 7:885–890, 1981.
19. Belohorsky B, Siracky J, Sandor L, Klauber E: Comments on the development of amenorrhea caused by myleran in cases of chronic myelosis. Neoplasm 7:397–403, 1960.
20. Bertani A, Riccio M, Bellligolli A: Vulvar reconstruction after cancer excision: The island groin flap technique. Br J Plast Surg 43:159–161, 1990.
21. Bigg SW, Kavoussi LR, Catalona WJ: Role of nerve sparing radical prostatectomy for clinical stage B2 prostate cancer. J Urol 144:1420–1424, 1990.
22. Bloom JR, Ross RD, Burnell G: The effect of social support on patient adjustment after breast surgery. Patient Counselling and Health Education 1:50–59, 1978.
23. Bolund G: Suicide and cancer: II. Medical and care factors in suicide by cancer patients in Sweden. J Psychosoc Oncol 3:31–52, 1985.
24. Bracken RB, Johnson DE: Sexual function and fecundity after treatment for testicular tumors. Urology 7:35–38, 1976.
25. Bracken RB, Smith KD: Is semen cryopreservation helpful in testicular cancer. Urology 15:581–583, 1980.
26. Bransfield DD: Breast cancer and sexual functioning: A review of the literature and implications for future research. Int J Psychiatry Med 12:197–211, 1983.
27. Breitbart W, Holland J: Psychosocial aspects of head and neck cancer. Semin Oncol 15:61–69, 1988.
28. Buchanan JD, Fairley KF, Barrie JU: Return of spermatogenesis after stopping cyclophosphamide therapy. Lancet 2:156–157, 1975.
29. Capone MA, Westie KS, Goode RS: Sexual rehabilitation of the gynecological cancer patient: An effective counseling model. In Vaeth JM, Blomberg RC, Adler L (eds): Frontiers of Radiation Therapy and Oncology. Basel, Karger, 1980, pp 123–130.
30. Chapman RM: Gonadal injury resulting from chemotherapy. Am J Ind Med 4:149–161, 1983.
31. Chapman RM: Effects of cytotoxic therapy on sexuality and gonadal function. Semin Oncol 9:84–94, 1982.
32. Chapman RM, Sutcliffe SB, Malpas JS: Cytotoxic induced ovarian failure in women with Hodgkin's disease. I. Hormone function. JAMA 242:1877–1881, 1979.
33. Chapman RM, Sutcliffe SB, Malpas JS: Male gonadal dysfunction in Hodgkin's disease. JAMA 245:1323–1328, 1981.
34. Chapman RM, Sutcliffe SB, Rees LH, et al: Cyclical combination and gonadal function: Retrospective study in males. Lancet 1:265–269, 1979.
35. Chapman RM, Sutcliffe SB, Rees L, et al: Prospective study: The effects of Hodgkin's disease and nitrogen mustard, vincristine, procarbazine and prednisolone on male gonadal function. Proc Am Soc Clin Oncol 20:321, 1979.
36. Chapman RM, Sutcliffe SB: Protection of ovarian function by oral contraceptives in women receiving chemotherapy for Hodgkin's disease. Blood 58:849–851, 1981.
37. Cheviakoff S, Calmera JC, Morgenfeld M, Mancini RE: Recovery of spermatogenesis in patients with lymphoma after treatment with chlorambucil. J Reprod Fertil 33:155–157, 1973.
38. Christensen DN: Postmastectomy couple counseling: An outcome study of a structured treatment protocol. J Sex Marital Ther 9:266–275, 1983.
39. Cirino E, Pepe G, Pepe F, et al: Sexual complications after abdominoperineal resection. Ital J Surg Sci 17:315–318, 1987.
40. Clifford E, Clifford M, Georgiade NG: Breast reconstruction following mastectomy: II. Marital characteristics of patients seeking this procedure. Ann Plast Surg 5:344–346, 1980.
41. Cole MP: Suppression of ovarian function in primary breast cancer. In Forrest APM, Kunkler PB (eds): Prognostic Factors in Breast Cancer. Edinburgh, E & S Livingston, 1968.
42. Correa RJ Jr, Gibbons RP, Cummings KB, Mason JT: Total prostatectomy for stage B carcinoma of the prostate. J Urol 117:328–329, 1977.
43. Craig TJ, Abeloff MD: Psychiatric symptomatology among hospitalized cancer patients. Am J Psychol 131:1323–1327, 1974.
44. Culp OS: Radical perineal prostatectomy: Its past, present and possible future. J Urol 98:618–626, 1967.
45. Culp DA, Graf RA, Hasctek R: Testicular tumor. J Urol 89:843–850, 1963.
46. Cust MP, Whitehead MI, Powels R, et al: Consequences and treatment of ovarian failure after total body irradiation for leukaemia. Br Med J 299:1494–1497, 1989.
47. Dean C, Chetty U, Forrest APM: Effects of immediate breast reconstruction on psychosocial morbidity after mastectomy. Lancet 1:459–462, 1983.

48. Derogatis L, Kourlesis SM: An approach to evaluation of sexual problems in cancer patient. CA Cancer J Clin 31:46–50, 1981.

49. Dhillon RS, Palmer BV, Pittam MR, Shaw HJ: Rehabilitation after major head and neck surgery—the patient's view. Clin Otolaryngol 7:319–324, 1982.

50. Disaia PJ, Creasman WT, Rich WM: An alternative approach to early cancer of the vulva. Am J Obstet Gynecol 133:825–832, 1979.

51. Donohue JP, Foster RS, Rowland RG, et al: Nerve sparing retroperitoneal lymphadenectomy with preservation of ejaculation. J Urol 144:287–292, 1990.

52. Drasga RE, Einhora LH, Williams SD, et al: Fertility after chemotherapy for testicular cancer. J Clin Oncol 1:179–183, 1983.

53. Dropkin MJ: Coping with disfigurement and dysfunction after head and neck cancer surgery: A conceptual framework. Semin Oncol Nurs 5:213–219, 1989.

54. Dupont WD, Page DL: Menopausal estrogen replacement therapy and breast cancer. Arch Intern Med 151:67–72, 1991.

55. Fallowfield LJ, Hall A: Psychosocial and sexual impact of diagnosis and treatment of breast cancer. Br Med Bull 47:388–399, 1991.

56. Farberow NL, Ganzler S, Cutter F, et al: An eight year survey of hospital suicide. Life Threatening Behav 1:184–201, 1971.

57. Finkle AL, Taylor SP: Sexual potency after radical prostatectomy. J Urol 125:350–352, 1981.

58. Forbes AP: Chemotherapy, testicular damage, and gynecomastia: An endocrine "black hole." N Engl J Med 229:42–43, 1978.

59. Fordney DS: Dyspareunia and vaginismus. Clin Obstet Gynecol 21:205–221, 1978.

60. Frank D, Dornbush RL, Webster SK, et al: Mastectomy and sexual behavior: A pilot study. Sex Disabil 1:16–26, 1978.

61. Gamba A, Romano M, Grasso IM, et al: Psychosocial adjustment of patients surgically treated for head and neck cancer. Head Neck 14:218–223, 1992.

62. Gerard D: Sexual functioning after mastectomy: Life versus lab. J Sex Marital Ther 8:305–315, 1982.

63. Gershenson DM: Menstrual and reproductive function after treatment with combination chemotherapy for malignant ovarian germ cell tumors. J Clin Oncol 6:270–275, 1988.

64. Gibbons W: In-vitro fertilization as therapy for male factor infertility. Urol Clin North Am 14:563–567, 1987.

65. Gloeckner MR, Startling JR: Providing sexual information to ostomy patients. Dis Colon Rectum 25:575–579, 1982.

66. Glucksmann A: The effects of radiation on reproductive organs. Br J Radiol 20(suppl 1):101–109, 1947.

67. Goin MK, Goin JM: Midlife reactions to mastectomy and subsequent breast reconstruction. Arch Gen Psychiatry 38:225–227, 1981.

68. Goldstein I, Feldman MI, Deckers PJ, et al: Radiation associated impotence. A clinical study of its mechanism. JAMA 251:903–910, 1984.

69. Goldstein MK, Teng NNH: Gynecologic factors in sexual dysfunction of the older woman. Clin Geriatr Med 7(1):41–61, 1991.

70. Goligher JC: Sexual function after excision of the rectum. Proc R Soc Med 44:824–827, 1951.

71. Gradishar W, Schilsky RI: Effects of cancer treatment on the reproductive system. Crit Rev Oncol Hematol 8:153–171, 1988.

72. Hahn EW, Feingold SM, Simpson L, et al: Recovery from aspermia induced by low dose radiation in seminoma patients. Cancer 50:337–340, 1980.

73. Hatch KD: Neovaginal reconstruction. Cancer 71:1660–1663, 1992.

74. Havenga K, Welvaart K: Sexual dysfunction in men following surgical treatment for rectosigmoid carcinoma. Ned Tijdschr Geneeskd 135:710–713, 1991.

75. Hientanen P, Lonnqvist J: Cancer and suicide. Ann Oncol 2:19–23, 1991.

76. Henderson BE, Paganini-Hill A, Ross RK: Decreased mortality in users of estrogen replacement therapy. Arch Intern Med 151:75–78, 1991.

77. Hilaris BS, Whitemore WF, Batata MA, et al: Implantation of prostate: Dose response considerations. Front Radiat Ther Oncol 12:82–90, 1978.

78. Hojo K, Sawada T, Moriya Y: An analysis of survival and voiding, sexual function after wide ileopelvic lymphadenectomy in patients with carcinoma of the rectum, compared with conventional lymphadenectomy. Dis Colon Rectum 32:128–133, 1989.

79. Hojo K, Vernava AM, Sugihara K, Katumata K: Preservation of urine voiding and sexual function after rectal cancer surgery. Dis Colon Rectum 34:532–539, 1991.

80. Hurny C, Holland JC: Psychosocial sequelae of ostomies in cancer patients. CA 36:170–183, 1985.

81. Hurwitz DJ, Zwiebel PC: Gluteal thigh flap repair of chronic perineal wounds. Am J Surg 150:386, 1985.
82. Hussey DH: The testicle. In Cox JD (ed): Moss' Radiation Oncology. 7th ed. Mosby, St. Louis, 1994, pp 559–589.
83. Jamison KR, Wellisch DK, Pasnau RO: Psychosocial aspects of mastectomy: I. The women's perspective. Am J Psychiatry 135:432–436, 1978.
84. Jewett HJ: The results of radical perineal prostatectomy. JAMA 210:324–325, 1969.
85. Jewett MAS, Kong YP, Godberg SD, et al: Retroperitoneal lymphadenectomy for testis tumor with nerve sparing for ejaculation. J Urol 139:1220–1224, 1988.
86. Jordan VC: Long term adjunct tamoxifen therapy for breast cancer: The prelude to prevention. Cancer Treat Rev 17:15–36, 1990.
87. Kaplan HS: A neglected issue: The sexual side effects of current treatments for breast cancer. J Sex Marital Ther 18:3–19, 1992.
88. Kiebert GM, De Haes JCJM, Van de Velde CJH: The impact of breast conserving treatment and mastectomy on the quality of life of early stage breast cancer patients: A review. J Clin Oncol 9:1059–1070, 1991.
89. Kilkku P, Gronroos M, Punnonen R: Sexual function after conization of uterine cervix. Gynecol Oncol 14:209–212, 1982.
90. Kopecky AA, Laskowski TZ, Scott R: Radical retropubic proctectomy in the treatment of prostate carcinoma. J Urol 103:641–644, 1970.
91. Koster META, Bersman J: Problems and coping behavior of facial cancer patients. Soc Sci Med 5:569–578, 1990.
92. Koukouras D, Spiliotis J, Scopa CD, et al: Radical consequences in the sexuality of male patients operated for colorectal carcinoma. Eur J Surg Oncol 17:285–288, 1991.
93. Koyama H, Wada T, Nishizawa Y, et al: Cyclophosphamide induced ovarian failure and its therapeutic significance in patients with breast cancer. Cancer 39:1403–1409, 1977.
94. Kreuser ED, Hetzel WD, Hiet W, et al: Reproductive and endocrine gonad functions in adults following multidrug chemotherapy for acute lymphoblastic or undifferentiated leukemia. J Clin Oncol 6:588–595, 1988.
94a. Kreuser ED, Harsch U, Hetzel WD, Schreml W: Chronic gonadal toxicity in patients with testicular cancer after chemotherapy. Eup J Cancer Clin Oncol 22:289–294, 1986.
95. Kumar PP, Good R, Rainbolt C, et al: Low morbidity following transperineal percutaneous template technique for permanent iodine 125 endocurietherapy of prostate cancer. Endocuriether Hyperther Oncol 2:119–126, 1986.
96. La Monica G, Audisio RA, Tamburini M, et al: Incidence of sexual dysfunction in male patients treated surgically for rectal malignancy. Dis Colon Rectum 28:937–940, 1985.
97. Lamb MA, Woods AF: Sexuality and the cancer patient. Cancer Nurs 4:137–144, 1980.
98. Lange PH, Narayan P, Fraley EE: Fertility issues following therapy for testicular cancer. Semin Urol 11:264–274, 1984.
99. Lasry JC-M, Margolese RG, Poisson R, et al: Depression and body image following mastectomy and lumpectomy. J Chronic Dis 40:529–534, 1987.
100. Leandri P, Rossignol G, Gautier JR, Ramon J: Radical retropubic prostatectomy: Morbidity and quality of life. Experience with 620 consecutive cases. J Urol 147:883–887, 1992.
101. Lee IP, Dixon RL: Effects of procarbazine on spermatogenesis determined by velocity sedimentation cell separation technique and serial mating. J Pharmacol Exp Ther 181:219–226, 1972.
102. Lee ECG, Maguire GP: Proceedings: Emotional distress in patients attending a breast clinic. Br J Surg 62:162, 1975.
103. LeFloch O, Donaldson SS, Kaplan HS: Pregnancy following oophoropexy and total nodal irradiation in women with Hodgkin's disease. Cancer 38:2263–2268, 1976.
104. Leiter E, Brendler H: Loss of ejaculation following bilateral retroperitoneal lymphadenectomy. J Urol 98:375–378, 1967.
105. Li FP, Fine W, Jaffe N, et al: Offspring of patients treated for cancer in childhood. J Natl Cancer Inst 62:1193–1197, 1979.
106. List MA, Ritter-Sterr C, Lansky SB: A performance status scale for head and neck cancer patients. Cancer 66:564–569, 1990.
107. Love RR: Antiestrogen chemoprevention of breast cancer. Crit Issues Res Prev Med 20:64–78, 1991.
108. Lushbaugh CC, Ricks RC: Some cytokinetic and histopathological considerations of irradiated male and female gonadal tissues. Front Radiat Ther Oncol 6:228–248, 1972.
109. MacGregor FS: Some psychosocial problems associated with facial deformities. Am Sociol Rev 16:629–638, 1951.

110. Maguire P: Breast conservation vs mastectomy: Psychological considerations. Semin Surg Oncol 5:137–144, 1989.
111. Maguire GP, Lee EG, Bevington DJ, et al: Psychiatric problems in the first year after mastectomy. BMJ 1:963–965, 1978.
112. Matus-Ridley M, Nicosis SV, Meadows AT: Gonadal effect of cancer therapy in boys. Cancer 55:2353–2363, 1985.
113. Meistrich ML, Chawla SP, da Cunha MF, et al: Recovery of sperm production after chemotherapy for osteosarcoma. Cancer 63:2115–2123, 1989.
114. Miller DG: Alkylating agents and human spermatogenesis. JAMA 217:1662–1665, 1971.
115. Miller PJ: Mastectomy: A review of psychosocial research. Health Soc Work 6:60–66, 1980.
116. Miller JJ, Williams GF, Leissring JC: Multiple late complications of therapy with cyclophosphamide including ovarian destruction. Am J Med 50:530–535, 1971.
117. Million RR: The lymphomatous disease. In Fletcher GH (ed): Textbook of Radiotherapy. Philadelphia, Lea & Febiger, 1980, pp 584–636.
118. Mittal B: A study of penile circulation before and after radiation in patients with prostate cancer and its effect on impotence. Int J Radiat Oncol Biol Phys 11:1121–1125, 1985.
119. Monga U, Bordelon G, Tan G: Sexuality and sexual adjustment of patients with head and cancer. Presented at the 36th Scientific Meeting of the American Society for Therapeutic Radiology and Oncology, San Francisco, October 3–6, 1994.
120. Morley GW, Lindenauer SM, Youngs D: Vaginal reconstruction following pelvic exenteration: Surgical and psychological considerations. Am J Obstet Gynecol 116:996–1002, 1973.
121. Morris J: Outcome following treatment for head and neck cancer: Beyond clinical assessment. Eur J Cancer 5:675, 1991.
122. Morris T, Greer HS, White P: Psychological and social adjustment to mastectomy: A two year follow up. Cancer 40:2381–2387, 1977.
123. Moth I, Andreasson B, Soren BJ, Bock JE: Sexual function and somatopsychic reactions after vulvectomy. Dan Med Bull 30:27–34, 1983.
124. Nilsson LO, Kock NG, Kylberg F, et al: Sexual adjustment in ileostomy patients before and after conversion to continent ileostomy. Dis Colon Rectum 24:287–290, 1981.
125. Ofman US, Auchincloss SS: Sexual dysfunction in cancer patients. Curr Opin Oncol 4:605–613, 1992.
126. Peck WS, McGreer JT, Kretschmar NR, et al: Castration of the female by irradiation. Radiology 34:176–186, 1940.
127. Peeling WB: Phase III studies to compare goserelin with orchiectomy and with diethylstilbestrol in treatment of prostatic carcinoma. Urology 33(suppl):45–52, 1989.
128. Polivy J: Psychological effects of mastectomy on a woman's feminine self-concept. J Nerv Ment Dis 164:77–87, 1977.
129. Pontes JE, Huber R, Wolf R: Sexual function after radical prostatectomy. Prostate 8:123–126, 1986.
130. Pruyin JFA, De Yong PC, Bosman LJ, et al: Psychosocial aspects of head and neck cancer—a review of the literature. Clin Otolaryngol 11:469–474, 1986.
131. Quinlan DM, Epstein JI, Carter BS, Walsh PC: Sexual function following radical prostatectomy: Influence of preservation of neurovascular bundles. J Urol 145:998–1002, 1991.
132. Qureshi MS, Pennington JH, Goldsmith HJ, et al: Cyclophosphamide therapy and sterility. Lancet 2:1290–1291, 1972.
133. Ray GR, Cassady JR, Bagshaw MA: Definitive radiation therapy of carcinoma of the prostate: A report on 15 years of experience. Radiology 106:407–418, 1973.
134. Ray GR, Trueblood HW, Enright LP, et al: Oophoropexy: A means of preserving ovarian function following pelvic megavoltage radiotherapy for Hodgkin's disease. Radiology 96:175–180, 1970.
135. Redman JR, Bajorunas DR, Golsrein MC, et al: Semen cryopreservation and artificial insemination for Hodgkin's disease. J Clin Oncol 5:233–238, 1987.
136. Reed E, Sanger WG, Armitage JO: Results of semen cryopreservation in young men with testicular carcinoma and lymphoma. J Clin Oncol 4:537–539, 1986.
137. Renneker R, Cutler M: Psychological problems of adjustment to cancer of the breast. JAMA 148:833–838, 1952.
138. Rhamy RK, Wilson SK, Caldwell WL: Biopsy proven tumor following definitive irradiation for resectable carcinoma of the prostate. J Urol 107:627–630, 1972.
139. Richter P, Calamera JC, Morgenfeld MC, et al: Effects of chlorambucil on spermatogenesis in the human with malignant lymphoma. Cancer 25:1026–1030, 1970.
140. Rose DP, Davis TE: Ovarian function in patients receiving adjunct chemotherapy for breast cancer. Lancet 1:1174–1176, 1977.

141. Ross GT: Congenital anomalies among children born of mothers receiving chemotherapy for gestational trophoblastic neoplasms. Cancer 41:1317–1322, 1978.

142. Ross GT: Congenital anomalies among children born of mothers receiving chemotherapy for gestational trophoblastic neoplasms. Cancer 37:1043–1047, 1976.

143. Rowley MJ, Leach DR, Warner GA, Heller CG: Effect of graded doses of ionizing radiation on the human testis. Radiat Res 59:665–675, 1974.

144. Rustin G, Pektasides D, Bagshawe KD, et al: Fertility after chemotherapy for male and female germ cell tumors. Int J Androl 10:389–392, 1987.

145. Rutledge F, Sinclair M: Treatment of intraepithelial carcinoma of the vulva by skin excision and graft. Am J Obstet Gynecol 102:807, 1968.

146. Sabri S, Cotton LT: Sexual function following aortoiliac reconstruction. Lancet 2:1218–1219, 1971.

147. Sanger WG, Armitage JO, Schmidt MA: Feasibility of semen cryopreservation in patients with malignant disease. JAMA 244:789–790, 1980.

148. Sanger CK, Resnikoff M: A comparison of the psychological effects of breast savings procedures with the modified radical mastectomy. Cancer 48:2341–2346, 1981.

149. Santangelo ML, Romano G, Sassaroli C: Sexual function after resection for rectal cancer. Am J Surg 154:502–504, 1987.

150. Santoro A, Bondonna G, Valagussa P, et al: Long term results of combined chemotherapy-radiotherapy approach in Hodgkin's disease: Superiority of ABVD plus radiotherapy versus MOPP plus radiotherapy. J Clin Oncol 5:27–37, 1987.

151. Scammell GE, White N, Stedronska J, et al: Cryopreservation of semen in men with testicular tumor of Hodgkin's disease: Results of artificial insemination of their partners. Lancet 2:31–32 1985.

152. Schain WS: The sexual and intimate consequences of breast cancer treatment. CA 38:154–161, 1988.

153. Schain WS, Edwards BK, Groell CR, et al: Psychosocial and physical outcomes of primary breast cancer therapy: Mastectomy versus excisional biopsy and irradiation. Breast Cancer Res Treat 3:377–382, 1983.

154. Schain WS, Jacobs E, Wellisch DK: Psychosocial issues in breast reconstruction: Intrapsychic, interpersonal, and practical concerns. Clin Plast Surg 11:237–251, 1984.

155. Schover LR: The impact of breast cancer on sexuality, body image, and intimate relationships. CA 41:112–120, 1991.

156. Schover LR: Sexuality and fertility in urologic cancer patients. Cancer 60:553–558, 1987.

157. Schover LR, Evans RB, von Eschenbach AC: Sexual rehabilitation and male radical cystectomy. J Urol 136:1015–1017, 1986.

158. Schover LR, Evans RB, von Eschenbach AC: Sexual rehabilitation in a cancer center: Diagnosis and outcome in 384 consultations. Arch Sex Behav 16:445–461, 1987.

159. Schover LR, Fife M, Gershenson DM: Sexual dysfunction and treatment for early cervical cancer. Cancer 63:204–212, 1989.

160. Schover LR, Montague DK, Schain WS: Sexual problems. In DeVita VT, Hellman S, Rosenberg SA (eds): Cancer: Principles and Practice of Oncology. 4th ed. Philadelphia, JB Lippincott, 1993, pp 2464–2480.

161. Schover LR, Randers-Pehrson M: Sexuality and cancer—For the women who have cancer and her partner. Atlanta, American Cancer Society, 1991.

162. Schover LR, Randers-Pehrson M: Sexuality and cancer: For the men who have cancer and his partner. Atlanta, American Cancer Society, 1991.

163. Schover LR, von Eschenbach AC: Sexual and marital relationships after treatment for nonseminomatous testicular cancer. Urology 25:251–255, 1985.

164. Seibel MM, Freeman MM, Graves WL: Carcinoma of the cervix and sexual function. Obstet Gynecol 55:484–487, 1980.

165. Shamberger RC, Sherins RJ, Rosenberg SA: The effects of postoperative adjunct chemotherapy and radiotherapy on testicular function in men undergoing treatment for soft tissue sarcoma. Cancer 47:2368–2374, 1981.

166. Shapiro E, Kinsella TJ, Makuch RW, et al: Effects of fractionated irradiation on endocrine aspects of testicular function. J Clin Oncol 3:1232–1239, 1985.

167. Sherins RJ, DeVita VT Jr: Effect of drug treatment for lymphoma on male reproductive capacity. Studies of men in remission after therapy. Ann Intern Med 79:216–220, 1973.

168. Sherins RJ, Olweny CT, Ziegler JL: Gynecomastia and gonadal dysfunction in adolescent boys treated with combination chemotherapy for Hodgkin's disease. N Engl J Med 299:12–16, 1978.

169. Sherwin BB: A comparative analysis of the role of androgen in human male and female sexual behavioral specificity: Critical threshold and sensitivity. Psychobiology 16:416–425, 1988.

170. Slanina J: Long term side effects of irradiation in patients with Hodgkin's disease. Int J Radiat Oncol Biol Phys 2:1–19, 1977.

171. Sobrinho LG, Levine RA, DeConti RC: Amenorrhea in patients with Hodgkin's disease treated with antineoplastic agents. Am J Obstet Gynecol 109:135–139, 1971.

172. Spitz S: Histological effects of nitrogen mustard on human tumors and tissues. Cancer 1:383–398, 1948.

173. Stienberg MD, Juliano MA, Wise L: Psychological outcome of lumpectomy versus mastectomy in treatment of breast cancer. Am J Psychiatry 142:32–39, 1985.

174. Stellman RE, Goodwin JM, Robinson J, et al: Psychological effects of vulvectomy. Psychosomatics 25:779–783, 1984.

175. Stillerman AH: Sexual adjustment to mastectomy: Description comparison with partner's perspective and prediction of sexual adjustment [dissertation]. Dis Abstr Northwestern Univ, 1984.

176. Stillman RJ, Schinfeld JS, Schiff I, et al: Ovarian failure in long term survivors of childhood malignancy. Am J Obstet Gynecol 139:62–66, 1981.

177. Sutherland AM, Orbach CE, Dyk RB, Bard M: The psychological impact of cancer surgery: I. Adaptation to the dry colostomy: Preliminary report and summary of findings. Cancer 5:857–872, 1952.

178. Takasaki N, Okada S, Kawasaki T, et al: Studies on retroperitoneal lymph node dissection concerning postoperative ejaculatory function in patients with testicular cancer. Hinyokika Kiyo 37:213–219, 1991.

179. Tavel FR, Osius TG, Parker JW, et al: Retroperitoneal lymph node dissection. J Urol 89:241–245, 1963.

180. Thachil JV, Jewett MAS, Ridder WD: The effects of cancer and cancer therapy on male fertility. J Urol 126:141–145, 1981.

181. Tomic R, Bergman B, Damber JE, et al: Effects of external radiation therapy for cancer of the prostate on the serum concentration of testosterone, follicle stimulating hormone, luteinizing hormone and prolactin. J Urol 130:287–289, 1983.

182. Tomoda H, Furosawa M: Sexual and urinary dysfunction following surgery for sigmoid colon cancer. Jpn J Surg 15:355–360, 1985.

183. Van de Wiel HM, Weijmar Schultz WM, Hallensleben A, et al: Sexual functioning following treatment of cervical carcinoma. Eur J Gynaecol Oncol 9:275, 1988.

184. van Heeringen C, De Schryver A, Verbeek E: Sexual function disorders after local radiotherapy for carcinoma of the prostate. Radiother Oncol 13:47–52, 1988.

185. Van Thiel DH, Ross GT, Lipsett MB: Pregnancies after chemotherapy of trophoblastic neoplasms. Science 169:1326–1327, 1970.

186. Vera MI: Quality of life following pelvic exenteration. Gynecol Oncol 12:355–366, 1981.

187. Vincent CE, Vincent B, Greiss FC, Linton EB: Some marital sexual concomitants of carcinoma of the cervix. South Med J 68:52–58, 1975.

188. Vinokur AD, Threatt BA, Caplan RD, Zimmermann BL: Physical and psychosocial functioning and adjustment to breast cancer: Long term follow-up of a screening population. Cancer 63:394–405, 1989.

189. Vinokur AD, Threatt BA, Caplan RD, Zimmermann BL: Physical and psychosocial functioning and adjustment to breast conserving cancer treatment and mastectomy. Psychosomatics 31:33–39, 1990.

190. Vivani S, Santoro A, Ragri G, et al: Gonadal toxicity after combination chemotherapy for Hodgkin's disease: Comparative results of MOPP vs ABVD. Eur J Cancer Clin Oncol 21:601–605, 1985.

191. Von Eschenbach AC, Phamphilis TM, Kean TJ: Goals and potential for sexual rehabilitation. In Rodriguez DB (ed): Sexual Rehabilitation of the Urologic Cancer Patient. Boston, GK Hall & Co., 1981, pp 216–227.

192. Vose JM, Kennedy BC, Bierman PJ, et al: Long term sequelae of autologous bone marow or peripheral stem cell transplantation for lymphoid malignancies. Cancer 69:784–789, 1992.

193. Wabrek AJ, Wabrek CJ: Mastectomy: Sexual implications. Prim Care 3:803–810, 1976.

194. Walsh PC: Radical prostatectomy, prevention of sexual function, cancer control: The controversy. Urol Clin North Am 14:663–673, 1987.

195. Walsh PC, Donker PJ: Impotence following radical prostatecotmy: Insight into etiology and prevention. J Urol 128:492–497, 1982.

196. Walsh PC, Epstein JI, Lowe FC: Potency following radical proctectomy with wide unilateral excision of the neurovascular bundle. J Urol 138:823–827, 1987.

197. Walsh PC, Jewett HJ: Radical surgery for prostatic cancer. Cancer 45:1906–1911, 1980.
198. Walsh PC, Lepor H, Eggelston JC: Radical prostatectomy with preservation of sexual function. Prostate 4:473–485, 1983.
199. Walsh PC, Mostwin JL: Radical prostatectomy and cystoprostatectomy with preservation of potency. Results using a new nerve sparing technique. Br J Urol 56:694–697, 1984.
200. Walsh PC: Radical retropubic prostatectomy with reduced morbidity: An anatomic approach. NCI Monogr 7:133–137, 1988.
201. Walsh PC, Schlegel PN: Radical pelvic surgery with preservation of sexual function. Ann Surg 208:391–400, 1988.
202. Warne GL, Fairley KF, Hobbs JB, et al: Cyclophosphamide induced ovarian failure. N Engl J Med 289:159–1162, 1973.
203. Weijmar Schultz WCM, van de Wiel HBM, Bouma J, et al: Psychosocial functioning after the treatment of cancer of the vulva. Cancer 66:402–407, 1990.
204. Weinstein M, Roberts M: Sexual potency following surgery for rectal carcinoma: A follow-up of 44 patients. Ann Surg 185:295–300, 1977.
205. Weisman AD, Worden W: The fallacy of the post-mastectomy depression. Am J Med Sci 273:169–175, 1977.
206. Wellisch DK, Jamison KR, Pasnau RO: Psychological aspects of mastectomy: II. The man's perspective. Ann J Psychiatry 135:543–546, 1978.
207. Whitehead E, Shalet SM, Blackledge G, et al: The effect of combination chemotherapy on ovarian function in women treated for Hodgkin's disease. Cancer 52:988–993, 1983.
208. Whitelaw GP, Smithwick RH: Some secondary effects of sympathectomy with particular reference to disturbance of sexual function. N Engl J Med 245:121–130, 1951.
209. Yeager SE, Van Heerden JA: Sexual dysfunction following proctocolectomy and abdominoperineal resection. Ann Surg 191:169–170, 1980.
210. Zinreich ES, Derogatis LR, Herpst J, et al: Pretreatment evaluation of sexual function in patients with adenocarcinoma of the prostate. Int J Radiat Oncol Biol Phys 19:1001–1004, 1990.
211. Zuckerman S: The sensitivity of the gonads to radiation. Clin Radiol 26:1–15, 1965.

KEVIN G. SMITH, PhD
MARTIN GRABOIS, MD

CHRONIC PAIN AND SEXUALITY

From the Department of
  Anesthesiology (KGS)
  and
Department of Physical Medicine
  and Rehabilitation (MG)
Baylor College of Medicine
Houston, Texas

Reprint requests to:
Kevin Smith, PhD
6550 Fannin, Suite 1903
Houston, TX 77030

Chronic pain and sexual dysfunction are common problems confronted by physicians and other health professionals. Although the definition of chronic pain varies, a pain, in general, is considered chronic when it exceeds 3–6 months in duration.[16] Available statistics indicate that the incidence and cost of chronic pain in human suffering and economic loss is staggering.[3,30] Low back pain, for example, occurs in 50–80% of the general population of industrial societies.[30] It is estimated that 97 million Americans suffer from some kind of pain, at a total cost of about $79 billion per year in terms of lost work days and health care expenditures.[3] A majority of acute pain episodes remit without a physician's consultation. Low back pain, for example, is characterized by a high spontaneous remission rate, and it is equally characterized by a high recurrence rate.

An association between chronic pain and sexual dysfunction has been recognized;[21,22,28] however, few studies directly examine chronic pain and sexuality. A search using MEDLINE and PSYCLIT revealed very little published data on the subject. We attempted to gather additional information by conducting an informal survey. Leaders in the field of chronic pain research who were active in the American Pain Society and the American Academy of Pain Medicine were surveyed. Their responses, along with the additional literature searches, confirmed our initial impressions that a limited amount of work has been done in this area. This chapter summarizes material garnered from all of these sources, including a literature search, a survey of the leaders in the field of chronic pain, and observations from our own clinical practice.

FACTORS INFLUENCING SEXUALITY
IN PATIENTS WITH CHRONIC PAIN

Physical sexual activity has been known to precipitate, aggravate, or relieve pain. For example, coitus has been known to cause headaches[18] and to aggravate back pain.[28] In contrast, some patients report relief of pain and relaxation after sexual intercourse. Pain has been known to adversely affect sexual functioning in patients with ankylosing spondylitis,[9] rheumatoid arthritis,[40] and osteoarthritis.[5] The influence of pain in patients with arthritic conditions is discussed in greater detail in chapter 8.

The underlying pathophysiology of sexual dysfunction as it relates to chronic pain has not been studied extensively. A variety of chronic pain syndromes involving the perineum make sexual activity impractical. By definition, pudendal, genitofemoral, and ilioinguinal neuralgias interfere with sexual activity. Pudendal neuralgias are thought to be a cause of idiopathic vulvodynia.[20] Likewise, ilioinguinal and genitofemoral neuralgias also can lead to profound sexual dysfunction. Differentiating which nerves are involved and how to treat them sometimes requires a multidisciplinary approach involving the surgeon, neurologist, and anesthesiologist.[19]

Treatment interventions for chronic pain also can cause sexual dysfunction. Many of the medications prescribed for chronic pain will influence sexual performance. Excessive consumption of drugs, including prescribed opiates, is not uncommon in patients with chronic pain.[6,10] Sedatives, tranquilizers, and narcotics all may suppress sexual desire and cause erectile difficulties. If, however, pain symptoms and the associated emotional consequences are relieved with the medications, some patients will experience an improvement in sexual function. Abuse of prescription or illicit drugs is often a significant factor in decreased physical, psychological, and sexual functioning.

For patients undergoing invasive procedures, hypogastric and ilioinguinal blocks and the placement of a caudal epidural catheter can cause erectile dysfunction. For example, surgical interventions may damage the neural, endocrinal, and vascular control of erections. Sexual dysfunction may occur after lumbar sympathectomy.[19] Unilateral denervation is generally considered to have no effect on sexual function. In a study carried out by Whitelaw and Smithwick,[39] 12 men were submitted to unilateral removal of L1–3 ganglia. Seven of the 12 men described significant disturbance in sexual functioning, with either erectile difficulties and/or problems with ejaculation.

Cordotomy is another procedure that has been performed in patients with chronic pain. In one study,[31] a 4% incidence of sexual dysfunction was reported due to the complications of percutaneous cordotomy; a decrease occurred in voluptuous sensations about the genitals on the side rendered analgesic by the procedure. Impotence was reported only occasionally, even with bilateral cordotomies. The iatrogenic effects of pain treatment should be considered when a patient presents with pain and sexual dysfunction. This also raises questions for the clinician and patient about the relative benefit of pain relief through invasive procedures and the potential risk of sexual dysfunction with this approach.

The reduction in frequency of sexual activity can be caused by many factors other than medical treatment. The most likely causes include physical incapacity, real or perceived aggravation of pain, disinterest, a poor relationship with the partner, medications, and psychological problems either resulting from or preceding the onset of pain. Depression is common in patients with chronic pain, and depression may lead to or contribute to sexual dysfunction. Fear of aggravating the pain during sexual intercourse will influence sexual activity. If increased pain is frequently associated with sexual dysfunction, performance anxiety (i.e., inability to achieve or maintain an adequate erection) can also reduce the number of sexual encounters. So far, none of these factors have been systematically studied in patients with chronic pain.

CHRONIC PAIN AND MARITAL ADJUSTMENT

Pain complaints can indicate or precipitate a more severe problem with the marital relationship. While the relationship between sexual dysfunction and chronic pain may be underrepresented in the literature, the relationship between marital dysfunction and chronic pain is well known.[29] Since the earliest studies of women with pelvic pain,[11,12] researchers have studied marital adjustment in these patients. In these studies, sexual and marital dysfunction overlapped significantly.[11,12,17,18,22–25,28,29,36] They found that patients with pain had poorer marital adjustment than controls. Likewise, one study examined differences in marital dysfunction in pain patients with demonstrable organic lesions versus those with no observed organic pathology.[24] The patients with no organic basis for their pain complaint were more dysfunctional than the patients with actual organic findings. Despite these results, the relationship between pain and marital or sexual dysfunction remains unclear. While it is true that pain can be a psychological symptom,[22] some studies suggest that sexual maladjustment is simply the result of the pain itself.[20,27]

When one spouse is in pain, the other can also suffer. Studies of pain patients and their spouses have noted a correlation in psychopathology.[1,32] Block[2] monitored the skin conductance and heart rates of 16 people viewing their pain-patient spouses. Painful displays were associated by increased skin conductance by the viewing spouses. Spouses with higher marital satisfaction showed a greater increase in skin conductance than spouses who were not as satisfied with their marriages. These studies show that it is certainly possible for spouses and other family members to experience a physiological response to the "chronic illness behavior" of the person in pain.[2] It is also plausible that some spouses may avoid closeness and intimacy in order to avoid physiological discomfort.[12] Several authors have suggested that the symptom of pain can serve a communicative role between the patients and the people around them.[23,24] As the pain exerts its effects on others, it in turn is influenced in its expression by the expectations and responses of others.

Withdrawal from the sexual liaison can be a way of demonstrating the authenticity of pain, communicating anger toward the demanding spouse, and expressing unmet needs to be nurtured.[28] Problems become compounded when repeated medical and surgical work-ups are negative but the patient still complains of pain. In these circumstances, the spouse may question how much of the pain is actually physical. With a spouse's feeling of obligation and a need to care for the "medically ill" person, these conditions can bring a couple to a superficial harmony or what some authors have referred to as "pseudomutuality" or "sick role homeostasis" with cumulating conflicts underneath. It is often difficult to define the primary and secondary causes of decline in marital and sexual functioning. A reduction in sexual activity can be due to pain or to the spouses' response to pain behavior.

In most cases, the decline in marital functioning is due to a combination of factors. Spouses of patients with chronic pain may discourage patients from engaging in certain physical activities. They may also withdraw affection and attention or may increase demands on the patients in response to increased "well behavior." Changes in roles and responsibilities also may influence sexuality. Family members may not be supportive of the patient's attempts to resume former roles and duties if doing so leads to fewer satisfying activities for themselves.[12,28]

One of the few studies that directly examined marital and sexual adjustment in chronic pain patients was conducted by Osborne and Maruta.[28] In this study, 50 married chronic pain patients and their spouses were interviewed independently; 70% of the patients had a history of chronic back and/or extremity pain, and 78% reported either elimination or reduction in sexual activity. Approximately half of the people in each group reported experiencing sexual dysfunction after the onset of the pain problem. Two thirds of the patients reported pain after sexual activity, and a majority of the spouses of these patients recognized the increase in pain in the affected spouse. This patient group tended to maximize the frequency of sexual activity before pain and minimize the frequency of sexual activity after pain. The results of this study, although small, provide clear evidence for the impact of chronic pain on sexual functioning.

In addition to sexual dysfunction, marital satisfaction can be affected by the patient's irritability, depression, use of medication, inability to work, and associated financial problems. In other cases, couples have reported that pain "brought us closer together."[28] Before pain, 80% of both patients and spouses in Maruta's and Osborne's study were satisfied with their adjustment.[21] After pain, the rate of satisfaction dropped to one third, and approximately half of both the patients and spouses expressed dissatisfaction with their level of marital adjustment. In another study by Maruta and Osborne,[22] sexual activity and marital adjustment were examined in 66 married patients with a history of chronic pain of nonmalignant origin for six months or more. Thirty-two percent of the women and 44% of the men reported deterioration in the overall marital relationship; 60% of the men and 56% of the women noted deterioration in sexual adjustment in marriage. Only 5% of women and 4% of men experienced an improvement in their overall marital adjustment. More recently, Monga et al.[26] presented the preliminary results of sexual functioning in 27 patients with pain lasting more than 6 months. Among these patients, 72% reported that they were sexually active; 31% engaged in sexual intercourse at least once a week and 50% in masturbation. About 45% of the men experienced erectile dysfunction, and 32% had difficulty achieving orgasm. Half described the quality of their present sexual functioning as poor. Among the patients who were sexually active, 55% were moderately to extremely satisfied with their personal relationships with their sexual partners. A similar result was found for women. A majority of the women were sexually active; two of the four patients described having multiple orgasms, and all were extremely interested in sexual activities. These results indicate that although sexual dysfunction does exist for patients with chronic pain, many remain relatively satisfied with the quality of their sexual relationships.

PSYCHOSEXUAL DISORDERS AND SEXUAL ABUSE

In addition to sexual dysfunction as a consequence of pain and its related treatments, physicians have observed the comorbidity of other psychosexual disorders and chronic pain. Herr[15] presented a case report of a woman with back pain who requested help with problems related to sexual identity and gender reassignment. Rehabilitation goals in these cases can be influenced by concerns about sexual identity. The patient's ability to set clear goals can be impaired if continued ambivalence and confusion about identity exists. These patients often desire to make career choices that they perceive to be congruent with their preferred sexual identity. In our experience, confusion over career choices is often linked to continued ambivalence related to sexual identity. Patients need counseling to address these concurrent and interrelated medical, psychosocial, and career-related issues.[4,38]

An association between chronic pain and a history of spouse or childhood sexual abuse has been well documented. Researchers have shown a history of spouse and/or sexual abuse in patients with chronic pain,[13] pelvic pain,[37] headache,[7] and gastrointestinal disorders.[39] While this relationship has been well established, the exact causal nature is less clear. One study showed a higher incidence of women who were abused among patients with pain complaints for which no clear cause could be identified.[13] However, patients with chronic pain with clear causes, such as trauma, and objective organic findings also can present with a history of sexual abuse. In our view, the causal relationship in these cases is less evident. However, it is certainly possible that a person with a history of childhood sexual abuse may cope less effectively and be more at risk for developing maladaptive behavior patterns such as chronic pain syndrome or posttraumatic stress disorder. The treatment of pain in patients with a history of sexual abuse is not substantially different, but a sensitivity on the part of treating clinicians concerning issues of childhood sexual abuse and its many effects can enhance the physician-patient relationship, lead to better patient management, and promote successful treatment outcome.

EVALUATION AND MANAGEMENT

It is important to recognize that chronic pain may lead to sexual problems and at times may be a reflection of underlying psychological or familial distress. Questions about sexual functioning should be included as a part of any complete physical history. Premorbid functioning of the patient's psychological and marital relations should be explored. Because chronic pain may be associated with a reduction in the frequency and quality of sexual encounters, the interviewer should directly ask about the frequency of sexual activity, the means of sexual expression, and the satisfaction in sexual activity both currently and before the onset of pain. If possible, the interviewer should include both partners in these evaluations.

Assessment of the quality of the marital relationship is often vital in understanding not only the pain problem but also sexual-related issues. It is important to assess the effects of pain on the marital relationship and the degree of marital satisfaction before and after the onset of the pain problem. Exploring sexual activities is a sensitive area; it can be helpful to open the interview by stating that people with pain often find that their marital relationship is affected by pain. A subsequent question about how the couple may view the effects of chronic pain on their relationship may be less threatening. It is also important to find out what they believe would happen to the sexual relationship if the pain got better.

At times chronic pain may bring the partners closer through increased emotional intimacy or increased time together. For others, pain complaints can be used as an excuse for not engaging in sexual activity when the real reason is primary sexual dysfunction or marital discord. Successful treatment of the pain may threaten an otherwise satisfactory arrangement. If such issues become apparent, they need to be addressed as part of the total management of chronic pain. Aspects of the patient's pain problem that may be reinforcing to family members also need to be identified. If a psychologist is not a part of the multidisciplinary team, a referral would be appropriate to address these issues.

Once the history of sexual dysfunction and other factors have been elicited, treatment alternatives can be explored. In many cases, the use of multiple medications or substances is a common culprit. Reduction of narcotics or sedatives can be accomplished as part of a comprehensive chronic pain management program. If these problems persist, the patient should be referred to an alcohol or substance abuse program. In selected cases, in which major psychosocial issues have been delineated, psychotherapy should be considered. Various psychotherapeutic approaches are discussed in more detail in chapter 17. The patient and partner can be counseled about the need to plan sexual activities at times when the pain is at a minimum. The timing of pain medications may need to be adjusted so that there is maximum relief of pain around the time when sexual encounters are expected to occur. Further, pain medication can be taken about half an hour prior to sexual activity. However, this may remove the element of spontaneity that is important in any relationship. Advice on alternative positioning should be provided, especially in patients with limited range of motion. An excellent guide to various positioning options is provided by Herbert.[14] Unfortunately, no research has been carried out to assess the practical aspects and beneficial effects of any specific position. Relaxation exercises and hypnotic techniques may be helpful to control the pain and enhance the sexual experience. Other useful approaches include stretching exercises, massage, and movement therapy. Finally, the definition of sexual activity can be broadened to include activities other than sexual intercourse.

SUMMARY

Chronic pain and sexual dysfunction are common problems confronted by physicians and other health care providers. Physical sexual activity has been known to precipitate, aggravate, or relieve pain. A reduction in frequency of sexual activity can be caused by many factors, including physical incapacity, aggravation of pain, disinterest, a poor relationship with the partner, marital discord prior to the onset of pain, medications, and psychological problems either resulting from pain or preceding the onset of pain. So far, none of these factors have been systematically studied. Although the relationship between sexual dysfunction and chronic pain may be underrepresented in the literature, the relationship between marital dysfunction and chronic pain is well known. While it is true that pain can be a psychological symptom, sexual maladjustment in some cases is simply the result of the pain itself. Many of the treatment interventions for patients with chronic pain can cause sexual dysfunction in patients undergoing invasive procedures, including surgery, and in patients taking excessive amounts of sedatives, tranquilizers, and narcotics. The iatrogenic effects of pain treatment should be considered when a patient presents with sexual dysfunction. It is important to include questions about sexual functioning as a part of any complete physical history. Assessment of the quality of the marital relationship is often vital in understanding not only the pain problem but issues related to sexual functioning.

More research is needed to examine the effects of chronic pain on marital and sexual satisfaction. Specifically, studies examining the impact of various treatment modalities on the sexual functioning of chronic pain patients is needed.

REFERENCES

1. Ahern D, Follick M, Adams A: Emotional and marital distress in spouses of chronic low back pain patients. Pain (suppl 2):S15, 1984.
2. Block A: An investigation of the relationship of the spouse to chronic pain behavior. Psychosom Med 43:395–402, 1981.
3. Bonica J: General considerations of chronic pain. In Bonica JJ (ed): The Management of Pain, Vol 2. Philadelphia, Lea & Febiger, 1990, pp 181–183.
4. Chubon RA: Addressing concurrent transexuality, disability, and career-related problems: The case of Jackie/Jack. Career Dev Q 37:108–112, 1988.
5. Currey HLF: Osteoarthritis of the hip joint and sexual activity. Ann Rheum Dis 29:488–493, 1970.
6. De Leon G, Wexler HH: Heroin addiction: Its relation to sexual behavior and sexual experience. J Abnorm Psychol 81:36–38, 1973.
7. Domino JV, Haber JD: Prior physical and sexual abuse in women with chronic headache: Clinical correlates. Headache 27:310–314, 1987.
8. Drossman D, Leserman J, Nachman G: Sexual and physical abuse in women with functional or organic gastrointestinal disorders. Ann Intern Med 113:828–833, 1990.
9. Elst P, Sybesma T, van der Stadt RJ, et al: Sexual problems in rheumatoid arthritis and ankylosing spondylitis. Arthritis 27:217–220, 1984.
10. Gomez-Marrero J, Feria M, Mas M: Stimulation of opioid receptors suppresses penile erectile reflexes and seminal emission in rats. Pharmacol Biochem Behav 31:393–396, 1978.
11. Gidro-Frank L, Gordon T, Taylor H Jr: Pelvic pain and female identity. Am J Neurol Neurosurg Psychiatry 25:1184–1202, 1960.
12. Gidro-Frank L, Gordon T: Reproductive performance of women with pelvic pain of long duration. Fertil Steril 7:440–447, 1956.
13. Haber JD, Roos C: Effects of spouse abuse and/or sexual abuse in the development and maintenance of chronic pain in women. In Fields HL, et al (eds): Advances in Pain Research and Therapy. Vol 9. New York, Raven, 1985, pp 889–895.
14. Herbert L: Sex and Back Pain. Edina, MN, Educational Opportunities, 1987.
15. Herr EL: Career counseling in a case of sexual identity change: Jackie/Jack. Career Dev Q 37:102–107, 1988.
16. International Association for the Study of Pain: Classification of chronic pain: Description of chronic pain syndromes and definitions of pain states. In Merskey H (ed): Pain (suppl 3):S1, 1986.
17. Kreitman N, Sainsbury P, Pearce K, Costain W: Hypochondriasis and depression outpatients at a general hospital. Brit J Psychiatry 3:607–615, 1965.
18. Lance JW: Headaches related to sexual activity. J Neurol Neurosurg Psychiatry M39:1226, 1976.
19. Loeser JD, Sweet WH, Tew JM Jr, van Loveren H: Neurosurgical operations involving peripheral nerves. In Bonica JJ (ed): The Management of Pain, Vol 2. Philadelphia, Lea & Febiger, 1990, p 2055.
20. Magni G, DeBertolini C: Chronic pain as a depressive equivalent. Postgrad Med 73:79–85, 1983.
21. Maruta T, Osborne D: Sexual activity in chronic pain patients. Psychosomatics 19:531–537, 1978.
22. Maruta T, Osborne D, Swanson D, Halling J: Chronic pain patients and spouses: Marital and sexual adjustment. Mayo Clin Proc 56:307–310, 1981.
23. Merskey H: Psychiatric patients with persistent pain. Psychosom Res 9:299–309, 1965.
24. Merskey H, Boyd D: Emotional adjustment and chronic pain. Pain 5:173–178, 1978.
25. Mohamed SN, Weisz GM, Waring EM: The relationship of chronic pain to depression, marital adjustment, and family dynamics. Pain 5:285–292, 1978.
26. Monga TN, Tan G, Ostermann H, Grabois M: Sexuality in patients with chronic pain [abstract]. Presented at IRMA VII meeting Washington, DC, April 1994.
27. Norfleet M, Hammett B, Lichte S, et al: Helping families cope with chronic pain. In Wolberg L, Aronson M (eds): Group and Family Therapy. New York, Brenner/Mazel, 1982, pp 302–321.
28. Osborne D, Maruta T: Sexual adjustment and chronic back pain. Med Aspects Hum Sex 14:94–113, 1980.
29. Payne B, Norfleet M: Chronic pain and the family: A review. Pain 26:1–22, 1986.
30. Raj P (ed): Practical Management of Pain. Chicago, Year Book, 1986.
31. Rosomoff H, Papo I, Loeser J: Neurosurgical operations of the spinal cord. In Bonica JJ (ed): The Management of Pain, Vol 2. Philadelphia, Lea & Febiger, 1990, p 2070.
32. Shanfield SB, Herman EM, Cope DN, Jones JR: Pain and the marital relationship: Psychiatric distress. Pain 343–351, 1979.
33. Starling JR, Harms BA, Schroeder ME, Eichman PL: Diagnosis and treatment of genitofemoral and ilioinguinal entrapment neuralgia. Surgery, October:581–586, 1987.

34. Sternbach R, Wolf RC, Murphy RW, Akeson WH: Aspects of chronic low back pain. Psychosomatics 14:52–56, 1973.
35. Turner M, Marinoff S: Pudendal neuralgia. Am J Obstet Gynecol 165:1233–1236, 1991.
36. Violon A: The onset of facial pain. Psychother Psychosom 34:11–16, 1980.
37. Walker E, Katon W, Harrop-Griffiths J, et al: Relationship of chronic pelvic pain to psychiatric diagnoses and childhood sexual abuse. Am J Psychiatry 145:75–80, 1988.
38. Webb B, Betsy J: Back problems and a new life direction: The case of Jackie/Jack. Career Dev Q 37:99–101, 1988.
39. Whitelaw, Smithwick: In Aronoff GM (ed): Evaluation and Treatment of Chronic Pain. Baltimore, Urban & Schwarzenberg, 1985.
40. Yoshino S, Uchida S: Sexual problems of women with rheumatoid arthritis. Arch Phys Med Rehabil 62:112–123, 1981.

MAUREEN R. NELSON, MD

SEXUALITY IN CHILDHOOD DISABILITY

From the Departments of Physical
  Medicine and Rehabilitation
  and Pediatrics
Baylor College of Medicine
  and
Department of Physical Medicine
  and Rehabilitation
Texas Children's Hospital
Houston, Texas

Reprint requests to:
Maureen R. Nelson, MD
Chief
Department of Physical Medicine
  and Rehabilitation
Texas Children's Hospital
6621 Fannin Street
Mail Code 2-2590
Houston, TX 77030

The development of sexuality is a long-term process in any child, and it is additionally complicated in a child and adolescent with a disability. Sexuality has been described in many ways, most generally in broad terms describing a part of one's personality or self-concept. It includes one's feelings and expression of being a male or a female. This includes sexual drives and behaviors but certainly is not limited to them. Sexuality is influenced by personal, societal, and cultural factors that include physical, emotional, spiritual, and social portions of the personality.

Five percent of children are born with some type of physical or mental disability,[27] including Down syndrome, spina bifida, cerebral palsy, and neuromuscular diseases. Additionally, approximately 200,000 children have a serious traumatic brain injury each year, and about 1,110 children have a spinal cord injury each year. These disabilities will have an impact on the child's total development, including sexual development.

This chapter reviews current concepts of socialization of children, starting in infancy, including sexual aspects of socialization and the impact of disabilities on sexual development. Sex education for children with disabilities and sexual functioning in childhood-onset disabilities, including reproduction, also are addressed.

SEXUAL DEVELOPMENT

The steps of sexual development are almost universal. Although the rate at which they occur may vary, particularly in a child with disability, the sequence remains basically the same. Specific disabilities can lead to predictable variances or challenges in a child's development. Some of these variations are amenable to specific interventions by the parents or other caretakers.

Infants

In infancy, children experience their first relationships with other individuals. These lay a basis for the child's perception of all future relationships. Touch is a major factor that is believed to give children a feeling of security and bonding.[4] Mutual gaze, particularly with the mother, has been described as one of the primary means of creating a bond between the mother and child. For a child who is born with a severe visual defect, touch or other means must be substituted for the gaze to form a bond.[19] Holding and cuddling of a baby have been described not only as nurturing but as playing a role in future sexual development. A child learns to enjoy this activity.[28] Infants are also taking in food, smells, and other sensory input. They are beginning to learn a good deal about the world and its interactions. The basics of social interaction are believed to be in place within the first 6 months.[19] These positive interactions contribute to trusting others and beginning to develop a healthy social and sexual development.

Decreased holding and hugging of children, even if due to poor emotional or physical response from the child, which may be a result of increased tone or other physical problem, may led to an altered sense of self and an altered perception of touch by the child. Similarly, separation from the parent for extended periods for hospitalization or other reasons may lead the child to a feeling of confusion. Additonally, some children experience feeding difficulties, which leads to confusion in the association they should feel between feeding and pleasure.[11]

Toddlers

By the time children are 2 years old, they generally learn their gender identity, the fact that they are a boy or girl. A child at this stage is beginning to learn its gender role, the things it does and says to indicate that it is male or a female. Many experiences in childhood will contribute to a child's concept of what being a boy or girl means. This may be altered in a child with a disability. Additionally, with the extra demands placed on parents to take care of a disabled child's physical needs, they may not place as much emphasis on teaching about issues related to social skills and sexuality.[40] The parents are the initial teachers and role models in sexuality for a child.

As well as learning the differences between boys and girls during this age, children are learning the names of parts of the body. It is helpful to include the names of all parts of the body, including penis and breast. A child is also beginning to learn limits and the rules of social expectations. As their cognitive and language skills grow, they are learning skills for communication. Learning appropriate words to express one's self about sexual matters can contribute to preventing sexual abuse and exploitation.[4,29] With increased knowledge, the child may better recognize inappropriate behavior and be able to describe it to trusted adults.

Traditionally, children gain control over their bowel and bladder during the toddler phase. For some children, this will never be possible. Other children, however, will be able to participate in some manner in maintaining continence or helping to maintain clean clothes.

In children who undergo frequent physical examinations or physical therapy, some touching has been described as intrusive, clinical, and sometimes uncomfortable. With this can come feelings that one's body causes pain and that one's body is connected with unpleasant experiences.[38]

Preschoolers

Children during the preschool period are continuing to learn their sexual role and, by the time they enter school, have a fair idea of expectations for males and females. Children in the 3- to 5-year-old range generally have an increased awareness of sexuality, and the identification as a male or female is increased.[28] Social isolation may become a problem. Children with visible deficits are often rejected as playmates by healthy peers. A frequent problem involves not having a model of an adult with a similar disability to use as a standard for comparison.[40]

Privacy may be a problem for children with disabilities. They may need to be more closely supervised by caretakers, and, since children frequently learn from spontaneous physical interaction, this form of learning may be limited. The lack of privacy may affect the child's perception of his or her own body and of personal boundaries in regard to touch. A child with a physical disability is frequently handled by many people for various medical procedures or medical care. This touch, of course, is very different than the touch of a hug. Children may be partially or totally disrobed for the purpose of physical examination or treatment. It is very confusing for a child to be touched so much by strangers, and this may lead to confusion about public and private nudity and appropriateness of touch.[4]

Self-exploration of the genitals is a common activity for toddlers. Both boys and girls tend to do this after they have achieved the physical coordination to do so. For children with disabilities, not only is a lack of privacy a hinderance in this area but some children may not be able to reach their genitals, and others may have a lack of sensation. Children learn in spontaneous and innocent ways, but disabled children frequently have much less opportunity to learn in this manner than do other children.[4] Children need to be taught that masturbation is not carried out in public areas. Some researchers believe that this activity is important in preliminary learning of sexual self-image and sexual responsiveness for future activity as an adult.[28]

School-Age Children

Children in the school-age group turn their focus from themselves to the outside world. Children begin looking to their peer group for support, interaction, and information. They develop their social skills and compare ideas, including those about sexuality. Children with disabilities may have limited opportunities due to social isolation. Children who are blind will be deprived of learning the nonverbal signals that people give during communication. The child could give inadvertent nonverbal signals that may not be what he means and may actually be offensive.[19] Similarly, deaf children may have difficulty communicating with other children of their age.[12] Since blind and deaf children have limited opportunity to compare ideas with their peers and become socially isolated, they require special assistance maximizing their communication, particularly with other children.[11] Children with physical disabilities may also become socially isolated, either due to lack of mobility and physical skills or to overprotective family members and other providers of care. Having children participate in organized recreational and social activities such as sports, music, hobbies or other activities can assist them in overcoming some of these obstacles. Children of this age are learning the cultural roles for each gender. This is also a common time for a child to first develop a crush on an adult. It also is an important time for the child to find that there can be affection for someone outside the family and that they can find love in more than one place.[28]

Lack of information about sexuality can include the area of physical pubertal changes. Parents and others should teach children about the changes that will occur in puberty prior to their occurrence. Teaching about bodily changes, including menarche and nocturnal emissions, is helpful. It is also important for the child to understand the difference between what is considered appropriate in private versus in public.

Children with increased social isolation will need more information than other children because they have fewer opportunities for spontaneous learning, both in observing others and interacting among themselves.

Adolescents

Adolescence is a tumultuous time for any youngster. Bodies change during puberty, and secondary sex characteristics develop. Girls begin to menstruate generally between 10 and 13 years of age, and boys begin to have nocturnal emissions generally between 13 and 15 years of age. Our cultural emphasis on a perfect body is learned by almost every child by this time. It places a good deal of stress on any adolescent and is magnified with someone who has a physical disability. Looking or moving differently than one's peers is an exaggerated problem during adolescence. Some teens may have a precocious or delayed puberty. Variation from the physical developmental level of peers may add to the teen's stress. The adolescent with a physical disability must develop a body image that frequently includes a wheelchair, braces, or a crutch.[15] With the rapid changes seen in adolescence, the teen must find a balance between the positive and negative aspects of the body and feel comfortable with it. The balance is made more difficult for the teenager with physical disability.[5] Studies of teens with visible physical disabilities have reported that they saw themselves as lacking in romantic appeal and had poorer body images than others.[22] Adolescents with physical disabilities subconsciously may wonder if their defective bodies will be able to function sexually.[35,36] Teenagers with disabilities that are less visually apparent, who do not feel ill but may need periodic hospitalization or medical care, may deny their disability in their desire to be "normal." Additionally, without a visible handicap they may not receive the sympathy from the public that someone with a visible problem may obtain.[16]

Adolescence is a time for moving toward independence. This is made more difficult in people who are dependent on their parents for physical care. Lack of experience in self-care and overprotection may add to this problem. To minimize the problem, it is helpful to have children begin to participate in self-care activities within their abilities as early as possible and to gradually increase this participation as physical and cognitive abilities allow. Such an approach may help minimize rebellion, which can lead to serious physical and emotional problems during adolescence. One of the problems with teens attempting to gain independence is that experimentation and use of trial and error are common behaviors for doing so. These common ways to learn success in decision making may be limited in the adolescent with a disability. Having a physical disability or chronic illness also may lead to regression of personal development.[16] Children who grow up being dependent in their activities and in their daily care may learn a pattern of "learned helplessness" that may make them overly compliant and make achieving independence more difficult.[15]

Independence from parents is not only emotional but financial. For children who have minimal opportunities to learn job skills and who have significant potential medical costs, the financial aspect is an added difficulty. This is a very helpful time to have a role model of another adult, particularly one with a disability. Although such a role model often is not available in person, beginning recently, a disabled role model occasionally can be found in the mass media. Communication skills are growing and are of crucial importance for socialization. Social opportunities during adolescence are important in the rehearsal of adult gender roles. Teens try out various interactions to increase their capacity for friendship, intimacy, and their ideas about themselves. These rehearsals help develop a value system, including that related to sexual behavior, and aid in developing their sexual identity. Sexual behavior at this time is largely experimental and sporadic.[28] Around puberty many teens interact with others out of curiosity in genital manipulation and exploration. This may be with a person of the same or opposite sex. It is a demonstration of curiosity that is extremely common, particularly in boys.[23]

In looking at social and sexual activity and knowledge in adolescents with disability compared with others, several trends are evident. Results vary and are more positive in recent studies than in those performed ten or more years ago. However, teens and young adults with physical disabilities had much more frequently not been on a date than other teenagers, and those who did date did so less frequently than other teens. Additionally, a much higher percent of the disabled teens and young adults had not had sex, and more of those who were sexually active did not use birth control. Surprisingly few had spoken with a doctor or anyone else about specific sexual questions regarding their disabilty or about the chance of passing it along genetically. Despite receiving sex education at school, knowledge of anatomy, sexual function, and reproduction was lower in several groups of teens with disabilities than other teens.[6]

Social interaction and success are reportedly more related to the environment and to the family than to the severity of physical disability.[6,24,31] A significant factor in young women with disabilities having active social lives was their parental expectations. Unfortunately, only a small percentage of parents studied expected their daughters to be socially active.[30,31] Many parents did, however, promote impressive educational goals.[31] One study looking at disabled women and social and sexual experience showed that women with disabilities had dates, steady relationships, and sexual contact significantly later in life than controls. However, masturbation occurred at the same time for the two groups.[2,24] This was interpreted to indicate that the disabled young women and teens had a similar awareness and interest in sexual feelings but fewer social opportunities for expression.[31] Adolescent girls with chronic disease have been felt to be at a greater risk of pregnancy than other teens. This higher risk has been interpreted as a subconscious attempt on the girls' part to prove that they are "normal." Regardless of whether a higher risk of pregnancy exists, there certainly is a higher risk of complications with pregnancy or sexually transmitted diseases among disabled than other teens.[5]

Menarche is a more important time for girls with disabilities than for other girls. It may be perceived as a positive occurrence in which the body finally does something that it is supposed to do, just like every female body should.[32] Conversely, it may be unwelcomed by the parents as a sign of their disabled daughter's emerging sexuality and possible independence.[41] The girl may react to menarche with fear if she is unaware of menstruation; if she has been properly educated prior to menarche by her parents or others, she may accept this as a usual occurrence.

Social skills generally develop slowly throughout childhood and adolescence through both personal experience and observation. These skills include the ability to relate to others in different situations and the ability to understand various levels of meaning. Similarly, the ability to learn the range of human emotions and how to control one's reactions to them occurs through many positive and negative experiences.[41]

SEX EDUCATION

Sex education begins informally in very early life through information from and observation of the parents and the family environment. It is important to acknowledge that the child is a sexual being and to validate the child's or parent's concerns about sexuality.[11] Developmentally appropriate social and sexual information should be given to the children to reduce the risk of sexual exploitation and abuse.[4,29] Using language that is simple and appropriate and using repetition and audiovisual material can be helpful.[25] Structured, specific opportunities to learn social skills and sex information are important for individuals with disabilities due to their limited opportunity for everyday learning of these matters. With most disabilities there is a capacity to learn how to use social skills and information that will improve the quality of life.[14]

Prior to establishing and providing sex education programs in school or other environments, it is important to inform the parents and to address any concerns they may have. Parents of disabled and nondisabled children have raised the issue that teaching sex education will prematurely interest children in sex and involve them in sexual activity. Research has shown that this is not the case.[28] Parents of children with disabilities frequently fear that their children will be unable to establish a satisfactory relationship or they will be used or hurt if they do become involved. Varying values and moral systems also may be an area of concern for parents.

Sex education can progress along with a child's developmental status. It can go from a general gender identity program beginning in kindergarten, along with socialization and communication skills appropriate for the age, to addressing anatomy, physiology, responsible behavior, social consequences of behavior, sexually transmitted diseases, and contraception in an adolescent group. Sex education sometimes is included in a course such as family life, which looks at other aspects, including boy/girl differences, heredity, and dating.[28]

People with and without physical disabilities all make individual adjustments for their social and sexual needs. There are various ways to be sexually active and to express oneself sexually that vary with physical abilities and interests.[37] It is particularly important for adolescents with spinal cord injury or other disability that leads to a lack of genital sensation to understand this and to know that nongenital orgasms are possible.

There may be different approaches for special needs in sex education. Some approaches that have been used include (a) using sets of films demonstrating social behaviors, (b) role playing in a controlled situation, and (c) self-instruction in which the student models an activity after the instructor.[15] Another approach, called the "circle concept," teaches people with developmental delay or mental retardation about various aspects of sexuality, including appropriate social interactions. This is taught in a multisensory way using auditory/visual and motor inputs to deal with various social and sexual situations. This is a concrete and specific means to help the individual understand where various persons would properly fit in their social circle.[3] In a related area, programs have been proposed that use concrete steps to instruct young women with developmental disabilities or mental retardation about menstruation and how to take care of it.[7]

Sex education or counseling can be extremely specific depending on the individuals' physical condition, questions, and reproductive implications. For example, a woman with spastic diplegic cerebral palsy may be interested in information about spasticity in the vaginal area since she has spasticity in the adductors of the leg. She may ask about specific positions that may be more comfortable for sexual intercourse due to the spasticity in the lower extremities, and she may also have specific questions about genetics, pregnancy, and childbirth.[34]

Sex education may also include genetic counseling. Approximately 5% of babies born in the United States have some type of mental or physical disability, including physical anomalies that require surgical intervention.[27] If a potential parent has a disability, the risk for having a child with a disability is 5% plus the specific risk for the individual's disability. If the person's disability was due to trauma, there is no additional genetic risk. If, however, the disability is genetic, the additional risk can be evaluated. For each diagnosis a very specific input can and should be given to prospective parents.[27]

SOCIOSEXUAL OUTCOMES WITH SPECIFIC DIAGNOSES

Cancer can add stress to sexual development in a variety of manners. Its impact varies with the specific diagnosis and with the treatment. Some common malignancies seen in adolescence include acute leukemia, central nervous system tumors, lymphomas, and bone tumors. Treatment can change the teens' body image in an array of ways. Alopecia is an infamous side effect of treatment for many types of cancer. Skin changes, including acne, dermatitis, and pruritus can result from irradiation and from several types of chemotherapy. Amputations may be involved, particularly in bone tumors, and may drastically change the teens' body image. For boys, testicular biopsy and radiation may be part of the treatment for acute leukemia. Nausea and vomiting, which are present in several types of chemotherapy and radiation, add to the list of problems.[23]

Some types of chemotherapy may cause temporary changes in ovulation or spermatogenesis. Since these agents may produce abnormalities of the fetus, the teen must understand that chemotherapy does not serve as birth control. The use of contraceptives is essential in sexually active teens on chemotherapy. Contraceptives must be carefully chosen depending on diagnosis, treatment, and current problems. A gynecologist should be consulted.[23]

Turner syndrome results in a defective or missing X chromosome in women with resultant dysgenetic ovaries and physical malformation, with normal external genitalia. Puberty does not usually occur spontaneously because the ovaries do not produce a normal amount of estrogen. Women with Turner syndrome are infertile and markedly short. However, they have been noted to have more traditionally feminine behavior characteristics both in childhood and adulthood. They are less physically active and aggressive. They are frequently treated with androgens in an attempt to increase their growth and then later treated with cyclic estrogen and progesterone replacements. There are several theories of why the behavior in Turner syndrome is more traditionally feminine. The theories include illness effect, being separated from one's age group, the effect of physical anomalies, self-perception of being fragile, being less attractive and rejected by the peer group, hormone exposure, and short height.[9]

Children with hearing impairment miss information while growing up. They have a decreased ability to understand social cues and have difficulty with reading. Children who know only sign language are restricted in the ability to interact with individuals who can hear. Sexual information must be very specific and graphic to be understood.[10]

Visual impairment can cause serious deficits in understanding because children cannot see to imitate what others around them do. In conversation, they miss nonverbal cues, including facial expressions. Blind children cannot see how male and female bodies are different or how they change with puberty. Without vision, children may have difficulty forming basic concepts and generalizations.[19] Touching is infrequent in the American culture, which can be a problem for children with visual deficit.

Teens who have severe visual deficit have difficulty even seeing who is around them at school or a party to know who they would be interested in speaking with. Even if they are interested in an individual, it is physically difficult for them to get to a person they cannot see, and it is difficult to get away from a person. In our society, eye contact is a frequent initiating event for social interaction. This cannot occur if one cannot see.

People who become deaf (adventitiously deaf), particularly those who become deaf after they have learned speech and language (postlingually deaf), will have some advantages over those who are congenitally deaf or who lost their hearing prior to acquiring speech and language (prelingually deaf) (Table 1).[12]

DIAGNOSIS-SPECIFIC PROBLEMS WITH SEXUAL FUNCTIONING

A number of childhood-onset disabilities lead to predictable and specific deficits in sexual functioning. The deficits can be in the area of actual ability to perform sexual activities, fertility, or difficulties using contraception. Some difficulties in sexual functioning in childhood-onset disabilities such as as spinal cord injury or traumatic brain injury are covered in other chapters.

Of all the pediatric-onset disabilities, by far the most research into sexuality is in spina bifida (myelomeningocele or SB). Although a fair amount of research has been done in both teens and adults with SB, the majority of it relies on self-report for its description of anatomic functioning. There appears to be a consensus that the majority of males are able to obtain erections, but there is variability on descriptions of the predictability of erections by spinal cord level involvement or bulbocavernosus or anocutaneous reflexes. Diamond et al. reported that 89% of men injured at a level at or below T10 and with a positive anocutaneous reflex had erections, but only 14% of men injured at levels above T10 and with a negative anocutaneous reflex were able to do so.[8] However, Jumper et al. did not find any correlation with level of lesion, bulbocavernosus reflex, rectal tone, or perineal sensation. They did note that most of the erections were reported as random, spontaneous events that occurred without physical stimulation. They also reported that over half of the patients had seminal emissions. In this group, there also was no change in the expected pattern of pubertal development, with most changes occurring at the expected rate. There were normal levels of testosterone, and penile and testes length was within normal limits.[20] A placement of an artificial

TABLE 1.   Obstacles in Sexual Development

Diagnosis	Infants	Toddlers	Preschoolers	School-age Children	Adolescents
Cerebral palsy	Increased tone with resultant poor response to holding and hugging	Spasticity and decreased mobility may interfere with toilet training	Lack of coordination Lack of mobility	Lack of mobility May have communication difficulties	Body image
Spina bifida	Decreased sensory input	Bowel/bladder training	May lack genital sensation Lack of mobility	Lack of mobility	Body image
Neuromuscular disease	May have decreased tone and poor response to holding	As in infancy	Lack of strength Lack of mobility	Lack of mobility	Body image
Blindness	Cannot gaze at mother/caretaker to form bond	Difficulty in learning body parts, overall body composition and differences between bodies of different ages and of the opposite gender	Less understanding of public/private behavior differences	Miss nonverbal cues	As in school age
Deafness	Decreased/no auditory input	Learning names of body parts	Communication deficits	Communication with peers	As in school age

urinary sphincter around the neck of the bladder does not alter sexual development or sexual function.[20] Although there is decreased fertility in men, there have been reports of fatherhood.[21] This decreased fertility has been poorly quantitated.

There is no decrease in fertility in women with SB. However, pregnancy may increase urinary tract infections and urinary incontinence and may exacerbate back pain. The presence of genital sensation is variable. Joint contractures may interfere with positioning for sexual activities as well as the use of some birth control devices, including the diaphragm and intrauterine device. Birth control pills should not be used if circulation problems have been reported.[32] The risk of spina bifida is 3% in the offspring of individuals with spina bifida and 0.1% in the general population.[21] A decreased percentage of females and even fewer males are sexually active compared with the general population.[21,33]

Cerebral palsy (CP) actually represents a broad spectrum of physical disabilities as opposed to one defined, specific physical problem. In CP, there is no adverse effect on genital sensation, menstruation or fertility. Sexual intercourse and masturbation may be difficult due to spasticity and contractures. With creative positioning, however, even individuals with severe spasticity and contractures can be sexually active. However, sexual stimulation and arousal can increase spasms and athetoid movements.[17,26,32] The spasticity, along with pelvic, upper and lower extremity contractures, may make dealing with menstruation and birth control a challenge. Barrier contraceptive methods may be impossible due to pelvic, lower extremity, or hand contractures, spasticity, or athetoid movements. Birth control pills are also generally not used if an individual is using a wheelchair the majority of the time.[17] During the birth process there may be an increase in muscle spasticity and some difficulty in having the mother bear down. However, obstetrical outcome is similar to that in the general population.[13,29]

Severe scoliosis (over 55°) has been described as interfering with positioning during sexual activities. The use of barrier methods of contraception, fetal growth, and labor may be difficult. This severe degree of scoliosis does not generally occur in the absence of other neuromuscular disorders.[17]

In neuromuscular diseases there is a wide spectrum of physical involvement. Menstruation, genital sensation, fertility, and pregnancy are unaffected. Muscular weakness and contractures of the lower extremities and back may interfere with sexual positioning, masturbation, and management of menstruation. Birth control pills are not generally used for contraception in individuals who are using a wheelchair for all mobility. Delivery may be difficult due to muscular weakness and physical contractures. Genetic counseling is essential.[26,32]

Cystic fibrosis may cause some predictable problems in sexual activity in both men and women. Sexual functioning is largely intact with normal genital sensation and sexual functioning. However, women may have dyspareunia as a result of inadequate lubrication. Oral contraceptives are generally not used in individuals with severe involvement. Men have good sexual function, but approximately 85% are sterile as a result of associated anomalies. Sexual activity may bring on acute coughing spells or pulmonary distress.[6,27]

Women with Down syndrome have normal menstruation and physical functioning for sexual activities and the ability to go through pregnancy and delivery. However, men with Down syndrome are infertile.[25] Due to their dysgenetic ovaries, females with Turner syndrome do not go through puberty spontaneously, and they are infertile.[9]

CONCLUSION

Sexuality is a part of human personality that encompasses the physical, social, spiritual, and emotional realms. In children and adolescents with a disability, developing that aspect of the personality can be even more of a challenge than it is for all children. By being aware of specific deficits and how to circumvent those areas, we can help children and their parents more readily develop a well-rounded personality and physical functioning. By modifying sex education to compensate for areas that may have been missed due to social isolation or physical deficits, particularly to include a larger social component, we can help children learn appropriate behavior, interactions, and responsibility. By acknowledging specific problems in sexual function, including development, actual sexual abilities, reproduction, and contraceptive needs, we can help parents to help their children become more knowledgable adolescents and adults.

REFERENCES

1. Beckmann CRB, Gittler M, Barzansky BM, et al: Gynecological health care of women with disabilities. Obstet Gynecol 74:75–79, 1989.
2. Blum RW, Resnick MD, Nelson R, et al: Family and peer issues among adolescents with spina bifida and cerebral palsy. Pediatrics 88:280–285, 1991.
3. Champagne MR, Walker-Hirschm LW: Circles: A self-organization for teaching appropriate social/sexual behavior to mentally retarded/developmentally disabled persons. Sex Disabil 5:172–177, 1982.

4. Cole SS, Cole TM: Sexuality, disability, and reproductive issues through the lifespan. Sex Disabil 11:189–205, 1993.
5. Coupey SM, Cohen MI: Special considerations for health care of adolescents with chronic illnesses. Pediatr Clin North Am 31:211–219, 1984.
6. Cromer BA, Enrile B, McCoy K, et al: Knowledge, attitude and behavior related to sexuality in adolescents with chronic disability. Dev Med Child Neurol 32:602–610, 1990.
7. Demetral GD, Driessen J, Goff GA: A proactive training approach designed to assist developmentally disabled adolescents deal effectively with their menarche. Sex Disabil 6:38–46, 1983.
8. Diamond DA, Rickwood AMK, Thomas DG: Penile erections in myelomeningocele patients. Br J Urol 58:434–435, 1986.
9. Downey J, Erhardt AA, Morishima A, et al: Gender role development in two clinical syndromes: Turner syndrome versus constitutional short stature. J Am Acad Child Adolesc Psychiatry 26:566–573, 1987.
10. Edmonson B: Disability and sexual adjustment. In Van Hasselt VB, Strain PS (eds): Handbook of Developmental and Physical Disabilities. New York, Pergamon, 1988, pp 91–106.
11. Evans J, Conine T: Sexual habilitation of youngsters with chronic illness or disabling conditions. J Allied Health 14:79–87, 1985.
12. Fitz-Gerald M, Fitz-Gerald D: The potential effects of deafness on sexuality. Sex Disabil 3:177–183, 1980.
13. Foley J: The offspring of people with cerebral palsy. Dev Med Child Neurol 34:972–978, 1992.
14. Geiger RC, Knight SE: Sexuality of people with cerebral palsy. Med Aspects Hum Sex 9:70–83, 1975.
15. Goldberg RT: Toward an understanding of the rehabilitation of the disabled adolescent. Rehabil Lit 42:66–74, 1981.
16. Greydanus DE, Demarest DS, Sears JM: Sexuality of the chronically ill adolescent. Med Aspects Hum Sex 19:36–52, 1985.
17. Greydanus DE, Demarest DS, Sears JM: Sexual dysfunction in adolescents. Semin Adolesc Med 1:177–187, 1985.
18. Hayden PW, Davenport SLH, Campbell MM: Adolescents with myelodysplasia: Impact of physical disability on emotional maturation. Pediatrics 64:53–59, 1979.
19. Hicks S: Relationship and sexual problems of the visually handicapped. Sex Disabil 3:165–176, 1980.
20. Jumper BM, McLorie GA, Churchill BM, et al: Effects of the artificial urinary sphincter on prostatic development and sexual function in pubertal boys with meningomyelocele. J Urol 144:438–442, 1990.
21. Cass AS, Bloom BA, Luxenberg M: Sexual function in adults with myelomeningocele. J Urol 136:425–426, 1986.
22. King GA, Shultz IZ, Steel K, et al: Self-evaluation and self-concept of adolescents with physical disabilities. Am J Occup Ther 47:132–140, 1993.
23. Klopovich PM, Clancy BJ: Sexuality and the adolescent with cancer. Semin Oncol Nurs 1:42–48, 1985.
24. Kokkonen J, Saukkonen AL, Timonen E, et al: Social outcome of handicapped children as adults. Dev Med Child Neurol 33:1095–1100, 1991.
25. Kreutner AL: Sexuality, fertility, and the problems of menstruation in mentally retarded adolescents. Pediatr Clin North Am 28:475–480, 1981.
26. Leavesley G, Porter J: Sexuality, fertility and contraception in disability. Contraception 26:417–441, 1982.
27. Rhine SA: Genetic counseling and evaluation of recurrence for people with physical disabilities. Sex Disabil 11:221–228, 1993.
28. Robinault IP: Sex, Society, and the Disabled: A Developmental Inquiry into Roles, Reactions, and Responsibilities. New York, Harper & Row, 1978.
29. Rousso H: Special considerations in counseling clients with cerebral palsy. Sex Disabil 11:99–108, 1993.
30. Rousso H: Affirming adolescent women's sexuality. West J Med 154:629–630, 1991.
31. Rousso H: Daughters with disabilities: Defective women or minority women? In Fine M, Asch A (eds): Women with Disabilities: Essays in Psychology, Culture, and Politics. Philadelphia, Temple University Press, 1988, pp 139–171.
32. Shaul S, Bogle J, Hale-Harbaugh J, et al: Toward intimacy: Family planning and sexuality concerns of physically disabled women. In Task Force on Concerns of Physically Disabled Women (eds): Toward Intimacy. 2nd ed. New York, Human Sciences Press, 1984, pp 34–57.

33. Shurtleff DB, Sousa JC: The adolescent with myelodysplasia: Development, achievement, sex and deterioration. In McLaurin RL (ed): Myelomeningocele. New York, Grune & Stratton, 1977, pp 809–830.

34. Steinbock EA, Zeiss AM: Sexual counseling for cerebral palsied adults: Case report and further suggestions. Arch Sex Behav 6:77–83, 1977.

35. Strax TE: Psychological issues faced by adolescents and young adults with disabilities. Pediatr Ann 20:507–511, 1991.

36. Strax TE: Psychological problems of disabled adolescents and young adults. Pediatr Ann 17:756–761, 1988.

37. Thornton CE: Sex education for disabled children and adolescents. In Bullard DG, Knight SE (eds): Sexuality and Disability: Personal Perspectives. St. Louis, Mosby, 1991, pp 229–234.

38. Thorton V: Growing up with cerebral palsy. In Bullard DG, Knight SE (eds): Sexuality and Disability: Personal Perspectives. St. Louis, Mosby, 1991, pp 26–30.

39. Woodhead JC, Murph JR: Influence of chronic illness and disability on adolescent sexual development. Semin Adol Med 3:171–176, 1985,

40. Ziff SF: The sexual concerns of the adolescent woman with cerebral palsy. Issues Health Care Women 3:55–63, 1981.

41. Winch R, Bengstron L, McLaughlin J, et al: Neonatal status of infants born to women with cerebral palsy. Devel Med Child Neurol 59:37–38, 1989.

FAE H. GARDEN, MD
DONNA M. SCHRAMM, MD

THE EFFECTS OF AGING AND CHRONIC ILLNESS ON SEXUAL FUNCTION IN OLDER ADULTS

From the Department of Physical
Medicine and Rehabilitation
Baylor College of Medicine
Houston, Texas

Reprint requests to:
Fae H. Garden, MD
Department of Physical Medicine
and Rehabilitation
Baylor College of Medicine
6624 Fannin Street, Suite 2330
Houston, TX 77030

Personal events and societal influences shape the gendered being into a unique sexual being throughout childhood, adolescence, and early, middle, and late adulthood. In late adulthood, sexual physiology may change, and at least for women, sexuality loses its procreative function. However, many authors[5,10,22,48] argue that sexual activity for older adults still provides a spectrum of functions: a recreational and pleasuring opportunity, an outlet of self-expression and actualization of the individual, an opportunity for companionship, physical nearness, and intimate communication during shared activity. One author stresses that sexual activity is a "key of life" that maintains two intimate persons' relationship and improves the bond.[10] However, physiologic changes, chronic disease and medications, implied or inferred social biases, and the loss of spouse and friends hinder sexuality in the elderly. This chapter discusses the effects of societal opinion, physiologic changes, and chronic illness and medications on sexual function in older people, and it presents the benefits to elderly people of continued sexual activity.

MYTHS AND BENEFITS OF SEXUAL ACTIVITY IN THE ELDERLY

Sexual activity serves procreation, but beyond this primal need, sexual activity fulfills individual pleasuring needs of one's self or of a partner and provides intimacy and companionship with obvious rewards. Researchers studying geriatric sexuality argue that sexual activity alone or with a partner fulfills various self-actualizing needs of the individual, from control and pleasure to companionship. Comfort explains that sexual activity is "mental, social, and physical preservation of the individual, even the elderly individual."[10] Described activities range widely from masturbation to petting to intercourse. Health care professionals who will render care or counseling to elderly people must affirm and acknowledge that sexual activity even without the possibility of reproduction may be beneficial.

Having established the benefits of sexual activity, we also must dispel the myths and societal prejudice that shroud sexual activity of older adults, particularly disabled older adults, and that contributes to the asexual vision many people, including health care professionals, have of the elderly. When held by medical professionals, these preconceived notions may affect our treatment approach to elderly people with sexual dysfunction or to the elderly people with chronic disease and concerns about sexual activity. Woodard and Rollin[55] have described ten commonly held beliefs about sexuality and disability in older adults. Perhaps the most widely held of these beliefs is that older disabled people are not interested in sex and that they should learn to adjust to a life of celibacy, especially after the age of 60.[55]

Even without the context of disability, aging and sexual activity by elderly participants is regarded negatively by society. Evaluating television cartoons, Bishop[6] found that while aging figures appeared infrequently, they were characterized negatively. In a similar study of a different social medium, birthday cards, Demos revealed that both aging and sexual activity in the elderly were portrayed unfavorably.[13] In a study of more sophisticated subjects, midwestern college students in the 1970s, Pocs found that the students underestimated or denied that parents participated in recreational, solitary, or extramarital sexual activity; in fact, even the married students did not improve their estimation of their parents' sexual activity.[41] Interestingly, a study of elderly women by Portnova[42] revealed prejudice among the elderly regarding sexual activity: The elderly people were found to be biased against sexual activity by nursing home occupants. Aging and sexual activity by the aged is denied, disavowed, or limited widely in society and sometimes even by the elderly themselves.

The myths regarding sexuality in the elderly are numerous, and the reasons they are perpetuated are complex. Representative statements of the misconceptions related to elderly sexuality include "desire ends at menopause," "sexual activity robs vital essences," and "sexually active older people are immoral." The reasons offered for the perpetuation of these incorrect characterizations are diverse. Byers[9] has proposed that young adults disavow and discourage sexual activity in older adults or parental figures because of subliminal oedipal conflicts, monetary motivations when a parent's sexual partner may compete for an inheritance, and because the older person may be managed and manipulated more easily in isolation. Some workers[5] cite a Victorian heritage, in which sexual activity was considered sinful and uniquely for reproduction, as the origin in this era of negativity toward nonreproductive sexuality in elderly people.

The "sexual revolution" of the 1960s and 1970s is credited with relaxing society's bias against sexual activity by the elderly. Arluke[2] reviewed handbooks on aging written before and after 1970 and found that in later books approval of sexual activity and dating more than doubled and that the number of pages devoted to sexual information almost tripled; it was not clear whether omission or disapproval is found in the remainder of the works.

This discussion of the benefits and societal perceptions of sexual activity for elderly people will allow a more perceptive review of the scientific data regarding the sexual interest, physiology, and activity of older adults.

HISTORICAL PERSPECTIVE
OF GERIATRIC SEXUALITY STUDIES

Although literature concerning sexuality and the aging is occasionally contradictory, it is generally accepted that sexual interest and activity does not automatically diminish with advancing age and may continue almost indefinitely.[27] In 1926 Raymond Pearl, as cited by Comfort,[10] was one of the first investigators to examine sexuality in septuagenarians, but Kinsey's publications of the 1940s and 1950s are cited as the most extensive objective study of sexuality.[26,27] These cross-sectional studies found that sexual activity, or coital frequency, declined with advancing age.

In 1968 Pfeiffer[40] noted that many elderly people regularly engaged in sexual activity but that the percentage of those doing so declined significantly with age. In people 78 or older, only 20% indicated that they regularly participated in sexual activity. The frequency of sexual activity among people 60 to 90 years old was reported to vary from once a month to three times a week. Older men reported greater sexual activity than elderly women. However, Pfeiffer found that sexual interest was maintained and reported by more than 40% of the women. The women in Pfeiffer's study reported that the primary limiting factor in sexual activity was lack of a partner. Pfeiffer and Davis[39] have noted that the ratio of women to men is 130 to 100 for people between the ages of 65 and 74; for those older than 75, the ratio increases to 178 to 100. These studies have been critiqued for their cross-sectional design and averaging of individual activity patterns.

Longitudinal studies of individuals' sexual activity have suggested that the activity patterns among individual relationships are stable over time.[20] Methodological and statistical considerations are also discussed in this study.[20]

Labby[29] has noted that the earlier a person began sexual activity in adulthood, the more likely that person was to continue activity into old age. Masters and Johnson[32] note that the best indicator of sexual activity in aging is previous activity in early and middle adulthood. No significant decrease in behavior was noted just on the basis of increased physiologic age. Only 10% of people older than 60 express no interest in sexual activity.[32] While cross-sectional studies suggest a decline in sexual activity, longitudinal studies suggest stability of the individual's sexual activity. Interest in sexual activity is preserved for many.

At this time, we believe that impotency is not the natural consequence of time. Many elderly persons stop sexual activity because of lack of a partner or a disease process.[10] When using the term *sexual problems*, some authors[44] attribute 50% of age-related "problems" to psychological factors such as loss of self-esteem and retirement in men and empty-nest syndrome in women. Other authors[33,35] referring to sexual dysfunction in men state that 60% of performance dysfunction is physiologic and that physiologic dysfunction related to vascular, metabolic, and neurologic derangement increases with age. Masters and Johnson report that restoration of sexual function is possible in many cases regardless of age.[32]

CHANGES IN THE SEXUAL RESPONSE WITH AGING

Changes in Men

The five components of normal male sexual function are libido, erection, ejaculation, orgasm, and detumescence.[57] The control of libido, or "interest," is influenced by poorly described mental processes and testicular androgens, which both may be affected by aging. Masters and Johnson are credited with making the first direct observations of age-related physiologic changes in the sexual response.[32] The phases of excitement, plateau, orgasm, and resolution are variably affected in a given individual as a result of aging. There appears to be a steady decline in the duration as well as the intensity of each phase. A reduced speed of arousal is often the first change in sexual function noted by aging men.[17] An acute or chronic illness has a more profound effect on the speed of sexual arousal in older people than one would expect to find in younger individuals.[17] Erections are delayed and less firm; ejaculations are shorter, less forceful, and of decreased volume; and the refractory period increases.[31]

Erectile changes in aging men are common and a source of great concern. Many older men require more time to achieve full penile engorgement. The sensitivity of the glans penis in detecting the difference between vibration and static touch decreases with age.[38] The change in penile length is less marked, and the fully erect penis may be less rigid than in the individual's younger years. Loss of collagen tissue as well as progressive arteriosclerosis are partially responsible for this phenomena. The usual darkening of the glans penis may not be as noticeable and elevation of the testicles is less obvious than in similar occurrences in younger men.[17] A change in coital position may be necessary if the erect penis is at a reduced angle. Cardiopulmonary changes inherent to the aging process may result in an excessively increased respiratory rate, tachycardia, and elevation of blood pressure.

Erectile dysfunction in the elderly may result both from psychological and physiologic problems. The presence of nocturnal or morning erections can be useful in differentiating between these two causes. Monitoring with penile plethysmography may be useful in some cases. The duration of erection during sleep decreases steadily with aging. While an adolescent may spend 3 hours erect (38% of time asleep) during an average evening of sleep, by age 65 a healthy man will have erections during 20% of his sleep time.[45] When impotence is due to physiologic processes such as diabetes, treatment options should be identified and discussed. Treatment alternatives include surgically implanted penile prostheses, external impotence management devices, and injectable and oral medications.

The sensation associated with ejaculation is frequently reported by older patients to be less intense. As the contractile strength of the prostate decreases with aging, so does the amount of viscosity of the ejaculate. Decreases of up to 50% of previous ejaculate volume have been noted by some men.[17] The postejaculation refractory period becomes significantly prolonged, sometimes lasting for days to weeks in men older than 70.[8] This phenomenon is a normal part of the aging process and should be explained to patients in a straightforward manner.

Elderly men who engage in sexual activity may have questions about their reproductive capability. Testicular biopsies have demonstrated active spermatogenesis in 50% of men older than 70.[45] Degenerative changes in the seminiferous tubules and germ cells are also evident.

Although sexual desire is maintained in many individuals, diminished libido may occur, and physiologic causes include alterations in sensation as well as hormonal levels. Diminished libido may be due to alterations in the sensations of vision, hearing, and smell. Testosterone, the primary hormone associated with sexual desire, is produced at all ages, but levels decrease gradually after the age of 20. An accelerated decline in testosterone levels occurs after the sixth decade.[8] Plasma testosterone normally rises during coitus,[18] and this response may be blunted in older individuals. Androgen replacement in older men—used to treat sexual dysfunction including decreased sexual desire—has met with limited success. Changes that do occur in men receiving this treatment are often attributed to either a placebo effect or an improvement in the patient's sense of well-being.[24]

Psychological factors also may decrease libido. Men who notice a decrease in their sexual desire are often influenced by negative social attitudes toward sexuality in the elderly. Many of these men were raised during a time when sex education and sexual expression were considered immoral. They may have concerns that their continued sexual desires could label them as "dirty old men." It is the role of the counselor to help allay these fears and educate older adults about the natural changes in sexuality with aging. Bringing the partner into the discussion is essential to foster the idea of closeness and continued intimacy.

Of interest in elderly men with sexual dysfunction is the role of dopamine agonists, such as L-dopa and bromocriptine, in increasing sexual drive and sexual activity.[19] Outside the central nervous system, dopaminergic receptors have been found in the pelvis, vas deferens, and penis. The effects of dopaminergic agents in increasing sexual activity may be central or peripheral, and at this point, related dysfunction is believed to be secondary to diminished availability of the neurotransmitter rather than alterations of the receptors.

Aging men may be affected at one or many phases of the sexual response. Alterations in libido may be related to hormonal or sensory losses or psychological inhibition. The phases of erection and ejaculation may be affected by alterations to the somatic, or autonomic, nervous system or vascular and metabolic derangement. Detumescence is prolonged with aging. Many organic causes of male sexual dysfunction are correctable.

Changes in Women

In contrast to the large body of literature addressing male sexuality, the literature addressing female sexuality is limited, possibly because of cultural bias but also probably because of the methodologic difficulties in measuring female sexual response and in diagnosing female sexual dysfunction.[36] Mooradian[36] addresses the factors altering sexual behavior in older women, and he divides these into anatomic changes in genitalia and breasts, hormonal changes, concurrent disease and medication use, and psychological factors.

Changes in vaginal size and lubrication often are blamed for sexual dysfunction. Vaginal dryness and resultant dyspareunia are common problems cited by postmenopausal women. Vaginal lubrication is a primary function of the Bartholin glands, which lose some of their effectiveness with aging. Estrogen deficiency leads to thinning and brittleness of the vaginal tissues. Use of antihistamines and decongestants will lead to dryness of the mucous membranes. Vaginal expansion during sexual arousal is decreased and contributes to the problem of uncomfortable intercourse.

Bachman[3] has suggested the use of oil- or water-based lubricants, such as K-Y jelly, just before intercourse to help women with atrophic vaginitis. An over-the-counter moisturizing gel in a tampon applicator called Replens is marketed by Columbia Laboratories and can be inserted into the vagina three times a week. Through the use of water-filled polymers that adhere to the vaginal cells, a layer of moisture is maintained that may improve comfort during intercourse. Regular performance of Kegel exercises will help to improve vaginal tone and strengthen pelvic muscles.

Estrogen deficiency contributes to vaginal dryness and diminished size as well as other changes in sexual function. The onset of menopause and its associated hormone deprivation is directly related to problems in women's interest in sex and performance. A decrease in coital frequency has been associated with low serum estrogen levels.[2] In one study,[11] a serum estradiol level of 35 pg/mL or lower was found to be a critical value that predicted dwindling frequency of intercourse. Most of the women who have intercourse at least once a week had estradiol levels above this value. Orgasmic capability may decrease in some postmenopausal women. For estrogen-deficient women, the uterine contractions that naturally occur during orgasm may be painful.[53] The development of urinary stress incontinence as a result of pelvic relaxation and tissue atrophy can profoundly adversely affect the woman and her partner.

When it has been determined that estrogen deficiency has resulted in these sexual problems, and when no medical contraindications exist, estrogen replacement therapy is often instituted. Estrogen replacement, either oral or topical, retards atrophic changes in the genitalia and stimulates vaginal secretions.

Androgens, primarily produced in the adrenal glands, are not adversely affected by menopause. The sexual stimulating properties of testosterone may play a large role in postmenopausal libido once estrogen levels have dropped.[17] The addition of androgen to postmenopausal hormonal replacement therapy is controversial. Sexual arousal is enhanced and sexual fantasies may increase when postmenopausal women are given androgens.[50]

Chronic illness adversely affects sexual function. Decreased muscle strength and bulk as well as movement limitations caused by osteoarthritis and osteoporosis contribute to the development of sexual dysfunction. Planning sexual activity for times when the patient is less fatigued can enhance interest and enjoyment.

Data describing psychological factors related to sexual interest and activity in postmenopausal women are complex and at times contradictory. In a group of women age 50 and older, 79% of postmenopausal women noted a decrease in sexual interest.[2] This finding has been disputed by others,[29] who indicate that women's interest in sex often intensifies after menopause, especially when they have the feeling that sexual activity is acceptable and can be continued in later life. The freedom from the risk of pregnancy and the absence of children in the house may help encourage continuation of sexual activity past menopause.[29]

Women in the United States can expect to live approximately 29 years past the age of menopause.[53] Since women tend to live longer than men, they may spend the last few years of their lives without a male partner. Women are more likely than men to cease sexual activity or to substitute masturbation for intercourse after the loss of their long-term sex partner.[29]

Similar to men, in the absence of chronic disease and an available partner, female sexual behavior may not change with age. Many sexual dysfunctions in women, if they do occur, may be remediable with exogenous or topical estrogens.

THE EFFECTS OF PHYSICAL ILLNESS

Chronic illness accounts for much of the decline in sexual function with aging.[37] In the elderly, diseases of the genitourinary tract and reproductive system have the greatest effect on sexual function. These are followed by endocrine disease, cardiovascular disease (see chapter 7), and respiratory disease.[12] The effects of cerebrovascular disease on sexual function are discussed in chapter 4.

Genitourinary Disorders

Benign prostatic hypertrophy in men and hysterectomy in women, as well as other female gynecological disorders detailed elsewhere,[58] compound the problem of sexual dysfunction in the elderly.

Benign prostatic hypertrophy develops in nearly 50% of men. Many fear that surgical treatment will impair sexual function.[12] Transurethral resection of the prostate (TURP) may result in retrograde ejaculation of semen into the bladder due to external sphincter damage. While this will interfere with fertility, it does not adversely affect physical sensation or erection. In many cases, impotence associated with TURP is psychological in origin.[12] A complete urologic work-up may be needed to differentiate psychological from organic causes of impotence. Other surgical approaches to the prostate that require an open incision are associated with an increased incidence of sexual dysfunction. The suprapubic and retropubic prostatectomies result in impotence in up to 20% of patients and the perineal approach is associated with up to a 50% rate of impotence.[52]

Because of the myth that hysterectomy results in a "loss of femininity," women may develop problems with their sexual identity postoperatively. The surgery results in shortening of the vagina and eliminates uterine contractions during orgasm. If the patient's preoperative sexual relationships were enjoyable and if her partner is supportive, these changes should not cause much problem.[52]

Endocrine Disorders

Endocrine disorders and their sequelae may result in sexual dysfunction. Primary hypothyroidism and diabetes mellitus and its sequelae are discussed here.

Primary hypothyroidism, more common in women, is manifested by lethargy, depressed motor and intellectual function, and cold intolerance. It frequently results in diminished libido and potency. While thyroxine therapy may eliminate many symptoms, sexual function can remain impaired.[17]

Sexual dysfunction is a common complication in patients with diabetes mellitus. Nearly 50% of diabetic men have been found to be impotent as a result of this endocrinopathy.[52] The impotence may be unrelated to the age of onset, severity of illness, or medication control.[8] The exact pathophysiology of erectile dysfunction in diabetic men has not been clearly defined. In many cases, organic causes are mixed with significant psychological overlay. One sex clinic has claimed that some diabetic patients with secondary impotence of up to 7 years were cured within 2–7 weeks of therapy.[43] A careful sexual history with particular attention to the onset of impotence, occurrence of nocturnal erections, masturbation, and alcohol intake should be obtained. Measurements of vascular dilatation during REM sleep by nocturnal penile plethysmography are useful in differentiating psychological from organic impotence.[23] The use of a surgically implanted rigid or inflatable penile prosthesis is helpful in cases of proven organic impotence. Patients may be offered one of a number of commercially available external impotence management devices in cases in which surgery is not acceptable.[56]

Patients and spouses may differ in their acceptance of these devices, and both should be included in the decision-making process prior to prescription.

Diabetic neuropathy can result in the development of retrograde ejaculation. Patients may complain of having a "dry orgasm" followed by the passage of cloudy urine. Reassurance from the physician that this is a physiologic rather than a psychological problem may be helpful.

The cause and prevalence of sexual dysfunction in diabetic women is unclear. Early studies[56] indicated that 35% of diabetic women had orgasmic dysfunction compared with controls. In contrast to male diabetics, there was a strong correlation between sexual dysfunction and duration of the disease. Later studies[16,47] have disputed these findings and have suggested that diabetic women show little impairment in their sexual response. In a study[4] of the sexual response of type I (insulin-dependent) diabetics, libido and orgasmic problems as well as impaired vaginal lubrication were related to elevated blood sugar levels. Furthermore, when women developed diabetes after entering into a relationship, their sexual response was more likely to become impaired.

Vascular Disorders

Cardiovascular[12,21,30] and cerebrovascular diseases[7,34,51] and their effects on sexual function are discussed in chapters 4 and 7.

Hypertensive men and women are at risk of developing sudden cardiac or cerebrovascular problems. Medical control of severe hypertension lowers but does not eliminate this risk. Drug therapy of hypertension, however, is often complicated by sexual dysfunction. The ACE-inhibitors, such as captopril, are among the least likely class of antihypertensives to cause erectile impairment.[49]

Degenerative Joint Disease

Pain and stiffness caused by this disorder can have an adverse effect on sexual function. Timing analgesic administration to coincide with likely times of sexual intimacy can be helpful.[17] Couples frequently must be counseled to adopt changes in their usual sexual position to allow comfortable intercourse.

Mental Illness

Depression, anxiety, and psychoneurosis are common psychological illnesses in the elderly. The presence of chronic illness or social isolation combined with depression can result in feelings of apathy and hopelessness. In this setting, it is not uncommon to find patients suffering from a loss of interest in sex. Psychotherapy and psychotropic drugs may improve the depression; libido does not always return.[17]

Confusion, a nonspecific symptom in many older people, also has been associated with the loss of sexual response. Individuals suffering from disinhibition, on the other hand, may display an increased sexual drive and occasional inappropriate attempts at sexual outlet.[17] Hypersexuality may also be part of the manic phase of a bipolar disorder.

Drug-Induced Sexual Dysfunction

Many of the drugs commonly prescribed to the elderly can result in sexual dysfunction by pharmacologically altering neurotransmission, hormonal function, or vascular flow.

Besides the antihypertensive medications, psychoactive agents such as tranquilizers and antidepressants often have significant sexual side effects. In some cases, sexual problems may have led to the depression and anxiety for which the drugs were prescribed. Decreased libido, impotence, and difficulty with ejaculation have been reported with the use of major tranquilizers.[54] Thioridazine (Mellaril), because of its alpha-adrenergic receptor antagonism, is a strong inhibitor of ejaculation. It is also known to cause vaginal dryness. Chlorpromazine (Thorazine) is associated with a dose-related loss of libido and impotence.[49] Among the antidepressants, trazodone (Desyrel) may result in priapism. The sedative and anticholinergic properties of these drugs can lead to decreased libido and impotence.[54]

Imipramine (Topfranil) and amitriptyline (Elavil) can cause painful ejaculation.[15] The minor tranquilizers, especially benzodiazepines such as diazepam (Valium), reduce libido by their depressive effect on the limbic system, septal region, and brain-stem reticular formation.[54]

Controlled studies have shown that chronic or excessive alcohol intake results in increased time to obtain an erection, increased time to ejaculation, and decreased orgasmic pleasure. These problems were noted to correlate positively with blood alcohol levels.[54]

Nicotine, by its vasoconstrictive action, can adversely affect potency.[54] The presence of atherosclerotic peripheral vascular disease often magnifies the problem.

COUNSELING ELDERLY PATIENTS

When asked about their need for sexual counseling, nearly half of the patients on a rehabilitation medicine service wanted to discuss sexual problems with a hospital staff member prior to discharge. Most of these patients expressed a preference for a like-sexed physician as the person with whom they would be most willing to discuss sexual concerns.[46] Unfortunately, few physicians incorporate a sexual history and physical into their routine examination, which often is a reflection of the doctor's lack of comfort with discussing sexuality issues. Many elderly people were raised in an environment where sexuality was not openly discussed. They are often reluctant to mention their sexual problems without a doctor's prompting. In an effort to circumvent this stalemate, Bray has suggested that the person who is to provide sexual education and counseling services should be comfortable with sexuality issues.[16] In many centers, this person is a nurse, social worker, or therapist. A thorough knowledge of the effects of aging on sexuality is essential to provide effective services.

An accurate and detailed sexual history and physical examination is an essential step in identifying potentially reversible causes of sexual dysfunction. Once this has been completed, appropriate counseling can be integrated into the rehabilitation process. One popular method for providing sexual counseling is the PLISSIT model,[1] which allows counselors to provide four different levels of intensity when addressing a patient's sexual concerns. The levels include Permission, Limited Information, Specific Suggestions, and Intensive Therapy.

Permission. Many geriatric patients will benefit from a general discussion of sexual concerns and reassurance that continuation of sexual activity is permissible. The counselor should refrain from making value judgments about a patient's sexual behavior. If the counselor identifies the possibility for an adverse outcome, such as risk of a heart attack or stroke, as a result of these behaviors, they are obligated to bring these concerns to the patient's attention.[8] Open discussion of sexual issues will reassure patients that the changes they are experiencing are part of the normal aging process.

Limited Information.   Some patients will require more than verbal reassurance in order to accept changes in their sexuality. Counselors should have a supply of educational materials in the form of books, pamphlets, and videotapes that can be used to provide information in layman's terms about sex and the aging process. Patients should be given the opportunity to discuss what they have read or watched.

Specific Suggestions.   At this level of counseling, patients are given assistance, for example, in the form of prescriptions for vaginal lubricants or suggestions on variations on their usual coital position. Elderly men whose partners are premenopausal should be advised about the need for birth control if pregnancy is not desired.

Specific sexual difficulties can usually be identified in the sexual history. Patients and their partners can use the suggested strategies to adapt their sexual behavior to the changes occurring with aging.

Intensive Therapy.   Certified sex therapists are probably the most qualified to provide assistance at this level. The therapy is time-intensive and requires the provider to have a thorough understanding of human behavior. Sex therapy should be considered when the first three levels of the PLISSIT model have not been successful.

SUMMARY

Sexual functioning, as with all other phenomena of aging, is of concern to rehabilitation professionals. Sexual responsiveness can be adversely affected by poor health, anxiety, and social myths. In the absence of these factors, older individuals may reasonably expect their sexual activity and enjoyment to be life-long. Many older people will seek help from the medical community when sexual problems arise. For this reason, members of the rehabilitation team who are comfortable discussing sexual issues with patients should be identified and trained to help the geriatric patients understand the normal changes with aging so that they do not fear losing their sexuality. The sexual concerns of an increasingly older population should be treated as a major part of geriatric rehabilitation programs.

REFERENCES

1. Annon JS: The PLISSIT Model: A proposed conceptual scheme for behavioral treatment of sexual problems. J Sex Educ Ther 2:1–15, 1976.
2. Arluke A, Levin J, Suchwalko J: Sexuality and romance in advice books for the elderly. Gerontology 24:415–418, 1984.
3. Bachman GA: Sexual dysfunction in postmenopausal women: The role of medical management. Geriatrics 43:79–83, 1988.
4. Bahen-Auger N, Wilson M, Assalian P: Sexual response of the type I diabetic women. Med Aspects Human Sex 94–100, October 1988.
5. Bates-Jensen B: Sexuality and the elderly. J Enterost Ther 16:158–163, 1989.
6. Bishop JM, Krause DR: Depictions of aging and old age on Saturday morning television. Gerontology 24:91–94, 1984.
7. Bray G: Sexual functioning in the stroke survivor. Arch Phys Med Rehabil 62:286–288, 1981.
8. Bray G: Sexuality in the aging. In Williams TF (ed): Rehabilitation in the Aging. New York, Raven, 1984, pp 81–94.
9. Byers JP: Sexuality and the elderly. Geriatr Nurs 4:293–297, 1983.
10. Comfort A, Dial LK: Sexuality and aging. Clin Geriatr Med 7:1–7, 1991.
11. Cutler W, Garcia S, McCoy N: Perimenopausal sexuality. Arch Sex Behav 16:225–234, 1987.
12. Dagon EM: Problems and prospects with sexuality and aging. Wis Med J 80:37–39, 1981.
13. Demos V, Jache A: When you care enough: An analysis of attitudes toward aging in humorous birthday cards. Gerontology 21:209–215, 1981.
14. Driver JD, Detrich D: Elders and sexuality. J Nurs Care 15:8–11, 1982.
15. Drugs that cause sexual dysfunction. Med Lett Drugs Ther 25:73, 1979.

16. Ellenberg M: Sexual aspects of the female diabetic. Mt Sinai J Med 44:495–500, 1977.
17. Felstein I: Sexual function in the elderly. Clin Obstet Gynecol 7:401–420, 1980.
18. Fox CA: Recent research in human coital physiology. Br J Sex Med 42:32–34, 1978.
19. Frajese G, Amalfitano M, Magnani A, et al: Neuroendocrine correlates in elderly sexual behavior. J Endocrinol Invest 8(suppl 2):17–21, 1985.
20. George K, Weiler SJ: Sexuality in middle and late life. Gen Psychiatry 38:919–923, 1981.
21. Hellerstein HK, Friedman EH: Sexual activity and the post coronary patient. Arch Intern Med 125:987–999, 1970.
22. Hogan R (ed): Human Sexuality: A Nursing Perspective. New York, Appleton-Crofts, 1980.
23. Karacan I, Williams RL, Thornby JI: Sleep-related tumescence as a function of age. Am J Psychiatry 132:932–937, 1975.
24. Kassel V: Long-term care institutions. In Weg R (ed): Sexuality in Later Years. New York, Academic Press, 1983, pp 167–184.
25. Kinsey AC, Pomeroy WB, Martin CE: Age and sexual outlet. In Kinsey AC, Pomeroy WB, Martin CE (eds): Sexual Behavior in the Human Male. Philadelphia, WB Saunders, 1948, pp 218–262.
26. Kinsey AC, Pomeroy WB, Martin CE: Sexual Behavior in the Human Female. Philadelphia, WB Saunders, 1953.
27. Kofoed L, Bloom JD: Geriatric sexual dysfunction. J Am Geriatr Soc 30:437–440, 1982.
28. Kolodny RC: Sexual dysfunction in diabetic females. Diabetes 20:557–559, 1971.
29. Labby DH: Aging's effects on sexual function. Postgrad Med 78:32–43, 1985.
30. Mackey FG: Sexuality and heart disease. In Comfort A (ed): Sexual Consequences of Disability. Philadelphia, G Stickley Co, 1978.
31. Mallett EC, Badlani GH: Sexuality in the elderly. Semin Urol 5:141–145, 1987.
32. Masters WH, Johnson V: Sex and aging—expectations and reality. Hosp Pract 21:175–198, 1986.
33. Melman A: Evaluation of the first 70 patients in the center for male sexual dysfunction of Beth Israel Medical Center. J Urol 131:53–57, 1984.
34. Monga TN, Lawson JS, Inglis J: Sexual dysfunction in stroke patients. Arch Phys Med Rehabil 67:19–22, 1986.
35. Montague DK: Diagnostic evaluation, classification and treatment of men with sexual dysfunction. Urology 14.545, 1979.
36. Mooradian AD, Greiff V: Sexuality in older women. Arch Intern Med 150:1033–1038, 1990.
37. Mulligan T, Retchin SM, Chinchilli VM, et al: The role of aging and chronic disease in sexual dysfunction. J Am Geriatr Soc 36:520–524, 1988.
38. Newman HF: Vibratory sensitivity of the penis. Fertil Steril 21:791–793, 1970.
39. Pfeiffer E, Davis GC: Determinants of sexual behavior in middle and old age. J Am Geriatr Soc 20:151–158, 1972.
40. Pfeiffer E, Verwoerdt A, Wang H: Sexual behavior in aged men and women. I. Observations on 254 community volunteers. Arch Gen Psychiatry 19:753–758, 1968.
41. Pocs O, Godow A, Tolone W, et al: Is there sex after 40? Psychol Today 11(1):54–56, 1977.
42. Portonova M, Young E, Newman MA: Elderly women's attitudes toward sexual activity among their peers. Health Care Int 5:289–298, 1984.
43. Renshaw DC: Sexual problems in old age and disability. Psychosomatics 22:975–985, 1981.
44. Richardson JD: Sexuality and our older patients: A brief look at myth and reality. Aust Fam Phys 17:648–650, 1988.
45. Riehl RA, Vaughn ED: Genitourinary disease in the elderly. Med Clin North Am 67:445–461, 1983.
46. Sadoughi W, Lashner M, Fine HL: Sexual adjustment in a chronically ill and physically disabled population: A pilot study. Arch Phys Med Rehabil 52:311–317, 1971.
47. Schreiner-Engel P, Schiavi RC, Victorisz R: Diabetes and female sexuality: A comparative study of women in relationships. J Sex Marital Ther 11:165–175, 1985.
48. Sedgwick R: Myths in human sexuality: A social-psychological perspective. Nurs Clin North Am 10:539–550, 1975.
49. Sexual problems in the elderly: The use and abuse of medications. A geriatrics panel discussion. Geriatrics 44:61–71, 1989.
50. Sherwin B, Gelfand M: The role of androgen in the maintenance of sexual functioning in oopherectomized women. Psychosom Med 49:397–409, 1987.
51. Sjogren K, Danber JE: Sexuality after stroke with hemiplegia. Scand J Rehabil Med 15:55–61, 1983.
52. Spennrath S: Understanding the sexual needs of the older patient. American Urologic Association Allied Journal April/Jun:10–17, 1983.
53. Steege JF: Sexual function in the aging woman. Clin Obstet Gynecol 29:462–469, 1986.

54. VanArsdalen KN, Wein AJ: Drug-induced sexual dysfunction in older men. Geriatrics 39:63–70, 1984.
55. Woodard WS, Rollin SA: Sexuality and the elderly: Obstacles and options. J Rehabil 47:64–68, 1981.
56. Zasler ND: Managing erectile dysfunction with external devices. Pract Diabetol 8:1–9, 1989.
57. Rousseua PC: Sexual changes and impotence in elderly men. Am Fam Physician 34:131–136, 1986.
58. Goldstein MK, Teng NNH: Gynecologic factors in sexual dysfunction in the older woman. Clin Geriatr Med 7:41–61, 1991.

HUSAM GHUSN, MD

SEXUALITY IN INSTITUTIONALIZED PATIENTS

From the Baylor College of
   Medicine
      and
Houston VA Medical Center
Houston, Texas

Reprint requests to:
Husam Ghusn, MD
Houston VA Medical Center
Geriatrics and Extended Care
   (110)
2002 Holcombe Blvd.
Houston, TX 77030

The number of patients occupying beds in nursing homes is expanding. Currently, there are close to 19,000 nursing homes and 1.5 million to 2 million nursing home beds.[24] The number of nursing home residents is expected to more than double over the upcoming 30 years and is estimated to reach 5.2 million by the year 2040. In 1980, 13% of nursing home residents were younger than 65, 15% between 65–74, 35% between 75–84, and 37% were 85 and older. In the future, the proportion of nursing home residents 85 and older is expected to increase, with a reciprocal decrease in the number of 65–84-year-old residents. In the year 2000, 9% of nursing home residents are expected to be younger than 65, 10% between 65–74, 33% between 75–84, and 47% older than 84. Many nursing home residents have severe impairments in their basic activities of daily living. More than 40% are dependent in eating, toileting, transferring, and dressing skills, and more than 90% are dependent in bathing. In addition, more than half of nursing home residents suffer from dementia. During the first week of admission, physicians should assess the rehabilitation potential of nursing home residents. Although some may benefit from a modified restorative rehabilitation program, almost all can benefit from an ongoing maintenance rehabilitation program.

Significant changes in role relationships are forced on patients and their significant other as they enter into the new environment of nursing homes.[2] Because these drastic changes occur in unfamiliar surroundings, patients may be subject to "emotional malnutrition." Some elders adjust well and develop new friendships with other nursing home residents and are thus able to maintain positive rewarding interpersonal relationships.[10] Most commonly, amid all their needs, the sexuality of institutionalized elderly people is often ignored or misinterpreted. In nursing homes, a significant proportion of elderly patients continue to have sexual thoughts and believe that patients their age should be allowed to be sexually active. Yet, their sexual activities are affected by several factors, including a multitude of chronic diseases, functional and sexual disabilities, presence of a willing and capable partner, and lack of privacy, especially in an institutionalized setting. In addition, patients living in nursing homes must deal with the nursing home staff, some of whom have misconceptions about the sexual needs of older people and try to enforce their own moral values on nursing home residents. Health care providers should be cognizant of the sexual needs of elderly people and the benefits of expressing their sexual thoughts on their health and social well being. Sexual needs of elderly people can be addressed by providing the proper environment, such as private space, in which to exercise such needs or through rechanneling sexual energy and thoughts into more practical activities. Such activities can be a source of love, warmth, and sense of well being to this unfortunate group of elders who cannot live independently. Despite a slowly increasing wealth of information about sexuality of nursing home residents, much remains to be learned. Researchers studying sexuality in nursing homes face several difficulties due to the reluctance of patients to talk about their sexuality[26] or the unwillingness of nursing home administrators to allow researchers to interview patients about such issues. Some nursing home residents are offended by such research topics and react in a hostile manner.[28] Studies are needed that are designed to better understand the impact of suppressing or supporting sexual feelings in nursing homes on the health and well being of their residents.

SEXUAL ACTIVITIES AND INTERESTS

Several studies indicate that most nursing home residents are not sexually active. Mulligan et al. reported that among 116 men with partners, despite moderately strong libido and the preference for vaginal intercourse, 80% no longer engaged in coitus. Five men reported that they had intercourse while on home visits approximately once a month, and one man averaged once per year.[21] Among 51 male and 55 female nursing home residents, Fonzo et al.[11] indicated that sexual activity had been interrupted in most women, except for a low percentage of wealthier women (4%). A total of 39% of men and 69% of women reported total absence of sexual fantasies. However, 25% of the men residing in the same nursing homes reported sexual intercourse once a month, and 7.8% reported sexual intercourse once a week. None reported any sexual intercourse at a frequency of more than once a week.[11] Similarly, another study of 63 nursing home residents in Wisconsin indicated that most of the residents no longer engaged in sexual activities. A total of 75% of the women and 31% of the men claimed that they do not fantasize. About 10% indicated that they masturbate.[28]

Although the intensity of sexual satisfaction may change with age due to physiologic and social factors, elderly people in nursing homes still experience pleasure during sexual intercourse.[11] Fonzo et al.[11] interviewed 51 male and 55 female residents of six nursing homes regarding sexual satisfaction and compared them to elders living at home. Only 3% of the men in nursing homes reported high pleasure during intercourse as compared to 42% of elders living at home. All women living at home and all nonwealthy women living in nursing homes reported no sexual pleasure during intercourse. No reasons were given. Frequency of intercourse, functional status, and age all positively correlated with sexual satisfaction. However, sexual satisfaction does not always correlate with sexual activity. Despite the relatively low sexual activity among veterans with partners in a Veterans Affairs Medical Center nursing home and the lack of sexual activity among those without partners, both groups indicated that they are reasonably satisfied with their sexual life.[21] Residents without partners were even more satisfied than those with partners, possibly because of lesser expectations.[21]

Despite the above, many institutionalized elders remain interested in their sexuality, especially if they have partners. Mulligan et al.[21] reported on the sexual interests of 61 men who were residing in a Veterans Affairs Medical Center nursing home in Richmond, Virginia. Men with partners were significantly younger than men without partners (mean age 67.7 and 74.8, respectively). Similarly, nursing home residents who had partners were more functional than those without partners (Barthel Index 50 vs. 67). In general, men with partners reported greater sexual interest, but those without reported that their interest would be greater if they had a partner. Residents with or without partners had the same sexual preferences. About 65% preferred vaginal intercourse; 21% preferred hugging and caressing; 5% preferred kissing; and only 2% preferred masturbation.

ATTITUDES

Residents of Nursing Homes

Although nursing home residents may not be sexually active themselves, they still support sexual rights for patients of their age. Among 63 Wisconsin nursing home residents, 39% of the men and 53% of the women felt that sex was not for someone of their years.[28] However, 81% of the men and 75% of the women felt that older people should be allowed to have sex despite the fact that they were not personally sexually active. Similarly, Fonzo et al. reported that 51% of male and 36% of female nursing home residents believed that people of their age should be allowed to have sexual intercourse. Although the practice of masturbation is reported to be low among some nursing home residents,[28] 46% of men believed masturbation is normal. However, a similar percentage (42%) had negative attitudes toward masturbation. In contrast, 17% of women felt that masturbation is normal and 61% had negative attitudes toward masturbation.

Elderly nursing home residents may have different perceptions about sexual activity than the young. When asked whether they think sex is different for men and women, 50% of men and 30% of women said that they believe that it is different; 23% of men and 39% of women said that they did not know.[28] In several studies,[11,28] men indicated they want to have sex because it is natural. Women agreed to that in one study; however, in others they believed that it should be done because of love (61% of women), pleasure (19%) or to please a partner (40%).[11] None of the men in either study believed that sex should be carried out to please their partner (Table 1). The majority of men and women seem to think that the opposite gender wants to have sex because it is natural; however, some women believed that men wanted sex because it is their marital duty (28%).[28] None of the men believed that women participated in sex to fulfill their marital duties, and only 4% considered it a marital duty for themselves.[28]

Sexual interests and preferences of older people are a continuation of lifelong patterns and are directly related to the expectations of the society in which they

TABLE 1. Reasons for Participating in Sexual Intercourse as Reported
by Nursing Home Residents

	Men (%)		Women (%)	
	Wasow et al.*	Fonzo et al.*	Wasow et al.*	Fonzo et al.*
Natural	58	75	35	33
Love	4	61	17	61
Pleasure	11	59	8	19
Please partner	0	0	3	40
Procreate	8	12	3	28
No answer	4	20	25	23

* Percentages add up to more than 100 because respondents may have provided more than one answer. Total number in Wasow study = 63; total number in Fonzo study = 106.

live.[23] Thus, some nursing home residents may not be interested in expressing their sexuality in such settings. Paunonen et al.[25] studied 50 elderly nursing home residents living in a small rural town in Finland (41 women and 9 men); the majority were 70–79 years old. Only 20% of the respondents indicated that it is natural and proper for old people to have a sex life. Almost half held the opinion that old people do not need sex, and 12% believed that sex is shameful and sinful. However, almost all the respondents (90%) wanted to show affection to other people, even though the proportion of those who said they had the opportunity to do so was much smaller. The influence of prior beliefs or societal expectations may even prohibit discussions about sexuality. Paunonen and Häggman[25] indicated that 16% of the subjects felt that sexuality is a strictly private matter that they would prefer not to talk about with anyone else.

Attitude of Nursing Home Staff

Sexual problems can be a source of concern not only to fellow residents and family members but also to nursing home staff.[17] Incidents and behaviors identifed as sexual and as "causing problems" can be categorized into three general categories: (1) sex talk, (2) sexual acts, and (3) implied sexual behavior[27] (Table 2). A total of 123 incidents were identified during a survey of registered nurses, licensed practical nurses, nurses aides, and orderlies working in an extended care facility.[27] Five incidents (4%) of implied sexual behavior were reported by the nursing home staff. Requesting unnecessary genital care was the most reported event. Thirty-five incidents (28%) of sex talk were recalled, with describing past sex acts being the most frequent. Among 71 incidents of sexual acts, masturbating

TABLE 2. Sexual Incidents as Reported by Nursing Home Staff

Implied sexual acts	Sexual acts
Requesting unnecessary genital care	Masturbating publicly
Reading pornography openly	Touching staff's buttocks and thighs
	Sexual talk and showing of genitalia
Sexual talk	Touching staff's breasts
Describing past experiences	Grabbing staff's buttocks, thighs, and breasts
Suggesting sex encounters	Showing genitalia
Lamenting sex losses	Deep kiss when hugged
Using foul language	Taking off clothes inappropriately
	Touching another patient's genitalia
	Sexual intercourse with visitor

TABLE 3.   Sexual Behavior Perceived as Acceptable by Nursing Staff

Social Arrangements	Physical Contact	Masturbation
Mixed social events	Hugs, kisses on cheek, forehead	Permit it in private
Visits with friends	Same-gender genital care	Permit it but do not encourage it
Expressions of kindness, love		

in public was the most reported event, representing 27% of the incidents of sexual acts. Touching the buttocks and thighs of staff members and sexual talk with showing of genitalia were reported by 18% and 17% of the respondents, respectively. Sexual intercouse with a visitor was reported by one registered nurse. Public masturbation was the most troublesome event, and was reported by 25% of the respondents; 25% of the nursing home residents were thought to create such incidents.

The few sexual activities that are acceptable to nursing home staff (Table 3) include: (1) limited physical contact between staff and patients; (2) masturbation in privacy; (3) verbal expressions of kindness and love to patients by staff; and (4) genital care of patients by staff of the same gender.[27] Half of nursing home staff consider hugging, hand holding, and kissing on the cheek or forehead as appropriate behaviors between patients and staff. Mixed social events and visits with women friends were recommended by a few respondents.[27]

Not only is the type of sexual activity scrutinized by nursing home staff, but the location of the activity is equally important. Commons et al.[5] studied 131 mental health professionals (69 males and 58 females) ages 25–79 with positions ranging from mental health workers to psychiatrists who were employed by state institutions for the mentally ill. Approval of sexual activities was strongly related to location, with activities occurring on the grounds of the institution disapproved much more than activities in the bedroom. Contrary to expectation, respondents approved more highly of a female patient rather than a male patient initiating sexual activity with a consenting partner of either sex. There was a strong tendency for male homophobia. Male-initiated activity with a consenting partner was considered least therapeutic. The least tolerable was a male initiating activity with another male. (In this study, mental health professionals dealing with mentally ill patients did not consider sexual activity to be therapeutically beneficial. The form of sexual activity was significant, but little distinction was made between the therapeutic value of hugging or having sex. Staff seemed to be concerned about any form of sexual activity occurring between patients.) Mental health professionals were more concerned with the location and form of the activity rather than competence, degree of consent, or gender of initiating or other client.

FACTORS INFLUENCING SEXUAL ACTIVITY

To be sexually active, people need to have the interest, ability to carry out sexual activity, an interested and able partner, and an environment that allows such activities to take place. In one study, loss of interest was more frequent in female (28%) than male nursing home residents (8%).[28] Similarly, in the study by Fonzo et al.,[11] none of the men reported loss of interest, but 13% of the women cited it as a reason for their inactivity. Decreased libido and ability to perform is multifactorial and is commonly due to disease or pharmacologic interventions.

Despite the age-related physiologic changes consisting of increased sexual response time, an increased sexual refractory period, thinning of vaginal walls, and reduced ejaculatory urgency, there is no known age limit to sexual activity.[28] In fact, inability to perform was reported only by 15% of men in nursing homes. None of the women reported inability to perform as a problem.[11] Several processes that affect sexual function are described below.

Vascular Factors.   Some residents clearly retain interest in being sexually active but are not able to do so. Impotence in the older man is multifactorial, with vascular disease being the most common cause in men older than 50. In addition, the size of penile venous channels increases with age, leading to venous leakage and, thus, premature detumescence. For women, the rate, amount, and speed of vaginal lubrication may decrease due to the associated decrease in vaginal blood flow.

Endocrine Factors.   Following the peak in serum testosterone in the second and third decades of life in males, there is a gradual decline throughout life. Although testosterone levels are relatively lower in older men, unequivocal hypogonadism is uncommon. The main physiologic changes occurring in women during menopause is the decrease in estrogen production by the ovaries. Consequently, vaginal walls become thinner, the uterus becomes smaller, and breast size may decrease. Vaginal atrophy can be associated with dyspareunia, fissuring of the vaginal wall, and vaginal bleeding following intercourse.

Neural Changes.   In addition to hormonal and vascular changes, neural changes are observed, including decreased sensitivity to light touch in the penile area, which explains the need for greater penile stimulation. A gradual decline in the number of nocturnal penile tumescence events per night as well as the association of nocturnal penile tumescence with the rapid eye movement stage of sleep is observed with aging. Although healthy elders may report continued morning erections, these erections are usually diminished both in rigidity and duration. Healthy male elders who retain erectile function usually require more direct penile stimulation to achieve erection and often have difficulty maintaining it.[19]

Orgasms in elderly women can be delayed or painful due to intense uterine contractions. All of these factors may lead to sexual dysfunction and lead to loss of sexual interest in elderly women. Men may misinterpret dyspareunia as rejection and, as a result, develop erectile dysfunction. Furthermore, elderly men may not be able to sustain an erection long enough for their female partners to develop lubrication and orgasm. Fortunately, some of these changes are reversible with treatment, as outlined below.

Chronic Diseases.   In addition to the previously mentioned physiologic changes taking place as part of the aging process, chronic diseases contribute significantly to the sexual disorders seen in older adults. Endocrine disorders associated with impotence include thyroid disorders, diabetes mellitus, Cushing's syndrome, and prolactinomas. Diabetes is complicated by impotence in more than half of cases. Sexual dysfunction in diabetics can present as retrograde and premature ejaculation. Malnutrition, frequently seen in nursing homes, is associated with hypothalamic pituitary dysfunction and primary testicular failure. Micronutrient alterations such as zinc, folate, or B12 deficiency all contribute to the sexual dysfunction of the institutionalized patient. Dementia may cause loss of sexual interest. However, patients with Alzheimer's disease or multiinfarct dementia may have increased libido associated with inappropriate sexual activity such as self-exposure, inappropriate sexual gestures to nursing home staff, or public masturbation. Arthritis, common among nursing home patients, may diminish sexual enjoyment due to discomfort in certain positions and limited range of motions in joints such as the hips. It may lead to severe painful cramps. Ejaculatory problems and erectile failure have been reported in patients with Parkinson's disease. Urinary incontinence may lead to embarrassment and sexual dysfunction. Cerebrovascular accidents with resultant hemiplegia is a common cause of sexual disability among nursing home residents.[18] Similarly, cancer may affect elders physically and psychologically. The effects of both of these disease categories are discussed in this issue. Interestingly, despite the high bprevalence of such conditions in nursing homes, lack of performance was reported due to poor health in only 19% of residents.[28]

Pharmacologic Factors. Several surveys indicate that, on average, nursing home residents are prescribed 6–8 drugs and that some are prescribed 20 different medications simultaneously. Medications are a cause of sexual dysfunction in at least 25% of cases. Heterocyclic antidepressants can lead to decreased libido, erectile dysfunction, retrograde ejaculation, and anorgasmia. Neuroleptics, commonly used in institutionalized settings, can lead to decreased libido due to the associated hyperprolactinemia. Drugs with high anticholinergic activity can cause erectile dysfunction and ejaculatory impairment. Anxiolytics have been reported to interfere with ejaculation and achievement of orgasm. Antihypertensives, commonly prescribed in the elderly, including diuretics, sympatholytics, reserpine, alpha and beta blockers, and direct vasodilators have been implicated as a cause of impotence in many patients. In addition, H2 blockers, metoclopramide, anticonvulsants, carbonic anhydrase inhibitors, opioids, chemotherapeutic agents, and alcohol all may lead to sexual dysfunction.[9]

Psychological Factors. Psychological and social factors may contribute to sexual inactivity. Self-image is an important factor affecting sexual activity. The majority of men (58%) and women (78%) residing in nursing homes feel sexually unattractive.[28] Paunonen et al.[25] reported that only half of the nursing home residents were satisfied with their physical appearance—an important variable in one's level of sexual activity. In addition to their general appearance, which they frequently consider "asexual," many elders develop a negative identity due to depression, dependence, and physical losses. Moreover, a higher adherence to religion is associated with a decreased knowledge about sex. Institutionalized elders are most susceptible to these changes and suffer not only from personal physical limitations that hinder the free expression of sexuality, but are also in a social environment not conducive to enhancement of either their ego or sexual identities. Institutionalized settings pose significant logistic obstacles to elders attempting to maintain their identity, self-esteem, and sexuality.

Life in nursing homes is perceived by the residents as monotonous. The need for love, being loved, and continuing to be the object of attention and affection is very common among nursing home residents.[13] Women, especially, have complained about loneliness and feelings of abandonment and uselessness that were derived from lack of love. Paunonen et al.[25] reported that 52% of the nursing home residents he studied felt lonely, 58% felt neglected, and 66% felt they were not needed often or sometimes.

Sexuality is expressed in nontraditional ways. For young people, vaginal intercourse may be the objective, but for disabled nursing home residents, fellowship and a warm embrace may be the goal. Mulligan et al.[20] indicated that 90% of the residents continue to hug or kiss their spouses. Thus, nursing home residents resort to other ways of expressing their sexuality. Most find hugs and kisses a good way of ventilating their sexual feelings.

Partner Availability.   Although physiologic and psychological changes may lead to difficulties for some individuals, they cannot solely explain the decreased or nonexistent sexual activity in people of either gender. The most common reason for sexual inactivity among the institutionalized elder is the lack of a partner (27% of men and 33% of women),[28] whereas the patient's own illness accounted for the sexual inactivity of 8% of men and 6% of women in one nursing home. Similar percentages of nursing home residents lacking partners were reported by Fonzo et al.[11] (20% of men and 36% of women). Other studies indicated that loss of interest (47% of men and 27% in women) was the most common reason for sexual inactivity, followed by partner's death.[11] Another reason, separation from partner, was reported in 12% of men and 6% of women.[11]

Environmental Factors.   Availability of a partner is not all that is required to be sexually active. Privacy is necessary and, as a rule, is absent in nursing home settings. White et al.[29] reported on the sexual practices of 269 residents (84 men and 185 women) of 15 nursing homes in two Texas counties, both with large urban and rural centers. Although 91% of the residents were sexually inactive, 43 of 250 respondents (17%) said they would be interested in being sexually active but lacked opportunity (partner or privacy). Twenty one (8%) were sexually active and interested. There was a significant relationship between sexual interest-disinterest and sexual activity-inactivity.

Physical dysfunction is an impediment to only selected sexual activities. Elders are still able to participate in romantic conversation, dancing, kissing, caressing, oral sex, or even mutual genital stimulation. However, nursing home residents may be faced with other barriers inherent to the environment they live in that hinder the expression of their sexuality. An example of one such barrier is the attitudes of nursing home staff. In nursing homes, unmarried patients are often separated on the basis of sex. Private activities are condemned when seen by staff. As elders lose their independence, they may gradually relinquish the opportunity for sexual expression because others may label their actions as inappropriate. According to Maslow,[15] "we may be meeting the needs of the elder for food and safety but failing to meet their need to feel loved." Institutions are responding to constraints placed on them by families. Children of nursing home residents, or their next of kin, may pressure staff to forbid sexual contact because of their strong belief that older people should be asexual.[14]

RISKS AND BENEFITS OF SEXUAL ACTIVITIES IN NURSING HOMES

Although sexual activity can be beneficial physically and psychologically,[28] it may be associated with risks for abuse, especially among patients who have cognitive and/or physical deficits. An example of adverse psychological consequences is the experience of another loss: a partner being transferred or discharged to another facility or dying. The risk for physical injury is low since most of the "sexual activities" in residents with deficits are limited to hugging, kissing, or hand holding.

In nursing homes, staff members are particularly worried about the issue of consent. Competency can be difficult to assess. Assessment techniques that help determine whether a patient can consent to such an activity have been outlined by Lichtenberg.[14] In general, informed consent requires the following three conditions: (1) lack of physical or psychological coercion; (2) mental competence; and (3) awareness of risks and benefits.

TABLE 4. Guidelines to Determine Whether Sexual Contact Should Be Allowed

Patient's awareness of the relationship
  Is the patient aware of who is initiating sexual contact?
  Does the patient believe that the other person is a spouse and thus acquiesces to a delusional belief, or are they cognizant of the other's identity and intent?
  Can the patient state what level of sexual activity with which they would be comfortable?

Patient's ability to avoid exploitation
  Is the behavior consistent with formerly held beliefs/values?
  Does the patient have the capacity to say no to any uninvited sexual contact?

Patient's awareness of potential risks
  Does the patient realize that this relationship may be time-limited?
  Can the patient describe how they will react when the relationship ends?

Guidelines to test these three necessary conditions are outlined in Table 4. An assessment of the patient's formal beliefs and the ability to say no to uninvited sexual activities helps to determine whether the patient can avoid exploitation. Patients' awareness of the identity of their partner and ability to define their relationships and level of the sexual activities with which they are comfortable can be used as a measure of competence. Consenting to perform or agree to certain tasks requires different levels of competency. It is important to avoid the use of the principle of global judgment when deciding whether a particular resident can perform a particular activity.[4] Often partial, context-specific nature of competency should be recognized. The decision to participate in sexual activity is based on an old learning process. Patients may be able to understand the implications of such actions, but at the same time may not be able to take more sophisticated decisions. According to one report, the above assessment guidelines were used in five cases, and in four of the five, the patients were not aware of the relationship and could not avoid exploitation.[14] In the fifth case, the patient was found to be competent. These two groups differed in their mini-mental-state exams; people who were found competent scored about 21/30, and those who were found incompetent scored an average of 7/30. This indicates that patients with mildly low scores on a mini-mental exam may still be competent to decide whether to participate in a relationship.

Sexual contact has the potential to be physically and psychologically beneficial. Sexual activity helps people stay in good physical condition, is helpful to arthritic patients, and helps reduce physical and psychological stress.[28] In addition, introducing a heterosexual living arrangement in nursing homes—for spouses or others who have decided to engage in a relationship—can lead to improved behavior, improved self-care, and increased resident satisfaction.

THERAPEUTIC STRATEGIES

Several strategies can be used to enhance the expression of sexuality in institutionalized settings. Beforehand, however, the following goals should be achieved:

1. Clinicians should be aware of the myths and realities of sexuality of institutionalized adults. They should be taught that sex can help maintain the physical and psychological well being of older adults.

2. Health care professionals and the lay public should be educated about the sexual needs of institutionalized patients. Care providers should realize the importance of sexual expression and, thus, should not limit such opportunities.

3. Nursing personnel and recreation therapists play key roles in this effort. Certainly, impaired elders must be shielded from abuse. However, this should not be extrapolated to discouragement of sexual expression among all nursing home residents.

4. Mental health professionals must reexamine their own prejudices to clarify their decision-making about institutional policies. They need training on competence assessment and its use in decision making.

5. Institutional health care policies must be changed in order to provide high quality life to nursing home residents. This includes avoidance of restrictions of normal life activities such as sexual expression among interested patients. Use of quiet rooms or conjugal-visit rooms is one example.

6. Family members can help improve the life of their loved ones by avoiding the imposition of their own biases. Similarly, physicians must avoid imposing their own biases or the biases of family members on their patients. Instead, they must provide objective suggestions to interested nursing home residents for healthier ways of expressing their sexuality.

The patient, physician, health workers, and significant other (when indicated) should decide together whether the patient is able to participate in healthy sexual activity. To arrive at such decisions, the previously mentioned guidelines can be used to determine competence.[14] If the patient is interested in pursuing sexual activity but suffers from sexual dysfunction, the reason for the sexual dysfunction should be determined. Correctable causes, including illnesses and medication, should be addressed to enhance the sexual function of interested patients. For some patients, all that is needed is education about the various sexual activities in which they could participate, including allowing enough time for vaginal lubrication, estrogen replacement therapy when indicated, direct penile stimulation, and alternative positions for intercourse. To maintain sexual capacity and performance, patients need to participate in regular sexual activity.[16] Unfortunately, the physical slowing is often misunderstood and sexual activity may be halted instead of adjusted to the aging process.

For people who cannot engage in normal sexual activities but remain interested in expressing their sexuality, alternative outlets for sexual expression can be designed. An example of such activities was outlined by Citron et al.[3] in a Jewish nursing home in New York: belly dancing on Father's Day. The comment on this activity by the resident writers for the home's literary paper was titled: Belly Dancers Wiggle Into The Hearts of Residents. Comments included: "It was a glorious day for the Levindale residents as well as all the visitors and performers!" Additional activities to enhance sexual identities of residents included a men's club that sponsored activities such as discussing sports, politics, and religion and a luncheon for men only. Similarly, the women's club discussed provocative issues such as abortion and the women's liberation movement. Additional activities included cooking, crocheting, and knitting—reflections of their former role as a housewife. All of these activities helped maintain and restore the ego strength essential for sexual identities of nursing home patients.

Patients who are not competent to participate in sexual activity and who manifest inappropriate sexual behavior such as public masturbation can be a management problem. These patients should be educated about other ways of expressing their sexual activities. However, in most cases the patients are not able to fully comprehend the consequences of their action. Medications such as tranquilizers have been tried with some success. However, their benefits are usually accompanied by undesirable side effects, such as induction of extrapyramidal symptoms by the major tranquilizers, the most serious being tardive dyskinesias. Some tranquilizers, such as chlorpromazine, can cause excessive sedation, ataxia, and hypotension, leading to falls and possible fractures. Similarly, benzodiazepines may lead to paradoxical agitation, depression, confusion, instability, and incontinence. Physical restraints and incarceration in rooms are not recommended. Because of all these associated side effects, attempts at modifying the hormonal status of these patients with the use of antiandrogens have been tried with some success. Antiandrogens have been used in the treatment of sex offenders.[6,12,22] Both medroxyprogesterone acetate and cyproterone acetate have been used with good success at controlling sexual fantasies and sexual actions of these patients. Medroxyprogesterone acts through reduction in testosterone and luteinizing hormone levels to hypogonadal levels.[1] Medroxyprogesterone acetate has been tried in four institutionalized demented male patients who were engaged in disruptive sexual behavior not responsive to major and minor tranquilizers.[7] It was initially given intramuscularly at a dose of 300 mg/week for 1 year, and the dose was adjusted until a therapeutic effect was achieved. Subjects displayed a rapid decrease in sexual acting out within 10–14 days. Side effects were not noted. Patients had mild to moderate deterioration in their cognitive skills, which was an expected finding given the nature of their dementia. Although few younger transgressors may be resistant to even high doses of medroxyprogesterone acetate, most elderly patients do not need such high doses, and their symptoms could be controlled with much lower doses. Following 1 year of treatment, three patients did not have recurring symptoms when the treatment was discontinued. The fourth patient had recurring symptoms. His symptoms were less frequent and were managed by other nonpharmacologic techniques by the nursing staff. Serum testosterone levels return to pretreatment levels 4 weeks following discontinuation of medroxyprogesterone acetate. Similarly, cyproterone acetate has been used successfully in the treatment of hypersexuality and sexual deviation.[8,22] Results were similar to surgical castration. However, the loss of libido is usually more rapid due to the inhibitory action on adrenal testosterone.

CONCLUSION

Although elders in nursing homes continue to be interested in expressing their sexuality and believe that they have the right to participate in sexual activities, most nursing home elders are sexually inactive. Lack of sexual performance is due to a multitude of reasons, including lack of a partner, nonconducive environment, or inability to sexually perform in the traditional sense due to age-related changes, illnesses, or medications. Currently, nursing home staff and family members do not view sexual activities of nursing home elders favorably, and they impose significant restrictions on them. Family members and nursing home staff may benefit from further education about the sexual needs of older adults and the potential benefits of sexual activity to their health. For nursing home residents who are interested in pursuing their former sexual activities, nursing home staff and health professionals should be understanding, supportive, and nonrestrictive. Patients who cannot engage in sexual activities can be taught to channel their sexual energy into other activities that could provide them with a source of love and warmth. Recreational therapists and other nursing home staff can help design and implement such activities. For noncompetent nursing home residents who are thought to be at risk for harming themselves or others while pursuing their sexual needs, behavior modifications through the use of medroxyprogesterone acetate or cyproterone acetate can be achieved. Long-term care institutions and health care professionals should always aim at increasing the autonomy of nursing home residents, especially when it comes to such a basic need as their sexuality.

REFERENCES

1. Berlin FS, Meinecke CF: Treatment of sex offenders with antiandrogenic medication: Conceptualization, review of treatment modalities, and preliminary findings. Am J Psychiatry 138:601–607, 1981.
2. Berkman B, Rehr H: Social needs of the hospitalized elderly: A classification. Social Work 17:80, 1972.
3. Citron H, Kartman LL: Preserving sexual identity in the institutionalized aged through activities. Activities Adaptation and Aging 3:55–63, 1982.
4. Collopy B: Autonomy in long term care: Some crucial distinctions. Gerontologist 28:10–18, 1988.
5. Commons ML, Bohn JT, Godon LT, et al: Professionals' attitudes towards sex between institutionalized patients. Am J Psychother 46:571–580, 1992.
6. Cooper AJ: Progestogens in the treatment of male sex offenders: A review. Can J Psychiatry 31:73–79, 1986.
7. Cooper AJ: Medroxyprogesterone acetate (MPA) treatment of sexual acting out in men suffering from dementia. J Clin Psychiatry 48:368–370, 1987.
8. Davis TS: Cyproterone acetate for male hypersexuality. J Intern Res 2:159–163, 1974.
9. Deamer RL, Thompson JF: The role of medications in geriatric sexual function. Clin Geriatr Med 7:95–111, 1991.
10. Dominick JR, Greenblaat DL, Stotsky BA: The adjustment of aged persons in nursing homes: I. The patient's report. J Am Geriatr Soc 16:63–77, 1968.
11. Fonzo D, Carosi V, Quadri R, et al: Sexuological problems in nursing-homes: A methodology for investigation. J Endocrinol Invest 8(suppl 2):131–141, 1985.
12. Gagne P: Treatment of sex offenders with medroxyprogesterone acetate. Am J Psychiatry 138:644–646, 1981.
13. Kass MJ: Sexual expression in the elderly in nursing homes. Gerontologist 18:372–378, 1978.
14. Lichtenberg PA, Strzepeek DM: Assessments of institutionalized dementia patients' competencies to participate in intimate relationships. Gerontologist 30:117–120, 1990.
15. Maslow AH: Motivation and Personality. New York, Harper & Row, 1970.
16. Masters W, Johnson V: Human Sexual Inadequacy. Boston, Little, Brown & Co., 1970.
17. McCartney JR, Izeman H, Rogers D, Cohen N: Sexuality and the institutionalized elderly. J Am Geriatr Soc 35:331–333, 1987.
18. Mooradian AD: Geriatric sexuality and chronic diseases. Clin Geriatr Med 7:113–131, 1991.
19. Mulligan T, Katz PG: Erectile failure in the aged: Evaluation and treatment. J Am Geriatr Soc 36:54–62, 1988.
20. Mulligan T, Modigh A: Sexuality in dependent living situations. Clin Geriatr Med 7:153–160, 1991.
21. Mulligan T, Palguta R: Sexual interest, activity, and satisfaction among male nursing home residents. Arch Sex Behav 20:199–204, 1991.
22. Namer M: Clinical applications of antiandrogens. J Steroid Biochem 31:719–729, 1988.
23. Newman G, Nichols GR: Sexual activities and attitudes in older persons. JAMA 173:117–119, 1960.
24. Ouslander JG, Osterweil D, Morley J: In Demographics and Economics of Nursing Home Care. New York, McGraw-Hill, 1991.
25. Paunonen M, Häggman-Laitila A: Sexuality and the satisfaction of sexual needs. A study on the attitudes of aged home-nursing clients. Scand J Caring Sci 4:163–168, 1990.
26. Pfeiffer E: Geriatric sex behavior. Med Aspects Hum Sex 3:19–28, 1969.
27. Szasz G: Sexual incidents in an extended care unit for aged men. J Am Geriatr Soc 31:407–411, 1983.
28. Wasow M, Loeb MB: Sexuality in nursing homes. J Am Geriatr Soc 27:73–79, 1979.
29. White CB: Sexual interest, attitudes, knowledge, and sexual history in relation to sexual behavior in the institutionalized aged. Arch Sex Behav 11:11–21, 1982.

MARGARET A. NOSEK, PhD

SEXUAL ABUSE OF WOMEN WITH PHYSICAL DISABILITIES

From the Center for Research
  on Women with Disabilities
Department of Physical Medicine
  and Rehabilitation
Baylor College of Medicine
Houston, Texas

Reprint requests to:
Margaret A. Nosek, PhD
Director, Center for Research
  on Women with Disabilities
Department of Physical Medicine
  and Rehabilitation
Baylor College of Medicine
One Baylor Plaza
Houston, TX 77030

Inquiry into the sexual abuse of women with disabilities is one of the most complex, controversial, and disturbing challenges facing rehabilitation researchers. It brings to the table a combination of many unresolved issues in the studies of abuse, disability, and the status of women. As a dimension of the general study of abuse, disability has barely been acknowledged. As a dimension of the general study of disability, abuse has only recently surfaced as a problem and has yet to be the subject of rigorous scientific inquiry. To bring to light the importance of this problem and to set forth some parameters for further investigation into its magnitude and impact, this chapter reviews the literature on the sexual abuse of women with disabilities and presents the findings of a qualitative study of sexuality issues among women with physical disabilities in which the experience of abuse emerged as an unexpectedly strong and ominous theme. There will be a special focus on the effect of having a disability on increasing a woman's vulnerability to sexual abuse.

METHODOLOGIC ISSUES IN ABUSE RESEARCH

Before reviewing the literature on sexual abuse of women with disabilities, it is necessary to establish the parameters by which abuse can be examined. The first and most fundamental of these is definitions. While some authors claim that there is currently no totally satisfactory or standard definition of abuse,[17,21] there have been many attempts to do so. Dorothea Glass is quoted as defining sexual assault as "any unwanted sexual activity; visual, verbal, physical, or where the victim is less than the age of consent." She further calls it "an act of aggression and hostility against a whole person; not just a sexual act or a bodily violation, but an indignity, an invasion, and violation of a person that affects the victim physically, psychologically, and socially; an assault which does not necessarily end when the assailant leaves or is caught."[1] Cole[10] defines sexual abuse as "when a person is manipulated, tricked, or forced into touch or sexual contact."

In the literature on sexual abuse of pregnant women, McFarlane, Parker, Soeken, and Bullock[23] define it simply as being forced to have sexual activities. The American Medical Association, in its *Guidelines on Domestic Violence*,[2] defines sexual abuse as any form of forced sex or sexual degradation. This includes trying to make a woman perform sexual acts against her will; pursuing sexual activity when she is not fully conscious or is not asked or is afraid to say no; hurting her physically during sex or assaulting her genitals; coercing her to have sex without protection against pregnancy or sexually transmissible diseases; and criticizing her and calling sexually degrading names.

The Adult Protection Act of 1988 defines abuse as offensive mistreatment—whether physical, sexual, mental, emotional, material, or any combination—that causes or is reasonably likely to cause the victim severe physical or psychological harm or significant material loss to his or her estate. This definition opens the door to court determination of consequences before a label of abuse can be invoked, thus allowing societal stereotypes about the sexuality of people with disabilities and preconceived notions of suffering due to disability to have a disproportionate negative effect when people with disabilities are involved in such court proceedings.

The most thoroughly considered and practical definitions of abuse have been formulated by Finkelhor and Korbin[15] in the context of child abuse—the portion of harm to children that results from human action that is proscribed, proximate, and preventable. By "proscribed," the authors mean action that is negatively valued at the same time it causes harm—thus eliminating harmful effects of well-intended medical procedures but including actions that are deviant, of harmful intent, or in violation of legal or social expectations. By "proximate," they mean that action must have a direct effect and not be removed by time or space. This definition distinguishes child abuse clearly from the social, economic, and health problems of international concern. It is flexible enough to apply to a range of situations in a variety of social and cultural contexts. Finkelhor and Korbin specifically define sexual abuse of children as any sexual contact between an adult and a sexually immature (socially as well as psychologically) child for the purposes of the adult's sexual gratification; or any sexual contact to a child made by the use of force, threat, or deceit to secure the child's participation; or sexual contact to which a child is incapable of consenting by virtue of age or power differentials, or the nature of the relationship with the adult. The issue of power differentials and relationships with other individuals will become salient later in the discussion of the disempowerment of people with disabilities.

Once a label of abuse has been attached to an incident, it is necessary to determine other parameters for purposes of description and comparison. Trickett and Putnam[39] recommend that the degree of trauma related to the severity of abuse can be indexed by (1) type of abuse, (2) age at onset, (3) frequency, (4) closeness of the relationship to the abuser, and (5) presence of physical violence, pain, and threats.

The study of sexual abuse is severely compromised by issues of documentation. Estimates vary on the percent of actual cases that are reported to authorities, depending on the age of the victim. A study of 245 women with disabilities conducted by the Canadian DisAbled Women's Network (DAWN)[34] found that of the cases of abuse identified by their participants 43% had been reported to police, social service agencies, parents, teachers, or spouses. This figure was acknowledged as high by the investigators because more than half of the participants were members of consumer advocacy groups. McFarlane et al.[23] cited a statistic from the U.S. Department of Justice that of actual cases of spousal abuse 43% were not reported to the police. Their study of abused pregnant women found that 7.3% reported abuse by a partner in a paper and pencil questionnaire but 29.3% reported abuse when interviewed by a nurse. Cases of child abuse are even more complicated to document, given a child's general lack of understanding and vocabulary related to sexual activities. For children with disabilities, particularly cognitive and communication disabilities, there are additional complicating factors related to documenting personal experiences.[22] In a survey of human service agencies' child and adult protective services in all 50 states, Camblin[9] reported that seven states had no standardized reporting form and only 26 states gathered information on preexisting disability status.

Many methodological flaws are evident in the literature on sexual abuse. Most studies violate Laws'[21] guideline for rigorous cross-sectional studies: (1) choose subjects and controls from homogeneous populations, (2) assess sexual abuse history with an instrument that consists of multiple questions describing specific events, (3) use an explicit definition of abuse, (4) measure potential confounds such as socioeconomic status, family dynamics, psychological symptoms, history of sexual and physical abuse in childhood, and adult sexual and physical assault, (5) use valid and reliable instruments to measure comorbid medical and psychological problems, and (6) have adequate statistical power to test associations and control for confounds. Ammerman et al.[3] cite three shortcomings of child abuse research: (1) heterogeneous samples, (2) failure to match participants on relevant variables, and (3) use of psychometrically weak assessment instruments. In an attempt to avoid some of these shortcomings, the study reported in this chapter focuses on women with physical disabilities and attempts to describe their specific accounts of sexual abuse according to parameters recommended above. Before presenting these findings, however, it is necessary to examine previous research related to sexual abuse of girls and women with disabilities to provide a context for interpretation.

SEXUAL ABUSE OF CHILDREN WITH DISABILITIES

The most valid and respected statistic on the prevalence of childhood sexual abuse was stated by Finkelhor:[14] 25% of female children and 9% of male children. Several studies report substantially higher rates among children with disabilities, although rates vary considerably, and no attempt is made to distinguish between the experience of children with physical versus cognitive disabilities. Doucette,[13] for example, reported in a study of women with a variety of disabilities that the women were about 1½ times more likely to have been sexually abused as children than nondisabled women. A survey of 62 women conducted by the Ontario Ministry of Community and Social Services[12b] found that 50% of women with disabilities reported being sexually assaulted as a child compared to 34% of women without disabilities. Sobsey and Doe,[36] citing a variety of studies, report that the incidence of all types of abuse among children with disabilities appears to be 4.43 times the expected value. A recent Congressionally mandated study conducted by the National Center on Child Abuse and Neglect[12a] documented physical and sexual abuse twice as often in children with disabilities compared with other children. Muccigrosso[25] claims that 90–99% of people with development disabilities have been sexually exploited by age 18, four times the rate in the nondisabled population. Mullins[27] claims that 50–90% of people with developmental disabilities are sexually abused. Despite these widely divergent estimates, the body of evidence strongly points toward a prevalence of sexual abuse of children with disabilities that far exceeds public awareness.

Much of the attention in the literature has been spent on examining reasons for this increased prevalence of abuse among children with disabilities. These studies, however, focus almost exclusively on children with developmental disabilities who have severe cognitive impairments. Some studies attribute causation of the abuse to stress imposed on the family by the child's disability.[8] In nearly half the cases examined in the study by the National Center on Child Abuse and Neglect,[12a] the disability was identified as the root of the abuse or neglect. There is a considerable body of literature, however, that fails to confirm disability itself as a risk factor in abuse and even documents an inverse relationship between level of severity of disability and incidence of abuse.[6,7,17,19,38,43] There is general agreement with Garbarino[17] that related factors of greater importance include psychological, social, and cultural aspects of the family and characteristics of the parents such as coping skills, parenting skills, their own history of maltreatment, interpersonal violence, and low level of social exchange. According to Sobsey and Varnhagen,[37] "in many cases, it may not be the actual disability that contributes to the increased risk, but rather a function of society's expectations and treatment of disabled people." It must also be acknowledged that children with disabilities have a much greater risk of residing in institutions, where significantly higher rates of abuse are well documented.[12,17]

For all the analysis of disability as an increased risk factor in sexual abuse, little attention has been paid to the effect of child abuse on victims who have disabilities. To interpret the findings presented later in this chapter, it is helpful to understand some of the findings in the general literature on child abuse. Early writings claimed that the sexual abuse of children rarely involved coercion or violence, that the abuse is of short duration, and it has minimal effect in terms of gross measure of functioning later in life (e.g., marriage and bearing children), and that even in offenses that involve a great deal of violence, there is rarely a profound long-term effect.[16] These statements have been soundly refuted by more recent research among psychological, sociologic, and developmental investigators. Trickett and Putnam[39] found that sexual abuse peaked in children age 7–8 years and had a mean duration of 2 years. They documented sequelae of childhood sexual abuse to be multiple personality disorders, borderline personality disorders, somatoform disorders (especially chronic pelvic pain), eating disorders, substance abuse, and some forms of chronic psychosis. Other negative effects include low self-esteem, impaired sense of control and competence, and increased negative affect. They stated that cognitive capabilities can mediate these negative outcomes. Forty percent of women with premenstrual syndrome report histories of sexual abuse.[32] Researchers at Washington University found that physical abuse dramatically increases the likelihood of abnormal aggression later in life and that a significant percentage of girls developed withdrawal behavior patterns.[35]

Garbarino[17] was one of the few to examine the long-term effect of abuse in a disability context. He claimed that the abuse of special children (children with disabilities) results in acute and chronic medical problems that impair development and substantially increase the risk of delinquency, psychiatric disorders, and sexual dysfunction.

SEXUAL ABUSE OF WOMEN WITH DISABILITIES

The incidence of sexual abuse among women in general has been fairly well documented;[2,23] however, only a few studies have examined the incidence among women with disabilities. The DisAbled Women's Network of Canada surveyed 245 women with disabilities and found that 40% had experienced abuse, including 12% who had been raped. Perpetrators of the abuse were primarily spouses (including ex-spouses) (37%) and strangers (28%), followed by parents (15%), services providers (10%), and dates (7%). As mentioned above, fewer than half were reported, due mostly to fear and dependency. Ten percent of the women had used shelters or other services, 15% reported that no services were available or they were unsuccessful in their attempt to obtain services, and 55% had not tried to get services.

The Center for Research on Women with Disabilities at Baylor College of Medicine conducted an informal survey of battered women's shelters in Houston and found 64% to be inaccessible to women in wheelchairs. Sobsey and Doe[36] conducted a study of 166 cases handled by the University of Alberta's Sexual Abuse and Disability Project. The sample was 81.7% women, 70% persons with intellectual impairments, and had a very wide age range (18 months–57 years). In 95.6% of the cases, the perpetrator was known to the victim; 44% of the perpetrators were service providers. (Eighty-six and 99% of the perpetrators were known to the victim in the National Center on Child Abuse and Neglect study and in Muccigrosso's study, respectively.) Seventy-nine percent of the individuals were victimized more than once. Treatment services were either inadequate or not offered in 73% of the cases.

The Ontario Ministry of Community and Social Services[12b] surveyed 62 women and found that more of the women with disabilities had been battered as adults than women without disabilities (33% versus 22%), but fewer had been sexually assaulted as adults (23% versus 31%).

While reliable statistics on the experience of sexual abuse among women with disabilities are sorely lacking, there has been some analysis concerning why these women might experience a greater vulnerability. The combined cultural devaluation of women and persons with disabilities is a major factor,[5] often further confounded by devaluations based on age.[20] Overprotection and internalized societal expectations are other significant contributors. For persons with developmental disabilities, Muccigrosso[25] lists the by-products of living in extremely overprotected environments as (1) lack of knowledge, (2) overcompliance and socialized vulnerability, (3) the unrealistic view that everyone is a friend, (4) limited social opportunities, (5) low self-esteem, and (6) limited or no assertiveness or refusal skills. Womendez and Schneiderman[41] characterize the experience of women with disabilities as having fewer opportunities to learn sexual likes and dislikes and to set pleasing boundaries. They may not date, go to parties, or engage in age-appropriate sexual activity, experiencing frequent rejection. Their first sexual experience may come much later in life. These limited opportunities prevent them from learning how to start a relationship; much of their information on sexuality is second-hand. Women with disabilities often perceive celibacy or violent sexual encounters as their only choices, believing no loving person would be attracted to them. Some believe that fate proclaims that they deserve what they get and that bad feelings (such as pain) are better than none. There is often disassociation of the self from the parts of the body being assaulted, rooted in frequent pain inflicted by doctors and "helpers," where privacy is denied, nakedness is the norm, and women are treated as if they are not human. Few human service workers validate the abuse experienced by these women. Several studies have documented low rates of receiving sexuality counseling or information among women with arthritis[42] and spinal cord injury.[4,40,44]

The vulnerability to sexual exploitation of persons with a variety of disabilities, as perceived by health care providers, was studied by Mullan and Cole.[26] Persons with a combination of mental retardation and physical disability were rated as the most vulnerable, followed by persons with mental illness, physical disability only, mental retardation only, intellectual impairment, and learning disability. The authors listed 12 ways health care providers create victims out of persons with disabilities: institutionalize, reward compliance, isolate, extend dependency, withhold information, discount signals, support or create double binds between individuals and their families, don't believe, don't regard as sexual, deny basic rights, deny privacy, and overmedicate or restrain chemically.

Many factors contribute to the vulnerability of women with disabilities to sexual abuse. Many questions remain, however, about the actual abuse experiences of these women, the role their disabilities play in the abuse, and the effect the abuse has on their lives.

A QUALITATIVE STUDY

The following is a presentation of findings from a qualitative study that details sexual abuse experiences reported in interviews with 11 women who have physical disabilities. While no conclusions can be drawn from this study about the relative incidence of abuse among women with disabilities compared with women without disabilities, the findings do shed some light on the complex interweaving of personal, social, cultural, and environmental factors that allow sexual abuse of women with disabilities to take place, often with a severe negative impact.

Description of the Study

The current study used the qualitative method of open-ended interviewing to identify primary themes and issues about the sexuality of women with disabilities. Members of the research team developed a generalized interview guide[33] based on a literature review and their own experience. Three researchers, all with disabilities themselves and trained in interviewing techniques, used the interview guide primarily as a reference to make sure that they covered key areas.

Thirty-one adult women with disabilities that resulted in functional impairments participated in the interviews. The participants were recruited through personal contact and by fliers distributed locally and nationally. Use of theoretical sampling[18] assured that the selection of individuals represented key variables hypothesized to affect sexual functioning, such as (1) type of disability, (2) age at onset of disability, (3) ethnicity, and (4) marital status. All interviews were recorded on audiocassette, transcribed, and checked by the interviewer for accuracy. Field notes providing context to the interviews, nonverbal reactions of participants, and reactions of the interviewers were written and included within the transcripts for analysis.

The racial groups represented in the sample included Caucasian (18), Asian (4), Hispanic (3), and African-American (6). Ages ranged from 22 to 69, with ages at onset of disability ranging from birth to 52. Disabilities included cerebral palsy, postpolio, spina bifida, amputation (bilateral upper limb, unilateral lower limb), rheumatic conditions (including rheumatoid arthritis and systemic lupus erythematosus), multiple sclerosis, spinal cord injury, traumatic brain injury, and stroke. Sexual orientation consisted of 29 heterosexuals and 2 lesbians. Fifteen of the participants were never married, 7 were divorced, and 9 were married at the time of the interview. Fourteen of them had children. Level of education attained was unrepresentatively high: 10 had graduate degrees, 7 had bachelors degrees, 10 had some college, and 4 had a high school education. Seventeen worked for pay, and 13 were considered unemployed but productive, i.e., involved in homemaking, educational, or volunteer activities. Only one was considered inactive.

Analytic induction and constant comparison[18] were the qualitative data analysis techniques employed. Analysis began with the research team reading each of the transcribed interviews and discussing the major themes, issues, and hypotheses in weekly research team meetings. As key concepts emerged from these discussions, the research staff listed and grouped them into major thematic areas: sense of self, family of origin, friendship, sex education, abuse, physical sexual functioning, environmental and social barriers, abuse, health issues, dating, marriage, parenting, and personal assistance issues. After identifying these major themes, at least two researchers coded all interviews by bracketing the thematic passages on the transcripts and recording the appropriate code or codes for that passage. They resolved disagreements about coding in team meetings and refined the coding scheme itself when needed. An indication of the validity of the major themes was the lack of required modifications as the analysis of interviews neared completion. To provide the basis for a rich descriptive presentation of the major themes, the staff extracted coded passages from the transcripts as "chunks" and grouped them by themes. Members of the research team then reviewed each set of thematic chunks and described findings along with hypotheses or explanations of the phenomena under study. A review team evaluated the process and findings monthly. A panel of national experts from the fields of rehabilitation, independent living, medicine, and sexuality critiqued the preliminry report.

Procedure for Analyzing Abuse

After further analyzing themes extracted from the data, the research team identified five major thematic categories: sense of self, sexuality information, relationships, barriers, and health and physical functioning. The category of barriers consisted of factors that inhibited or prevented the development of positive sense of self, access to sexuality information, satisfactory relationships, and optimal health and physical functioning. There were three subcategories: environmental barriers, social barriers, and abuse.

The pricipal investigator returned to transcripts of the original interviews to identify specific reports of abuse experiences. For each abuse experience reported by each participant, the investigator determined the type of abuse as sexual, physical, or emotional, with the understanding that physical abuse includes emotional abuse, and sexual abuse includes both physical and emotional abuse. The type of abuse was charted along with the perpetrator, the age at which it occurred or began, frequency/duration (for example: once, many times, years, life-long), and a description of the abuse, including whether alcohol or drug abuse was involved. The research team examined and discussed this information until they reached consensus on designations within each parameter.

Using inductive techniques, the team processed this information with basic demographic and disability data on the participants and with a profile of each interview in order to interpret the disability-relatedness and impact of the abuse experiences. The team interpreted disability-relatedness by considering whether the experience occurred after the onset of disability and by asking such questions as: "Had this individual not had a disability, would the abuse have occurred?" and "Did factors related to the disability create psychological, behavioral, social, physical, or environmental conditions that made the abuse more likely to occur?" They interpreted impact as very low, low, moderate, severe, or very severe, according to predetermined guidelines based on the participants' own words. The first consideration was the length of the presentation of the experience by the participant and the number of times to which it was referred throughout the interview; second was the emotional intensity expressed during the presentation of the experience; third was the degree to which the participant said the experience affected her life physically, emotionally, or socially. The team interpreted the impact to be low for those who mentioned an event once in passing, without elaboration, with little emotional intensity, and with no statements that attributed to the experience a significant interference with developmental processes. The interpretation of severe impact was reserved for experiences that participants discussed at length or mentioned more than once in the interview, using strong, emotion-filled language, and with statements indicating a serious, long-lasting interference with their physical, emotional, or social functioning.

The research team identified an abuse experience as sexual if it involved unwanted physical contact to the participant's genitals or breasts, contact of any part of her body with the genitals of the perpetrator, or if the participant used such words as "raped," "molested," or "incested" in reporting the experience. The question of exhibitionism as abuse did not arise since no such experiences were reported in this study. For young children, the question of whether the contact was wanted was considered moot if the participant used the language of abuse to describe it. Willfulness on the part of the perpetrator was not considered, only the participant's perception of the experience as sexual abuse.

Data Related to Sexual Abuse

Of the 31 women in the study, more than one-third (11) reported experiencing sexual abuse. All totaled, 25 of the participants reported 55 separate experiences of abuse; 15 of which were sexual, 17 physical, and 23 emotional. Following are brief profiles of the women reporting sexual abuse.

#1: Emily, a 37-year-old, married Caucasian woman with no children, had polio at age 4 that severely affected all four limbs and her ability to breathe independently during sleep. She has a bachelor's degree and is working full-time. During her college years, she met a man from out of town on an airplane and, along with her female roommate, accepted an invitation to go out to dinner with him. After they had all consumed considerable alcohol, he told her he wanted her to become his mistress since he had previously had a good sexual experience with a woman who also had polio. When the roommate left to use the restroom, the man began fondling the participant's foot and placed it on his penis under the table. Since she was using her manual wheelchair instead of her power wheelchair in order to travel in his car, she was unable to pull away from his grasp. When her roommate returned, Emily talked him into taking them back to the dorm. This was the only abuse experience she reported. It was interpreted as disability-related, based on the perpetrator's reasons for approaching the participant and her inability to physically escape the situation. Although it frightened her considerably at the time and she had told only a few people about it over the years, the fact that she did not express lasting negative feelings about herself as a result of this experience indicates that it had a low impact on her development and later relationships.

#2: Elena, a 26-year-old Hispanic woman, had polio at age 1 that affected her ability to walk. She is married and was pregnant at the time of the interview. She had attended college and is working. Her mother raised her and two sisters in an upper-class family in South America. According to Elena, there were strong feelings of shame in the family toward her disability. As a child, her mother frequently took her to faith healers and physicians who performed numerous surgeries. She said, "I always felt that my body didn't belong to me." Her sister arranged for a boy to visit Elena in their home when Elena was 14 years old and had had no sexual experience. She hid her crutches and tried to look normal. On a later visit, he forced her to perform oral sex. When asked whether it was unusual in that culture for a young man to be that aggressive, she replied, "Oh yeah because all the men that I knew . . . they respect the woman until they get married." Her statement about not feeling ownership of her body, combined with her statement that his behavior was uncharacteristically aggressive in their culture and social class, led the researchers to interpret this experience as disability-related. The team interpreted it to have had a moderate impact, because she labeled it as an "unfortunate incident" yet used strong language such as "violent" and "totally disgusting" in describing it.

#3: Beatrice, a never-married, 33-year-old Caucasian woman, has had cerebral palsy from birth. She has a graduate degree but was not working at the time of the interview. Her parents raised her in a strong Catholic environment. Her father encouraged her to overcome her shyness and invite boys in whom she was interested to her house. She initially denied having any abuse experiences but, on reflection, said that when she was a teenager at summer camp, a boy fondled her breasts in a manner she didn't like. The researchers concluded that this was not disability-related in that it is often part of the developmental processes of sexual experimentation and setting boundaries. The fact that Beatrice only thought to mention this incident after reflection and described it in neutral terms with little detail indicates that it had a low impact.

#4: Ginny, a 46-year-old Caucasian woman, is married and has two children. At her birth, her arms were broken and amputated above the elbow by an alcoholic doctor. At the time of the interview, she was attending college but not working. She was raised in a low-income, poorly educated, rural family. She said that her mother rejected her and shamed her about her disability. There were 9 experiences of abuse in her interview, predominantly emotional. Two of the experiences were sexual: being molested as a child by an uncle and being raped at age 12 by a stranger. The research team considered both experiences to be not disability-related. Vulnerabilities related to her disability were outweighed by other risk factors in her life, such as her family demographics and persistent psychological violence. Her cursory description of the first experience indicates a low impact. The second experience, on the other hand, was interpreted as having a severe impact because, in her words, it made her feel "ashamed and dirty." She shut off her feelings after that and was convinced that sex was the only thing men would ever want from her.

#5: Patsy, a 36-year-old, never-married Asian woman, had polio at the age of 16 months and subsequently developed severe scoliosis. She has a master's degree and is unemployed but volunteers at a local advocacy office. Her family was very caring and supportive during her childhood; she lived with them at the time of the interview. She has never had a romantic or sexual relationship. She came to the U.S. just before college and believes the doctor at the immigration physical exam may have molested her by fondling her breasts. Her description of the experience suggests a routine breast exam, but her perception was of being molested. The experience itself was interpreted by the researchers to be an ordinary occurrence that was not disability-related, although her perception of it as a molestation was related to the social isolation and lack of sexuality information that resulted from her disability. She did not give many details of the experience or describe any persistent negative feelings subsequent to it, indicating that it had a low impact.

#6: Josephine, a 36-year-old Caucasian lesbian, has had severe juvenile rheumatoid arthritis since age 3. She considers herself married to her lover and has been very active in a support group for lesbians with disabilities. She has a doctorate and is working. She is the eldest of three siblings in a fairly happy family, but was frequently sick and in special schools or had a home tutor until ninth grade. In addition to reporting experiences of physical and emotional abuse by personal attendants, she reported being sexually abused while in a hospital for surgery at age 7. In that her disability required her to be hospitalized frequently, thereby increasing the likelihood of experiencing sexual abuse, the researchers interpreted this experience to be disability-related. She said that all the lesbians she knows were victims of incest or sexual abuse in hospitals. Her implication that lesbianism is related to sexual abuse and the impassioned language used in that discussion indicate that this experience had a severe impact.

#7: Heather, a 37-year-old African American woman, has had juvenile rheumatoid arthritis since age 12. She has never married, has a bachelor's degree, and is working. She was raped more than once by her stepfather before the onset of her arthritis. She reported becoming more introverted after being raped. When she told her mother about these experiences, her mother did not believe her. Neither parent ever acknowledged that the rape had occurred. She never received counseling until the 1980s, when the memories started resurfacing. Although he has had numerous dating relationships, she has never engaged in sexual activity due to religious beliefs. This abuse experience was interpreted as not disability-related since it occurred before the onset of her disability. Her repression of the memories, the strong language she used in describing the experiences, and the process of dealing with it later in life indicate a severe impact.

#8: Geraldine, a 26-year-old Caucasian woman, incurred a spinal cord injury (paraplegia) and a traumatic brain injury in an accident at age 15. She was married twice, divorced once, and has a young daughter. She has a high school education and was not working at the time of the interview. She described herself as a juvenile delinquent and wild in her youth. Her interview revealed four experiences of sexual abuse, all involving drugs or alcohol. The first three occurred in her teen years after acquiring a disability. In the first, she went to a bar at age 17 and met two brothers with whom she drank. Afterward, they went to the brother's apartment to smoke marijuana. The apartment was upstairs, and the brothers carried her. Once inside, they threw her on the bed, stripped her, and tried to rape her. When she stopped fighting them, they stopped and took her home. In the second and third experiences, she met men in bars on various occasions; one she referred to as the "hatchet man" and another as the "convict." She felt coerced into sexual activity with them. The fourth experience occurred as an adult. In her words, she was "sexually harassed" into doing cocaine and having sex with a high official in the contracting company where she worked. In an attempt to end the sexual harassment, she married her first husband, who turned out to be physically and emotionally abusive. The first three of these experiences may be disability-related because they reflect the excessive risk-taking behavior and impaired judgment that sometimes accompanies traumatic brain injury. Additionally, in the first experience her spinal cord injury limited her escape options. The fourth experience is more difficult to interpret because, while it reflects some of the same risk-taking behavior, there was nothing in her description indicating any relationship between the sexual harassment and her disability. The research team interpreted it to be not disability-related. The length of her descriptions and her use of strong language in the first and fourth experiences indicate a moderate impact. She mentioned the second and third experiences almost in passing, indicating a low impact.

#9: Della, a never-married, 26-year-old Caucasian woman, incurred a traumatic brain injury at age 16 that requires her to use crutches for walking. She had attended college and is working. She reported one experience of abuse, a date rape in college. In describing her response to it, she said, "Nothing happened because I didn't get pregnant," and she did not let it affect her. This indicates a low impact. The experience was interpreted by the research team to be not disability-related; it was viewed as a typical case of date rape.

#10: Sally, a 43-year-old, divorced Caucasian woman with no children, has had epilepsy and a back injury since age 24. She attended college and is working. She reported being sexually "tortured" repeatedly with a hair brush at age 5 by her 7-year-old brother and his friend. After the incidents were discovered, the whole family became over-protective of her. In her words, "it tore the family up" when she identified the brother as the perpetrator. She repressed the memory for 33 years, but for all that time she carried the hair brush with her. Both of her parents had been sexually abused as children, and she suspected her brother had been abused by his friend's sister. Her experience was not disability-related since it occurred before her back injury and onset of epilepsy. The strong language of abuse she used to describe the experience and her efforts to deal with it later in life indicate a severe impact.

#11: Lin, a 43-year-old, divorced Asian woman with two children, has had rheumatoid arthritis since age 28, She reported being sexually abused by a relative beginning at age 8 when she entered puberty. The abuse stopped only when he moved away. She said that she was caught between Eastern and Western cultures, that the Eastern way teaches children to do everything an adult says, that any adult in the house is the parent. For most of her life she wouldn't let male friends touch her. She didn't remember the abuse experiences until after her divorce. The researchers interpreted this to be non-disability-related since it occurred before the onset of her disability. Her detailed discussion of this experience and her analysis of it in relation to culture, using strong language with words of frustration, indicate that it had a severe impact.

Discussion

The experiences reported by these 11 women with disabilities verify many of the observations stated in the literature. The fact that more than one third of the women interviewed in this study had experienced sexual abuse of one form or another points to a problem of significant proportions. Examining these experiences according to Trickett and Putnam's[39] parameters of type of abuse, age at onset, frequency, closeness of the relationship to the abuser, and presence of physical violence, pain, and threats, gives greater insight into the nature of the abuse.

Among the 15 experiences reported, there was considerable variety in the type of sexual abuse, including fondling (3), coerced sexual activity (3), forced oral sex (1), sexual assault (5), and rape (3). Six of these experiences occurred in childhood, six in teen years, and three in adulthood. The large majority were single incidents. Of the four experiences that extended over months or years, three involved abuse by a relative and one was sexual harassment in the workplace. Perpetrators were predominantly dates (7), followed by relatives (4), with single reports of abuse in a hospital, in a work place, by a stranger, and by a physician. Two experiences reported by the same individual involved alcohol and drug abuse. Twelve experiences involved violence, pain, or threats. The three that did not appeared to have a very low impact, with two occurring in a dating situation and one in a medical setting that the researchers interpreted as ordinary but the participant interpreted as frightening.

The question of disability-relatedness was clear-cut in only three experiences, where the abuse occurred before the onset of disability. In six other experiences, the researchers interpreted the situation as one common to women in general. It is important to note, however, that in the situation of Ginny (#4), the effect of disability seemed to be far outweighed by the pervasive psychological violence in her family in creating her vulnerability to the two sexual abuse experiences she reported. Six experiences were interpreted by the research team as disability-related. Important factors in these reports were the inability to escape a situation due to architectural inaccessibility (Geraldine, #8, being carried up to a second-floor apartment) and a lack of adaptive equipment (Emily, #1, being in a manual wheelchair she could not propel). Emily's experience also shows the effect of social stereotypes on creating vulnerable situations. Her date was attracted to her specifically because she had polio. Josephine's (#6) experience illustrates the increased risk for sexual abuse in disability-related institutional settings. Geraldine's (#8) experiences were difficult to interpret because, although some may claim that high risk-taking behaviors may characterize women without disabilities, her particular behaviors may reflect impaired judgment that sometimes accompanies brain injury.

Based on the participants' own words, the researchers interpreted seven of the experiences to have had a low impact, three moderate, and five severe. All but two of the severe-impact experiences involved sexual assault or rape and tended to extend over time. The manifestation of the impact was in feelings of worthlessness, dirtiness, and hopelessness regarding prospects of having future satisfying relationships.

Some interesting findings on the role of culture emerged from this study. Two of the participants specifically mention cultural factors in recounting their experience. Elena (#2) indicated that in her social class and culture (Hispanic), the man's behavior toward her was quite different from behavior she observed toward her sisters and peers. Lin (#11) stated that in Asian cultures, children are taught to obey every adult very strictly, thus creating a vulnerable situation for her when she was repeatedly confronted by a mal-intended adult relative.

Many of the observations made by Womendez and Schneiderman[41] about the lack of opportunity for women with disabilities to understand their sexuality and have opportunities to develop social interaction skills and a positive self-concept have been illustrated in these case examples. Several of the participants expressed feelings of helplessness to prevent the abuse and had an attitude of submission to the experience. This reflects perceptions of disempowerment, not only in situations where a power differential is evident, as in a hospital or adult authority situation, but also in dating relationships.

In the process of interviewing the 31 women participating in this study, many experiences emerged that had all the hallmarks of abuse but could not technically be labeled abuse. A majority of the participants had experienced very frightening, frustrating, and psychologically damaging interactions with medical professionals. They reported repeated episodes of painful, insensitive handling and failure of physicians to address their questions and concerns. In addition to recounting the direct interaction as a negative event, they expressed intense feelings of abandonment and hopelessness; they were unable to perceive control of their health status and care. Technically, however, this cannot be considered abuse according to Finkelhor and Korbin's[15] requirement that the action be proscribed. In a medical context, any action by a professional is deemed by society to be well-intended. If actions by a professional have a negative impact, they could be considered malpractice but not abuse. There is a need for further discussion of this ethical dilemma. The severe, long-term, negative effect of inappropriate treatment in a medical context by women with physical disabilities deserves attention as an abuse issue and should not be devalued to the status of malpractice.

Previous work by the research team examined the findings of this qualitative study from the perspective of wellness.[30] Concepts of resilience and lines of resistance and defense found in the wellness models of Cowen[11] and Neuman,[29] respectively, are particularly relevant to the investigation of abuse among women with physical disabilities. For this population, the numerous environmental and attitudinal barriers and various abuses they regularly face can be viewed as stressors, forces that can hone resilience or cause defeat. Constant exposure to negative feedback (women with disabilities are ugly, worthless, a burden to society, and unable to ever fulfill their proper role as women); the absence and, in some cases, withholding of information about one's body; and environmental barriers compounded by a lack of appropriate assistive technology are not factors most people have to deal with in their daily lives. Personal elements, such as strong feelings of competence and high self-esteem, and sociocultural elements, such as encouraging, supportive family and friends, have an inestimable value in counteracting these negative forces.

The setting of boundaries, or in Neuman's terms, lines of resistance and defense, emerged as an important part of the resilience displayed by some of the participants in this study. Their boundaries were constantly threatened by insensitive behaviors of medical professionals and overwhelming overprotectiveness by family. The abuse they experienced caused a hardening of defense mechanisms. Because the cause of the abuse or barriers cannot be removed, in some cases the issue becomes one of management and minimizing the negative impact as much as possible.

The women interviewed who experienced abuse but were able to develop a positive sense of sexual self tended to be able to recognize their experiences as abusive and took action to reduce or eliminate them or to neutralize their impact. Some of the women interviewed had been so poorly informed about sexuality and life in general that they did not recognize the abuse until much later. The women who took action to end the abuse did so through divorce, counseling, avoidance, and escape. It is a major life challenge for women who have had these experiences to come to terms with them and develop positive sexuality in spite of them. For those with very limited life options, denial becomes the least damaging means of coping available to them.

Women in this study who exhibited characteristics of wellness had learned to reduce their vulnerability. They recognized what type of situation to avoid, be it with a date or a relative, in order to protect their emotional and physical health. Some of the participants who experienced long-term childhood abuse reported learning survival skills, such as talking their way out of it, seeking emotional support outside the family, and learning how to have backup support available if a situation ever became life-threatening.

Discussions about strategies for preventing sexual abuse of women with physical disbilities have just begun. Researchers, clinicians, and consumers all decry the lack of attention paid to this need in families, school systems, and social service systems. The following is a list of suggestions, drawn primarily from the work of Sandra Cole,[10] describes actions that could be taken by social service workers and clinicians to prevent sexual abuse.

1. Learn to recognize the signs of abuse.
   a. Certain types of injuries (reported or observed)
   b. Behavioral extremes, hyperactivity, mood swings
   c. Sleep disturbances, nightmares
   d. Eating disturbances, loss of weight
   e. Somatic disorders
   f. Fear of intervention
2. Listen to, believe, and act on accounts of abuse.
3. Do everything within your power to prevent institutionalization.
4. Do everything within your power to create opportunities
   for quality personal assistance.
5. Acknowledge the sexuality of women with disabilities.
6. Acknowledge the basic human rights of women with disbilities.
7. Teach a healthy questioning of authority figures.
8. Teach independent behaviors.
9. Teach healthy sexuality.
10. Reinforce a positive sense of self.

CONCLUSION

There is an asexual, dependent, passive stereotype of women with physical disabilities that, in many ways, may lie more at the root of the vulnerability to sexual abuse faced by these women than the disability itself. There is ample evidence in the literature, as confirmed by this qualitative study, that these vulnerabilities do exist. What is seriousiy lacking, however, are data on the incidence and prevalence of sexual abuse in women with physical disabilities. Research that analyzes the experience of abuse according to recommended definitions and parameters, in correlation with other personal, social, cultural, and environmental variables, will make a major contribution to understanding the many risk factors that disability imposes on women's lives.

ACKNOWLEDGMENT

The author would like to acknowledge the contribution of the research team at the Baylor College of Medicine's Center for Research on Women with Disabilities in the preparation of this report. Members of the team included Diana H. Rintala, PhD; Mary Ellen Young, PhD; Carol Howland, BA; Jama L. Bennett, MEd; and C. Don Rossi, MS. This research was conducted under funding from the National Institutes of Health (grant 1 R01 HD30166-01).

REFERENCES

1. Aiello D, Capkin L, Catania H: Strategies and techniques for serving the disabled assault victim: A pilot training program for providers and consumers. Sex Disabil 6:135–144, 1983.
2. American Medical Association: Diagnostic and treatment guidelines on domestic violence. Chicago, AMA, 1992.
3. Ammerman RT, Cassisi JE, Hersen M, Van Hasselt VB: Consequences of physical abuse and neglect in children. Clin Psychol Rev 6(4):291–310, 1986.
4. Beckmann CR, Gittler M, Barzansky BM, Beckmann CA: Gynecologic health care of women with disabilities. Obstet Gynecol 74:75–79, 1989.
5. Belsky J: Child maltreatment: An ecological integration. Am Psychol 35:320–335, 1980.
6. Benedict MI, White RB, Wulff LM, Hall BJ: Reported maltreatment in children with multiple disabilities. Child Abuse Neglect 14:207–217, 1990.
7. Benedict MI, Wulff LM, White RB: Current parental stress in maltreating and nonmaltreating families of children with multiple disabilities. Child Abuse Neglect 16:155–163, 1992.

8. Bristol MM, Schloper E: A developmental perspective on stress and coping in families of autistic children. In Blacker J (ed): Severely Handicapped Young Children and Their Families. Orlando, Academic Press, 1984, pp 91–142.
9. Camblin LD Jr: A survey of state efforts in gathering information on child abuse and neglect in handicapped populations. Child Abuse Neglect 6:465–472, 1982.
10. Cole SS: Facing the challenges of sexual abuse in persons with disabilities. Sex Disabil 7:71–88, 1986.
11. Cowen EL: In pursuit of wellness. Am Psychol 46:404–408, 1991.
12. Crossmaker M: Behind locked doors: Institutional sexual abuse. Sex Disabil 9:201–220, 1991.
12a. Disabled children are abused most [National Center on Child Abuse and Neglect survey]. The Washington Post, October 7, 1993, A16.
12b. Disabled women more likely to be battered [Ontario Ministry of Community and Social Services survey]. The Toronto Star, April 1, 1987, F9.
13. Doucette J: Violent Acts Against Disabled Women. Toronto, DisAbled Women's Network, 1986.
14. Finkelhor D: Sexually victimized children. New York, Free Press, 1979.
15. Finkelhor D, Korbin J: Child abuse as an international issue. Child Abust Neglect 12:3–23. 1988.
16. Gagnon J, Simon W: Sexual encounters between adults and children. New York, Sex Information and Education Council of the U.S., 1970.
17. Garbarino J: The abuse and neglect of special children: An introduction to the issues. In Garbarino J, Brookhouser PE, Authier KJ (eds): Special Children—Special Risks. The Maltreatment of Children with Disabilities. New York, Aldine 1987, pp 3–14.
18. Glaser BG, Strauss AL: Discovery of grounded theory: Strategies for qualitative research. New York, Aldine Publishing, 1967.
19. Glaser D, Bentovim A: Abuse and risk to handicapped and chronically ill children. Child Abuse Neglect 3:565–575, 1979.
20. Kreigsman KH, Bregman S: Women with disabilities at midlife. Rehabil Counsel Bull 29:112–122, 1985.
21. Laws A: Does a history of sexual abuse in childhood play a role in women's medical problems?: A review. J Women's Health 2:165–172, 1993.
22. Light J, Collier B, Parnes P: Communicative interaction between young nonspeaking physically disabled children and their primary caregivers. Augmentative Alternative Communication 1:74 83, 1985.
23. McFarlane J, Christoffel K, Bateman L, et al: Assessing for abuse: Self-report versus nurse interview. Public Health Nurs 8:245–250, 1991.
24. McFarlane J, Parker B, Soeken K, Bullock L: Assessing for abuse during pregnancy: Severity and frequency of injuries and associated entry into prenatal care. JAMA 267:3176–3178, 1992.
25. Muccigrosso L: Sexual abuse prevention strategies and programs for persons with developmental disabilities. Sex Disabil 9:261–272, 1991.
26. Mullan PB, Cole SS: Health care providers' perceptions of the vulnerability of persons with disabilities: Sociological frameworks and empirical analyses. Sex Disabil 9:221–242, 1991.
27. Mullins JB: The relationship between child abuse and handicapping conditions. J School Health 56:134–136, 1986.
28. [Reference deleted].
29. Neuman B. The Neuman systems model: Application to nursing education and practice. Norwalk, CT, Appleton-Century-Crofts, 1982.
30. Nosek MA, Howland CA, Young ME, et al: Wellness models and sexuality among women with physical disabilities. J Appl Rehabil Counsel 25:50 58, 1994.
31. [Reference deleted].
32. Paddison PL, Gise LH, Lebovits A, et al: Sexual abuse and premenstrual syndrome: Comparison between a lower and higher socioeconomic group. Psychosomatics 31:265–272, 1990.
33. Patton MQ: Qualitative Evaluation and Research Methods. 2nd ed. Newbury Park, CA, Sage, 1990.
34. Ridington J: Beating the "odds": Violence and women with disabilities (Position Paper 2). Vancouver, Canada, DisAbled Women's Network, 1989.
35. Schwartzbeck C: Abuse makes kids aggressive. The Houston Chronicle. May 22, 1993.
36. Sobsey D, Doe T: Patterns of sexual abuse and assault. Sex Disabil 9:243–260, 1991.
37. Sobsey D, Varnhagen C: Sexual abuse and exploitation of people with disabilities: Toward prevention and treatment. In Csapo M, Gougen L (eds): Special Education across Canada: Challenges for the '90s. Vancouver, Canada, Center for Human Development and Research, 1989.
38. Starr R, Dietrich KN, Fischhoff J, et al: The contribution of handicapping conditions to child abuse. Topics in Early Childhood Special Education 4:55–69, 1984.

39. Trickett PK, Putnam FW. Impact of child sexual abuse on females: Toward a developmental psychobiological integration. Psychol Sci 4:81–87, 1993.

40. White MJ, Rintala DH, Hart KA, Fuhrer MJ: Sexual activities, concerns, and interests of women with spinal cord injury living in the community. Am J Phys Med Rehabil 72:372–378, 1993.

41. Womendez C, Schneiderman K: Escaping from abuse: Unique issues for women with disabilities. Sex Disabil 9:273–280, 1991.

42. Yoshino S, Uchida S: Sexual problems of women with rheumatoid arthritis. Arch Phys Med Rehabil 62:122–123, 1981.

43. Zirpoli TJ, Snell ME, Loyd BH: Characteristics of persons with mental retardation who have been abused by caregivers. J Spec Educ 21(2):31–41, 1987.

44. Zwerner J: A study of issues in sexuality counseling for women with spinal cord injuries. Women Ther 1:91–100, 1982.

MANJU MONGA, MD

FERTILITY AND PREGNANCY IN DISABLED WOMEN

From the Division of Maternal
  Fetal Medicine
Department of Obstetrics,
  Gynecology and Reproductive
  Sciences
University of Texas Medical School
  at Houston
Houston, Texas

Reprint requests to:
Manju Monga, MD
Division of Maternal Fetal
  Medicine
Department of Obstetrics,
  Gynecology and Reproductive
  Sciences
University of Texas Medical School
  at Houston
6431 Fannin Street
Suite 3204
Houston, TX 77030

This work was supported in part by
the Burroughs Wellcome Fellowship of the American Association
of Gynecologists and Obstetricians
Foundation.

It has often been erroneously assumed that physically disabled individuals are not interested in pursuing sexually fulfilling relationships or are incapable of achieving pregnancy and effectively caring for newborn infants. This attitude is commonly held by health care professionals who care for women with disabilities, and it may be due, in part, to the paucity of available information concerning gynecologic and obstetric care of these women, which prevents health care providers from feeling competent in discussing these issues. This situation has led to a reluctance on the part of health care professionals to elicit questions or concerns from their patients regarding sexual activity and reproduction. A survey of 55 women with physical disabilities revealed that fewer than 20% were offered counseling or information about gynecologic issues following the onset of their disability.[7] Furthermore, none of the women with paralysis or obvious physical deformity received such information. If all aspects of health are to be addressed in the rehabilitative care of disabled women, extensive education of health care professionals is required.

Pregnancy is associated with rapid physical, hormonal, and emotional changes that may affect a woman's independence, body image and self-esteem. In a woman with disabilities, these effects may be more profound, resulting in "a double dose of disequilibrium."[16] In addition, some disabilities may adversely affect the pregnancy or may worsen during the course of pregnancy. Ideally, counseling should occur preconceptionally and should include discussion on the effect of the disability on pregnancy, labor, delivery, and the puerperium; the effect of current or anticipated medications on embryogenesis; and the antepartum, perinatal and long-term effects of pregnancy on the disability.[65] The health care team should also be familiar with medical interventions or lifestyle modifications that may optimize pregnancy outcome.

Similarly, gynecologic care of disabled women should be preceded by an assessment of the effects of the disability and current medications on the hormonal control of the menstrual cycle. Certain physical disabilities may limit the woman's ability to maintain menstrual or genital hygiene or to effectively use specific methods of contraception.[41] All of these issues need to be addressed in an open, nonjudgmental manner.

This chapter will discuss several aspects of reproduction in women with spinal cord injury, multiple sclerosis, rheumatoid arthritis, cancer, and diabetes mellitus.

SPINAL CORD INJURY

According to data collected in the National Spinal Cord Injury data base between 1973 and 1985, the annual incidence of spinal cord injuries is about 32 per million.[110] Spinal cord injury (SCI) occurs most commonly during the peak reproductive years: the mean age at the time of injury is 29 years; the median age is 25 years, and the mode is 19 years.[110] About 15–20% of SCI occurs in females.[122] Advances in rehabilitative care have allowed an increasing number of women with SCI to lead independent and normal lives, including sexual activity and pregnancy, however, little has been written about the effect of SCI on female reproduction. The literature is limited to several retrospective case series,[41,94,95,117–119,122] and reviews.[22,48,62,78,79,107]

Pregnancy in Women with Spinal Cord Injury

Fertility and spontaneous abortion rates are unaffected by spinal cord injury,[78] as is the incidence of congenital anomalies and stillbirth.[5] A team approach to the management of pregnant spinal cord patients had been recommended.[48] The team should include a primary care physician, obstetrician, urologist, neurologist, anesthesiologist, and rehabilitation personnel. It is important to recognize and prevent various complications of spinal cord injury that may negatively affect pregnancy (Table 1).

URINARY TRACT INFECTION

Most authors cite recurrent urinary tract infection as the most common complication of pregnancy in women with SCI, with a reported incidence of 35–94%.[5,22,41,54,119,122] Indwelling catheters and incomplete bladder emptying with urinary stasis predispose these women to developing urinary tract infections during pregnancy. Most of these infections are asymptomatic, but some patients will develop pyelonephritis, renal insufficiency, and calculi as sequelae. Pregnant patients with pyelonephritis are particularly susceptible to develop sepsis and adult respiratory distress syndrome.[40] In addition, pyelonephritis may be associated

TABLE 1. Complications of Pregnancy in Women with Spinal Cord Injury

Urinary tract infection	Anemia	Autonomic dysreflexia
Decubitus ulcers	Hypotension	Unattended birth
Thromboembolic phenomenon	Pulmonary compromise	Hyperkalemia

with premature uterine contractions.[47] Prevention and prompt treatment of even asymptomatic urinary tract infections is therefore of paramount importance, and urinary stasis should be avoided. Urinary cultures should be performed frequently, preferably at every antenatal visit. The value of prophylactic antibiotic coverage in these patients has been debated. Patients who have been treated for a documented urinary tract infection during pregnancy, or who are otherwise at increased risk for recurrent infections due to an indwelling catheter or a history of frequent urinary tract infections, should receive prophylactic antibiotics such as nitrofurantoin, cephalexin or ampicillin.[114]

Decubitus Ulcers

Decubitus ulcers are a frequent complication of SCI that may be exacerbated by pregnancy due to increased maternal weight and difficulty in executing transfers.[5,22,78,122] Meticulous skin care should be administered to sites at high risk for skin breakdown, such as the heels, sacrum, and ischium.[78] During labor and delivery, special care should be taken to position the patient with suitable padding and protection at pressure points. Decubiti may result in sepsis and increased catabolism, resulting in a nutritionally depleted state.[5]

Thromboembolic Disease

Pregnancy predisposes women to thromboembolic disease due to increased levels of vitamin K-dependent clotting factors, venous stasis resulting from increased venous distensibility and mechanical obstruction by the gravid uterus, and vessel wall injury in the case of operative delivery.[60] Pregnant women with SCI are theoretically at even greater risk for thromboembolic disease due to prolonged periods of immobilization. Since this has only rarely been reported,[54,81] clinical vigilance is indicated but prophylactic anticoagulation is not recommended.

Anemia

Early studies reported anemia as a major problem in women with SCI.[95] Anemia is exacerbated during pregnancy due to the physiologic increase in plasma volume, which is greater than the physiologic increase in red blood cell mass.[73] More recently, significant anemia has not been reported as a common complication of pregnancy in women with SCI.[5,122] Because iron supplementation may further compromise bowel function, concomitant administration of stool softeners has been recommended.[123]

Hypotension

In normal pregnancy, arterial blood pressure decreases due to a fall in systemic vascular resistance, beginning at 7 weeks of gestation, with a nadir at 24–32 weeks of gestation.[73] Further, cardiac output decreases by as much as 25% when turning from the left lateral to the supine position due to compression of the inferior vena cava by the gravid uterus and decreased venous return.[73] Pregnancy may thus exacerbate hypotension associated with the loss of autoregulatory vasoconstriction in women with SCI above the level of the splanchnic outflow tracts (T5).[22,78,122] Similarly, autonomic vasoconstriction to conserve heat and vasodilation to lower body temperature are absent: the patient is poikilothermic below the level of the lesion (unable to shiver or sweat) and should be appropriately protected if the ambient temperature is extreme.[22,78]

PULMONARY COMPROMISE

Pregnancy causes physiologic adaptations in respiratory and pulmonary function including an increase in oxygen consumption, an increase in minute ventilation due to an increase in tidal volume, a decrease in expiratory reserve volume, and a decrease in residual volume due to a 4-cm rise of the diaphragm.[28] Pregnancy does not affect vital capacity. SCI, especially at high levels, decreases vital capacity and respiratory reserve and is associated with a less forceful cough due to impaired intercostal and abdominal muscle function.[22] Therefore, women with SCI are at increased risk for respiratory compromise during pregnancy, including atelectasis and pneumonia. In patients at risk for these complications, early antenatal pulmonary function studies, arterial blood gas determination, respirology consultation, and intrapartum pulse oximetry should be considered.[22]

AUTONOMIC HYPERREFLEXIA

The most serious and potentially life-threatening complication that may affect pregnant women with SCI is autonomic hyperreflexia (also known as autonomic dysreflexia, autonomic stress syndrome, or the mass reflex). During pregnancy, this syndrome occurs in 60–85% of women with lesions above T7.[5,54,122] It is much less common in women with lesions below T7 but may occur if the lesion is incomplete with destruction of descending pathways and preservation of ascending ones.[22] Episodes of autonomic hyperreflexia are precipitated by noxious sensory stimuli such as contraction, distension, or manipulation of the cervix, uterus, bladder, and rectum.[78] Therefore, vaginal examination, bladder catheterization, disimpaction, and perineal distension may incite autonomic hyperreflexia. These noxious stimuli are transmitted via afferent, somatosensory, and viscerosensory pathways into the dorsal horns of the spinal cord. From there, the stimuli ascend in the spinothalamic tracts and posterior columns and initiate reflex sympathetic arcs that are not inhibited by higher, supraspinal centers.[22,78,119] This massive sympathetic hyperactivity, uninhibited by central nuclei below the level of the cord lesion, results in vasoconstriction, particularly of the splanchnic vascular bed, and severe systemic hypertension.[119] The aortic and carotid body baroreceptors respond to this intense hypertension by vagal stimulation, bradycardia, and arteriovenous (AV) conduction abnormalities, including first- and second-degree heart block and sinus arrest.[22] While marked hypertension, headache, and bradycardia are the hallmarks of autonomic hyperreflexia, centrally mediated vasodilatation occurs above the level of the cord lesion. This results in profuse sweating, blotching of the skin, piloerection, and increased cutaneous temperature above the level of the lesion.[22,54]

The morbidity and mortality associated with autonomic hyperreflexic episodes during pregnancy appear to be related to the severe systemic hypertension that can result in uteroplacental vasoconstriction with fetal distress,[1] or in maternal intracranial hemorrhage, coma, and death[66] (Table 2). The first steps for effective prevention and treatment of this disorder are a clear understanding of the precipitating causes (Table 3) and prompt recognition of presenting symptoms and

TABLE 2. Complications of Autonomic Dysreflexia

Uteroplacental vasoconstriction	Intracranial hemorrhage
Fetal distress	Coma
Asystole	Death

TABLE 3. Stimuli that May Precipitate Autonomic Dysreflexia

Manipulation of indwelling catheter	Uterine contraction
Vaginal speculum examination	Visceral distension (bladder, uterus, rectum)
Cervical examination	Perineal distension

TABLE 4. Symptoms and Signs of Autonomic Dysreflexia

Severe systemic hypertension	First-degree heart block
Headache	Second-degree heart block
Blurring of vision	Sweating
Nasal congestion	Piloerection
Bradycardia	Flushing

signs (Table 4). Bladder distension should be avoided by effective bladder drainage during the antepartum and intrapartum periods. Any manipulation of the cervix, vagina, bladder, or rectum (such as cervical examination, speculum examination, foley catheterization, or manual disimpaction of the rectum) should be preceded by the application of topical anesthetic jelly to reduce noxious stimulation.[78] Antenatal consultation with an obstetric anesthesiologist may be of benefit because blockade of the afferent impulses by early placement of an epidural catheter with infusion of epidural meperidine, bupivicaine, or a combination of fentanyl-bupivicaine has been shown to be effective prophylaxis for autonomic hyperreflexia.[22,92] The level of the epidural block may be difficult to determine due to lack of sensation below the level of the cord lesion, and it may be titrated to just above the perceived sensory level, recognizing that the patient may require ventilatory support if a high block is achieved.[62] Treatment of autonomic hyperreflexia involves removal of the noxious stimulus; epidural, spinal, or general anesthesia; and short-acting antihypertensive agents such as sodium nitroprusside, nitroglycerin, calcium channel blockers, or labetolol.[1] Distension of the perineum during the second stage of labor may precipitate autonomic hyperreflexia in a woman who was previously asymptomatic, and vigilance is especially important during this time. Forceps or vacuum assisted delivery may be used to shorten the second stage of labor if autonomic hyperreflexia occurs.[78] Cesarean section may be necessary in the case of recalcitrant autonomic hyperreflexia that is unresponsive to other measures and is usually followed by prompt resolution of symptoms.[78]

LABOR AND DELIVERY

While earlier reports suggested an increased incidence of preterm labor and a shorter duration of labor in SCI patients,[95,97,113] more recent data do not support this.[5,122] The pain of uterine contractions during the first stage of labor is transmitted through T11–L2.[24] Therefore, women with complete spinal cord lesions above the level of T10 will experience painless labor. However, they may be aware of contractions due to an increase in spasticity, flexor spasms, or clonus.[22] Otherwise, the onset of labor may be heralded only by symptoms of autonomic hyperreflexia or membrane rupture, and the possibility of undetected labor with unattended birth exists.[94] It has therefore been suggested that digital cervical examinations be performed at each antenatal visit after 26 weeks, with hospitalization if dilatation or effacement is found. Alternatively, uterine contractions can be monitored using home tocodynamometry.[1] Some clinicians advocate routine hospitalization at term to prevent unattended deliveries; however, this can be quite disruptive to the patient and her family.

Pain control can be achieved using intravenous analgesia or epidural anesthesia. In patients with high lesions and no perception of pain, early epidural placement is recommended to prevent autonomic hyperreflexia, as discussed above. If regional anesthesia has not been used, perineal infiltration with local anesthetic agents is recommended since perineal distension and episiotomy can stimulate a hyperreflexic episode.[22,92] The use of succinylcholine during endotracheal intubation in women with recent spinal cord injuries (within 1 year) has been associated with profound hyperkalemia due to the release of potassium from denervated muscle. Potassium levels should be monitored if general anesthesia is required.[92]

Operative delivery should be reserved for obstetric indications. Several reports indicate an increased incidence of forceps-assisted deliveries and cesarean sections for reduced pelvic diameter, uncontrollable hyperreflexia, and inability to bear down during the second stage.[41,54,94,118,119,122] Cesarean section can generally be performed using a transverse incision in the lower uterine segment unless a suprapubic cystotomy is present, necessitating a classical cesarean section.[3]

The use of nonabsorbable suture or delayed absorbable sutures to repair episiotomy sites was recommended in earlier studies due to an increased incidence of wound disruption and infection;[81,95,116] however, more recent reports have not supported this.[5,122]

There is no contraindication to breast feeding in women with SCI, although one report cited a decrease in milk production in women with lesions above T6.[21] Women with high lesions may experience some difficulty in comfortably positioning the infant.[21,107]

Gynecologic Issues in Women with Spinal Cord Injury

There are several reports about the effect of spinal cord injury on menstruation.[17,19,38] All report temporary amenorrhea in at least half of patients, which usually resolves to the preinjury menstrual pattern within several months. The cause of this transient amenorrhea is unknown, but it is believed to be stress, which alters hypothalamic stimulation of pituitary gonadotropins and results in anovulation.[64,78] The development of amenorrhea does not appear to be related to the level or completeness of the lesion. Neither is the level of the injury correlated with cycle length, duration of menses, or serum concentration of ovarian hormones.[86] Failure to resume the preinjury pattern of menstruation within several months of the injury should lead to an investigation of other possible causes. A survey performed by McCluer of 108 paraplegic women showed that 85% managed the hygienic aspects of menstruation independently as compared to 38% of 52 quadriplegic women.[64] She stated that "rehabilitation personnel should pay more attention to the hygienic aspects of menstruation as part of self-care training for disabled women."

Virtually no information exists on effective contraceptive methods that are easily used and well tolerated by women with SCI.[64,107] The oral contraceptive pill, while highly effective, is associated with an increased risk of deep vein thrombosis and may therefore be unsafe in these women. This has not been well studied. Barrier methods such as the diaphragm may be difficult to insert, and basal body temperature records are ineffective in predicting ovulation.[86] Condoms appear to be safe and effective. If the woman desires long-term contraception, she may choose injectable progesterone compounds such as medroxyprogesterone acetate, which provides contraception for 3 months but has been associated with complete disruption of the menstrual cycle and menstrual irregularity and may be difficult to manage.[71] Subdermal implants containing levonorgesterel (Norplant) are effective for up to 5 years unless removed earlier. Norplant is also associated with irregular menstrual periods.[71] Neither depomedroxyprogesterone acetate nor Norplant have been associated with a significantly increased risk of thromboembolic disease.

Conclusion

With improved rehabilitation and familial and societal support, it is likely that more women with SCI will elect to have children. The medical team caring for such women need to be aware of the potentially serious complications that may occur during pregnancy, labor and delivery. Prospective studies in this area are lacking. Finally, in order to better manage all aspects of health care in women with SCI, there is a need for prospective studies on the effect of SCI on gynecologic function, and on the most appropriate means of contraception in these women.

MULTIPLE SCLEROSIS

Multiple sclerosis (MS) is one of the most common chronic debilitating neurologic diseases that affects young people. The disease is more prevalent in women, with a peak incidence at age 20–40.[2] Therefore, reproductive-age women with MS often raise important questions about the effect of MS on pregnancy and the potential impact of pregnancy on the course of the disease.

Effect of Pregnancy on Multiple Sclerosis

Prior to 1950, pregnancy was reported to have a detrimental effect on MS. However, one prospective study[9] and several retrospective studies[8,42,85] since then have shown an improvement in MS during the antepartum period with some worsening during the postpartum months. Early retrospective studies compared the incidence of relapse in pregnant patients to a group of nonpregnant women who acted as controls.[85] They found that 11% of women experienced a relapse during pregnancy as compared to a baseline relapse rate of 28% in the nonpregnant controls. Thirty-two percent of the pregnant patients experienced a relapse during the first 6 months following delivery. Two retrospective cohort studies since 1988 have confirmed these findings[8,42] by describing the effect of pregnancy on multiple sclerosis as "relapse rate" (number of relapses per person per year). In each report, 52 women recalled the relapse rate prior to, during, and after each pregnancy. In Frith's study, the antepartum relapse rate was 0.30; the nonpregnant relapse rate was 0.53; and the postpartum relapse rate was 0.49.[42] Bernardi reported an antepartum relapse rate of 0.10 versus nonpregnant relapse rate of 0.65 and a postpartum relapse rate of 0.79.[8] The only prospective study to date followed eight women with MS and found that only one experienced a relapse during pregnancy (annualized relapse rate of 0.17).[9] During the immediate 6-month postpartum observation period, six of the eight women experienced relapses (annualized relapse rate of 1.74). Two population-based retrospective studies examined the effect of pregnancy on long-term disability in women with MS.[115,121] They found no association between the total number of pregnancies and the severity of disability.

The observed short-term beneficial effect of pregnancy on multiple sclerosis is not easily explained. The cause of MS is unknown but is postulated to involve an aberrant autoimmune response to some environmental stimulus (possibly a virus) in genetically predisposed individuals.[3] This results in T-lymphocyte-mediated destruction of myelin basic protein; demyelination in the periventricular white matter, spinal cord, brain stem, and cerebellum; and multiple neurologic deficits that cannot be explained by a single neuroanatomic lesion.[3] Some studies have shown an increase in the T helper-to-suppressor cell ratio in patients with MS.[3,90] It had been postulated that pregnancy lowered the T helper-to-suppressor cell ratio, thus decreasing the aberrant autoimmune response.[10] More recent data suggest that the total number of T cells and T cell subpopulations are unchanged during pregnancy and that the relative immunosuppression of pregnancy (which allows fetal tolerance) is due to the production of poorly defined immunosuppressor substances from the decidua and the trophoblast.[13] The observed decrease in relapse rate may be due to the immunosuppressive effects of alpha fetoprotein, pregnancy-associated plasma protein, alpha-2-pregnancy-associated glycoprotein, progesterone, and 1,25-dihydroxyvitamin D_3, which increase during pregnancy.[43]

A postpartum increase in relapse rate may be due to the sudden disappearance of these immunosuppressive substances following delivery. The exacerbation appears to be unaffected by breast feeding.[75] The postpartum period is often complicated by anemia, increased stress, and decreased sleep, all of which may be associated with MS relapse unrelated to pregnancy status.

There are no prospective data to support termination of pregnancy as a means of controlling MS or preventing relapse. In fact, most investigators agree that pregnancy does not alter the ultimate course of the disease.[10,115,121]

Effect of Multiple Sclerosis on Pregnancy

Fertility and rates of spontaneous abortions, stillbirth, and malformations are unaffected by MS.[9,25] There is an increased risk of MS in children of a person with MS, estimated at 3%.[100]

Urinary tract infections are common during pregnancy and occur more often in women with MS due to dysfunctional micturition. Cystitis, even if asymptomatic, should be treated promptly in pregnant women because pyelonephritis is a common sequela due to the physiologic changes of the urinary tract during pregnancy.[73] In patients with MS, prompt treatment is especially important because infection may exacerbate neurologic symptoms.[10] Women with recurrent urinary tract infections or those who require catheterization should be placed on suppressive antibiotic therapy.[114] Routine management of labor and delivery is indicated, with cesarean section reserved for the usual obstetric indications.[10,25] There is no contraindication to the use of magnesium sulphate for preeclampsia or betasympathomimetic agents for preterm labor. There is no contraindication to epidural or spinal analgesia during labor or to general anesthesia, if necessary.[92]

If a patient with MS has been treated with prednisone during the preceding year, she should receive 100 mg of hydrocortisone every 8 hours during labor or perioperatively if surgery is necessary. Prednisone and hydrocortisone are quickly metabolized by the placenta (unlike dexamethasone or betamethasone), and the theoretical risk of congenital malformations or adverse perinatal outcome is low. These steroids are classified as category B drugs by the FDA. Other immunosuppressive agents sometimes used to treat MS have not been studied as well.

Azathioprine, although associated with maternal liver toxicity, has been used without neonatal complications in pregnant women with renal transplants.[26] Azathioprine has been associated with transient neonatal chromosome breaks.[29] There are only limited case reports about the use of cyclosporin in pregnancy.

Gynecologic Issues in Women with Multiple Sclerosis

Contraceptive counseling in women with MS should consider that manual dexterity is required for correct placement of a diaphragm and that the risk of pelvic infection is increased in women using an intrauterine device.[71] There is no contraindication to the use of oral contraceptive pills. In fact, in a prospective study of the effect of oral contraceptives on experimental demyelinating disease in guinea pigs, Arnason demonstrated a beneficial effect of estrogen-dominant oral contraceptives.[4] This study has not been reproduced in humans. Women who are on immunosuppressive therapy are at increased risk of cervical and vulvar dysplasia and should have regular gynecologic examinations, including Pap smears.[105]

Conclusion

In summary, pregnancy does not appear to exacerbate MS and, in fact, may have a small beneficial effect on the relapse rate during the antepartum period. This is usually followed by postpartum exacerbation. There is no evidence that MS adversely affects the outcome of pregnancy or that long-term disability status is altered by pregnancy. The decision to carry a pregnancy should be based on the couple's desire for children after appropriate antepartum counseling and assessment of physical impairment and available sources of support.

RHEUMATOID ARTHRITIS

Many aspects of obstetric and gynecologic care in women with multiple sclerosis apply to women with disabling rheumatoid arthritis (RA). Seventy-five percent of women with RA will experience some improvement of the disease during pregnancy, and 95% will experience exacerbation during the postpartum period.[65] The reason for this pattern is unclear, but, as in MS, may be related to the placental and decidual production of immunosuppressive proteins or to modulation of the cellular immune system during pregnancy.

RA has not been shown to decrease the fertility rate. It may be associated with an adverse perinatal outcome in the 5% of women with RA and the serum autoantibodies anti-Ro (SSA) and anti-La (SSB).[63] The presence of maternal anti-Ro autoantibody is associated with the development of complete congenital heart block and the neonatal lupus syndrome. Therefore, pregnant women with RA should be screened for this antibody, and a fetal echocardiogram should be performed if the antibody is found.

One of the biggest concerns in pregnant women with RA is the potential risk posed by medications used to control the disease during pregnancy. Aspirin inhibits platelet cyclooxygenase function and prostaglandin synthesis, and chronic ingestion during pregnancy is associated with prolonged gestation, protracted labor, and increased blood loss.[111] Neonatal hemorrhage may also be increased.[11] Other nonsteroidal antiinflammatory agents, such as indomethacin, also inhibit prostaglandin synthesis and may inhibit the onset of labor. Maternal indomethacin has been linked to premature closure of the fetal ductus arteriosus and fetal pulmonary hypertension.[117a] There are few reports of gold therapy during pregnancy, and its use, therefore, is not recommended. Although there have been occasional reports of fetal retinopathy and congenital deafness following the use of antimalarial agents during pregnancy, the quantitative risk of these drugs is unknown. Two case series describing a total of 56 patients reported only one case of a small congenital ventricular septal defect after use of penicillamine during pregnancy.[25] As mentioned above, the use of prednisone or hydrocortisone has not been associated with fetal congenital anomalies, and other immunosuppressive drugs have been less well studied.

Labor and delivery are usually unaffected by rheumatoid arthritis; however, involvement of the temperomandibular joints or the larynx may impede endotracheal intubation during general anesthesia, and cervical spine disease places the mother at risk for vertebral subluxation.

CANCER

Cancer complicates approximately one in 1,000 pregnancies.[36] The most common malignancies diagnosed in pregnancy include lymphoma, melanoma, and cancers of the cervix, breast,, thyroid, ovary, brain, and colon.[102] The most common cancers that cause maternal deaths are those of the neurologic and hematopoeitic systems.[99] Unfortunately, only sparse data exist on the effect of cancer on the gravida or her fetus, often in the form of case series and retrospective reviews. Although a dissertation on the individual types of cancer and pregnancy is beyond the scope of this chapter, general management principles will be reviewed. Discussion of cancer and pregnancy should include the following: (1) Does pregnancy adversely influence maternal outcome? (2) Does the cancer pose a risk to the fetus? (3) Does the cancer treatment pose a risk to the fetus? (4) What is the effect of cancer treatment on future reproductive function?

The Effect of Pregnancy on Cancer

There is much controversy concerning the possible adverse effect of pregnancy on various forms of cancer, including breast cancer, malignant melanoma, and cervical tumors.[49,77,91,112] The literature suggests that in pregnant patients, the diagnosis of cancer is made when the disease is more advanced, and that stage-for-stage the prognosis is the same as in the nonpregnant state. The presence of a fetus has not been conclusively shown to advance the rate of tumor growth. Therefore, elective termination of pregnancy offers no clear therapeutic advantage to the mother. The challenge to the physician is to make an accurate and timely diagnosis, because a delay in diagnosis places the mother at increased risk for morbidity.

The Risk of Cancer to the Fetus

Patients and physicians often express concern about possible transplacental metastasis of the tumor to the fetus. Only 53 cases of malignancy metastatic to the products of conception were reported between 1866 and 1987.[33] Of these, only 12 actually metastasized to the fetus. The most common maternal tumor that metastasizes to the products of conception is malignant melanoma. Thirty percent of tumors that metastasize to the placenta and more than 50% of those that metastasize to the fetus are malignant melanomas.[33] The overall rate of fetal metastasis is so low as to eliminate this as an indication for elective abortion. The effect of cancer on general maternal condition, including poor nutrition, infection or thromboembolic disease, can adversely affect fetal outcome.[35]

The Effect of Cancer Therapy on the Fetus

SURGERY

Surgical procedures may be required for diagnosis or treatment of cancers in pregnancy. In general, the fetus is exposed to potential risks from the effect of anesthetic agents or from the surgery itself. Although the reasons are unclear, there appears to be an increased incidence of fetal loss after anesthesia in the first trimester of pregnancy.[37] Therefore, it has been recommended that surgery be deferred until the second trimester. However, because delay in surgery may compromise the maternal condition, the decision should be made on a case-by-case basis after consultation with the oncologists, neonatologists, and obstetricians. There is no significant difference in the rate of congenital anomalies between patients having surgery and controls, and no anesthetic drug has been definitively proven to be teratogenic in humans.[37] Extraabdominal procedures and intra-abdominal procedures that do not involve the reproductive tract are generally tolerated well, but uterine manipulation in the third trimester of pregnancy has been associated with preterm labor.[102] Intraoperative complications such as hypoxia, hypotension, and decreased uteroplacental perfusion should be avoided because these can adversely affect fetal outcome. This can often be achieved by lateral displacement of the uterus to avoid inferior vena caval compression.[39,46]

RADIATION THERAPY

The fetus may be exposed to radiation during diagnostic or therapeutic procedures in the management of cancer during pregnancy. The embryo is at risk for radiation injury due to its high rate of mitotic activity and cell differentiation, and exposure to radiation has well-defined effects based on the dose and gestational age.[6,12] Radiation during the preimplantation phase (up to 10 days of pregnancy) produces an all-or-none effect wherein spontaneous abortion is the most likely adverse consequence or the fetus is unaffected.[82] During the period of organogenesis (days 11–56 of pregnancy), the embryo is at increased risk of radiation injury and visceral or somatic damage, including microcephaly, mental retardation, retinal degeneration, cataracts, and genital and skeletal malformations.[27] Embryonic exposure to fewer than 5 rads has rarely been associated with anomalies.[12] In children born to women exposed to the atomic bomb during pregnancy, there was a 2.4% incidence of mental retardation after 10–50 rad exposure.[84] This rate increased to 18% in women exposed to 50–100 rads. The most critical window for exposure was between 8 and 15 weeks of gestation.[102] The effect of fetal exposure to radiation after 20 weeks of gestation is usually limited to low birthweight, anemia, and dermatologic changes, although an increased risk for childhood leukemia has been reported (relative risk 1.5).[12,102] Therapeutic abortion has been suggested if a fetus has been exposed to radiation at a dose of greater than 5–10 rads.[82,102]

CHEMOTHERAPY

Physiologic changes in blood volume, renal blood flow, and gastrointestinal motility may affect the absorption, distribution, and excretion of chemotherapeutic agents during pregnancy.[73] Since antineoplastic agents affect rapidly proliferating cells, they are potentially dangerous to the fetus.[76, 109] Most of the data regarding the teratogenic effect of chemotherapeutic agents are derived from experiments on pregnant laboratory animals, and little information is available in humans. In a 1960 review of 50 pregnant women who received anticancer chemotherapy, there

were eight cases of fetal abnormalities, 16 spontaneous abortions, and seven therapeutic abortions.[109] No anomalies were noted in infants whose mothers received
chemotherapy in the second or third trimesters of pregnancy. Similarly, a later
review reported 15 documented cases of fetal abnormalities in women receiving
chemotherapy in the first trimester of pregnancy as compared to none in 73 women
receiving treatment after the first trimester.[76] More recent reviews place the risk of
teratogenicity after first-trimester chemotherapy at 12.7–17%.[101] The first trimester
administration of folic acid antagonists (methotrexate and aminopterin) is most
commonly associated with spontaneous abortion or congenital abnormalities
(cranial dysostosis, hypertelorism, micrognathia, limb abnormalities, and cerebral
anomalies).[68,76,109,120] Alkylating agents also have been implicated in congenital
malformations after use during the first trimester.[76,103] Less information is
available about other chemotherapeutic agents, but their use should be limited to
life-threatening situations in the first trimester. Second- and third-trimester
chemotherapy is associated with low birthweight and pancytopenia.[76,103] The risk
of neonatal neutropenic sepsis and hemorrhage due to thrombocytopenia warrants
discussion among the neonatologists, obstetricians, and oncologists with regard to
the timing of chemotherapy with respect to anticipated delivery. No long-term
studies address possible delayed effects on the offspring, such as impaired growth,
development, reproductive function, or carcinogenesis. In summary, possible
damage to the fetus should be balanced against possible effects to the mother if
antineoplastic therapy is delayed.

Effect of Cancer on Future Reproductive Function

Data on the effect of chemotherapy on fertility are conflicting. Horning reported that only 55% of women resumed normal menses following chemotherapy
for Hodgkin's lymphoma.[53] Byrne reported no chemotherapy-related decrease in
female fertility with the exception of alkylating agents (especially cyclophosphamide)
which resulted in amenorrhea and ovarian failure after greater than 6 months of
use by women older than 35.[15] Gershenson reviewed outcome in women successfully
treated with antineoplastic agents for germ cell ovarian tumors and reported that
only 68% resumed regular menses.[44] In all reports, the susceptibility of the ovary
to radiation or chemotherapy appears to be related to dose, duration of treatment,
and age of the patient.

There appears to be little risk of fetal malformation in the offspring of women
previously treated with chemotherapy. These data are derived from reports of 596
women treated with methotrexate or actinomycin-D for gestational trophoblastic
disease,[45,98] and it is unclear if they also pertain to other antineoplastic therapy.

Few studies report the effect of subsequent pregnancies on long-term survival
in cancer patients. There is no evidence to suggest that 5- or 10-year survival rates
following breast cancer are altered in women who become pregnant as compared
with those who do not.[14,30,52,96] Women who do become pregnant tend to have had
low-grade tumors, probably reflecting self-selection, with patients who have a
better prognosis electing to have children.[51]

Conclusion

The diagnosis of cancer in pregnancy is fraught with physiologic, moral, and
ethical dilemmas and presents an emotional and stressful time for the patient and
the physician. Little data exist on which to base universal management schemes,
and treatment should be individualized based on the mother's condition, wishes,

and the gestational age. Prospective studies on the effects of pregnancy on the course of the disease and the fetal effects of cancer and its treatment are needed.

DIABETES

Diabetes mellitus is a complex disease that may lead to varied impairments and disabilities. Diabetes may deteriorate during pregnancy and may have a multitude of effects on the fetus. This is in contrast to gestational diabetes, which manifests as glucose intolerance during pregnancy and is associated with an increased incidence of fetal macrosomia but little other fetal or maternal morbidity. This discussion will focus on preexisting or overt diabetes mellitus (type 1 and type 2).

Effect of Pregnancy on Diabetes

DIABETIC RETINOPATHY

The severity of diabetic retinopathy is directly related to the duration and severity of diabetes and is believed to be a direct consequence of hyperglycemia.[59,106,109] In case-controlled studies of pregnant diabetic women, 15–30% developed signs of retinopathy during pregnancy, and deterioration occurred in 30% of those with preexisting retinal disease.[50,72] Rapid achievement of glycemic control may be associated with worsening retinopathy; however, tight metabolic control is necessary to decrease the risk of fetal malformations (see below). Preconceptional glycemic control and photocoagulation of proliferative vascular lesions is preferable because these women usually do well.[32,59] In most patients, the retinal deterioration regresses postpartum; however, prompt photocoagulation of recognized proliferative lesions is recommended during pregnancy, because this may reduce the rate of progression to blindness by 50%.[31,50]

DIABETIC NEPHROPATHY

A diagnosis of diabetic nephropathy is made if there is greater than 300 mg of protein in a 24-hour urine collection during the first half of pregnancy and there is no evidence of urinary tract infection.[88] In patients with preexisting diabetic nephropathy, proteinuria usually increases to levels greater than 3.0 g/day by the third trimester.[58,88] Hypertension develops in up to 32% of previously normotensive pregnant women with diabetic nephropathy, and the diagnosis of preeclampsia may be especially difficult to make due to preexisting proteinuria.[87,88] Renal function, proteinuria, and hypertension usually return to baseline in the postpartum period.[56,58] Pregnancies complicated by nephropathy are at increased risk for anemia, intrauterine growth retardation, preterm delivery, and perinatal morbidity and mortality, especially if severe proteinuria (> 5 g/day), renal failure (creatinine clearance ≤ 30 mL/min or serum creatinine > 5 mg/dL), or concomitant atherosclerotic heart disease are present.[58] Long term follow-up fails to show any effect of pregnancy on renal function.[88]

CARDIOVASCULAR COMPLICATIONS

Chronic hypertension complicates 10% of all diabetic pregnancies, and this is significantly increased in women with retinopathy or nephropathy.[20] Preeclampsia occurs in 12% of insulin-requiring diabetic patients versus 8% in nondiabetic gravidas.[74] The diagnosis is often difficult to make due to preexisting hypertension and proteinuria. Although coronary artery disease is rarely encountered in pregnant diabetic patients, it is associated with significant maternal and perinatal mortality.[80,104]

DIABETIC KETOACIDOSIS

Diabetic ketoacidosis, which threatens maternal and fetal well being, complicates 9.3% of pregnancies in diabetic women.[20] Common precipitating causes include emesis, beta adrenergic agonist administration, stress, infection, or patient neglect. The diagnosis is made by a clinical picture of hyperventilation, obtundation, dehydration, and hypotension accompanied by hyperglycemia and ketonemia. Abdominal pain and vomiting may be present. Prompt diagnosis and treatment of this condition is essential since correction of maternal ketoacidosis is associated with improvement in fetal biophysical status.[55]

Effect of Diabetes Mellitus on Pregnancy

OBSTETRICAL COMPLICATIONS

Pregnant diabetic patients are at increased risk for pyelonephritis, polyhydramnios (in up to 32% of pregnancies), preterm labor (31%) and spontaneous abortion (30% vs 15% in nondiabetic women).[20,69] The increased incidence of spontaneous abortion appears to be correlated with poor glycemic control in early pregnancy.[70]

Fetal and Neonatal Complications

CONGENITAL MALFORMATIONS

There is a two- to fivefold increase in the frequency of major congenital anomalies in infants of diabetic mothers, with a reported incidence of 4.7–8%.[50,74,83] The most common organ systems that are affected include cardiac, central nervous, and skeletal systems. These anomalies have been primarily correlated with maternal hyperglycemia during the early postconceptional period. Strict metabolic control during the very early period of gestation (< 24 days of conception) has been associated with a decreased incidence of major malformations.[89] Elevated glycosylated hemoglobins (> 8.5%) and elevated maternal fetal serum alpha-fetoprotein are directly correlated with malformation rates.[67,89] Diabetic patients should have detailed ultrasound and fetal echocardiographic assessment in the second trimester as a screen for congenital anomalies.

FETAL GROWTH ABNORMALITIES

Fetal macrosomia, defined as birthweight greater than the 90th percentile for gestational age, occurs in 30% of all diabetic patients.[50] The pathophysiology of this condition is thought to be related to maternal hyperglycemia, which stimulates fetal insulin production and, in turn, accelerates fetal growth. Improved glucose control appears to be highly correlated with normalization of birthweight.[57] Intrauterine growth restriction (or birthweight less than 10th percentile for gestational age) may complicate diabetic pregnancies with retinopathy or nephropathy due to underlying vascular disease.

PERINATAL MORTALITY AND NEONATAL MORBIDITY

Infants of diabetic mothers are at increased risk for prematurity and perinatal morbidity, including hyperbilirubinemia, hypoglycemia, respiratory distress, transient tachypnea, hypocalcemia, cardiomyopathy, and polycythemia.[50,74] The

TABLE 5. Outline of Management for Pregnant Diabetic Patients

Preconceptional counseling	Congenital anomalies
	Perinatal death
	Prematurity
	Neonatal complications
	Hypertension
	Progressive retinopathy
	Progressive nephropathy
Preconceptional glucose control	Nutritional assessment and modification
	Modification of insulin regimen for tight glycemic control
First trimester	Hemoglobin A_1c (glycosylated hemoglobin)
	Ultrasound to establish gestational age/viability
	Ophthalmologic assessment (repeat monthly or each trimester as indicated)
	24-hour urine protein/creatinine clearance (repeat monthly or each trimester)
	Electrocardiogram/echocardiogram if vasculopathy present
Second trimester	Maternal serum alpha-fetoprotein level
	Targeted ultrasound and fetal echocardiogram
Third trimester	Antenatal surveillance (as indicated based on severity and duration of diabetes)
	Ultrasound for estimated fetal weight (if poor glycemic control or as indicated)
Delivery	Based on glycemic control and maternal and fetal condition

reported perinatal mortality rate in diabetic women is approximately twice that in the nondiabetics, and the majority of deaths are related to stillbirth, congenital malformations, and respiratory distress syndrome.[50,74]

Conclusion

Preexisting diabetes mellitus is associated with significant maternal and fetal complications, and management should be coordinated in a tertiary care center if possible. The management of the pregnant diabetic is outlined in Table 5. A detailed discussion of the management of the pregnant diabetic is beyond the scope of this chapter, but the reader is directed to excellent recent reviews.[50,74,83]

SUMMARY

As rehabilitative care improves and women with disabilities are encouraged to pursue active, fulfilling lives with complete integration into society, we may see an increase in the number of disabled women who actively seek gynecologic and obstetric care. It is therefore imperative that health care professionals educate themselves with regard to the impact of pregnancy on these disabilities and possible means of optimizing pregnancy outcome. Prospective research is clearly required in the areas of contraception and gynecologic problems and maternal-fetal complications in these women.

REFERENCES

1. ACOG Committee Opinion, Committee on Obstetrics, Maternal and Fetal Medicine: Management of labor and delivery for patients with spinal cord injury. No. 83, May 1990. Int J Gynecol Obstet 36:253–254, 1991.
2. Adams RD, Victor M: In Principles of Neurology. New York, McGraw-Hill, 1989, pp 756–774.
3. Aminoff RJ: Neurologic disorders. In Creasy RK, Resnik R: Maternal Fetal Medicine: Principles and Practice. 3rd ed. Philadelphia, WB Saunders, 1994, pp 1071–1100.
4. Arnason BG, Richman DP: Effect of oral contraceptives on experimental demyelinating disease. Arch Neurol 21:103–107, 1969.
5. Baker ER, Cardenas DD, Benedetti TJ: Risks associated with pregnancy in spinal cord-injured women. Obstet Gynecol 80:425–428, 1992.

6. Beckman DA, Brent RL: Mechanism of known environmental teratogens: Drugs and chemicals. Clin Perinatol 13:649–687, 1986.
7. Beckmann CRB, Gittler M, Barzansky BM, et al: Gynecologic health care of women with disabilities. Obstet Gynecol 74:75–79, 1989.
8. Bernardi S, Grasso MG, Bertollini R, et al: The influence of pregnancy on relapses in multiple sclerosis: A cohort study. Acta Neurol Scand 84:403–406, 1991.
9. Birk K, Ford C, Smeltzer S, et al: The clinical course of multiple sclerosis during pregnancy and the puerperium. Arch Neurol 47:738–742, 1990.
10. Birk K, Smeltzer SC, Rudick R: Pregnancy and multiple sclerosis. Semin Neurol 8:205–213, 1988.
11. Bleyer WA, Au WY, Lange WA, et al: Studies on the detection of adverse drug reactions in the newborn. JAMA 213:2046–2053, 1970.
12. Brent RL: The effect of embryonic and fetal exposure to x-ray, microwaves, and ultrasound: Counseling the pregnant and nonpregnant woman about these risks. Semin Oncol 16:347–368, 1980.
13. Branch DW, Scott JR: Immunology of pregnancy. In Creasy RK, Resnik R (ed): Maternal Fetal Medicine: Principles and Practice. 3rd ed. Philadelphia, WB Saunders, 1994, pp 115–127.
14. Brown RN: Carcinoma of the breast followed by pregnancy. Surgery 48:862–874, 1960.
15. Byrne J, Mulvihill JJ, Myers MH, et al: Effects of treatment on fertility in long-term survivors of childhood or adolescent cancer. N Engl J Med 317:1315–1321, 1987.
16. Carty EA, Conine TA: Disability and pregnancy: A double dose of disequilibrium. Rehabil Nurs 13:85–87, 1988.
17. Comarr AE: Observations of menstruation and pregnancy among female spinal cord injury patients. Paraplegia 3:263–272, 1963.
18. Committee on Biological Effects of Ionizing Radiation, National Research Council: Other somatic and fetal effects. In Beir V (ed): Health Effects of Exposure to Low Levels of Ionizing Radiation. Washington, DC, National Academy Press, 1990, pp 352–371.
19. Cooper IS, Hoen TI: Metabolic disorders in paraplegic neurologies. Neurology 2:322–340, 1952.
20. Cousins L: Pregnancy complications among diabetic women: Review 1965–1985. Obstet Gynecol Surv 42:140–149, 1987.
21. Craig DI: The adaptations to pregnancy of spinal cord injured women. Rehabil Nurs 15:6–9, 1990.
22. Crosby E, St. Jean B, Reid D, et al: Obstetrical anesthesia and analgesia in chronic spinal cord-injured women. Can J Anaesth 39:487–494, 1992.
23. Cross LL, Meythaler JM, Tuel SM, Cross AL: Pregnancy, labor and delivery post spinal cord injury. Paraplegia 30:890–902, 1992.
24. Cunningham FG, MacDonald PC, Gant NF, et al: In Williams Obstetrics. 19th ed. Norwalk, CT, Appleton & Lange, 1993, pp 425–442.
25. Davis RK, Maslow AS: Multiple sclerosis in pregnancy: A review. Obstet Gynecol Surv 47:290–296, 1992.
26. Davison JM, Lindheimer MD: Renal disorders. In Creasy RK, Resnik R: Maternal Fetal Medicine: Principles and Practice. 3rd ed. Philadelphia, WB Saunders, 1994, pp 844–864.
27. Dekaban AS: Abnormalities in children exposed to x-irradiation during various stages of gestation: Tentative timetable of radiation injury to the human fetus. Part I. J Nucl Med 9:471–477, 1968.
28. de Swiet M: Pulmonary disorders. In Creasy RK, Resnik R (eds): Maternal Fetal Medicine: Principles and Practice. 3rd ed. Philadelphia, WB Saunders, 1994, pp 891–904.
29. de Swiet M: Rheumatologic and connective tissue disorders. In Creasy RK, Resnik R (ed): Maternal Fetal Medicine: Principles and Practice. 3rd ed. Philadelphia, WB Saunders, 1994, pp 1062–1070.
30. Devitt JE, Beattie WG, Stoddart TG: Carcinoma of the breast and pregnancy. Can J Surg 7:124–128, 1964.
31. Diabetic Retinopathy Study Research Group: Photocoagulation treatment of proliferate retinopathy. Clinical application of diabetic retinopathy study (DRS) findings; Report No. 8. Opthalmology 88:583–600, 1982.
32. Dibble CM, Kochenour NK, Worley RJ, et al: Effect of pregnancy on diabetic retinopathy. Obstet Gynecol 59:699–704, 1982.
33. Dildy GA, Moise KJ, Carpenter RJ, Klima T: Maternal malignancy metastatic to the products of conception: A review. Obstet Gynecol Surv 44:535–540, 1989.
34. Doll DC, Ringenberg QS, Yarbro JW: Management of cancer during pregnancy. Arch Int Med 14:2058–2064, 1988.
35. Doll DC, Ringenberg QS, Yarbro JW: Antineoplastic agents and pregnancy. Semin Oncol 16:337–346, 1989.

36. Donegan WL: Cancer and pregnancy. Cancer 33:194–214, 1983.
37. Duncan PG, Pope B, Cohen MM, Greer N: Fetal risk of anesthesia and surgery during pregnancy. Anesthesiology 64:790–794, 1986.
38. Durkhan JP: Menstruation after high spinal cord transection. Am J Obstet Gynecol 100:521–524, 1968.
39. Eckstein K, Marx GF: Aortocaval compression and uterine displacement. Anesthesiology 40:92–96, 1974.
40. Eriksen NL, Parisi VM: Adult respiratory distress syndrome and pregnancy. Semin Perinatol 14:68–78, 1990.
41. Feyi-Waboso PA: An audit of five years' experience of pregnancy in spinal cord damaged women. A regional unit's experience and a review of the literature. Paraplegia 30:631–635, 1992.
42. Frith JA, McLeod JG: Pregnancy and multiple sclerosis. J Neurol Neurosurg Psychiatry 51:495–498, 1988.
43. Gall S: Maternal adjustments in the immune system in normal pregnancy. Clin Obstet Gynecol 26:521–536, 1983.
44. Gershenson DM: Menstrual and reproductive function after treatment with combination chemotherapy for malignant ovarian germ cell tumors. J Clin Oncol 6:270–275, 1988.
45. Goldstein DP, Berkowitz RS, Bernstein MR: Reproductive performance after molar pregnancy and gestational trophoblastic tumors. Clin Obstet Gynecol 27:221–227, 1984.
46. Goodlin RC: Importance of the lateral position during labor. Obstet Gynecol 37:698–701, 1971.
47. Graham JM, Oshiro BT, Blanco JD, Magee KP: Uterine contractions after antibiotic therapy for pyelonephritis in pregnancy. Am J Obstet Gynecol 168:577–580, 1993.
48. Greenspoon JS, Paul RH: Paraplegia and quadriplegia: Special considerations during pregnancy and labor and delivery. Am J Obstet Gynecol 155:738–741, 1986.
49. Hacker NF, Berek JS, Lagasse LD, et al: Carcinoma of the cervix associated with pregnancy. Obstet Gynecol 59:735–746, 1982.
50. Hagay ZJ, Reece EA: Diabetes mellitus in pregnancy. In Reece EA, Hobbins JC, Mahoney MJ, Petrie RH (eds): Medicine of the Fetus and Mother. Philadelphia, JB Lippincott, 1992, pp 982–1020.
51. Harrington SW: Three-year to forty-year survival rates following radical mastectomy for carcinoma of the breast. West J Surg Gynecol Obstet 63:272–283, 1955.
52. Holleb AI, Farrow JH: The relation of carcinoma of the breast and pregnancy in 283 patients. Surg Gynecol Obstet 115:65–67, 1962.
53. Horning SJ, Hoppe RT, Kaplan HS, Rosenberg SA: Female reproductive potential after treatment for Hodgkin's disease. N Engl J Med 304:1377–1382, 1981.
54. Hughes SJ, Short DJ, Usherwood MM, et al: Management of the pregnant woman with spinal cord injuries. Br J Obstet Gynaecol 98:513–518, 1991.
55. Hughes AB: Fetal heart rate changes during diabetic ketosis. Acta Obstet Gynecol Scand 66:71–73, 1987.
56. Jovanovic R, Jovanovic L: Obstetric management when normoglycemia is maintained in diabetic pregnant women with vascular compromise. Am J Obstet Gynecol 149:617–623, 1984.
57. Jovanovic-Petersen L, Peterson CM, Reed GF, et al: Maternal postprandial glucose levels and infant birth weight: The Diabetes in Early Pregnancy Study. Am J Obstet Gynecol 164:103–111, 1991.
58. Kitzmiller JL, Brown ER, Phillippe N, et al: Diabetic nephropathy and perinatal outcome. Am J Obstet Gynecol 141:741–751, 1981.
59. Klein R: Recent developments in the understanding and management of diabetic retinopathy. Med Clin North Am 72:1415–1437, 1988.
60. Laros RK: Thromboembolic disease. In Creasy RK, Resnik R (eds): Maternal Fetal Medicine: Principles and Practice. 3rd ed. Philadelphia, WB Saunders, p 792.
61. Leavesley G, Porter J: Sexuality, fertility and contraception in disability. Contraception 26:417–437.
62. Lindan R, Leffler EJ, Bodner D: Urological problems in the management of quadriplegic women. Paraplegia 25:381–385, 1987.
63. Maddison P, Mogavero H, Reichten M, et al: Patterns of clinical disease associated with antibodies to nuclear riboucleprotein. J Rheumatol 5:407–411, 1978.
64. McCluer S: Reproductive aspects of spinal cord injury in females. In Leyson JF (ed): Sexual Rehabilitation of the Spinal-Cord-Injured Patient. Totowa, NJ, Humana Press, 1990, pp 181–196.
65. McEwan Carty E, Conine TA, Hall L: Comprehensive health promotion for the pregnant woman who is disabled. J Nurse Midwifery 35:133–141, 1990.

66. McGregor JA, Meeuwsen J: Autonomic hyperreflexia: A mortal danger for spinal cord-damaged women in labor. Am J Obstet Gynecol 151:330–333, 1985.
67. Miller E, Hare JW, Cloherty JP, et al: Elevated maternal hemoglobin A1c in early pregnancy and major congential anomalies in infants of diabetic mothers. N Engl J Med 304:1331–1334, 1981.
68. Milunsky A, Graef JW, Gaynor MF: Methotrexate-induced congenital malformation. J Pediatr 72:790–798, 1968.
69. Miodovinik M, Lavin JP, Knowles HC, et al: Spontaneous abortion among insulin-dependent diabetic women. Am J Obstet Gynecol 150:372–376, 1984.
70. Miodovinik M, Skillman C, Holroyde JC, et al: Elevated maternal glycohemoglobin in early pregnancy and spontaneous abortion among insulin-dependent diabetic women. Am J Obstet Gynecol 153:439–442, 1985.
71. Mishell DR: Contraception, sterilization, and pregnancy termination. In Herbst AL, Mishell DR, Stenchever MA, Droegemueller W: Comprehensive Gynecology. 2nd ed. St. Louis, Mosby-Year Book, 1992, pp 295–364.
72. Moloney JBM, Drury MI: The effect of pregnancy on the natural course of diabetic retinopathy. Am J Ophthalmol 93:745–756, 1982.
73. Monga M, Creasy RK: Cardiovascular and renal adaptations to pregnancy. In Creasy RK, Resnik R (eds): Maternal Fetal Medicine: Principles and Practice. 3rd ed. Philadelphia, WB Saunders, 1994, pp 758–767.
74. Moore TR: Diabetes in pregnancy. In Creasy RK, Resnik R (eds): Maternal Fetal Medicine: Principles and Practice. 3rd ed. Philadelphia, WB Saunders, 1994, pp 934–978.
75. Nelson IM, Franklin GM, Jones MC: Risk of multiple sclerosis exacerbation during pregnancy and breast feeding. JAMA 259:3441–3443, 1988.
76. Nicholson HO: Cytotoxic drugs in pregnancy. J Obstet Gynaecol Br Commonw 75:307–312, 1968.
77. Nisker JA, Shubert M: Stage IB cervical carcinoma and pregnancy: Report of 49 cases. Am J Obstet Gynecol 145:203–206, 1983.
78. Nygaard I, Bartscht KD, Cole S: Sexuality and reproduction in spinal cord injured women. Obstet Gynecol Surv 45:727–732, 1990.
79. Ohry A, Molho M, Rozin R: Alterations of pulmonary function in spinal cord injured patients. Paraplegia 13:101–108, 1975.
80. Olofsson P, Liedholm H, Sartor G, et al: Diabetes and pregnancy: A 21 year Swedish trial. Acta Obstet Gynecol Scand Suppl 122:3–56, 1984.
81. Oppenheimer WM: Pregnancy in paraplegic patients: Two case reports. Am J Obstet Gynecol 110:784–786, 1971.
82. Orr JW Jr, Shingleton HM: Cancer in pregnancy. Curr Probl Cancer 8:1–50, 1983.
83. O'Sullivan MJ, Skyler JS, Raimer KA, Abu-Hamad A: Diabetes and pregnancy. In Gleicher N (ed): Principles and Practice of Medical Therapy in Pregnancy. 2nd ed. Norwalk, CT, Appleton & Lange, 1992, pp 357–377.
84. Otake M, Dchull WJ: In utero exposure to A-bomb radiation and mental retardation: A reassessment. Br J Radiol 57:409–414, 1984.
85. Poser S, Poser W: Multiple sclerosis and gestation. Neurology 33:1422–1427, 1983.
86. Reame NE: A prospective study of the menstrual cycle and spinal cord injury. Am J Phys Med Rehabil 71:15–21, 1992.
87. Reece EA, Coustan DR, Hayslett JP, et al: Diabetic nephropathy: Pregnancy performance and fetomaternal outcome. Am J Obstet Gynecol 159:56–66, 1988.
88. Reece EA, Winn HN, Hayslett JP, et al: Does pregnancy alter the rate of progression of diabetic nephropathy? Am J Perinatol 7:193–197, 1990.
89. Reece EA, Gabrielli S, Abdalla M: The prevention of diabetes associated birth defects. Semin Perinatol 12:292–807, 1988.
90. Reinherz EL, Weiner HL, Hauser SL, et al: Loss of suppressor T cells in active multiple sclerosis. N Engl J Med 303:125–129, 1980.
91. Reintgen SM, McCarty KS, Vollmer R, et al: Malignant melanoma and pregnancy. Cancer 55:1340–1344, 1985.
92. Reisner LS, Nichols KP: Anesthetic considerations in the complicated obstetric patient. In Creasy RK, Resnik R (eds): Maternal Fetal Medicine: Principles and Practice. 3rd ed. Philadelphia, WB Saunders, 1994, pp 1173–1190.
93. Reynoso EE, Shepherd FA, Messner HA, et al: Acute leukemia during pregnancy: The Toronto leukemia study group experience with long-term follow-up of children exposed in utero to chemotherapeutic agents. J Clin Oncol 5:1098–1106, 1987.
94. Robertson DNS: Pregnancy and labour in the paraplegic. Paraplegia 10:209–212, 1972.

95. Robertson DNS, Guttman L: The paraplegic patient in pregnancy and labour. Proc Roy Soc Med 56:381–387, 1963.
96. Robinson DW: Breast carcinoma associated with pregnancy. Observations of 1128 cases of breast carcinoma. Am J Obstet Gynecol 92:658–666, 1965.
97. Rossier AB, Ruffieux M, Ziegler WH: Pregnancy and labour in high traumatic spinal cord lesions. Paraplegia 7:210–215, 1969.
98. Rustin GJ, Booth M, Dent J, et al: Pregnancy after cytotoxic chemotherapy for gestational trophoblastic tumours. BMJ (Clin Res) 288:103–106, 1984.
99. Sachs BP, Penzias AS, Brown DAJ, et al: Cancer related maternal mortality in Massachusetts, 1954–1985. Gynecol Oncol 36:395–400, 1990.
100. Sadovnick AD, Baird PA: Reproductive counselling for multiple sclerosis patients. Am J Med Genet 20:349–354, 1985.
101. Schapira DV, Chudley AE: Successful pregnancy following continuous treatment with combination chemotherapy before contraception and throughout pregnancy. Cancer 54:800–803, 1984.
102. Schwartz PE: Cancer in pregnancy. In Reece EA, Hobbin JC, Mahoney MJ, Petrie RH (eds): Medicine of the Fetus and Mother. Philadelphia, JB Lippincott, 1992, pp 1257–1284.
103. Sieber SM, Adamson RH: Toxicity of antineoplastic agents in man: Chromosomal aberrations, antifertility effects, congenital malformations, and carcinogenic potential. Adv Cancer Res 22:57–184, 1975.
104. Silfen SL, Wapner RJ, Gabbe SG: Maternal outcome in Class II diabetes mellitus. Obstet Gynecol 55:749–751, 1980.
105. Sillman F, Stanek A, Sedlis A, et al: The relationship between human papillomavirus and lower genital intraepithelial neoplasia in immunosuppressed women. Am J Obstet Gynecol 150:300–308, 1984.
106. Sinclair S, Nesler C, Schwartz S: Retinopathy in the pregnant diabetic. Clin Obstet Gynecol 28:536–552, 1985.
107. Sipski ML: The impact of spinal cord injury on female sexuality, menstruation and pregnancy: A review of the literature. J Am Paraplegia Soc 14:122–126, 1991.
108. Skyler JS: Complications of diabetes mellitus: Relationship to metabolic dysfunction. Diabetes Care 2:499–509, 1979.
109. Sokal JE, Lessmann EM: Effects of cancer chemotherapeutic agents on the human fetus. JAMA 172:1765–1771, 1960.
110. Stover SL: Spinal Cord Injury: The Facts and Figures. National SCI Data Base. Birmingham, University of Alabama, 1986, pp 1–40.
111. Stuart MJ, Gross SJ, Elrad H, Graeber JE: Effects of acetylsalicylic-acid ingestion on maternal and neonatal hemostasis. N Engl J Med 307:909–912, 1982.
112. Sumner WC: Spontaneous regression of melanoma: Report of a case. Cancer 6:1040–1042, 1953.
113. Swartz HA, Reichling BA: Hazards of radiation exposure for pregnant women. JAMA 239, 1907–1908, 1978.
114. Sweet RL, Gibbs RS: Urinary Tract Infection. In Sweet RL, Gibbs RS (eds): Infectious Diseases of the Female Genital Tract. 2nd ed. Baltimore, Williams & Wilkins, 1990, pp 267–289.
115. Thompson DS, Nelson LM, Burns A, et al: The effects of pregnancy in multiple sclerosis: A retrospective study. Neurology 36:1097–1099, 1986.
116. Tsoutsoplides GC: Pregnancy in paraplegia: A case report. Int J Gynecol Obstet 20:79–83, 1982.
117. Turk R, Turk M, Assejev V: The female paraplegic and mother-child relations. Paraplegia 21:186–191, 1983.
117a. Van den Veyver IB, Moise KJ: Prostaglandin synthetase inhibitor in pregnancy. Obstet Gynecol Surv 48:493–502, 1993.
118. Verduyn WH: Spinal-cord-injured women. In Leyson JF (ed): Sexual Rehabilitation of the Spinal-Cord-Injured Patient. Totowa, NJ, Humana Press, 1990, pp 197–206.
119. Wanner MB, Rageth CJ, Zach GA: Pregnancy and autonomic hyperreflexia in patients with spinal cord lesions. Paraplegia 25:482–490, 1987.
120. Warkany J: Aminopterin and methotrexate: Folic acid deficiency. Teratology 17:353–358, 1978.
121. Weinshenker BG, Hader W, Carriere W, et al: The influence of pregnancy on disability from multiple sclerosis: A population based study in Middlesex County, Ontario. Neurology 39:1438–1440, 1989.
122. Westgren N, Hultling C, Levi R, Westgren M: Pregnancy and delivery in women with a traumatic spinal cord injury in Sweden, 1980–1991. Obstet Gynecol 81:926–930, 1993.
123. Young BK, Katz M, Klein SA: Pregnancy after spinal cord injury: Altered maternal and foetal response to labor. Obstet Gynecol 62:59–63, 1983.

TIMOTHY B. BOONE, MD, PhD

EVALUATION AND MANAGEMENT OF IMPOTENCE IN PHYSICALLY DISABLED MEN

From the Scott Department of
 Urology
Baylor College of Medicine
 and
Spinal Cord Injury Unit
Houston VA Medical Center
Houston, Texas

Reprint requests to:
Timothy B. Boone, MD, PhD
6560 Fannin, Suite 1004
Houston, TX 77030

Erectile potency is a subjective term that can be defined as the ability to develop sufficient rigidity to achieve and sustain penetration until ejaculation. *Erectile failure* is also a subjective term; it is defined as an inability to achieve sufficient penile rigidity for the purpose of vaginal penetration and sustaining rigidity until ejaculation. Erectile failure also can be seen at awakening and during masturbation. Erectile failure may be temporary, situational, or present as a long-term symptom.

Because erectile failure is a subjective concept and every person it affects does not seek medical advice, little is known about the prevalence of erectile dysfunction in American men. Erectile dysfunction is common in older men and occurs in association with medical disorders such as diabetes, peripheral vascular disease, chronic renal failure, or pelvic surgery. The best estimates indicate that erectile dysfunction affects 8 million to 10 million adult men in the United States.[22,27,30] The incidence of impotence is 5% at age 40, 25% at age 65, 55% at age 75, and 75% at age 80.[35] Even though the incidence of erectile dysfunction is higher in older Americans, impotence should not be considered a normal aging process. Psychogenic impotence is often caused by psychological and physiologic factors. The anxiety associated with impotence may aggravate borderline erectile dysfunction. This psychological overlay may make the differential diagnosis difficult, and clinicians must understand the multifaceted nature of erectile function. When a defined neurologic event has occurred, premorbid erectile dysfunction should be reviewed, and the patient's and partner's psychological adjustment to the disability should be ascertained by asking when sexual function was last satisfactory to both parties.

Clinicians must remember that the frequency of intercourse changes with age. Men 60–64 years old have coitus an average of three times a month; men 75–79 years old average 1.7 times a month.[36] Overall, 74% of married men and 56% of married women were noted to be sexually active in a 1990 study by Diokno et al.[13] Sexual dysfunction in men age 80–100 often stems from a fear of poor performance and impotence and a lack of opportunity for sexual relationships. Because older patients often depend on intimate relationships for social support, the loss of sexual function can have a negative impact on their overall health and well being. These are all important considerations for assessing the degree of sexual dysfunction in aging persons.

All health care professionals should be appropriately educated with regard to the anatomic, physiologic, and psychological bases of human sexuality. The physiology of normal sexual function is presented in chapter 2.

A recent study demonstrated a low rate (25%) of doctor-initiated discussions with patients regarding sexual matters.[22] This indicates that the present level of doctor-patient communication regarding sexual function is far from satisfactory. The following discussion will center on various causes of erectile dysfunction and on options for management.

TYPES OF DYSFUNCTION

Vasculogenic Impotence

Vasculogenic impotence is the leading cause of erectile dysfunction. Arterial blood flow, cavernosal smooth muscle compliance, and venous occlusion represent major sources of potential vasculogenic erectile dysfunction. Goldstein[19] has attempted to classify vasculogenic impotence into two major groups: cavernosal artery insufficiency and corporal venoocclusive dysfunction. In patients with cavernosal artery insufficiency, the cavernosal artery systolic occlusion pressure is lower than 90 mm Hg, and the gradient between the brachial and cavernosal artery systolic pressure is 20 mm Hg. In corporal venoocclusive dysfunction, the corporal body pressure cannot be sustained at a normal rigidity. The mechanism of corporal venoocclusion appears to be mechanical trapping of blood within the lacunar emissary venules, leading to short-lived penile erections.

The hypogastric-cavernosal arterial tree may be damaged by trauma or atherosclerosis. Aortoiliac bypass surgery may diminish blood flow to the internal iliac arteries, leading to erectile dysfunction.[47] Several studies suggest that arterial disease in humans is the major factor contributing to erectile dysfunction associated with aging.[11,67] The paired cavernosal arteries develop intimal and medial fibrosis.[54] Studies in aging baboons have shown progressive fibrosis in the trabecular framework of the corporal smooth muscle.[5] Blunt perineal and pelvic trauma can injure the common penile or deep-cavernosal artery. In 1993, Lue reported observing severe arterial occlusive disease in young men with a history of chronic cocaine abuse.[34] Cocaine is thought to be an endothelial toxin that initiates severe arteriosclerosis. Arterial occlusive disease from atherosclerosis in the cavernosal arteries is associated with cigarette smoking, chronic hypertension, diabetes mellitus, hyperlipidemia, and a family history of coronary artery disease.

The corpora cavernosa have an internal framework consisting of type 3 collagen, which is very compliant and elastic. Aging, vascular ischemia, and diabetes mellitus stimulate replacement of type 3 with type 1 collagen, thereby leading to a significant decrease in tissue compliance.[49] This loss of compliance also is seen in the venous outflow system, where adequate compression of the emissary veins against the tunica albuginea is prevented and venous leak occurs with loss of penile rigidity. Peyronie's disease causes venous leak and erectile dysfunction. There is a failure to inhibit venous outflow. A fibrous plaque develops in the tunica albuginea and corpus cavernosum that sometimes causes penile curvature. This fibrous plaque associated with Peyronie's disease "holds" the emissary veins open, and the result is venous leak. The cause of Peyronie's disease is not known. Some studies suggest that most patients who suffer from vascular impotence actually have venous leak.[42,53]

Neurogenic Impotence

A variety of neurologic disorders cause erectile dysfunction. Central lesions (multiple sclerosis, cerebrovascular accident, temporal lobe epilepsy, and spinal cord injury) and peripheral lesions (diabetes mellitus and radical pelvic surgery) are associated with insufficient release of the neurotransmitters that relax the corporal sinusoids and increase arterial blood flow and in this way interfere with initiation of tumescence. The pathways involved in normal erectile function are reviewed in chapter 2. Central nervous system lesions affecting erectile dysfunction can be classified as sacral-infrasacral or suprasacral in origin. There are two mechanisms for initiating tumescence: reflexogenic and psychogenic. A spinal reflex pathway mediates reflexogenic erections. The afferent limb of the reflex originates in sensory receptors of the glans penis and penile skin with neurotransmission through the dorsal penile nerve to the sacral spinal cord. The efferent limb of the reflex begins in the sacral parasympathetic nuclei, with exiting fibers joining the pelvic nerve to innervate the cavernosal smooth muscle. Psychogenic erections begin with conscious arousal and activation of the preoptic anterior hypothalamic area, with projection along the brain stem to the thoracolumbar and sacral spinal cord centers governing penile erection. Disruption of these pathways at any level can cause erectile dysfunction. Suprasacral pathways may be affected in multiple sclerosis,[20] spinal cord injury or tumor,[7,9] Parkinson's disease,[59] cerebrovascular accident,[39] or transverse myelitis. Patients with cauda equina injury, sacral cord trauma, or neural injury following radical pelvic surgery may have significant sacral-infrasacral damage to erectile pathways. The cavernosal nerves emerge from the pelvic plexus near the rectum to travel laterally along the prostate until they penetrate the urogenital diaphragm and enter the corporal bodies. Radical prostatectomy for adenocarcinoma of the prostate will cause erectile dysfunction unless attempts are made to spare the nerves along the gland. Unless the cancer has reached the nerve bundles, this usually can be accomplished, with reported maintenance of erectile function in 50–90% of men (see chapter 2). Surgical therapy for bladder cancer (cystoprostatectomy) and rectal cancer (abdominoperineal resection) is associated with a high rate of postoperative impotence. Rarely, a treatable occult herniated disk is detected when a patient is evaluated for neurogenic impotence.[60]

Spinal Cord Injury

Suffering a spinal cord injury is a tremendous personal tragedy that challenges a patient's relationship with his partner.[66] Sexual dysfunction from such an injury should be addressed early in the rehabilitation process. Education and rehabilitation are crucial to the restoration of sexual lives and are especially important because the majority of spinal cord injuries are sustained by young adults. Numerous studies have focused on the erectile and ejaculatory function of spinal cord-injured men.[7,9,15,17,21,45,62] Unfortunately, most of the patients studied were surveyed by mail and were not examined using objective criteria to assess erectile function. The literature divides patients into those with upper and lower motor neuron injury and groups with complete and incomplete lesions (see chapter 3). Reflexogenic and spontaneous erections are common in patients with cervical and thoracic lesions. More than 90% of patients with upper motor neuron lesions have erectile function. However, only 20% can initiate psychogenic erections. Frequently, the quality of tumescence is poor and the timing is unpredictable, making intercourse impossible. Fewer than half report successful intercourse, and few patients can ejaculate.

Patients with lower motor neuron lesions do not have reflex erections and rarely have spontaneous erections. About 25% can initiate psychogenic erections, but they generally are brief and unsuitable for coitus. Spinal shock, which may last from several days to many months, usually causes parallel loss of bladder and erectile function. However, because 70% of patients will regain erectile function within 1 year of injury, definitive treatment (i.e., penile prosthetics) should not be undertaken during this initial period.

Endocrine Dysfunction

Hypogonadism is the most common endocrine-related cause of erectile dysfunction. Systemic diseases such as diabetes mellitus, renal failure, hypo- and hyperthyroidism, Cushing's disease, and hemochromatosis are often associated with hypogonadism and impotence.[63,64] About a third of men with endocrine-based impotency have primary testicular failure, and the remainder have hypothalamic-pituitary disease.[28] Although uncommon, elevation of prolactin levels responding to the presence of a prolactinoma can cause sexual dysfunction. Loss of libido is thought to be the cause of erectile dysfunction in men with hyperprolactinemia. Impotence in diabetic men is often a combination of neuropathy, microangiopathy, and hypogonadism. About 7–20% of patients with erectile dysfunction have diabetes mellitus,[43] and the incidence may be as high as 95% in diabetic men older than 70.[24] Impotence may be the presenting symptom of diabetes. Decrease in penile blood pressures[17] and abnormal penile brachial indices have been reported in diabetic patients. About 35–75% of impotent men with diabetes have decreased genital sensation and retrograde ejaculation, indicating severe autonomic neuropathy.[8]

Psychogenic Impotence

The past 30 years have seen less frequent diagnoses of psychogenic impotence and increased findings of organic causes for erectile dysfunction. The early theories of psychogenic impotence centered on performance anxiety and the spectator role in psychogenic erectile dysfunction.[37,71] Most investigators believe that erectile dysfunction has an organic cause in more than half of patients, with the incidence increasing in older patients.[63,64] Psychogenic causes for impotence include religious orthodoxy, sexual phobias or deviation, depression, obsessive-compulsive personality, widower's syndrome, poor body image, concern about aging, and the "Madonna-prostitute" syndrome.[32] The exact pathogenesis of psychogenic impotence is unknown, but most theories emphasize sympathetic overactivity and a fixed state of detumescence. Many psychological techniques are available to assist couples with psychogenic impotence. Referral to a sex therapist or psychotherapist is recommended.

INVESTIGATIONS

Many specialized tests for erectile dysfunction have been devloped over the past 10 years. Decisions about testing must be guided by the patient's history, social environment, desires, and expectations. Extensive vascular studies are not indicated in young spinal cord-injured patients without a history of pelvic trauma. Testing should always be goal-oriented.

History and Physical Examination

The medical and sexual history are the most important features in the diagnosis of erectile dysfunction. Lue has promoted the concept of goal-directed therapy for impotence, recognizing that the disorder is not life-threatening or an infectious disease.[33] Many specialized tests for erectile dysfunction have been developed over the last 10 years, and the work-up can be tailored to the patient's goals, motivation, physical health, and psychological condition. Decisions about testing must be guided by the patient's desires and expectations.

The opportunity to interview the partner is important in eliciting a reliable history and planning treatment. A detailed medical, surgical, marital, social, and sexual history and a careful review of the neurologic, cardiovascular, gastrointestinal, and genitourinary systems should be obtained. Special attention should be paid to current medications, a history of smoking, use of alcohol or recreational drugs, or a history of venereal diseases or pelvic or spinal trauma.

Numerous medications are associated with erectile dysfunction. Diuretics, exogenous hormones, H2 blockers, tricyclic antidepressants, and antihypertensive medications have all been linked to loss of sexual function (Table 1).[57] Slag et al. found that medications were the most frequent cause of impotence in an outpatient setting.[61] The vast array of medications may affect sexual function at various levels: loss of rigidity, decreased libido, or anejaculation. Drugs are commonly used to treat the cardiovascular system of elderly patients. Antihypertensive agents with the lowest incidence of impotence include calcium channel blockers, Prazosin, and angiotensin-converting enzyme inhibitors.

The physical examination should include evaluation of motor, sensory, and reflex function of the genitalia, lower extremities, and perineum. Secondary sexual

TABLE 1.   Medications and Sexual Dysfunction

Phenothiazines	Tricyclic Antidepressants	MAO Inhibitors	Antihypertensives	Others
Chlorpromazine	Imipramine	Pargyline	Reserpine	Cimetidine
Prochlorperazine	Amitriptyline	Phenelzine	Guanethidine	Heparin
Thioridazine	Doxepin		Clonidine	Digoxin
Perphenazine			Thiazide diuretics	Estrogen
Trifluoperazine			Beta-blockers	Clofibrate
			Hydralazine	Acetozolamide
			Methyldopa	Progestational agents
			Spironolactone	Chemotherapeutic agents

MAO – monoamine oxidase.

characteristics should be evaluated and testicular volume estimated to rule out possible endocrinologic factors. The S2 root contains the dorsal penile sensory fibers from the glans and motor fibers to the sphincter muscles. Sphincteric weakness and loss of penile sensation to pinprick are significant findings. Efferent bladder and erectile tissue innervation emerges from the S3 root. Patients with erectile dysfunction, normal penile sensation, and no vascular insufficiency should undergo urodynamic studies to address coexisting pathology at S3. For patients with a spinal cord injury, the level and completeness of injury should be evaluated, the presence or absence of rectal tone assessed, and the bulbocavernosus reflex tested. The quadriceps, Achilles tendon, and bulbocavernosus reflexes should always be tested. About 70% of normal men have an intact bulbocavernosus reflex on clinical examination.[6] Patients with diabetes, alcoholism, or other causes of peripheral neuropathy should undergo a careful examination to detect sensory loss in a stocking-and-glove distribution. Loss of sensation in the lateral aspects of the leg or foot in a patient with a herniated disk may correspond to bladder or erectile dysfunction resulting from nerve root compression.

Evaluation of the Endocrine System

The endocrinologic evaluation includes measurements of testosterone, prolactin, and thyroid function. A low serum testosterone measurement warrants further testing, including measurement of follicle-stimulating hormone (FSH), luteinizing hormone (LH), and pooled testosterone samples (taken 30 minutes apart since the serum level of testosterone oscillates during the day). Further testing to exclude occult systemic disease may include a complete blood count, creatinine, lipid profile, measurement of fasting blood glucose, and a urinalysis.

Nocturnal Penile Tumescence

Nocturnal erections are normal, nonsexually stimulating events associated with the frequency of rapid eye movement (REM) sleep. The neurologic basis of nocturnal penile tumescence (NPT) is not known, but many investigators assume that the release of tonic inhibitory activity of the central nervous system leads to NPT during REM sleep.[26] Because patients with psychogenic impotence have normal nocturnal erections (3–5 per night, 30 minutes duration), whereas organic erectile dysfunction is associated with marked impairment, NPT monitoring in a sleep laboratory has been used to distinguish psychogenic from organic impotence.[25] The duration of nocturnal erections ranges from 38 to 27 minutes in men in their 20s and 60s, respectively. A recent study showed that the frequency of nocturnal erections occurring during REM sleep remained constant and was not age-dependent.[56] Furthermore, the investigators found a decrease in rigidity by NPT testing in men older than 60 even though the men and their partners reported regular intercourse. Test results must be interpreted in conjunction with the patient's history and are not meant to replace it. NPT testing performed in a sleep laboratory uses polysomnography (to measure the quality and quantity of REM sleep) and other physiological parameters along with visual inspection and testing of the erect penis to assess erectile function. Medicolegal issues and associated sleep disorders are appropriate reasons for formal sleep laboratory testing. A compact ambulatory home monitor (RigiScan, Dacomed, Inc., Minneapolis) can be used to document penile rigidity and tumescence over 2–3 nights of recording. Allen and Brendler[1] concluded that the correlation between Snap Gauge and NPT is not good and that the nocturnal penile tumescence test is more accurate to

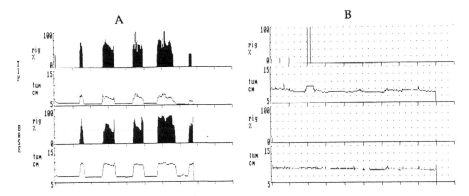

FIGURE 1. Ambulatory nocturnal penile tumescence monitoring. The tracing shows several rigid erections with adequate duration in a normal individual *(A)*. Significant abnormalities are detected in a 35-year-old man with multiple sclerosis *(B)*.

determine the clinical diagnosis. Figure 1 illustrates normal NPT testing in a healthy volunteer and testing in a 35-year-old man with neurogenic impotence from multiple sclerosis. Rings at the penile base and tip measure circumferential changes in diameter and calculate axial rigidity. Sustained rigidity of at least 70% with a duration of at least 10 minutes is considered normal.

Neurophysiologic Testing

Penile erection is primarily a vascular event combining arterial inflow and restricted venous outflow. Complex neural mechanisms involving the thoracolumbar and sacral spinal cord regulate penile blood flow. When the vascular and endocrinologic studies are normal, the indications for neurophysiologic testing include suspicion of neurogenic impotence based on the patient's history and physical examination, voiding dysfunction (usually areflexia) or abnormal NPT testing. Routine screening of all patients with neurophysiologic testing is not warranted or rewarding.[12,16]

The peripheral nervous system serving erectile function involves the pelvic and pudendal nerves. Their integrity can be tested by examining neurally mediated events that share common pathways controlling erectile function. Voiding dysfunction identified by a voiding cystometric study can be considered confirmation of abnormal pelvic nerve innervation to the bladder, implying similar loss of innervation to the penis. Bethanechol supersensitivity testing can be used to confirm parasympathetic denervation of the bladder.[3] The pudendal nerves supply sensation from the glans penis and penile skin and supply motor innervation to the bulbocavernosus, ischiocavernosus, and external urethral sphincter muscles. Sensory stimulation via the dorsal penile branch of the pudendal nerve plays an important role in the development and maintenance of penile erection.[23] The ability to increase genital stimulation to maintain a rigid erection may be an important feature of sexual function in aging men. The absence of this stimulation during NPT testing may account for the loss of rigidity reported in men older than 60.[56] Pudendal somatosensory and motor function can be tested to identify patients with neurogenic erectile dysfunction. Bulbocavernosal reflex (BCR) testing is useful in evaluating patients suspected of having pudendal neuropathy or a sacral spinal cord lesion.[6,48] Pudendal nerve conduction velocity can be measured, and its prolongation is correlated strongly with clinical neuropathy.[60] The entire pudendal afferent pathway may be studied by evoked potential testing or biothesiometry.

Somatosensory evoked potential (SSEP) testing provides objective neurophysiologic measurements and has been used for many years to study peripheral nerves. The dorsal penile nerve is stimulated and the response is recorded by surface electrodes placed at some site within the central nervous system. The afferent genitocerebral pathway begins with penile skin receptor stimulation and activation of pudendal sensory axons to sacral dorsal root ganglia. Ascending second-order fibers presumably transmit sensory input to the thalamus, where third-order fibers project to the contralateral primary sensory area located deep in the interhemispheric fissure.[10] Evoked potential wave forms are generated at a synapse or relay sites in the spinal cord and primary sensory cortex. Simultaneous surface recording over the sacral spinal cord allows the calculation of both peripheral and central conduction times, which can be helpful in localizing neurologic lesions.

Biothesiometry is an inexpensive, noninvasive method for detecting sensory abnormalities of the penis. A vibratory stimulus at a fixed frequency and variable amplitude is applied to the glans penis. The patient's perception threshold to the stimulus is noted. Normal biothesiometry and abnormal evoked potential testing suggest somatosensory receptor cell damage or collagen infiltration of the penile skin.[50] There are no direct neurophysiologic methods to assess the integrity of the efferent nerves to the penis. Diagnostic methods are being developed to address neurogenic erectile dysfunction at the target level.[65]

Penile Blood Flow

Because vasculogenic impotence is the leading cause of erectile dysfunction, several techniques have been developed to evaluate the vascular component of penile erection. Insufficient arterial inflow and venous leakage from the corpora cavernosa affect approximately 5 million men in the United States.[22] Arteriogenic, venogenic, and combined dysfunction constitute the major categories of vasculogenic impotence. Arteriography, penile plethysmography, Doppler ultrasound, and pharmacocavernosometry are the principal techniques for vascular testing of the penis and erectile dysfunction.

Arteriography remains the standard for investigation of the penile vasculature. Pudendal artery angiography and corpus cavernosography are reserved for the occasional patient who is considered for vascular surgery.[44] Internal pudendal or iliac arteriography is indicated in a limited number of young patients with suspected trauma to isolated segments of the arterial tree when arterial reconstruction is a primary consideration for treating arteriogenic impotence.

Since the 1970s, measurement of penile blood pressure has been used as a screening test for arteriogenic impotence. A rigid erection requires blood flow through the paired cavernosal arteries to sustain an intracavernosal pressure of at least 75 mm Hg.[67] The penile brachial pressure index (PBI) has been effective for detecting arterial disease. Penile blood pressure is compared with brachial blood pressure at rest and following exercise. The ratio of penile to brachial pressure, the PBI, should be at least 0.75. A ratio below 0.6 is diagnostic of vasculogenic impotence.[58] A reduction in the PBI following exercise indicates a vascular steal syndrome, which may be responsible for loss of penile rigidity during intercourse. Continuous-wave Doppler analysis measures pressure from all arteries in the penis rather than a single artery, thereby serving as a sensitive indicator of vascular disease. Furthermore, impotence should be considered a potential risk factor for arterial atherosclerotic vascular disease, and a low PBI has been associated syrongly with a subsequent major vascular event occurring within 2–3 years.[44]

Diagnostic injection of the cavernosal smooth muscle with relaxing drugs is one of the most popular methods of establishing the diagnosis of organic impotence. Failure to respond to vasoactive substances injected into the cavernous tissues is an indicator of arterial insufficiency, especially when duplex Doppler ultrasound shows a lack of arterial dilation with increased blood flow through the cavernosal arteries. Figure 2 demonstrates the simultaneous measurement of arterial diameter and velocity of blood flow following intracorporeal injection of papaverine, phentolamine, and prostaglandin E1 (Trimix). A normal rigid erection following injection implies normal arterial and venous anatomy and suggests psychogenic or neurogenic causes for impotence. Combining injections with visual sexual stimulation or masturbation can augment the erectile response and improve the vascular assessment.

Venoocclusive dysfunction, or "venous leak," may cause vasculogenic impotence by permitting unrestricted venous outflow in the face of adequate arterial inflow to the penis. A loss of trabecular expansion and compression of the subtunical venules from age-induced fibrosis of the fibroelastic framework can lead to venoocclusive dysfunction. Radiologic procedures can be performed to study the venous drainage of the penis. Dynamic cavernosography and cavernosometry

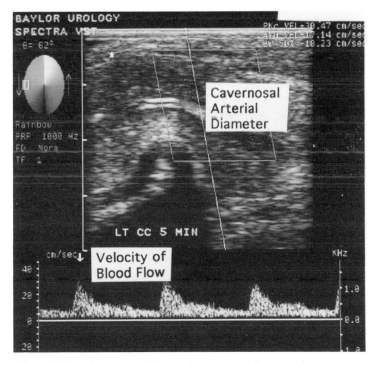

FIGURE 2.   Duplex ultrasonography of the cavernosal artery allows measurement of luminal diameter and velocity of penile blood flow.

are used to diagnose venous leakage. Heparinized saline is infused into the corpora cavernosa, and the flow rate to maintain a rigid erection is calculated; greater than 120 mL/min is abnormal.[69] Radiographic contrast can be added to demonstrate the site of venous leakage.

MANAGEMENT

Figure 3 outlines the diagnosis and management of impotence and is meant to serve as a broad outline of the thought process involved in evaluating a patient for erectile dysfunction. If the patient's history clearly suggests psychogenic cause, the patient and partner should be referred for professional counseling.

Medical Treatment

The medical treatment of impotence includes oral yohimbine, injections of testosterone, or intracavernous self-injections of vasoactive agents. Yohimbine is an alpha-2 adrenergic blocker with reputed action in the central nervous system to improve erectile function.[42] The greatest improvement with yohimbine treatment is seen in patients with psychogenic impotence. Testosterone therapy is appropriate only for patients with low testosterone levels. Oral forms of testosterone are ineffective and have been shown to increase serum lipids and to damage the liver. Furthermore, testosterone therapy may stimulate the growth of an occult prostate

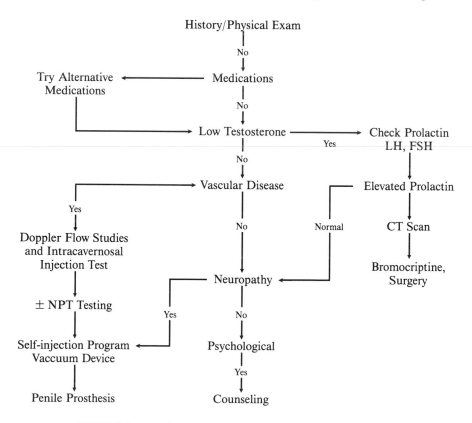

FIGURE 3.   Outline for diagnosis and management of impotence.

cancer. If the patient is hypoandrogenic, it is important to adhere strictly to a schedule of an annual rectal examination and measurement of serum prostate-specific antigen. Intramuscular testosterone enanthate or cypionate is given once a month.

INTRACAVERNOUS SELF-INJECTION THERAPY

Self-injection therapy successfully treats 70–80% of impotent men.[55] The endogenous release of transmitters can be mimicked by the intracavernosal injection of vasoactive drugs. Papaverine and phentolamine were the vasoactive agents first used in self-injection programs,[73] but the recent additon of prostaglandin E1 has led to triple drug therapy (Trimix) and reduced doses of papaverine and phentolamine.[68] Long-term use of papaverine and phentolamine may result in penile fibrosis in a small percentage of cases.[51] Reports of corporal tissue scar formation at higher doses of papaverine and phentolamine led to the addition of prostaglandin E1 to further reduce the strength of papaverine and phentolamine. Patients inject the minimal amount of Trimix required to achieve erection into the lateral penile shaft. These agents have no effect on the ability to ejaculate or achieve orgasm. Up to 95% of patients with spinal cord injury can be successfully treated with a self-injection program.[4,72] Patients with neurogenic impotence are very sensitive to the medication, and doses lower than those considered standard in an impotence clinic are usually prescribed. The risk of prolonged erection (priapism) is 3–10%, and the patient must be counseled about this possibility during training. Discomfort, burning sensation, and pain during the procedure have been reported.[14,68] Bleeding disorders, sickle cell disease, and poor manual dexterity are contraindications to self-injection therapy.

Vacuum Constriction Devices

Vacuum devices represent a new mode of therapy for erectile dysfunction.[18,46] A clear cylinder is placed over the penis, and a suction device creates a vacuum, drawing blood into the corporal tissue (Fig. 4). A constriction band is released from the base of the cylinder to the base of the penis to maintain the erection. Most patients can achieve sufficient rigidity for intercourse using vacuum constriction devices that offer the advantages of safety and relatively low cost. Penile hypothermia, constriction of scrotal and other tissues, and hematomas have been reported in some patients.[29] Most devices list for $300, and several models are available, including one with a battery-powered suction motor for patients with poor manual dexterity. Priapism has not been a problem. Total constriction time should be limited to 30 minutes. Patients with sensory deficits should be warned about prolonged constriction with the rings, because tissue ischemia and loss of

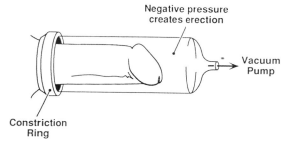

FIGURE 4. Vacuum-constriction device placed over the penis to create negative pressure drawing blood into the corporal tissues.

Negative pressure
creates erection

Vacuum
Pump

Constriction
Ring

the penis may result. Patients who favor this form of therapy require no further diagnostic testing.

Penile Prostheses

Penile prostheses are a surgical option for disabled patients with vasculogenic or neurogenic impotence. Three types have evolved over the past 20 years: rigid, semi-rigid or malleable, and hydraulic inflatables.[40,41] The rigid prosthetic rods have been replaced by malleable devices, which are associated with less material fatigue and lower risk of fracture. Perkash et al. have advocated use of the semi-rigid rods to prevent loss of condom catheters, and he reports a long-term failure rate of 8% with a 2% infection rate.[52] Perkash reported satisfactory intercourse in 68% of patients. These devices provide penile erection but do not affect the ability to have an orgasm. Early reports had shown that patients with spinal cord injury and reduced penile sensation had a high incidence of erosion (20%) with the semi-rigid devices.[53] The time to erosion varied from 5 days to longer than 3 years and often was associated with infection. Further experience with the inflatable devices showed a lower rate of erosion.[31] An inflatable penile prosthesis is shown in Figure 5. The three-piece device consists of two inflatable cylinders implanted in the corporal bodies, a pump located in the scrotum, and a fluid reservoir placed behind the abdominal wall. Penile prosthetics are not contraindicated in patients with disabilities such as spinal cord injury. However, patients must be selected carefully and receive counseling on the risks and benefits of prosthetic surgery.

Vascular Surgery

Various reconstructive procedures have been described.[20,23] In an overview of types and results of vascular surgical procedures for impotence,[19] Goldstein concluded that conventional procedures for venous ligation restored potency in only about 20% of cases and arterial reconstruction was effective in about 80% of a highly selected group of patients with arteriogenic impotence.

Arterial revascularization has a limited role in the treatment of arteriogenic impotence. Well-defined arterial lesions from trauma are amenable to reconstruction. However, most arteriogenic impotence results from aortoiliac occlusive disease. When the disease is proximal, it is often associated with claudication and hip pain. Reconstructive procedures to improve lower extremity blood flow have been noted

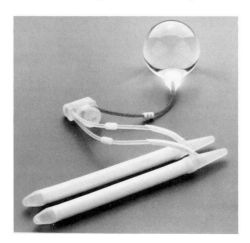

FIGURE 5. Inflatable penile prosthesis (Courtesy of American Medical Systems, Minneapolis).

to restore potency in up to 50% of patients with proximal aortoiliac occlusive disease.[38] Unfortunately, distal occlusive disease is quite common, and efforts to revascularize the corpora have failed in most series with long-term follow-up.

Penile venous ligation surgery to correct venous leak seemed to have a promising future when the first procedures were performed.[70] However, new venous collaterals often develop, and delayed surgical failure is common.

FERTILITY AND ELECTROEJACULATION

Ejaculatory failure occurs in up to 95% of spinal-cord injured patients, and until several years ago no techniques were available to treat this fertility problem. Fortunately, the advent of vibratory stimulation and electroejaculation has made semen collection possible in men with neurologic disorders.[2] Numerous pregnancies have been initiated using these techniques in conjunction with intrauterine insemination. A rectal probe with metal electrodes is used to deliver electrical current (electroejaculation) to postganglionic nerve fibers, stimulating emission and ejaculation. Vibratory stimulation is often successful in patients with lesions above T8. A vibrator is held against the penile shaft and glans for several minutes to induce ejaculation. The bladder is rinsed with a buffered solution to harvest retrograde portions of the ejaculate. Early reports indicate that time since injury has no significant effect on electroejaculatory success or the quality or quantity of recovered sperm. Furthermore, injury during prepubescence does not appear to prevent future success with electroejaculation. The development of electroejaculation has given new hope to potential young fathers with spinal cord injuries.

SUMMARY

Advances in the knowledge and understanding of erectile physiology over the last decade have improved the treatment of erectile dysfunction. Nerve-sparing procedures can be used in patients undergoing pelvic surgery. Orthoses or self-injection of vasoactive drugs can be used as nonsurgical approaches to erectile problems. When nonsurgical options are not acceptable or satisfactory results cannot be obtained, implantation of a penile prosthesis can be considered as an alternative. Arterial reconstructive and venous ligation procedures are available for selected patients.

REFERENCES

1. Allen R, Brendler CB: Sanp-Gauge compared to a full nocturnal penile tumescence study for evaluation of patients with erectile impotence. J Urol 143:51–54, 1990.
2. Bennett CJ, Seager SW, Vasher EA, et al: Sexual dysfunction and electroejaculation in men with spinal cord injury: Review. J Urol 139:453–457, 1988.
3. Blaivas JG: A critical appraisal of specific diagnostic techniques. In Krane RJ, Siroky MD (eds): Clinical Neuro-Urology. Boston, Little, Brown & Co., 1979, pp 69–109.
4. Bodner DR, Lindan R, Leffler E, et al: The application of intracavernosus injection of vasoactive medications for erections in men with spinal cord injury. J Urol 138:310–311, 1987.
5. Bornman MS, du Plessis DJ, Ligthelm AJ: Histological change in the penis of the Chacma baboon: A model to study aging penile vascular impotence. J Med Primatol 14:13–18, 1985.
6. Bors E, Blinn KA: Bulbocavernosus reflex. J Urol 82:128–130, 1959.
7. Bors E, Comarr AE: Neurological disturbances in sexual function with special reference to 529 patients with spinal cord injury. Urol Surv 10:191–222, 1960.
8. Broderick GA, Swartz S: Erectile dysfunction in diabetes. Hosp Pract 85–97, August 1991.
9. Chappelle PA, Durand J, Lancert P: Penile erection following complete spinal cord injury in men. Br J Urol 52:216–219, 1980.
10. Chippa KH, Ropper AH: Evoked potentials in clinical medicine. N Engl J Med 306:1205–1211, 1982.

11. Davis SS, Viosca SP, Guralnik M, et al: Evaluation of impotence in older men. West J Med 142:499–505, 1985.
12. Desai KM, Dembny K, Morgan H, et al: Neurophysiological investigation of diabetic impotence. Are sacral response studies of value? Br J Urol 61:68–73, 1988.
13. Diokno AC, Brown MB, Herzog AR: Sexual function in the elderly. Arch Intern Med 150:197–200, 1990.
14. Earle CM, Keogh EJ, Wisniewski ZS, et al: Prostaglandin E1 therapy for impotence, comparison with papaverine. J Urol 143:57–59, 1990.
15. Fitzpatrick WF: Sexual function in the paraplegic patient. Arch Phys Med Rehabil 55:221–227, 1974.
16. Fowler C, Ali Z, Kirby RS, Pryor JP: The value of testing for unmyelinated fibre, sensory neuropathy in diabetic impotence. Br J Urol 61:63–67, 1988.
17. Gaskell P: The importance of penile blood pressure in cases of impotence. Can Med Assoc J 105:1047–1051, 1971.
18. Gilbert HW, Gingell JC: Vacuum constriction devices: Second-line conservative treatment for impotence. Br J Urol 70:81–83, 1992.
19. Goldstein I: Overview of types and results of vascular surgical procedures for impotence. Cardiovasc Intervent Radiol 11:240–244, 1988.
20. Goldstein I, Siroky MB, Sax DS, Krane BJ: Neurologic abnormalities in multiple sclerosis. J Urol 128:541–545, 1982.
21. Griffith ER, Tomko MA, Timms RJ: Sexual function in spinal cord-injured patients: A review. Arch Phys Med Rehabil 54:539–543, 1973.
22. Handelsman H: Public health service assessment—Diagnosis and treatment of impotence. US Department of Health and Human Services, Washington, DC, 1990, Health Technology Assessment report 90-3457.
23. Herbert J: The role of the dorsal nerves of the penis in the sexual behavior of the male rhesus monkey. Physiol Behav 10:293–300, 1973.
24. Kaiser FE, Udhoji V, Viosca SP, et al: Cardiovascular stress tests in patients with vascular impotence [abstract]. Clin Res 37:89A, 1989.
25. Karacan I: Clinical value of nocturnal erection in the prognosis and diagnosis of impotence. Med Aspects Hum Sex 4:27–34, 1970.
26. Kessler WO: Nocturnal penile tumescence. Urol Clin North Am 15:81–86, 1988.
27. Kinsey AC, Pomeray WB, Martin OE: Sexual Behavior in the Human Male. Philadelphia, WB Saunders, 1948.
28. Korenman SG, Stanik-Davis S, Mooradian A: Evidence for a high prevalence of hypogonadotropic hypogonadism in sexually dysfunctional older men. Clin Res 35:182A, 1987.
29. Korenman SG, Viosca S, Kaiser FE, et al: Use of a vacuum tumescence device in the management of impotence. J Am Geriatr Soc 38:217–220, 1990.
30. Krane RJ, Goldstein I, Saenz de Tejada I: Impotence. N Engl J Med 321:1648–1659, 1989.
31. Light JK, Scott FB: Management of neurogenic impotence with inflatable penile prosthesis. Urology 17:341–343, 1981.
32. LoPiccolo J: Diagnosis and treatment of male sexual dysfunction. J Sex Marital Ther 11:215–219, 1986.
33. Lue TF: Patient's goal-directed impotence management. Urol Grand Rounds 29:1–5, 1989.
34. Lue TF: Male erectile dysfunction. Am Urol Assoc Postgrad Course, 1993.
35. Martin CE: Sexual activity in the aging male. In Money J, Musoph H (eds): Handbook of Sexology. New York, Elsevier, 1977.
36. Masters WH: Sex and aging—expectation and reality. Hosp Pract 15:175–198, 1986.
37. Masters WH, Johnson VE: Principles of the new sex therapy. Am J Psychiatry 133:548–554, 1976.
38. Metz P, Frimodt-Moller C, Mathiesen FR: Erectile function before and after arterial reconstructive surgery in men with occlusive arterial leg disease. Scand J Thorac Cardiovasc Surg 17:45–50, 1983.
39. Monga TN: Sexuality post stroke. Phys Med Rehabil State Art Rev 7:225–236, 1993.
40. Montague DK: Experience with semirigid rod and inflatable penile prostheses. J Urol 129:967–968, 1983.
41. Montague D: Periprosthetic infections. J Urol 138:68–69, 1987.
42. Morales A, Surridge DHC, Marshall PG, Fenemore J: Nonhormonal pharmacological treatment of organic impotence. J Urol 128:45–47, 1982.
43. Morley JE: Impotence. Am J Med 80:897–905, 1986.
44. Morley JE, Korenman SG, Kaiser FE, et al: Relationship of penile brachial pressure index to myocardial infarction and cerebrovascular accidents in older men. Am J Med 84:445–448, 1988.

45. Munro D, Horne HW, Paull DP: The effect of injury to the spinal cord and cauda equina on the sexual potency of men. N Engl J Med 239:903–911, 1948.
46. Nadig PW, Ware JC, Blumoff R: Noninvasive device to produce and maintain an erection-like state. Urology 27:126–131, 1986.
47. Ohshiro T, Kosaki G: Sexual function after aortoiliac vascular reconstruction: Which is more important, the internal iliac artery or hypogastric nerve? J Cardiovasc Surg 25:47–50, 1984.
48. Padma-Nathan H: Neurologic evaluation of erectile dysfunction. Urol Clin North Am 15:77–80, 1988.
49. Padma-Nathan H, Cheung D, Perelman J, et al: The effects of aging, diabetes and vascular ischemia on the biochemical composition of collagen found in the corpora and tunica of potent and impotent men [abstract]. Int J Impotence Res 2:75, 1990.
50. Padma-Nathan H, Levine F: Vibratory testing of the penis. J Urol 137:201A, 1987.
51. Padma-Nathan H, Payton T, Goldstein I: Treatment for organic impotence: Alternatives to the penile prosthesis. Am Urol Assoc Update 6:2–7, 1987.
52. Perkash I, Kabalin JN, Lennon S, Wolfe V: Use of penile prostheses to maintain external condom catheter drainage in spinal cord injured patients. Paraplegia 30:327–332, 1992.
53. Rossier AB, Fam BA: Indication and results of semirigid penile prostheses in spinal cord injury patients: Long term follow-up. J Urol 131:59–62, 1984.
54. Ruzbarsky V, Michal V: Morphologic changes in the arterial bed of the penis with aging. Invest Urol 15:194–199, 1977.
55. Saenz de Tejada I: The physiology of erection, signposts to impotence. Contemp Urol 4:52–68, 1992.
56. Schiavi RC, Schreiner-Engel P: Nocturnal penile tumescence in healthy aging men. J Gerontol 43:146–150, 1988.
57. Shabsigh R: Is a drug effect part of your patient's complaint of impotence? Contemp Urol 5:51–58, 1993.
58. Silber SJ: Impotence. Adv Intern Med 30:359–385, 1984.
59. Singer C, Weiner WJ, Sanchez-Ramos JR: Autonomic dysfunction in men with Parkinson's disease. Eur Neurol 32:134–140, 1992.
60. Siroky MB, Sax DS, Krane RJ: Sacral signal tracing: The electrophysiology of the bulbocavernosus reflex. J Urol 122:661–664, 1979.
61. Slag MF, Morley JE, Elson MK: Impotence in medical clinic outpatients. JAMA 249:1736–1740, 1983.
62. Smith EM, Bodner DR: Sexual dysfunction after spinal cord injury. Urol Clin North Am 20:535–542, 1993.
63. Spark RF, White RA, Connolly PB: Impotence is not always psychogenic: Newer insights into hypothalamic-pituitary-gonadal dysfunction. JAMA 243:750–755, 1980.
64. Spark RF, Wills CA, Royal M: Hypogonadism, hyperprolactinemia, and temporal lobe epilepsy in hyposexual men. Lancet 1:413–417, 1984.
65. Stief CG, Djamilian M, Anton P, et al: Single potential analysis of cavernous electrical activity in impotent patients: A possible diagnostic method for autonomic cavernous dysfunction and cavernous smooth muscle degeneration. J Urol 146:771–776, 1991.
66. Urey JR, Henggeler SW: Marital adjustment following spinal cord injury. Arch Phys Med Rehabil 68:69–74, 1987.
67. Virag R: Arterial and venous hemodynamics in male impotence. In Bennett AM (ed): The Management of Male Impotence. Baltimore, Williams & Wilkins, 1982, pp 108–125.
68. Waldhauser M, Schramek P: Efficiency and side effects of prostaglandin E1 in the treatment of erectile dysfunction. J Urol 140:525–527, 1988.
69. Wespes E, Delcour C, Struyven J, Schulman CC: Cavernometry-cavernography: Its role in organic impotence. Eur Urol 10:229–232, 1984.
70. Wespes E, Schulman CC: Venous leakage: Surgical treatment of a curable cause of impotence. J Urol 133:796–798, 1985.
71. Wolpe J: Psychotherapy by Reciprocal Inhibition. Stanford University Press, 1958.
72. Wyndaele JJ, de Meyer JM, de Sy WA, Claessens H: Intracavernous injection of vasoactive drugs: One alternative for treating impotence in spinal cord injury patients. Paraplegia 24:271–275, 1986.
73. Zorgniotti AW, Lefleur RS: Auto-injection of the corpus cavernosum with a vasoactive drug combination for vasculogenic impotence. J Urol 133:39–41, 1985.

GABRIEL TAN, PhD
ROSIE BOSTICK, PhD

SEXUAL DYSFUNCTION AND DISABILITY: PSYCHOSOCIAL DETERMINANTS AND INTERVENTIONS

From the VA Medical Center
  and the Department of Psychiatry
  and Behavioral Sciences (GT)
  and
Department of Physical Medicine
  and Rehabilitation (RB)
Baylor College of Medicine
Houston, Texas

Reprint requests to:
Gabriel Tan, PhD
VA Medical Center
Psychology Service (116B)
2002 Holcombe Blvd.
Houston, TX 77030

This chapter begins with a literature review of the psychological and psychosocial impact of disability as it pertains to one's sexuality. A review of the literature on the treatment of sexual dysfunction follows. The purpose of the review is not to chronicle sexual dysfunction but to update the readers on this important topic. It serves as a reminder that, with or without a disability, sexual dysfunctions are quite prevalent. The chapter concludes with suggestions for key elements to be included in a comprehensive program of sexuality for the physically challenged.

PSYCHOLOGICAL AND PSYCHOSOCIAL IMPACT OF DISABILITY ON SEXUALITY

In 1980 in its International Classification of Impairments, Disabilities, and Handicap, the World Health Organization described a three-category definition of disability that included biologic, functional, and psychosocial elements of disability. Sexuality is viewed as an aspect of human relationships, and therefore, sexual functioning and dysfunction cannot be adequately understood outside the realm of human functioning and the psychosocial impact of being disabled. Geiger[15] argues that sexual activity is primarily a cerebral and, therefore, psychological event. It may or may not involve genital stimulation and sensation. Despite the contributions of recent medical breakthroughs in such areas as prosthetic implants and intracavernous injection therapy, there is a danger of focusing too much attention on the mechanics of enabling sexual intercourse and minimizing the psychological effects and psychosocial context of sexual dysfunction. Singh and Magner[56] pointed out that although up to 70% of individuals with spinal cord injuries were capable of some degree of sexual activity, many did not engage in sexual activities due to psychological factors relating to body image, increased dependency, and feelings of inferiority. This finding is not peculiar to individuals with spinal cord injuries; individuals with other disabling conditions tend to avoid a sexually active life for the same reason.

Cole and Cole[10] classified disabling conditions into four major categories (Table 1). They used age of onset and the progressive or stable nature of the disability to develop a construct of disability and sexuality.

Disabling conditions may be congenital or acquired (type 1–type 4). The age at which a person is disabled is a highly significant factor in sexual development.[26] The impact of congenital disability on a child's development and development of sexuality is covered in chapter 11. Individuals born with congenital disabilities often have dramatically different initial sexual self-awareness than individuals who become disabled as adults. The presence of the disability fosters an "overprotective" environment that inhibits ordinary physical and social exploration, thereby depriving the child of normal sexual experiences. Exploration of sexuality is often delayed or overshadowed by physical and economic dependency on parents or guardians. Cole reported: "They may find themselves in an adult world, wanting to be sexually sophisticated but lacking the requisite education."[10]

Many professionals think that the sexual concerns of persons who are physically challenged do not differ significantly from those of the able-bodied.[26] People who are physically challenged are men and women first and disabled second. However, those with acquired or type 3 or 4 disabilities are often faced with the "comorbidity" of dealing with the loss of a former state of "well-being" as well as the loss or impairment of sexual functioning. Depending on the nature and type of disability, the role of organic determinants on sexual dysfunction vis-a-vis psychological and psychosocial determinants varies. Even when clinicians suspect that a dysfunction has an organic cause, they would be wise to also explore the possibility of underlying psychological factors. Sexual dysfunctions in persons with physical disabilities usually have a primary and a secondary factor. Trieschmann[64] strongly advises that both be evaluated and treated.

TABLE 1. Classification of Disability

Classification	Sequelae
Type 1 disabilities Pre-adolescent nonprogressive (before puberty)	Limb amputation, congenital loss of organ of special sensation, congenital brain injury, deafness
Type 2 disabilities Pre-adolescent progressive (before puberty)	Juvenile rheumatoid arthritis, childhood onset diabetes mellitus, cystic fibrosis, degenerative diseases
Type 3 disabilities Post-adolescent or adult nonprogressive	Traumatic spinal cord injury, brain injury, disfiguring burns, amputation
Type 4 disabilities Post-adolescent progressive	Degenerative diseases, stroke, cancer, arthritis, lung disease, diabetes mellitus, end-stage renal disease

Adapted from Cole T, Cole S: Rehabilitation of problems of sexuality in physical disability. In Kottke F, Lehmann J (eds): Krusen's Handbook of Physical Medicine and Rehabilitation. 4th ed. Philadelphia, WB Saunders Co, 1990, pp 988–1008.

A common denominator is the psychological and psychosocial impact that disability and chronic medical conditions tend to extol from their survivors, much like an unwelcome and unexpected trauma. It has been the assumption, although not well documented, that individuals often go through stages of grieving for losses that may include a physical component (such as loss of ability to ambulate), a cognitive component (such as decreased capacity to concentrate, process information, and solve problems), a sexual component (such as loss of erectile or orgasmic capacity), and a vocational component (such as loss of ability to perform the premorbid occupation). The importance of each of the above losses, either singly or in combination, will vary with each individual. For example, in a society where self-worth is often defined by occupation and employment provides a structure for daily routine and meaningful pursuit, the loss of vocation may have a highly devastating effect on the individual's reason for living.

As the individual traverses the rehabilitation hurdles, the need for understanding and support from others cannot be overemphasized.

Psychosocial influences often act to inhibit attempts to maintain or develop sexual relationships.[60] They may occur in the form of: (1) maladaptive cognitive factors such as masculinity/femininity concerns, fear of failure (performance anxiety), rejecting the "wellness" model and succumbing to the sick role, negative body image/self-concept, anticipation of pain, and irrational beliefs; (2) interpersonal relationships such as social skills, courtship, marriage, and family; and (3) general psychological status, including depression, anxiety, psychosis, and history of sexual trauma.

Maladaptive Cognitive Factors

Religious, cultural, and socializing factors have dichotomized sex roles as feminine and masculine and have assigned corresponding sex role stereotypes. A man is judged to be strong, independent, competent, and sexually aggressive. A woman is correspondingly judged to be passive, dependent, submissive, warm, and sexually passive.[66] Two common stereotypes are "woman-homemaker" and "man-provider." The fallacy in ascribing to this point of view occurs when one is no longer able to perform in said stereotypical fashion. For example, if the physically challenged male is unable to initiate or play an active sexual role, is he no longer masculine? Or if he is unable to achieve erectile competence is he no longer masculine? What about the physically challenged female? If she has difficulty assuming the homemaker role, is she no longer feminine?

Fear of failure or performance anxiety becomes a self-fulfilling prophecy. The more one becomes a spectator in the sexual arena, the more likely one is to experience disappointment with one's performance. Negative thoughts become "blocks" that inhibit the physically challenged from attempting to reestablish themselves as sexual beings. Kaplan[23] labeled this process of development of negative blocks as resistance. She believed that the concept of resistance had far-reaching consequences. It pertained to anxiety generated by facing one's problems, giving up defenses, and changing one's behavior. Many individuals experience guilt and anxiety in the presence of success and pleasure. The anticipation or achievement of sexual success arouses a negative response in some individuals, thereby mobilizing resistance to treatment/change.

People often hide behind "the sick role" to avoid having to assume expected responsibilities and obligations. A key component of the sick role is the individual's inability to achieve wellness by an act of decision or will. This may be reflected in thoughts that sick people cannot have sexual relationships or the myth that people with disabling conditions are not interested in sex, cannot perform sexually, and are not desirable as sex partners.[29,60,62]

Beauty and perfection are prized in this society. Romano,[48] who has done much to overcome the gender bias in reporting about the sexuality and sexual needs of women with disabling conditions, writes that physical imperfection is often equated with asexuality socioculturally. She indicates that this belief is often internalized by those with disabling conditions, thereby causing them to feel ashamed for the perceived imperfection as well as the basic need for sexual intimacy with others. Negative thoughts of this type are likely to inhibit sexual functioning. It is an inescapable fact that some disabling conditions alter the appearance of the individual in ways that cannot be restored. The body image of many individuals with disabling conditions must now encompass scars, atrophy, prostheses, and other attachments. This altered body image accompanies the physically challenged into any intimate relationship.

Pain is a constant threat in some conditions, including arthritis, spinal cord injuries, and burns. Many individuals may avoid sexual activity for fear of producing further pain. Often, simple information about changing positions, judicious use of pillows, or extra clothing will eliminate this problem.

Negative thoughts of death and beliefs about further injury are common. Ignorance and misinformation can be just as inhibiting to sexual exploration. Individuals with heart and lung disease often report feelings of depression, reduced self-esteem, and preoccupation with life or death.[10] These perceptions are obvious deterrents to sexual health. Proper sexual counseling will help to alleviate unfounded fears.

Another maladaptive belief is that sex is for young people. Sexual discrimination against the elderly continues to exist.[61] Sexual needs of able-bodied elderly people are often overlooked. Those with physically challenging conditions are viewed as too old and too infirm to be concerned about sex. Many are not given the option of discussing sexual concerns. Although women do not experience much shift in their sexual capacity, aging men may experience a decline in orgasm. However, frequent and enjoyable erections can be maintained. The normal aging process does not automatically signal the onset of erectile and ejaculatory failure.

Interpersonal Relationships

As the disabled have grown in numbers, they have surfaced as a new minority group.[13] Probably the most fundamental dilemma for all minorities is determining whether to try to establish intimate relationships within "their own kind" or to venture out to a wider circle of people.[50] A different picture emerges with nonvisibly disabled individuals. They may refuse to be identified with the disabled and develop different social and psychological strategies to cope with their disabilities. Some disabled individuals have been able to transcend their disability and view themselves and others as human beings—attractive or unattractive, interesting or uninteresting, compatible or incompatible personalities rather than disabled or nondisabled.

Individuals with a disabling condition often find themselves in situations where a great deal of tact and social skills are needed. Even with the Americans with Disabilities Act, individuals often must navigate a difficult course using only personal skills to avoid discomfort and overcome personal, social, and architectural barriers. Attitude toward those with disabilities has been well studied.[11] Stigmatization of the disabled is not only limited to the general public but is evident among health professionals as well.[10,11] Stigmatization by health professionals might serve to discourage those with disabling conditions as they seek to establish satisfying interpersonal and intimate relationships.

The quality and nature of the relationship existing at the time of onset of the disabling condition merit scrutiny. Sexual dysfunction does not occur in a vacuum. Spence[60] and Kaplan[22] point out the importance of the partner in the relationship. Sexual interaction involves a dyadic situation in which two people provide a constant source of influence over the other's behavior. Partners may react in a number of ways to the occurrence of a sexual problem. Physical disability may have a marked impact on the couple's marriage. Many stressors exist requiring adaptations on the part of both partners in areas outside of the sexual arena. Until a reasonable degree of homeostasis has been reestablished in the relationship, sexual activity may be additionally compromised. A major commitment is required of both partners to discuss the changes the disability has brought into the relationship and to decide on ways to compensate for these changes. It is inadvisable to attempt sex therapy unless a reasonably affectionate relationship exists between the couple.[22] Spence[60] points out that for couples whose sexual relationship was previously unsatisfactory, the physical disorder may provide a convenient excuse for giving it up altogether. In addition, marital relationships that were distressed prior to the onset of a disabling condition do not fail exclusively because of sexual dysfunction of one partner but because the general fabric of the relationship has been weakened and could not tolerate the additional stress of the disability.

General Psychological State

An individual's premorbid personality has been found to be a fairly reliable predictor of the manner in which an individual with an acquired disability will cope with the disability.[9] Conscientious individuals who have attained a higher level of psychosexual and personality maturation show more motivation to adjust to their disability.

General satisfaction with life, high self-esteem, and sexual behaviors characterized by mutual openness and experimentation will promote an active and satisfying sex life.[57] Persons who report greater emotional distress are more likely to also have low interpersonal satisfaction, to be unemployed, and to have less active lifestyles.[28]

Depression and anxiety are the most commonly cited forms of psychopathology that accompany chronic illness.[46,60,61] Renshaw[46] writes that besides depression, three important "As" are causes of sexual dysfunction in people with diabetes: alcohol, anxiety, and anger.

Excessive use of alcohol causes sexual dysfunction in both sexes. Excessive anxiety, whether "performance anxiety" as discussed above or from other sources—fear of discovery, sexually transmitted diseases, or divine punishment—suppresses enjoyable effective sexual expression. Finally, anger between partners may successfully block sexual responses.

A variety of traumatic events predating the onset of a disability may lead to sexual dysfunction, including incest and rape. Spence[60] and Higgins[19] found that early adverse sexual experiences continued to plague a minority of survivors, and the authors felt that this possibility should be investigated during the assessment process. Higgins[19] considers it a "biological fallacy" to neglect psychological and sociological variables involved in sexual disturbances.

We often think of dependency as being dependent on another for emotional, economic, and social support and assistance to achieve a reasonable degree of independence. In the case of people with disabling conditions, the concept of dependence is broadened to encompass the medical regimen, including the dialyzer, ventilator, renal homograft, other mechanical devices, medical personnel, social services, and family.[1] The task of balancing dependence and independence, passivity and activity, sickness and health underlies many patients' adaptation to a disabling condition and affects their sexual adjustment.

PSYCHOLOGICAL TREATMENT OF SEXUAL DYSFUNCTION

A number of excellent books and reviews on the treatment of various sexual dysfunctions are available.[31,41,69] Much of the data in this section has been extracted from these publications. Unfortunately, most of the literature in this area does not examine the special needs of the physically challenged. Programs that purport to deal with sexual dysfunction among those with disability primarily have included sex education and general counseling. There is little published research that systematically evaluates the effectiveness of these interventions. Most textbooks on sexual dysfunctions among the general population are organized by the nomenclature of the Diagnostic and Statistical Manual of American Psychiatric Association, Third Edition, Revised (DSM-III-R),[3] which classifies sexual dysfunctions into categories of sexual desire disorders (hypoactive and hyperactive sexual desires) and sexual aversion disorder, sexual arousal disorders (female sexual arousal disorder and male erectile disorder), orgasm disorder (inhibited female orgasm, inhibited male orgasm, premature ejaculation), sexual pain disorder (dyspareunias and vaginismus), and sexual dysfunction NOS (not otherwise specified).

In the DSM-III-R toxonomy,[3] a diagnosis of sexual disorder is not made if the sexual dysfunction can be attributed entirely to organic factors such as a physical disorder or medication. It is accepted that some incidences of sexual dysfunction may have both an organic and a psychogenic cause.

Sexual Desire Disorder

Sexual desire disorder implies deviation from what the individual, spouse, and society consider as normative. Numerous treatment protocols have been proposed and tested. In addition to being among the most prevalent and perplexing sexual complaints facing health care professionals, desire problems present a theoretical challenging "new frontier." There is little agreement among the experts concerning the role of psychological, intrapsychic, and interpersonal determinants of libido. Although research efforts in recent years have focused on the role of hormones in particular, the findings have been inconsistent and ambiguous.[32]

Special clinical skills are required to assess the multitude of factors potentially contributing to this common complaint. Rosen and Leiblum[49] have proposed a clinical decision-making model in which primary and secondary low desire are differentiated, as well as a variety of individual and systemic issues.

A variety of treatment approaches for problems of sexual desire were advanced in the late 1970s and early 1980s. Kaplan[21] advocated a psychoanalytically based treatment. In contrast, Schover and LoPiccolo[52] reported a high success rate using a cognitive-behavioral approach. Rosen and Leiblum[49] drew a sociological script theory in dealing with problems of desire discrepancy between spouses. Other investigators, including Verhulst and Heiman,[65] recommended family-system approaches to desire disorders. Interest in pharmacologic intervention started in the 1980s as Bancroft and Wu[8] and Sherwin, Gelfand, and Bender[55] reported positive outcome of androgen replacement therapy. Research using antidepressant and dopamine agonist drugs to enhance desire also have been reported.[47]

How successful are these therapies in treating sexual desire complaints? In a random survey of sex therapists and counselors, Kilmann[25] reported that problems of desire required the greatest number of treatment sessions and that fewer than 50% of clients reported a successful treatment outcome for their desire difficulty. Other investigators have reported much higher success rates. For example, LoPiccolo and Freidman,[33] Schwartz and Masters,[53] and Apfelbaum[5] all reported success rates as high as with other sexual dysfunction.

Despite favorable outcome studies, it is difficult to know exactly what in the treatment protocol works since most reported protocols are multidimensional. This has led many experts to emphasize the value of incorporating biologic, psychological and interpersonal elements into the treatment of sexual desire disorder.

Perhaps the lack of clarity and specificity in the research literature lies in the lack of agreement among researchers and clinicians regarding the conceptualization and treatment of sexual desire. For example, should the focus be on the individual patient, or should desire discrepancies within the couple be addressed? How can desire be measured? Are there norms for men and women, young and old? Nevertheless, what is clear is that low sexual desire leads to significant problems for individuals and couples, and these problems are amenable to psychological therapies.

Sexual Aversions

Considered to be a subtype of sexual desire disorder, sexual aversion takes on the characteristic of phobias and panic disorder. For example, Kaplan[22] has linked sexual aversion to panic disorder. Anxiety is the common core, and treatment protocols should integrate biologic, cognitive behavioral, and interpersonal approaches. Patients should be evaluated for the use of antidepressants and other medications to reduce anxiety when it is clear that the phobic response is so strong that it interferes with responsivity to psychological therapies.

Treatment protocols should address the phobic aspects of the disorder as well as the sexual dysfunction. LoPiccolo and Friedman's model[33] consists of experiential/sensory awareness, insight, cognitive restructuring, and behavioral interventions. Ballenger's integrated model[7] is similar but incorporates psychodynamic elements aimed at calming a multimodal hypersensitivity.

In a review by Gold and Gold,[16] only one outcome study mentioning sexual aversion could be found. This is expected since sexual aversion has only been recently included in the DSM-III-R as a category of sexual dysfunction. However, due to the high success rate in treating phobias and panic disorders, the success of therapies for sexual aversion is expected to be high for patients showing no concomitant sexual dysfunction (80–85%) and less successful when other sexual problems coexist (6–70%).[16]

Female Sexual Arousal Disorder

Lack of sexual arousal in women is a prevalent problem.[59] Nearly half of a community sample of women reported difficulty becoming aroused.[59] Yet, clinicians often prefer to conceptualize women with sexual problems as experiencing inhibited orgasm rather than inhibited arousal. Sexual arousal disorders may be global or situational and may or may not be lifelong. A lifelong disorder is considered primary and a situational disorder secondary.

The cause may be related to physiologic changes accompanying psychobiologic life stages and the related life stresses and developmental demands. The current state of knowledge does not permit a degree of specificity by which hormonal or other physiologic effects can be separated from psychological ones. Intrapersonal, interpersonal, and societal factors are other likely contributing causes,[21,24,38] as are the effects of childhood sexual abuse.[35]

The treatment protocol typically consists of directive sex therapy approaches in which patients are instructed to take an active role in their treatment program; examples are Masters and Johnson's program for orgasmic dysfunction,[37] LoPiccolo's program of masturbation training,[33] and Kaplan's program for general sexual dysfunction.[24]

Outcome research on sexual arousal in women is lacking, in part because clinicians and researchers have not agreed that arousal is important and do not have good instruments with which to measure it. Sexual arousal disorder in women tends to be underdiagnosed and, perhaps, misdiagnosed as orgasmic disorder.[38]

Male Erectile Disorder

Krane et al.[27] estimated that 10 million men in the United States have some form of erectile disorder. Spector and Carey[59] estimated the prevalence rates of erectile difficulty to be 3–9%. This prevalence rate is higher than 9% for men with chronic diseases and physical disabilities. Erectile dysfunction may be biogenic or psychogenic, primary or secondary, and lifelong or situational. The relative contribution of biogenic and psychogenic factors varies from case to case.

Relative to other sexual disorders, erectile dysfunction has witnessed enormous progress in vascular and neural assessment techniques and in vascular, pharmacologic, and surgical treatments. For a description of a comprehensive examination of erectile dysfunction and medical treatments, see Tiefer and Melman.[63]

Erectile failure invariably elicits great consternation in men of all ages, who typically view the disorder as a blow to their masculine adequacy. Treatment for psychogenic insufficiency runs the gamut from behavioral to psychodynamic approaches. Althof[2] suggests that primary impotence of psychogenic origin is best treated by psychotherapy since it frequently suggests conflicts regarding gender, sexual orientation, or paraphilic interests. The literature includes long lists of possible psychological factors contributing to the cause and maintenance of erectile disorders. If secondary impotence exists, the couple is usually interviewed together, and the focus is on the resolution of a particular conflict or event that may be interfering with the couple's sexual life. Sensate focus exercises are prescribed along with educational information and suggestions. Concurrent medical interventions such as auto-injection therapy or an external vacuum device may be helpful in some cases.

Studies on the psychological treatment of erectile dysfunction, and at long-term follow-up, have shown positive outcomes when organic cases have been screened out.[14] However, most of these treatment protocols combine a variety of procedures, including Masters and Johnson-style ingredients such as sensate focus, communication and interaction skills training, rational emotive therapy

(RET), psychotherapy, and masturbation. Thus far, the available outcome data do not make it possible to specify an ideal package of interventions; nor is it possible to delineate a most efficient format.

Female Orgasm Disorder

According to the DSM-III-R, approximately 30% of women have inhibited female orgasm. Although the figures vary from study to study, most estimates indicate that a considerable number of women do not experience orgasm.[59] Objecting to the confusion that often arises from classifying orgasmic dysfunction into a primary versus secondary disorder, Schover et al.[51] has developed a multi-axial system that contains seven categories for the orgasm phase axis: anhedonic orgasm, anorgasmic (total), anorgasmic except for masturbation, anorgasmic except for partner manipulation, anorgasmic except for masturbation and partner stimulation, anorgasmic except for vibrator or other mechanical stimulations, and infrequent coital orgasm.

For primary orgasmic dysfunction, directed masturbation training appears most effective. LoPiccolo[33] reported 95% success in having patients achieve orgasm through masturbation, 85% by direct genital stimulation by partner, and 40% through penile-vaginal intercourse following the treatment program.

Secondary inorgasmic problems are much more complicated to treat. Psychoanalytic, object-relations, cognitive-behavioral, and systems theory all offer conceptual approaches for treating these problems. Recent trends favor viewing the couple or the sexual relationship rather than the patient as the target of treatment.

Female inhibited orgasm has been widely researched. The most common criterion for treatment success has been self-report of orgasm. Only a few researchers have reported measures of satisfaction with sexual function.[23] Jayne[20] questioned the practice of equating orgasmic ability to treatment success since women often prefer the emotional closeness and intimacy associated with intercourse to masturbation despite the fact that orgasmic reliability is superior with masturbation.

Inhibited Male Orgasm

Inhibited male orgasm occurs much less frequently than premature ejaculation and erectile dysfunction. Subtypes of inhibited male orgasm are shown in Table 2. Emission phase disorders and retrograde ejaculations probably are completely biogenic.

A number of interventions have been used to treat men with inhibited orgasm: vibrator and electrical stimulation, a variety of sexual exercises, and a

TABLE 2. Subtypes of Inhibited Male Orgasm

Delayed orgasmic response
Absent orgasmic response
Incomplete orgasmic response
Emission phase disorder
Contractile or expulsion phase disorders
Squirtless seminal dribble
Retrograde ejaculation
Anesthetic ejaculation

Adapted from Kothari P: For discussion: Ejaculating disorders—a new dimension. Br J Sex Med 11:205–209, 1984.

range of general psychotherapeutic techniques,[12] Few controlled outcome studies are available. Dekker's[12] review of the few uncontrolled studies found suggests generally poor results and inconclusive findings. While some patients benefit substantially, many are only "somewhat improved" or unchanged.

Premature Ejaculation

Epidemiologic studies suggest that premature ejaculation may be one of the most common forms of sexual dysfunction.[59] However, there are serious problems with the definition of what constitutes premature ejaculation. For instance, Masters and Johnson's[37] classic definition "...as occurring when, on more than half of the occasions of intercourse, the women does not experience orgasm" defines the disorder in terms of the partner's reaction, thus relying on the partner's orgasmic latency, a phenomenon even less well understood than ejaculatory control. It is, therefore, not surprising that no reliable or objective measure exists and that the complaint of premature ejaculation is based almost exclusively on self-report.

The treatment protocol originally suggested by Semans[54] and elaborated by Masters and Johnson[37] has been widely used. The Semans stop-start technique consists of cycles of manual stimulation by the partner until the male experiences sensations indicative of forthcoming ejaculation, at which point the stimulation is stopped; it is restarted once the arousal subsides. This cycle is repeated with some variation until increased ejaculatory control is reported. The Masters and Johnson protocol is more elaborate in that it moves from "sensate focus" to the female-superior position and lateral-coital positions. Intense therapy sessions, and in some cases, social seclusion of the couple are also used.

The research on premature ejaculation is surprisingly extensive.[41] Cognitive and behavioral treatments, variations of "brief therapy," and eclectic approaches have all reported good success.[41] Other studies[36] have concluded that premature ejaculation can be treated by a group therapy format and by paraprofessionals. With a variety of procedures available, the outlook for successful treatment is good.

Sexual Pain Disorders

Two major categories of sexual pain disorders are dyspareunias and vaginismus. Dyspareunia is defined by a recurrent pattern of genital pain before, during, or immediately after coitus. Vaginismus is a sexual disorder that results from involuntary contraction of the vaginal muscles during attempted penetration.

Dyspareunia is a common complaint to gynecologists. For pain secondary to dyspareunia, women are more likely to seek medical help than a sex therapist. Organic sources and psychological variables have been alternatively proposed as the major factors in the cause of dyspareunia.

Psychogenic dyspareunias can often be treated with simple interventions such as use of artificial lubrication. Changing sexual positions to a female-superior position allows more control by the woman. When anxiety plays a central role, systematic desensitization is often used. A typical course might involve prohibition of intercourse; initial finger exploration of the vagina, first by the woman, then by her partner; sensate focus exercises increasing to 20 contractions four times per day; and self-dilation 1 week later.[45] Communication training and cognitive procedures also have been used. Lazarus[30] believed that although traumatic factors (e.g., sexual assaults or abuse) and developmental issues (e.g., an upbringing that invested sex with shame and guilt) may be significant in some instances, the majority of patients are likely to reveal relational conflicts. Like sexual arousal in women, dyspareunia is poorly researched with few outcome studies.[45]

There is some consensus in the field that, unlike dyspareunias, which may be caused by both organic and psychogenic factors, vaginismus is a psychosomatic condition that results from contraction of the circumvaginal muscles and is caused by fear of penetration. The statistics on vaginismus vary markedly.[45]

Treatment of vaginismus typically focuses on the elimination of vasospasm and fear. Psychoanalytic therapy, traditional sex therapy, and behavior therapy all have been found to be successful.[45,69] EMG biofeedback and hypnosis have also been successfully applied.[45] The success rate is very high despite the fact that vaginismus has remained a research orphan.[45] Clinical reports suggest that the important and necessary treatment components include progressive dilation, partner cooperation and support, provision of accurate information, and emphasis on sensual pleasuring and relaxation.[45]

SEX EDUCATION AND COUNSELING FOR THE PHYSICALLY CHALLENGED

Only recently have rehabilitation professionals devoted serious attention to improving sexuality of disabled patients. Early studies indicated that a disabled patient's sexuality was primarily seen as a problematic management issue. As late as in the 1970s, medical practitioners who attended to patients with spinal cord injury invariably shared the opinion that once individuals take to the wheelchair, their sexual activity is at an end. However, this state of affairs has changed. Several private and public rehabilitation centers are including sex education and counseling as part of their comprehensive rehabilitation programs.

The Sexual Attitude Reassessment (SAR) workshops[44] were precursors in the field of sex education for people with disabling conditions, their significant others, and professionals working in this medical specialty. The workshops were held over 2 days and covered a wide variety of information on sexual lifestyles of a diverse society. The goal was to desensitize the participants and open up a dialogue between the disabled and those with whom they interacted.

The PLISSIT model,[4] as shown in Table 3, was among the first indications of an organized attempt to improve the sexuality of the disabled. Adapted from the literature on treatment of sexual dysfunction, this model provided a conceptual framework to aid professionals counseling persons with disabilities regarding their sexual problems.

At level 1, permission is given to the individual with sexual concerns to openly discuss these issues. They are reassured that it is normal to have questions about their sexuality and to resume an active sex life. The goal of level 2 is to dispel sexual myths and concerns by providing patients with factual information about their conditions and concerns. In level 3, specific suggestions such as sensate focus exercises and brief counseling are provided. These suggestions are tailored to

TABLE 3. The PLISSIT Model

Level 1	P	Permission
Level 2	LI	Limited Information
Level 3	SS	Specific Suggestions
Level 4	IT	Intensive Therapy

the individual's particular condition and problems to circumvent. Most patients will need intervention only at levels 1–3. When severe and deep-seated problems are involved regarding sexual difficulties, level 4 (intensive therapy) is indicated. Level 4 interventions require the services of specially trained professionals.

No new models have been proposed in the literature since the PLISSIT. Williams[68] argues that there have been two parallel strands of development with respect to sexuality and disability. The first has been the empowerment of disabled people through political strategies to present disability not as a problem but an opportunity for unique experiences. One outcome of this movement has been the creation of the Association to Aid the Sensual and Personal Relationships of People with a Disability (formerly SPOD).

A second movement has been to recognize gender bias in discussions of disability and sexuality. The field of rehabilitation is replete with examples of this gender bias. An example has been the surge in biomedical/mechanical devices such as electroejaculation, vacuum suction, and penile prostheses, but the same enterprise appears to be lacking with respect to female needs. For a more detailed account of gender issues, refer to the work of Bullard and Knight.[26]

It is becoming the rule rather than the exception to have sexuality related education and/or intervention programs in major rehabilitation facilities. Many facilities start by educating both their professional and paraprofessional personnel to maximize the chances of patients getting consistent information.[10,44,58] Rabin[44] points out that educating personnel about sexuality and disability will also allow them the opportunity to examine their own convictions and attitudes toward the following: sexuality in general, sexuality in the disabled, masturbation, homosexuality, pre- and extramarital sex, abortion, and divorce.

Health professionals tend to rank the importance of a sex life higher than spinal cord-injured males do.[18,43,67] These studies show that while sex is important to these patients, it is not among their top two areas of concern.

Many of the spinal cord injury services provide information on sexuality and disability to their patients and medical personnel. The format for the dissemination of this information differs among medical centers. The Texas Institute of Rehabilitation and Research at Houston uses the Challenge Program, which it has developed to provide sex education. While there is no set model to follow, these programs appear to contain several crucial elements. First, they try to get disabled patients to talk openly about their sexuality and, in the process, feel validated. The patients should be encouraged to express their needs, concerns, and fears about their disability and expressions of intimacy.[10] Second, the shift is toward broadening the focus of sexuality away from preoccupation with the act of sexual intercourse. Thus, the achievement of orgasm through sexual intercourse is not the sole purpose of intervention but the expression of mutually satisfying sexual behavior involving the coordination of both mind and body. The rebuilding of a positive self-image and sexual identity should be the primary purpose of education and counseling rather than the physical relief of sexual frustration. Third, professionals and the patients alike must understand the patients' sexual experiences prior to as well as after the disability. When the disability is congenital or lifelong (type 1 or type 2), there is often a need to educate the patients about sexuality in general and their sexuality in particular to compensate for a background of deprivation.

Nosek[40] is conducting a National Institutes of Health–funded project on sexuality among women with physical disabilities from a wellness perspective (see chapter 14). Preliminary findings indicate that areas of sexuality can be grouped into five domains: (1) having positive sexual self-concept, (2) having sexual information, (3) having positive, productive relationships, (4) managing barriers (social, environmental, emotional, physical, and sexual abuse), and (5) maintaining optimal health and physical sexual functioning.

There is clearly a need for more and better information and counseling for women,[40] especially women with spinal cord injuries.[10] In follow-up studies, many women reported that the sexuality information provided during rehabilitation was inadequate or that they wished they had more counseling.

Following the rehabilitation model, a multidisciplinary approach is important in providing a comprehensive program of sex education and counseling (assessment, treatment, and long-term follow-up care of sexual functioning). A necessary adjunct to this team is a panel composed of peers of the target group.[17] Most programs have at least four components: educational, counseling, medical/surgical, and functional retraining. While the first three of these components are easily understood, functional retraining may require further elucidation. For individuals with motoric and sensory involvement, retraining and/or orthotic assistance may be needed for the "activities of daily living" of sexual activity.

Health professionals providing education and counseling to disabled people no longer need to wish that more information was available. A nonanecdotal body of knowledge is amassing in referred journals and medical texts. Underscoring the coming of age of this topic, the journal *Sexuality and Disability* in 1993 devoted an issue exclusively to the topic of sexual counseling for people with disabilities. This issue also contains a SIECUS annotated bibliography of available printed material on the subject. Rabin's[44] *Sensuous Wheeler* provides the reader with an extensive list of resources and references.

The following outline summarizes elements of comprehensive programs for the disabled.

Elements of a Comprehensive Program for the Physically Challenged
A Summary

I. Sex education tailored to the specific disabling condition
   A. Targeted toward the caregiving staff and the patients and their families
II. A comprehensive and interdisciplinary program that assesses the following:
   A. Primary and secondary sexual dysfunction and their organic and psychogenic cause, avoiding exclusive focus on one or the other
   B. Detailed premorbid sexual functioning
   C. Impact of disabling conditions in terms of the three elements as outlined by Spence:[60]
      1. Maladaptive cognitive factors
      2. Interpersonal relationships
      3. General psychological states
III. A coordinated intervention program that contains the following elements:
   A. Addresses both primary and secondary sexual dysfunction
   B. Maximally involves partners and significant others
   C. Combines the essence of the PLISSIT model and the wellness model
   D. Focuses on helping patients cope with the impact of the disabling conditions
   E. Includes these domains:
      1. Having positive sexual self-concept
      2. Having sexual information

3. Having positive productive relationships
4. Managing barriers (social, environmental, emotional, physical, and sexual abuse)
5. Maintaining optimal health and physical sexual functioning

F. When appropriate, treatment procedures for sexual dysfunctions as applied to the general population should be used and tested for effectiveness with physically challenged patients

IV. A built-in program evaluation and outcome research element that would begin to systematically test out the efficacy of each element/procedure/technique of this program

REFERENCES

1. Abram H, Hester L, Sheridan W, Epstein G: Sexual functioning in patients with chronic renal failure. In LoPiccolo J, LoPiccolo L (eds): Handbook of Sex Therapy. New York, Plenum Press, 1978, pp 411–419.
2. Althof SE: Psychogenic impotence: Treatment of men and couples. In Leiblum SR, Rosen RC (eds): Principles and Practice of Sex Therapy. 2nd ed. New York, Guilford Press, 1989, pp 237–264.
3. American Psychiatric Association: Diagnostic and Statistical Manual of Mental Disorders–Third Edition–Revised. Washington, DC, American Psychiatric Association, 1987.
4. Annon J, Robinson C: Behavioral treatment of sexual dysfunctions. In Sha'ked A (ed): Human Sexuality and Rehabilitation Medicine. Baltimore, Williams & Wilkins, 1981, pp 104–118.
5. Apfelbaum B: An ego-analytic perspective on desire disorders. In Leiblum SR, Rosen RC (eds): Sexual Desire Disorders. New York, Guilford Press, 1988, pp 75–106.
6. Ballard DG, Knight SE: Sexuality and Physical Disability—Personal Perspectives. St. Louis, Mosby, 1981.
7. Ballenger JC: Toward an integrated model of panic disorder. Am J Orthopsychiatry 59:284–293, 1989.
8. Bancroft J, Wu FCW: Changes in erectile responsiveness during androgen therapy. Arch Sex Behav 12:59–66, 1983.
9. Bracken M, Shepard M: Coping and adaptation following acute spinal cord injury: A theoretical analysis. Paraplegia 18:74–85, 1980.
10. Cole T, Cole S: Rehabilitation of problems of sexuality in physical disability. In Kottke F, Lehmann J (eds): Krusen's Handbook of Physical Medicine and Rehabilitation. 4th ed. Philadelphia, WB Saunders Co, 1990, pp 988–1008.
11. Daniels S: Correlates of attitudes toward the sexuality of the disabled person in selected health professionals. Sex Disabil 1:112–126, 1978.
12. Dekkar J: Inhibited male orgasm. In O'Donohue W, Geer JH (eds): Handbook of Sexual Dysfunctions. Boston, Allyn & Bacon, 1993, pp 279–301.
13. Eisenberg M: Disability and stigma. In Eisenberg M, Griggins C, Duval R (eds): Disabled People as Second Class Citizens. New York, Springer, 1982, pp 3–12.
14. Everaerd W: Male erectile disorder. In O'Donohue W, Geer JH (eds): Handbook of Sexual Dysfunctions. Boston, Allyn & Bacon, 1993, pp 201–224.
15. Geiger RC: Neurophysiology of sexual response in spinal cord injury. Sex Disabil 2:257–266, 1979.
16. Gold SR, Gold RG: Sexual aversions: A hidden disorder. In O'Donohue W, Geer JH (eds): Handbook of Sexual Dysfunctions. Boston, Allyn & Bacon, 1993, pp 83–102.
17. Griffith E, Cole S, Cole T: Sexuality and sexual dysfunction. In Rosenthal M, Griffith E, Bond M, Miller J (eds): Rehabilitation of Adults and Children with Traumatic Brain Injury. Philadelphia, FA Davis, 1990, pp 206–224.
18. Hanson R, Franklin M: Sexual loss in relation to other functional losses for spinal cord injured males. Arch Phys Med Rehabil 57:291–303, 1990.
19. Higgins G: Aspects of sexual response in adults with spinal cord injuries. A review of the literature. In LoPiccolo J, LoPiccolo L (eds): Handbook of Sex Therapy. New York, Plenum Press, 1978, pp 387–410.
20. Jayne J: A two-dimensional model of female sexual response. J Sex Marital Ther 7:3–30, 1981.
21. Kaplan HS: Disorders of Sexual Desire. New York, Brunner/Mazel, 1979.
22. Kaplan HS: Sexual Aversion, Sexual Phobias, and Panic Disorders. New York, Brunner/Mazel,

1987.

23. Kaplan HS: The Illustrated Manual of Sex Therapy. New York, New York Times Book Co., 1975.
24. Kaplan HS: The New Sex Therapy. New York, Brunner/Mazel, 1974.
25. Kilmann PR, Boland JP, Norton SP, et al: Perspectives of sex therapy outcome: A survey of AASECT providers. J Sex Marital Ther 12:116–128, 1986.
26. Knight S: The sexual concerns of the physically disabled. Presented at the Mind & Medicine Symposia, San Francisco, February 16–17, 1985.
27. Krane RJ, Goldstein I, de Tejada IS: Impotence. N Engl J Med 321:1648–1659, 1989.
28. Krause J, Crewe N: Long term predication of self reported problems following spinal cord injury. Paraplegia 28:186–202, 1990.
29. Lambert V, Lambert C: Psychosocial Care of the Physically Ill: What Every Nurse Should Know. Englewood Cliffs, NJ, Prentice-Hill, 1985.
30. Lazarus AA: Dispareunia: A multimodel psychotherapeutic perspective. In Leiblum SR, Rosen RC (eds): Principles and Practice of Sex Therapy. 2nd ed. New York, Guilford Press, 1989.
31. Leiblum SR, Rosen RC (eds): Principles and Practice of Sex Therapy. 2nd ed. New York, Guilford Press, 1989.
32. Letourner E, Donohue W: Sexual desire disorders. In O'Donohue W, Geer JH (eds): Handbook of Sexual Dysfunctions. Boston, Allyn & Bacon, 1993.
33. LoPiccolo J, Lobitz WC: The role of masturbation in the treatment of orgasmic dysfunction. Arch Sex Behav 2:163–171, 1972.
34. LoPiccolo J, Friedman JM: Broad spectrum treatment of low sexual desire: Integration of cognitive, behavioral, and systemic therapy. In Leiblum SR, Rosen RC (eds): Sexual Desire Disorders. New York, Guilford Press, 1988.
35. Maltz W, Holman B: Incest and Sexuality. Lexington, MA, Lexington Books, 1987.
36. Marks J: Behavioral psychotherapy in general psychiatry: Helping patients help themselves. Br J Psychiatry 150:593–597, 1986.
37. Masters WH, Johnson VE: Human Sexual Inadequacy. New York, Little, Brown & Co., 1970.
38. Morkoff PJ: Female sexual arousal disorder. In O'Donohue W, Geer JH (eds): Handbook of Sexual Dysfunctions. Boston, Allyn & Bacon, 1993.
39. Morkoff PJ: Sex bias and POD. Am Psychol 44:73–75, 1989.
40. Nosek MA, Howland CA, Young ME, et al: Wellness models and sexuality among women with physical disabilities. Presented at the TIRR Taboo Topics in Rehabilitation: Sexuality and Substance Abuse, Houston, November 12–13, 1993.
41. O'Donohue W, Geer JH (eds): Handbook of Sexual Dysfunctions. Boston, Allyn & Bacon, 1993.
42. O'Donohue W, Letousneau E, Geer JH: Premature ejaculations. In O'Donohue W, Geer JH (eds): Handbook of Sexual Dysfunctions. Boston, Allyn & Bacon, 1993.
43. Phelps G, Brown M, Chen J, et al: Sexual experience and plasma testosterone levels in male veterans after spinal cord injury. Arch Phys Med Rehabil 64:47–52, 1983.
44. Rabin B: The Sensuous Wheeler: Sexual Adjustment for the Spinal Cord Injured. San Francisco, Multi Media Resource Center, 1980.
45. Reid R, Lininger T: Sexual pain disorders in the female. In O'Donohue W, Geer JH (eds): Handbook of Sexual Dysfunctions. Boston, Allyn & Bacon, 1993.
46. Renshaw D: Impotence in diabetics. In LoPiccolo J, LoPiccolo L (eds): Handbook of Sex Therapy. New York, Plenum Press, 1978, pp 433–440.
47. Riley AJ, Riley EJ: Cholinergic and andrenergic control of human sexual responses. In Wheatley D (ed): Psychopharmacology and Sexual Disorders. New York, Oxford University Press, 1982.
48. Romano M: Counseling the spinal cord injured female. In Sha'ked A (ed): Human Sexuality and Rehabilitation. Baltimore, Williams & Wilkins, 1981, pp 157–166.
49. Rosen RC, Leiblum SR: A sexual scripting approach to problems of desire. In Leiblum SR, Rosen RC (eds): Sexual Desire Disorders. New York, Guilford Press, 1988.
50. Satilios-Rothschild C: Social and psychological parameters of friendship and intimacy for disabled people. In Eisenberg M, Griggins C, Duval R (eds): Disabled People as Second Class Citizens. New York, Springer, 1982, pp 40–51.
51. Schover L, Friedman J, Wieler S, et al: Multiaxial problems in oriented system for sexual dysfunctions: An alternative to DSM-III. Arch Gen Psychiatry 39:614–619, 1982.
52. Schover LR, LoPiccolo J: Treatment effectiveness for dysfunction of sexual desire. J Sex Marital Ther 8:179–197, 1982.
53. Schwartz MF, Masters WH: Inhibited sexual desire: The Masters and Johnson Institute treatment model. In Leiblum SR, Rosen RC (eds): Sexual Desire Disorders. New York, Guilford Press, 1988, pp 229–242.

54. Semans JH: Premature ejaculation: A new approach. South Med J 49:353–357, 1956.
55. Sherwin BB, Gelfand MM, Bender W: Androgen enhances sexual motivation in females: A prospective, crossover study of sex steroid administration in the surgical menopause. Psychosom Med 47:339–351, 1988.
56. Singh SP, Magner T: Sex and self: The spinal cord-injured. Rehabil Lit 36:2–10, 1975.
57. Siösteen B, Liundquist C, Blomstrand C, et al: Sexual ability, activity, attitudes and satisfaction as part of adjustment in spinal cord injured subjects. Paraplegia 28:285–295, 1990.
58. Smith I: Shattering the myths: Sexuality in rehabilitation. Rehabil Manage 2:28–34, 1989.
59. Spector JP, Carey MP: Incidence and prevalence of sexual dysfunctions: A critical review of the empirical literature. Arch Sex Behav 19:389–408, 1990.
60. Spence SH: Psychosexual Theory: A Cognitive-Behavioral Approach. New York, Chapman & Hall, 1991.
61. Sviland M: Helping elderly couples become sexually liberated: Psychosexual issues. In LoPiccolo J, LoPiccolo L (eds): Handbook of Sex Therapy. New York, Plenum Press, 1978, pp 351–360.
62. Thomas E: Problems of disability from the perspective of role theory. J Health Hum Behav 7:2–14, 1966.
63. Tiefer L, Melman A: Adherence to recommendations and improvement over time in men with erectile dysfunction. Arch Sex Behav 16:301–309, 1987.
64. Trieschmann R: Spinal Cord Injuries: Psychological, Social and Vocational Adjustment. New York, Pergamon Press, 1980.
65. Verhulst J, Heiman J: A systems perspective on sexual desire. In Leiblum SR, Rosen RC (eds): Sexual Desire Disorders. New York, Guilford Press, 1988, pp 243–270.
66. Weinberg S: Human sexuality and spinal cord injury. Nurs Clin North Am 17:407–419, 1982.
67. White M, Rintala D, Hart K, et al: Sexual activities, concerns and interests of men with spinal cord injury. Arch Phys Med Rehabil 71:255–231, 1992.
68. Williams C: Sexuality and disability. In Ussher JM, Baker CD (eds): Psychological Perspectives on Sexual Problems. New York, Routledge, 1993.
69. Wincze JP, Carey MP: Sexual Dysfunction: A Guide for Assessment and Treatment. New York, Guilford Press, 1991.

INDEX

Entries in **boldface** type signify complete articles.

555